TSUBASA

27

CLAMP

TRANSLATED AND ADAPTED BY
William Flanagan

LETTERED BY
Dana Hayward

BALLANTINE BOOKS · NEW YORK

A Del Rey Manga/Kodansha Trade Paperback Original

Tsubasa, volume 27 copyright © 2009 CLAMP
English translation copyright © 2010 CLAMP

Published in the United States by Del Rey, an imprint of The Random House Publishing Group, a division of Random House, Inc., New York.

DEL REY is a registered trademark and the Del Rey colophon is a trademark of Random House, Inc.

Publication rights arranged through Kodansha Ltd.

First published in Japan in 2009 by Kodansha Ltd., Tokyo

ISBN 978-0-345-52071-5

Printed in the United States of America

www.delreymanga.com

9 8 7 6 5 4 3 2 1

Translator/Adapter—William Flanagan
Lettering—Dana Hayward

Contents

Tsubasa crosses over with *xxxHOLiC*. Although it isn't necessary to read *xxxHOLiC* to understand the events in *Tsubasa*, you'll get to see the same events from different perspectives if you read both series!

Honorifics Explained

Throughout the Del Rey Manga books, you will find Japanese honorifics left intact in the translations. For those not familiar with how the Japanese use honorifics and, more important, how they differ from American honorifics, we present this brief overview.

Politeness has always been a critical facet of Japanese culture. Ever since the feudal era, when Japan was a highly stratified society, use of honorifics—which can be defined as polite speech that indicates relationship or status—has played an essential role in the Japanese language. When you address someone in Japanese, an honorific usually takes the form of a suffix attached to one's name (example: "Asuna-san"), is used as a title at the end of one's name, or appears in place of the name itself (example: "Negi-sensei," or simply "Sensei!").

Honorifics can be expressions of respect or endearment. In the context of manga and anime, honorifics give insight into the nature of the relationship between characters. Many English translations leave out these important honorifics and therefore distort the feel of the original Japanese. Because Japanese honorifics contain nuances that English honorifics lack, it is our policy at Del Rey not to translate them. Here, instead, is a guide to some of the honorifics you may encounter in Del Rey Manga.

-san: This is the most common honorific and is equivalent to Mr., Miss, Ms., or Mrs. It is the all-purpose honorific and can be used in any situation where politeness is required.

-sama: This is one level higher than "-san" and is used to confer great respect.

-dono: This comes from the word "tono," which means "lord." It is an even higher level than "-sama" and confers utmost respect.

-kun: This suffix is used at the end of boys' names to express familiarity or endearment. It is also sometimes used by men among friends, or when addressing someone younger or of a lower station.

-chan: This is used to express endearment, mostly toward girls. It is also used for little boys, pets, and even among lovers. It gives a sense of childish cuteness.

Bozu: This is an informal way to refer to a boy, similar to the English terms "kid" and "squirt."

Sempai/Senpai: This title suggests that the addressee is one's senior in a group or organization. It is most often used in a school setting, where underclassmen refer to their upperclassmen as "sempai." It can also be used in the workplace, such as when a newer employee addresses an employee who has seniority in the company.

Kohai: This is the opposite of "sempai" and is used toward underclassmen in school or newcomers in the workplace. It connotes that the addressee is of a lower station.

Sensei: Literally meaning "one who has come before," this title is used for teachers, doctors, or masters of any profession or art.

-[blank]: This is usually forgotten in these lists, but it is perhaps the most significant difference between Japanese and English. The lack of honorific means that the speaker has permission to address the person in a very intimate way. Usually, only family, spouses, or very close friends have this kind of permission. Known as *yobisute*, it can be gratifying when someone who has earned the intimacy starts to call one by one's name without an honorific. But when that intimacy hasn't been earned, it can be very insulting.

Chapitre.211
The Burned-in Smile

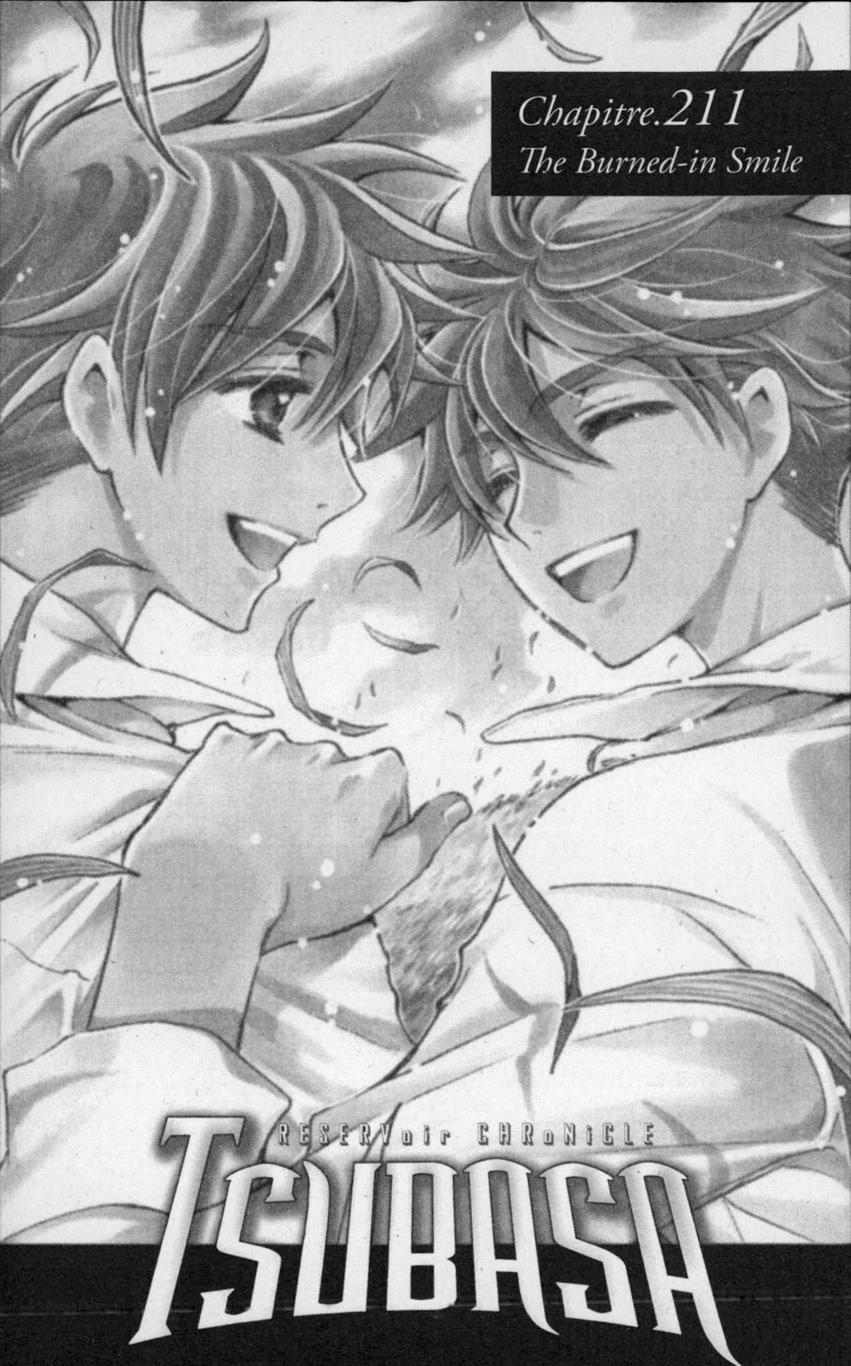
RESERVoir CHRoNiCLE
TSUBASA

ツバサ

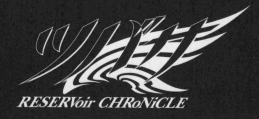

RESERVoir CHRoNiCLE

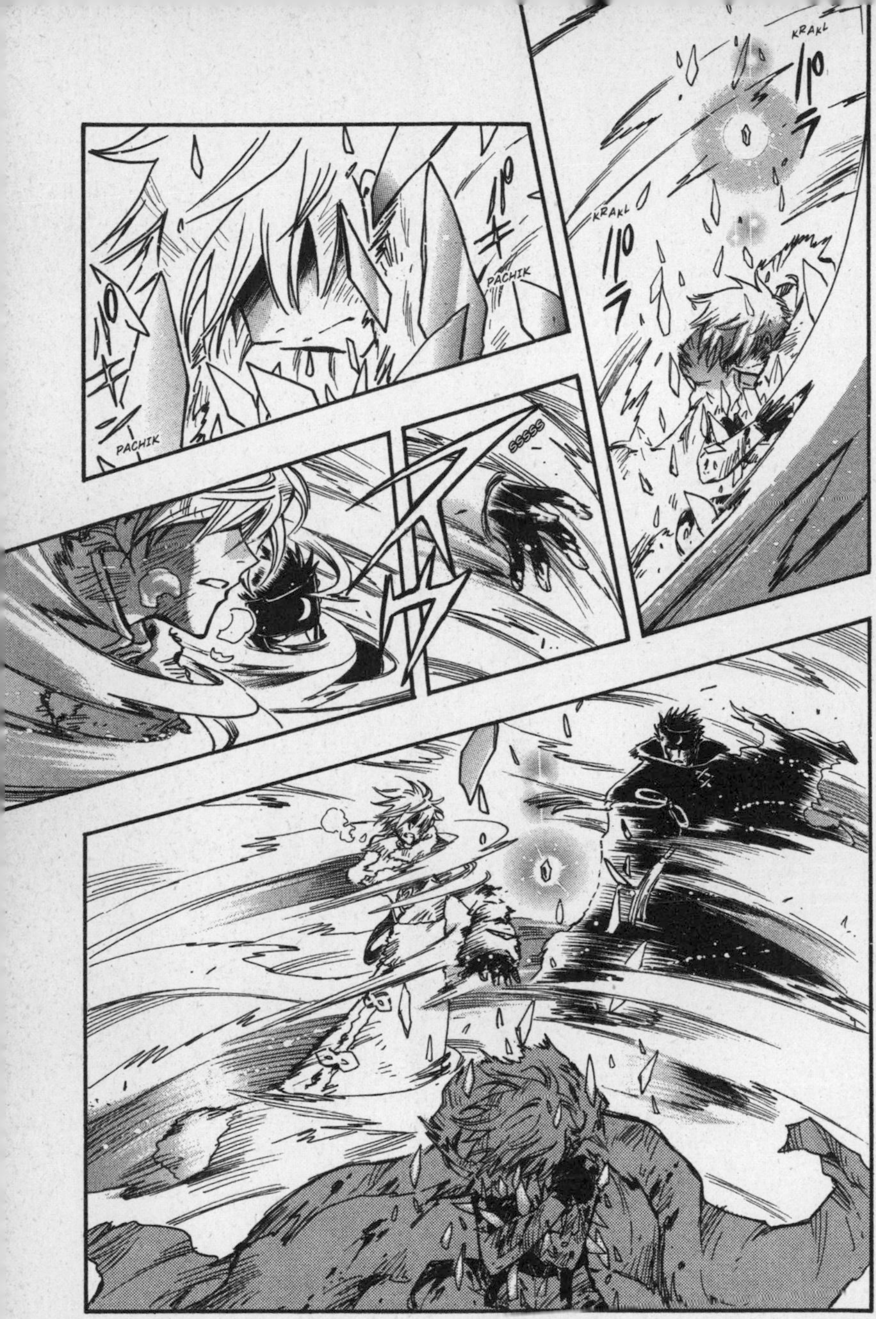
KRAKL
KRAKL
PACHIK
PACHIK
SSSSS

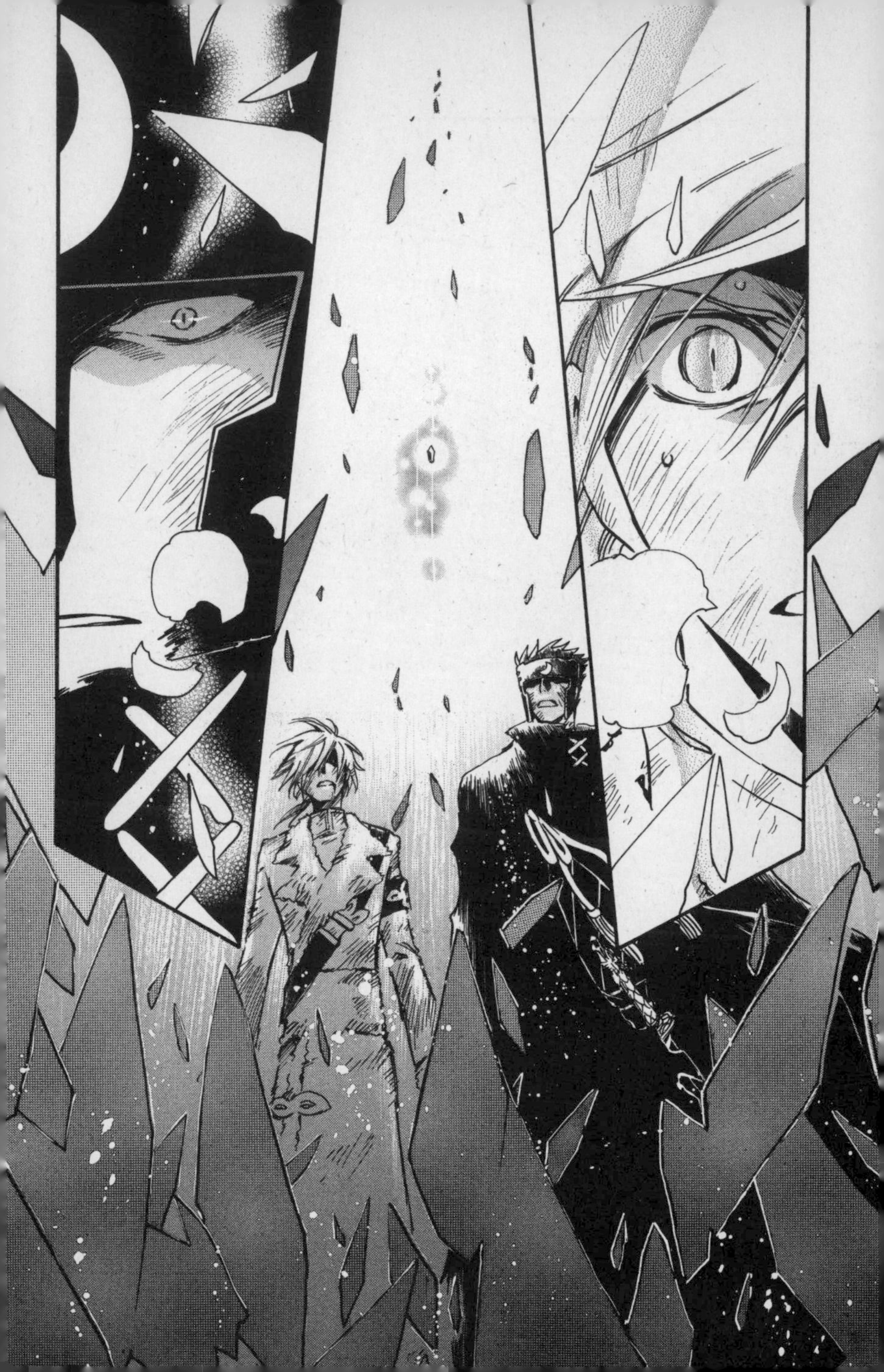

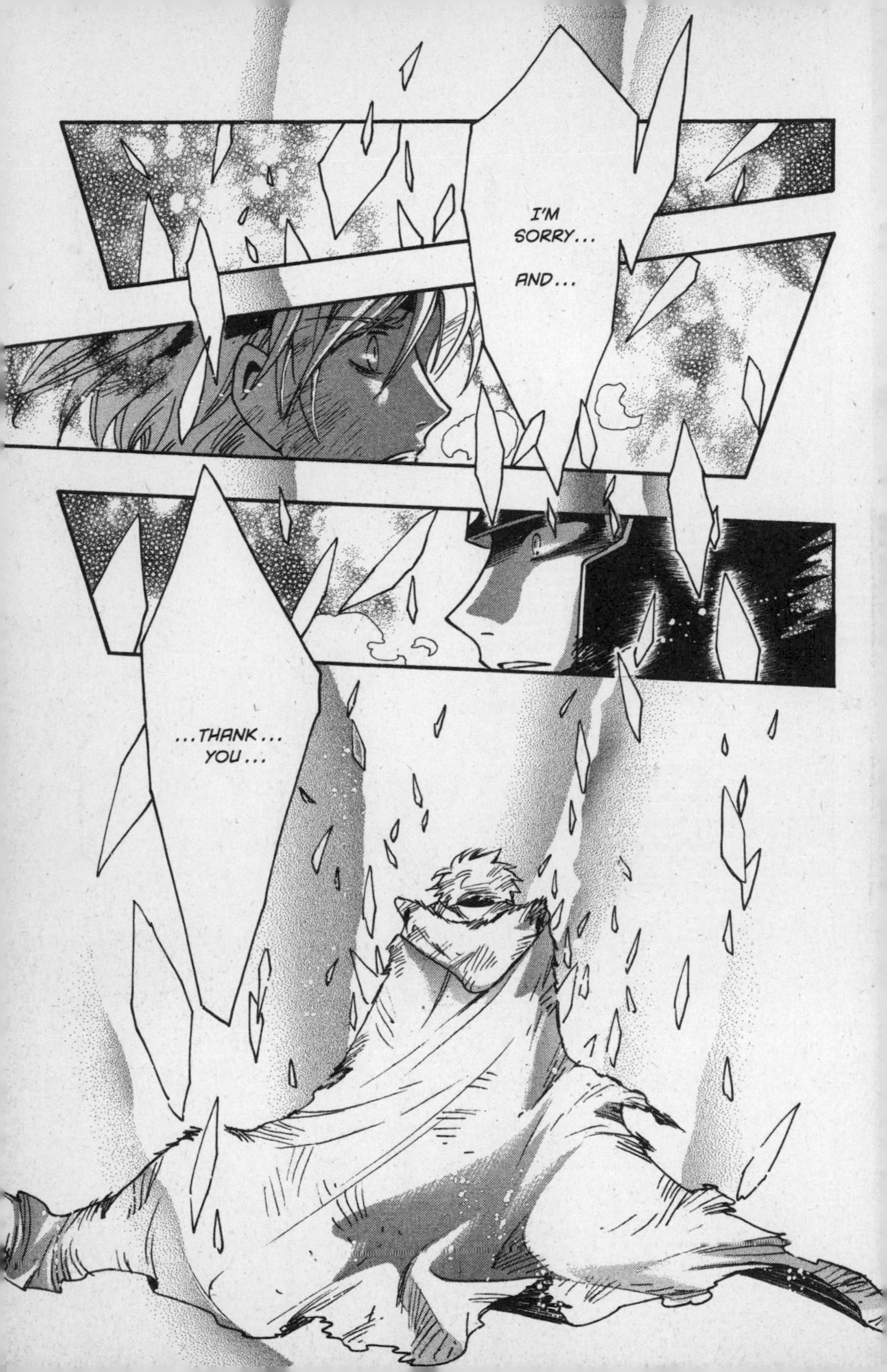
I'M SORRY...
AND...
...THANK... YOU...

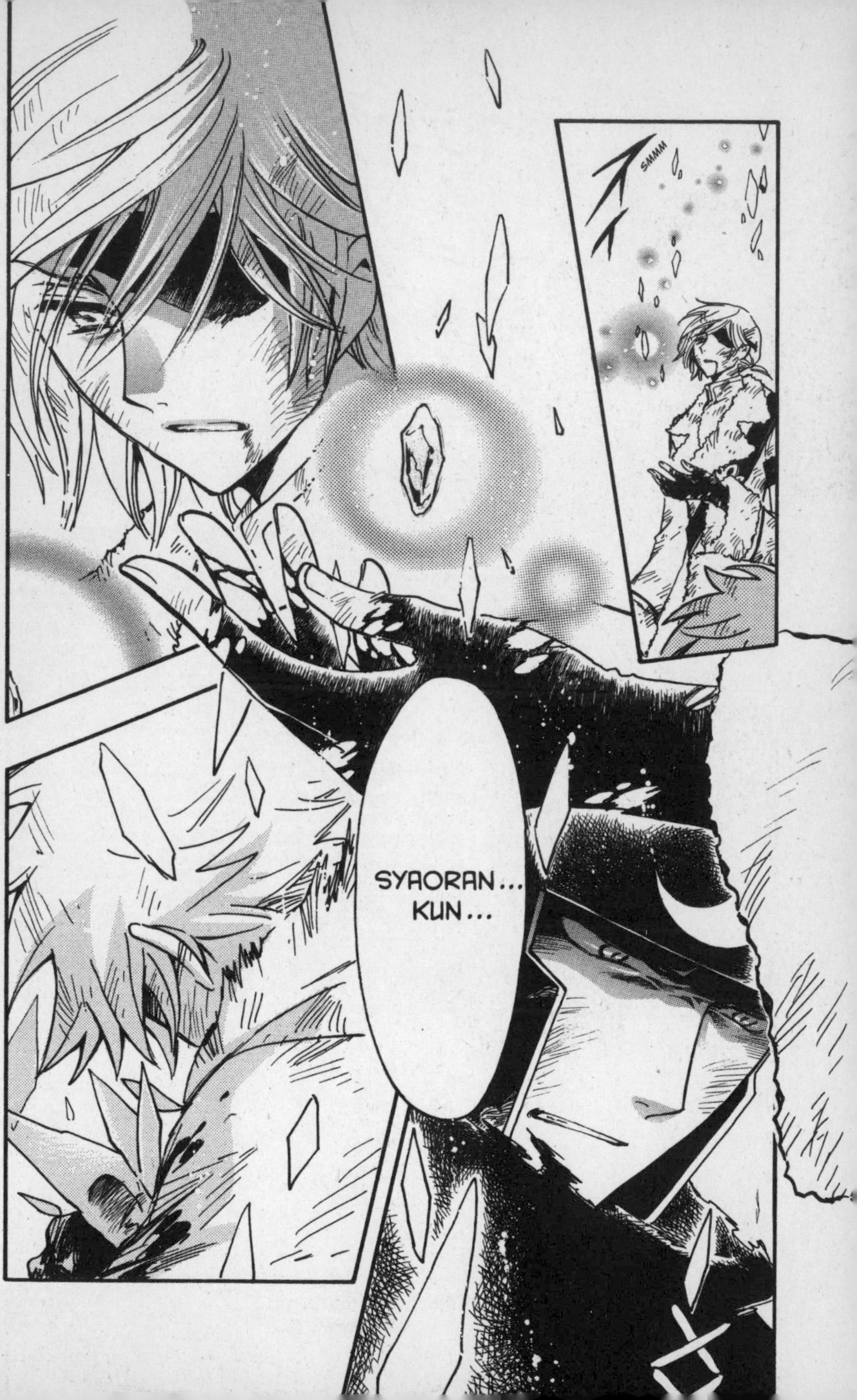
SMMM
SYAORAN... KUN...

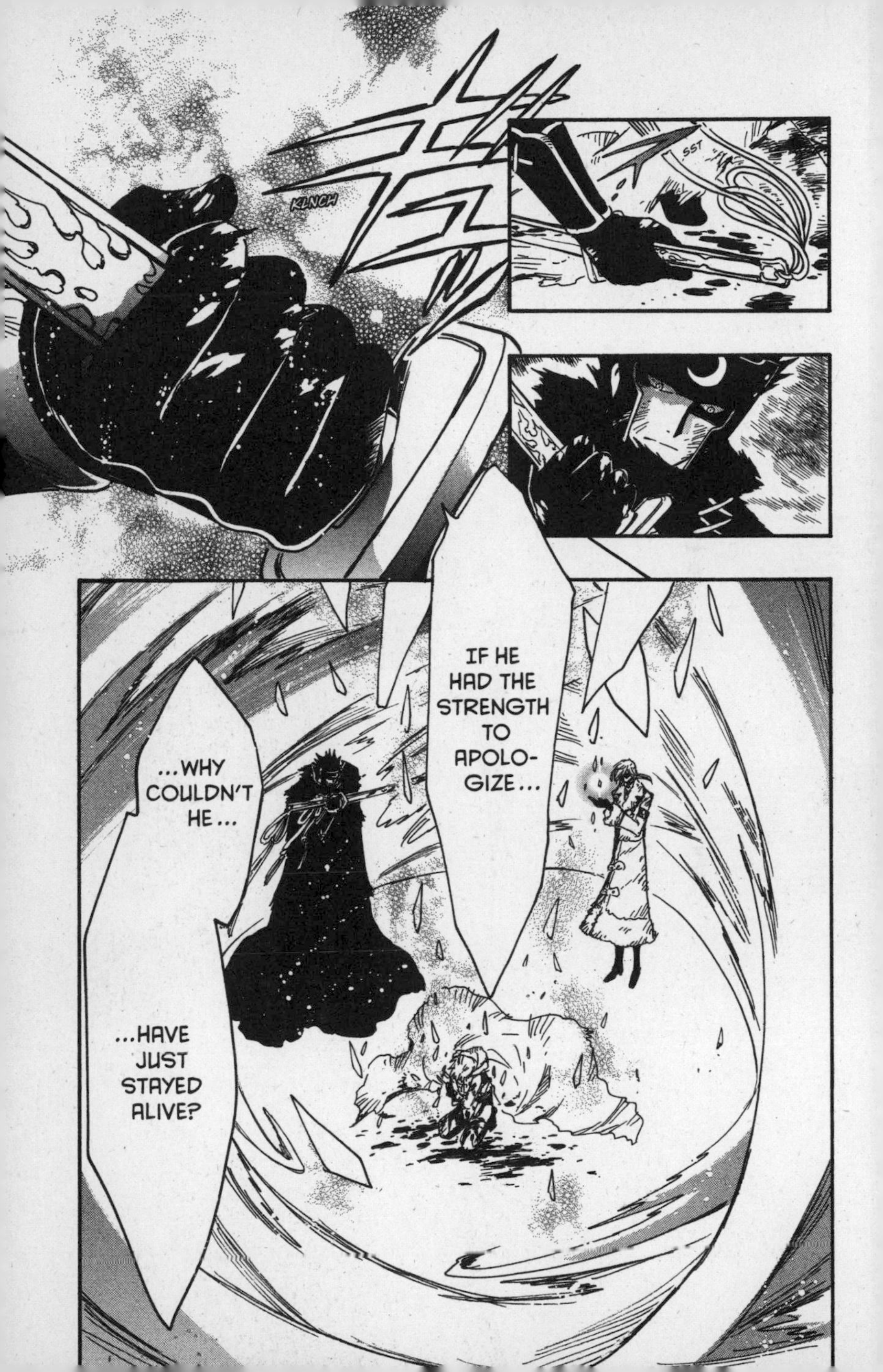
SST
KLNCH
IF HE HAD THE STRENGTH TO APOLO-GIZE...
...WHY COULDN'T HE...
...HAVE JUST STAYED ALIVE?

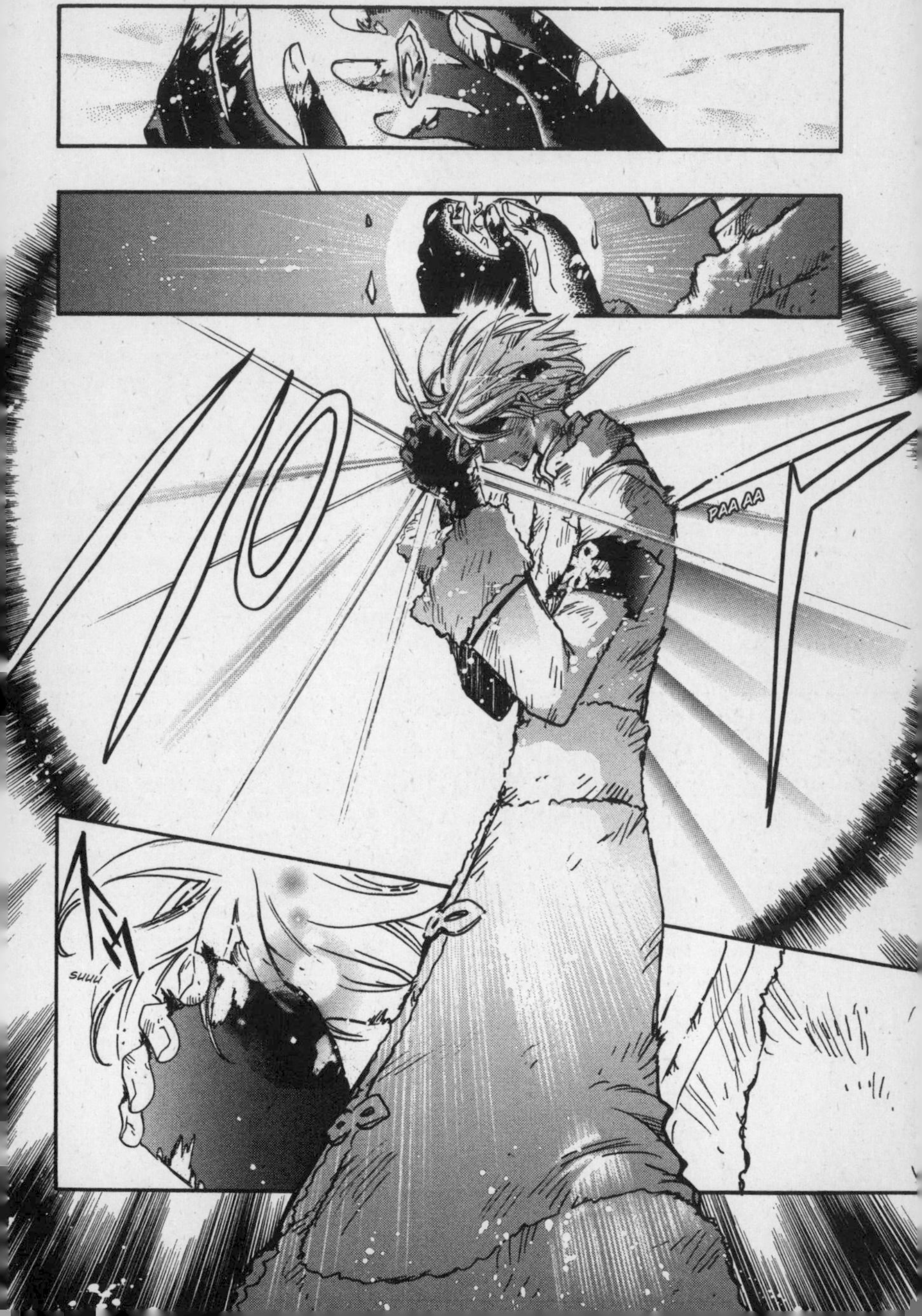
PAA AA
SUUU

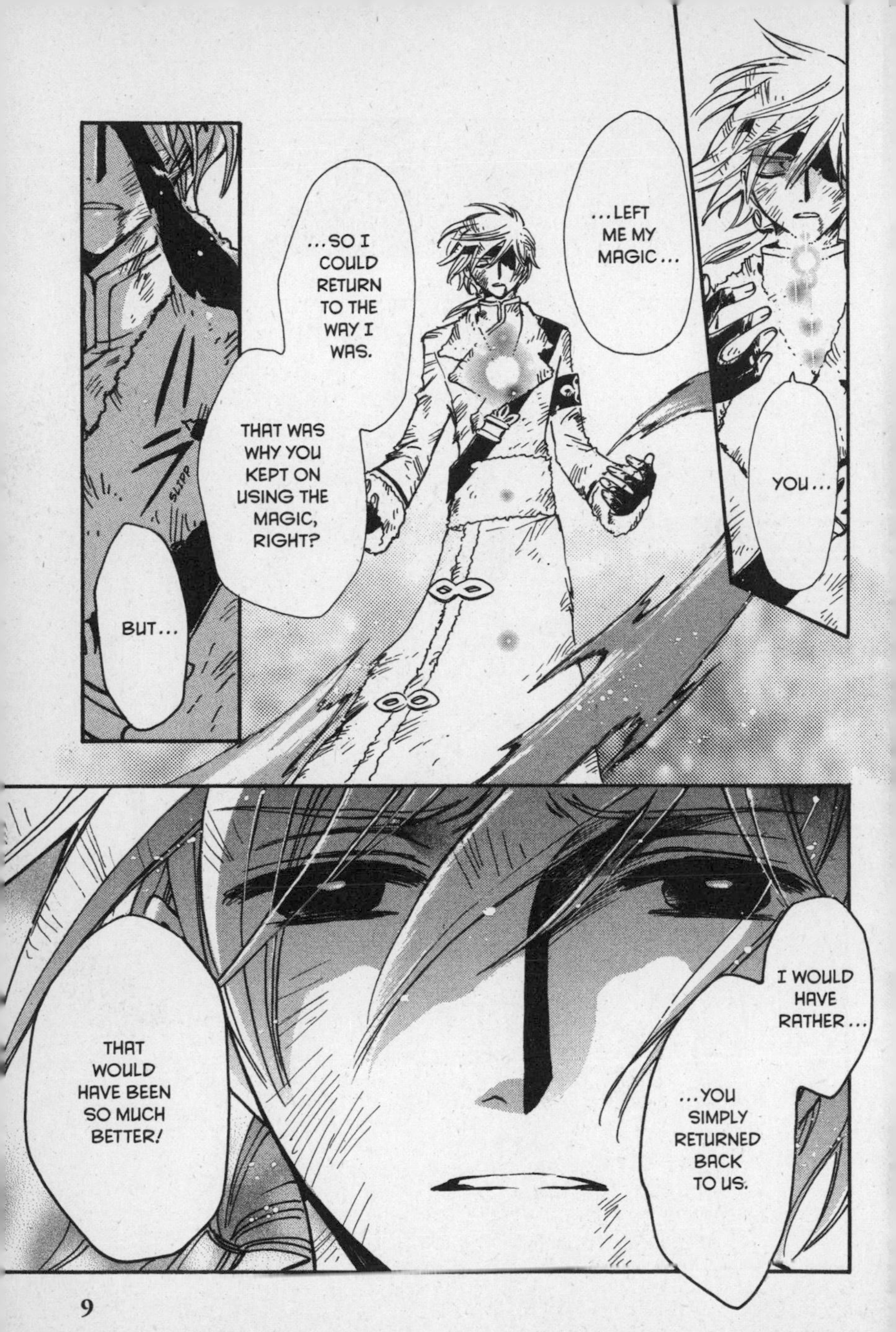
YOU...
...LEFT ME MY MAGIC...
...SO I COULD RETURN TO THE WAY I WAS.
THAT WAS WHY YOU KEPT ON USING THE MAGIC, RIGHT?
SLIPP
BUT...
I WOULD HAVE RATHER...
...YOU SIMPLY RETURNED BACK TO US.
THAT WOULD HAVE BEEN SO MUCH BETTER!

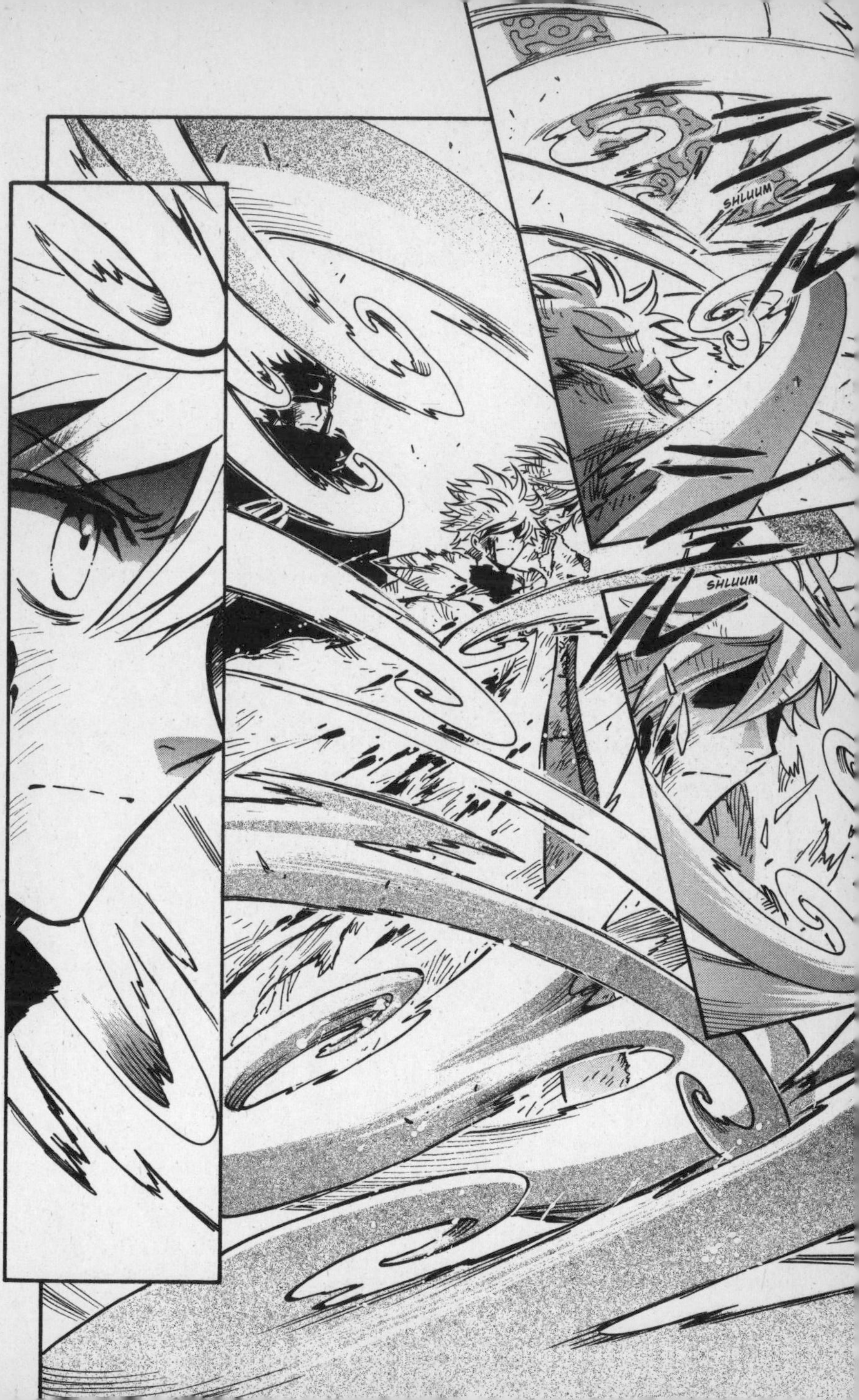
SHLUUM
SHLUUM

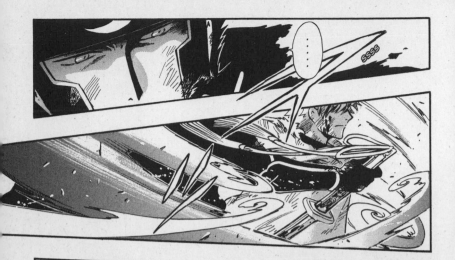

THIS MAGIC...

...IS WHAT CONNECTS THIS SPACE AND TIME WITH THAT MAN'S DIMENSION.

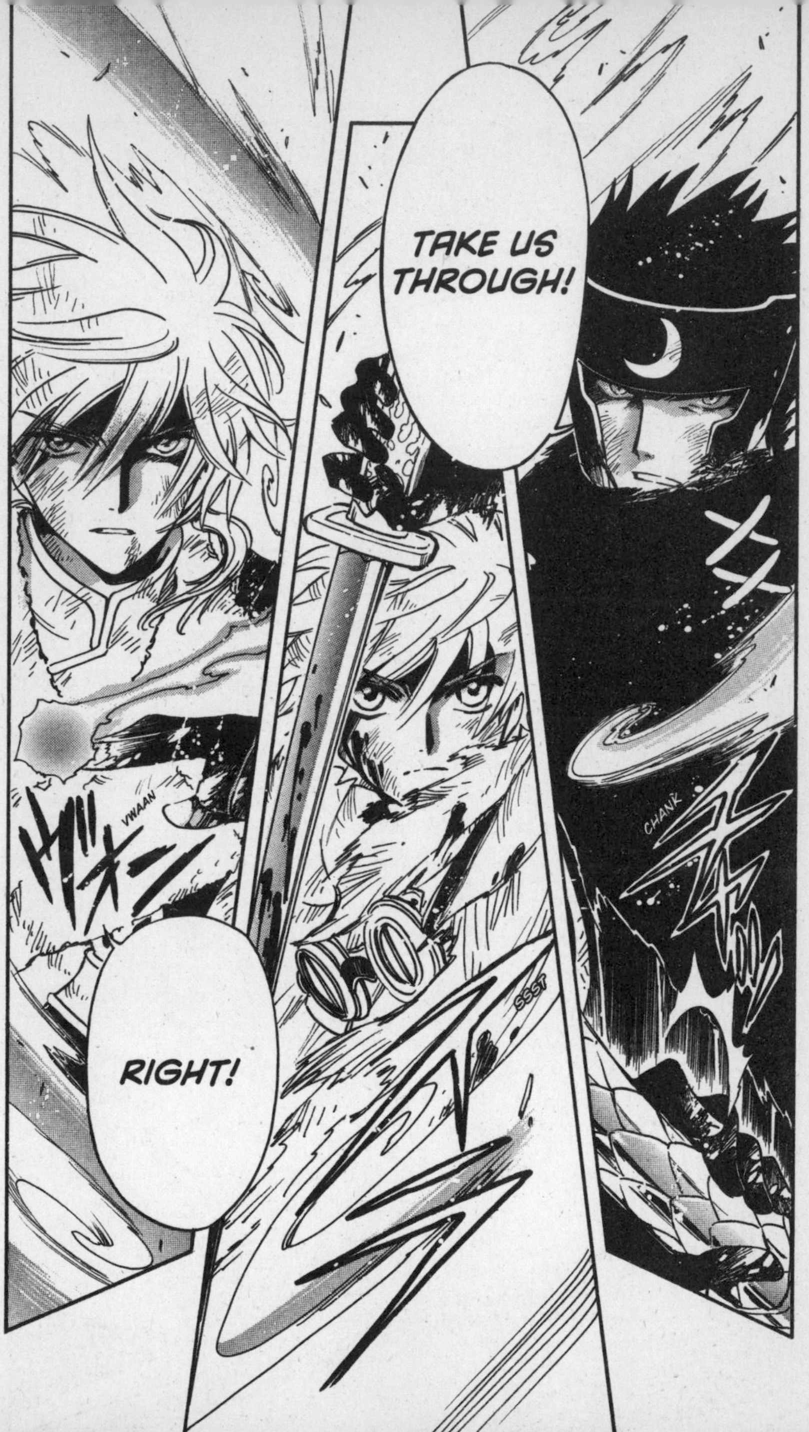
TAKE US THROUGH!
CHANK
SSST
VWAAN
RIGHT!

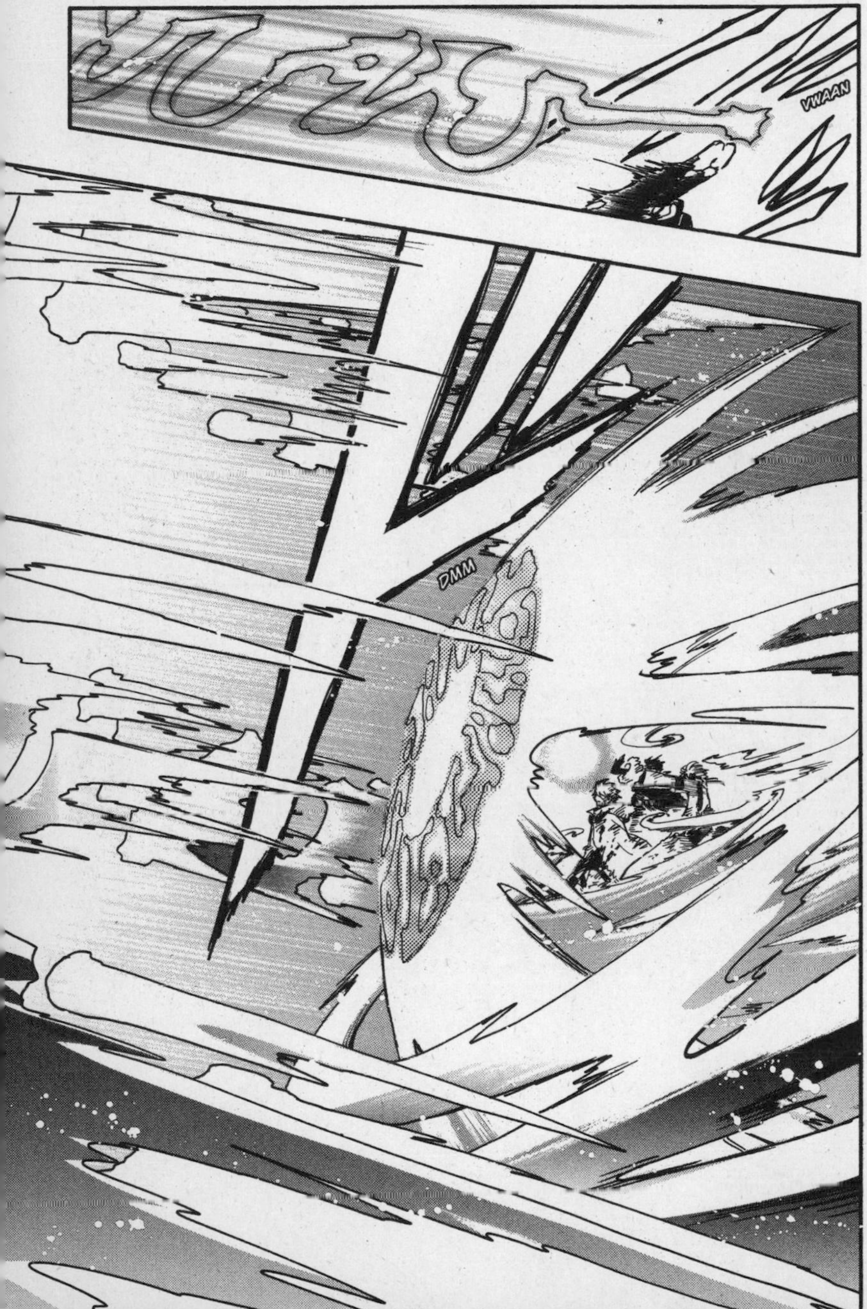
VWAAN
DMM

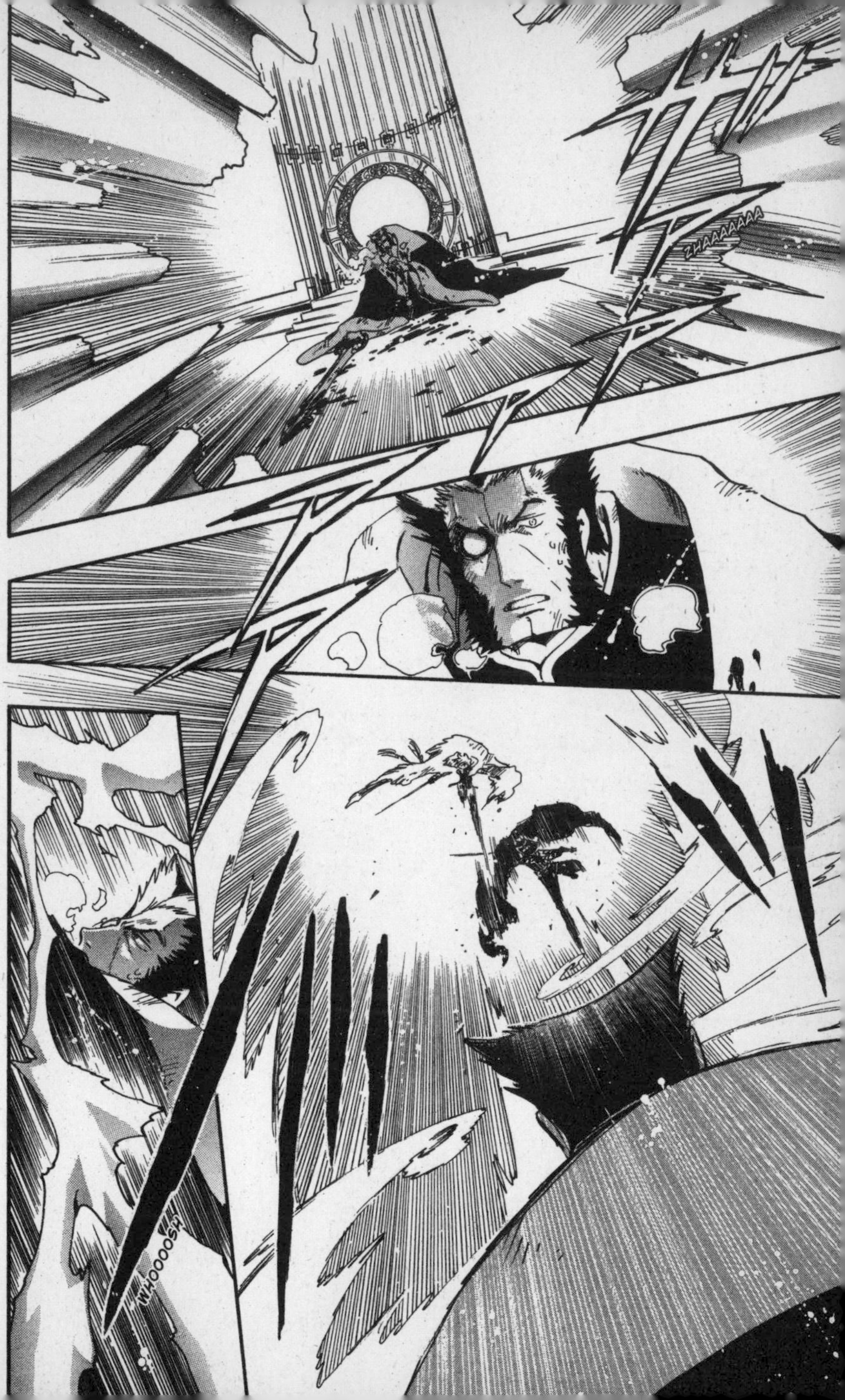
ZHAAAAAAA
WHOOOOSH

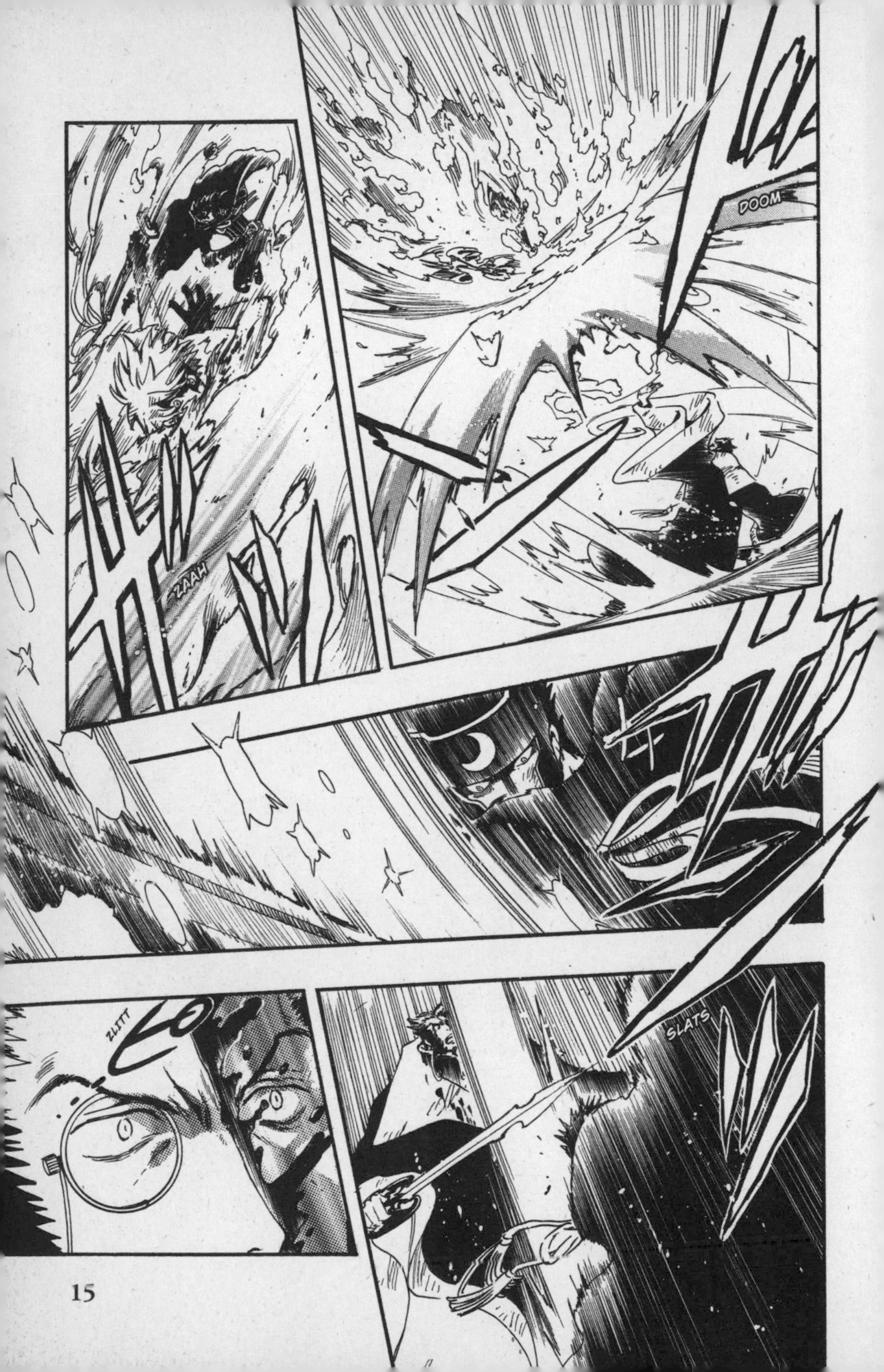
DOOM
ZAAH
SLATS
ZLITT

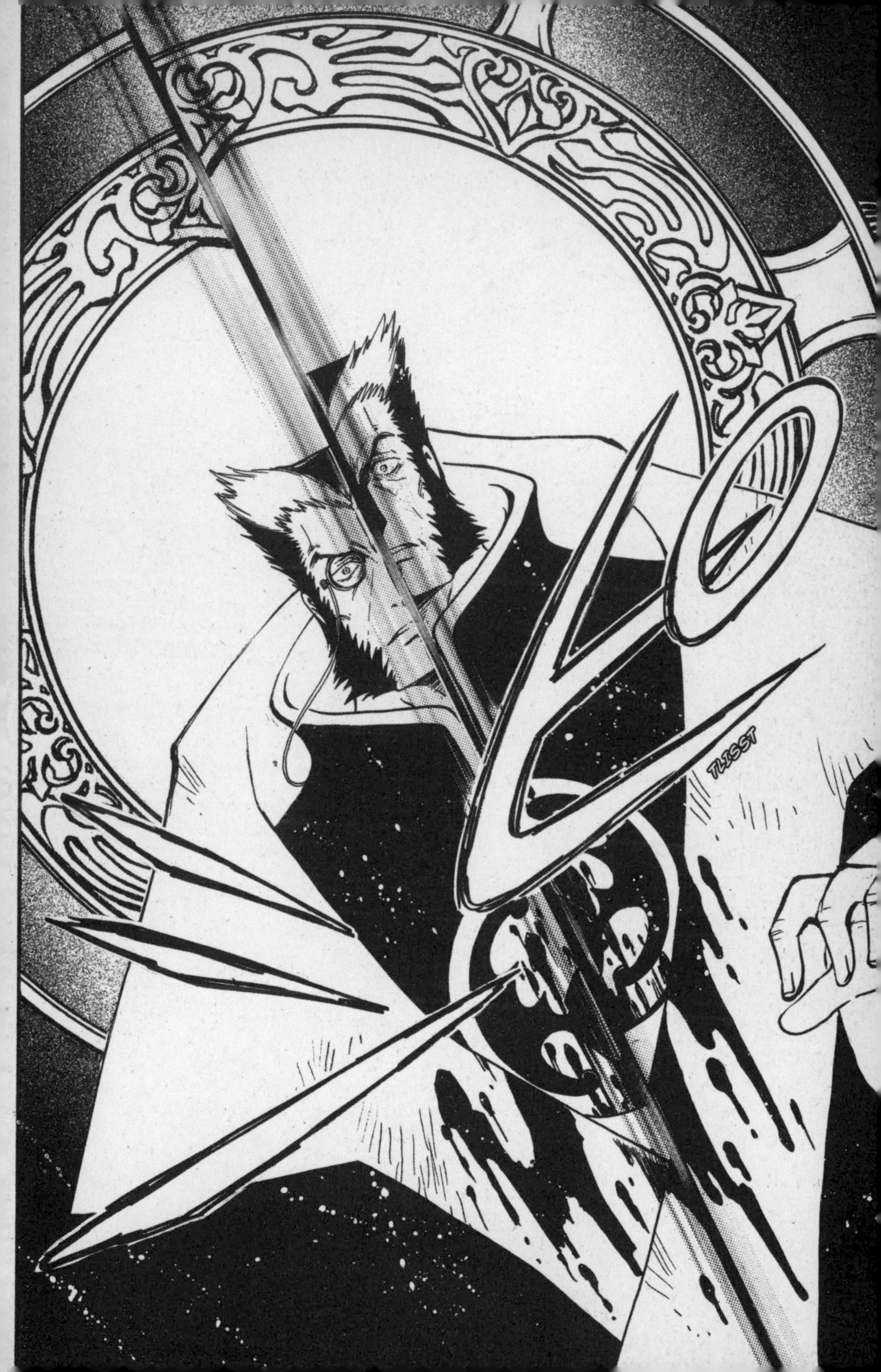
TLISST

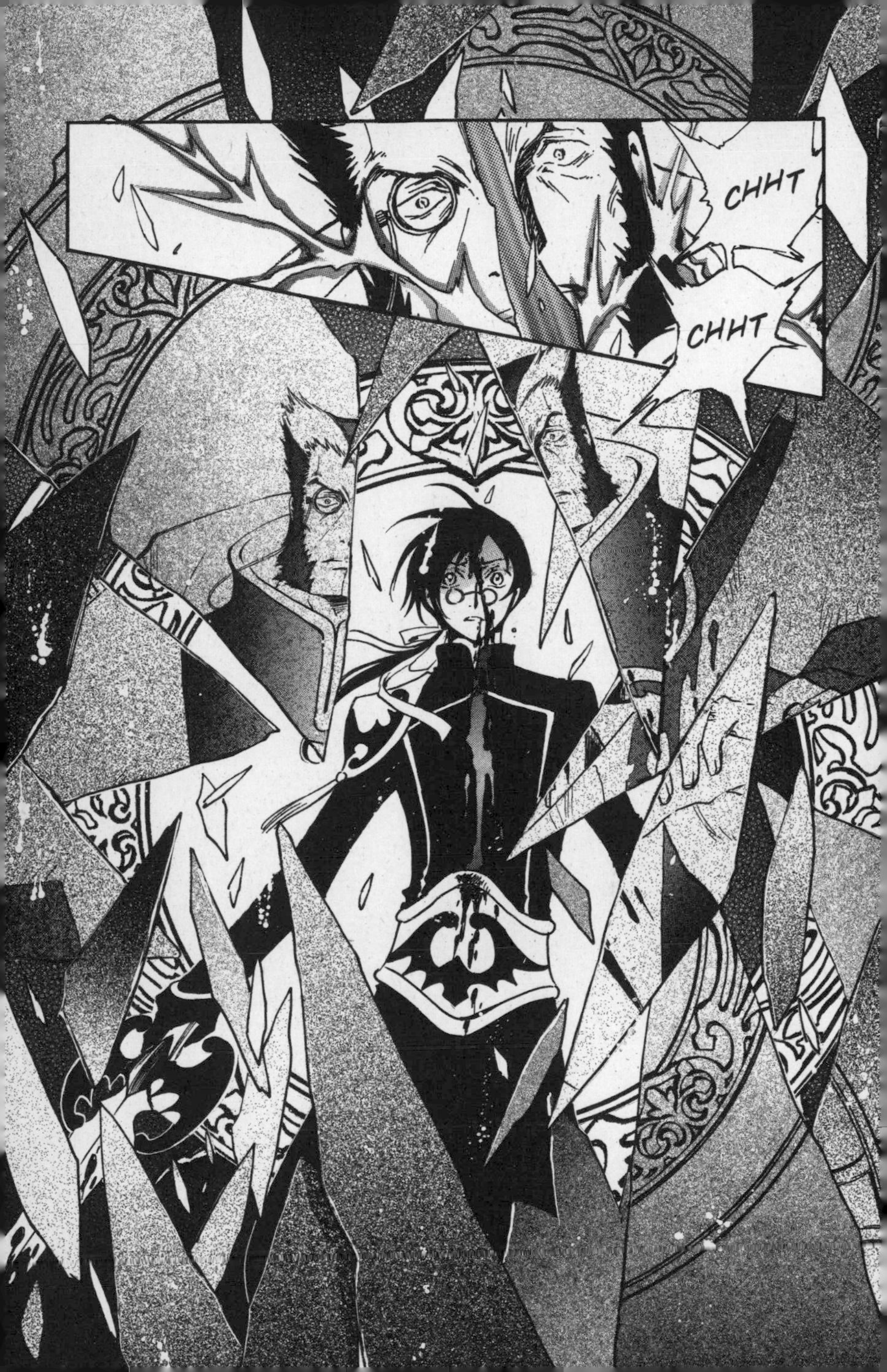
CHHT
CHHT

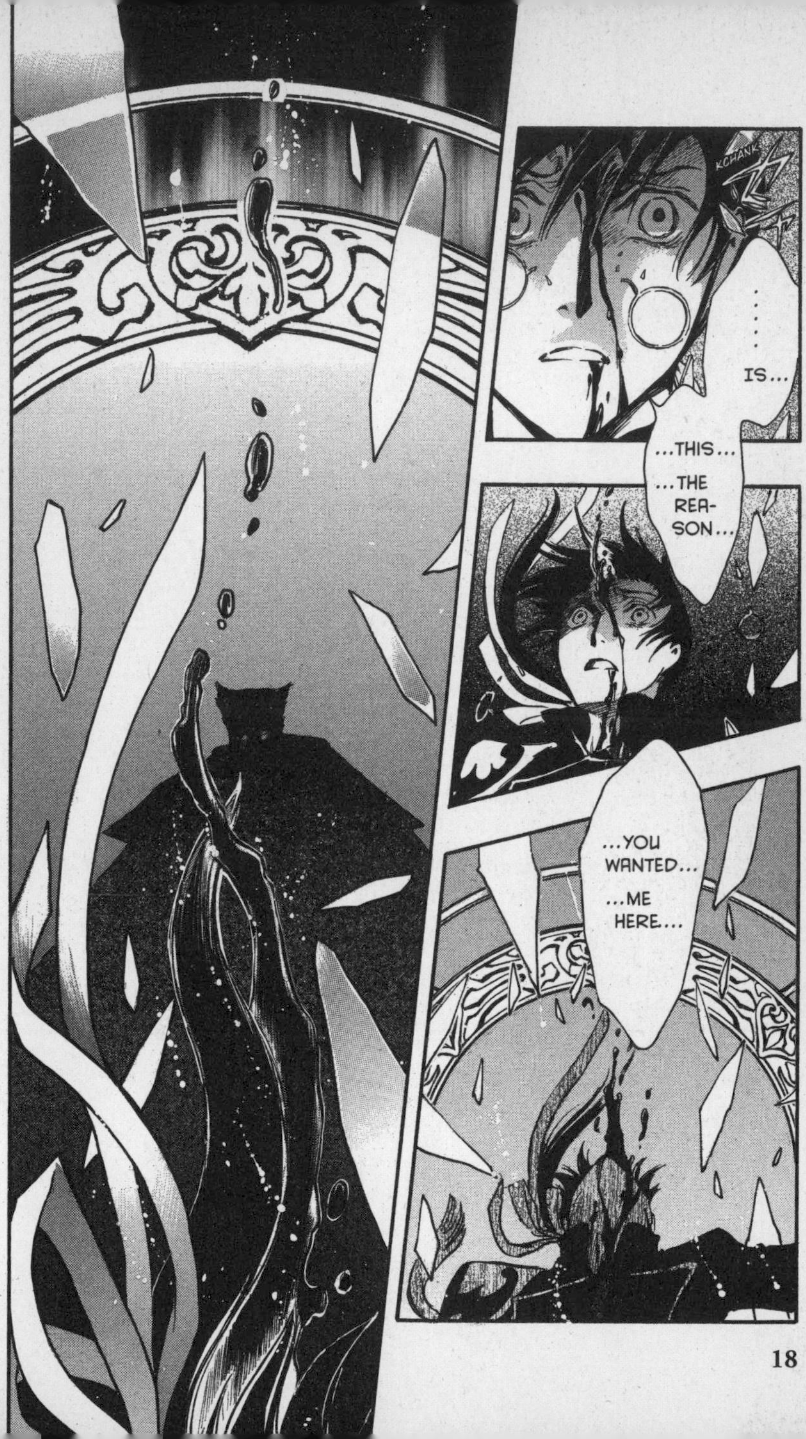
KCHANK
......
IS...
...THIS...
...THE REA-SON...
...YOU WANTED...
...ME HERE....

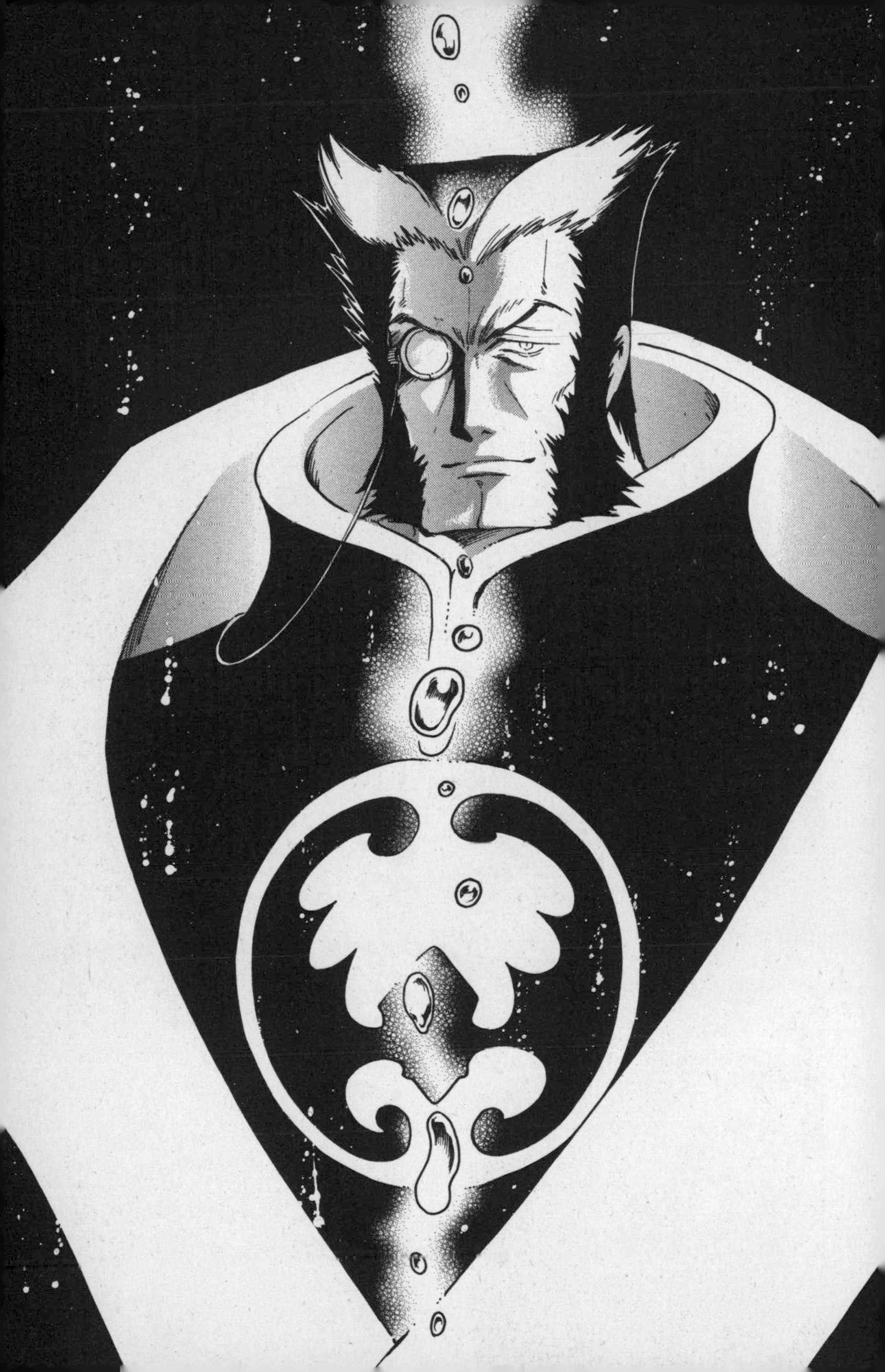

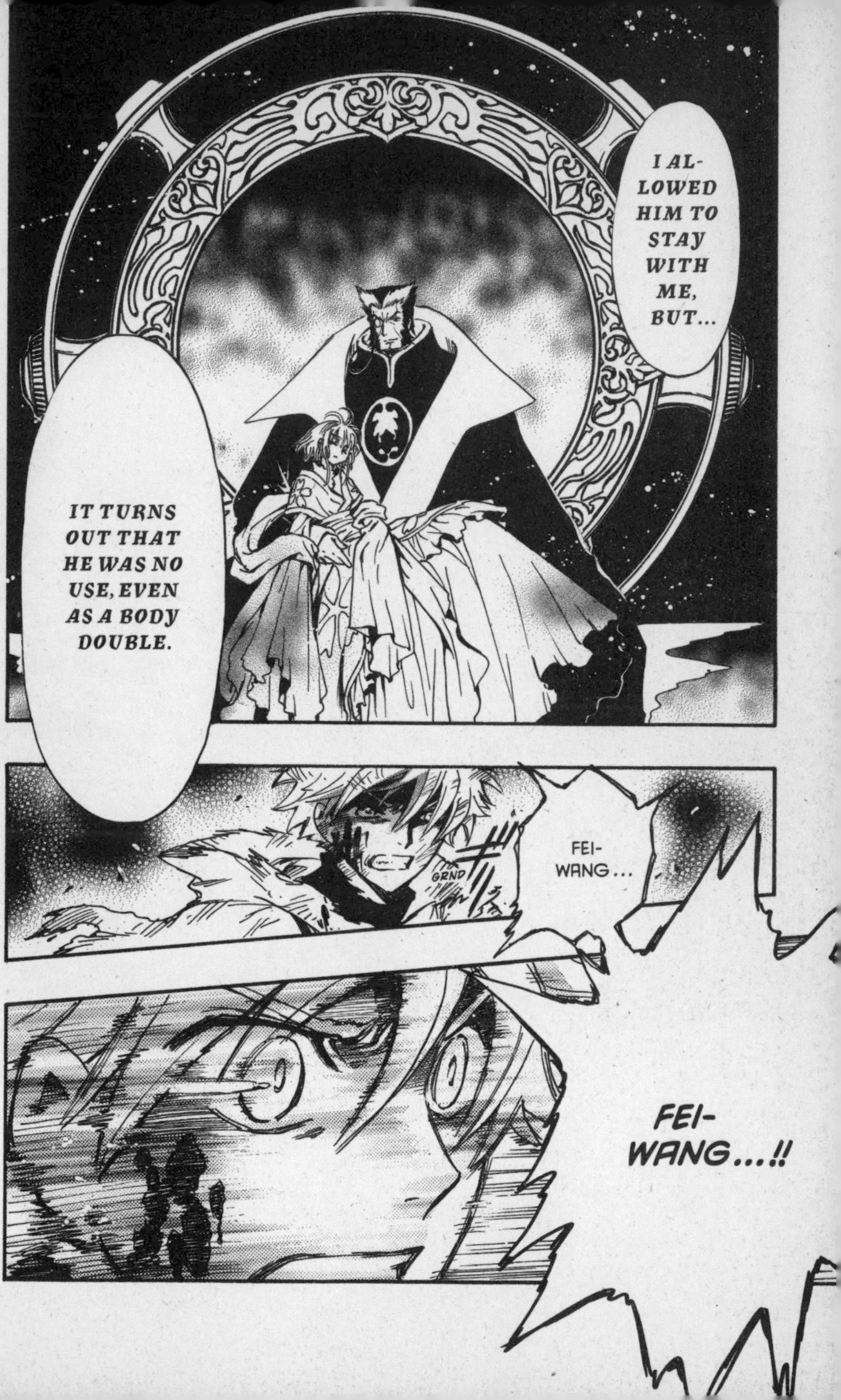
I AL-LOWED HIM TO STAY WITH ME, BUT...
IT TURNS OUT THAT HE WAS NO USE, EVEN AS A BODY DOUBLE.
FEI-WANG...
GRND
FEI-WANG...!!

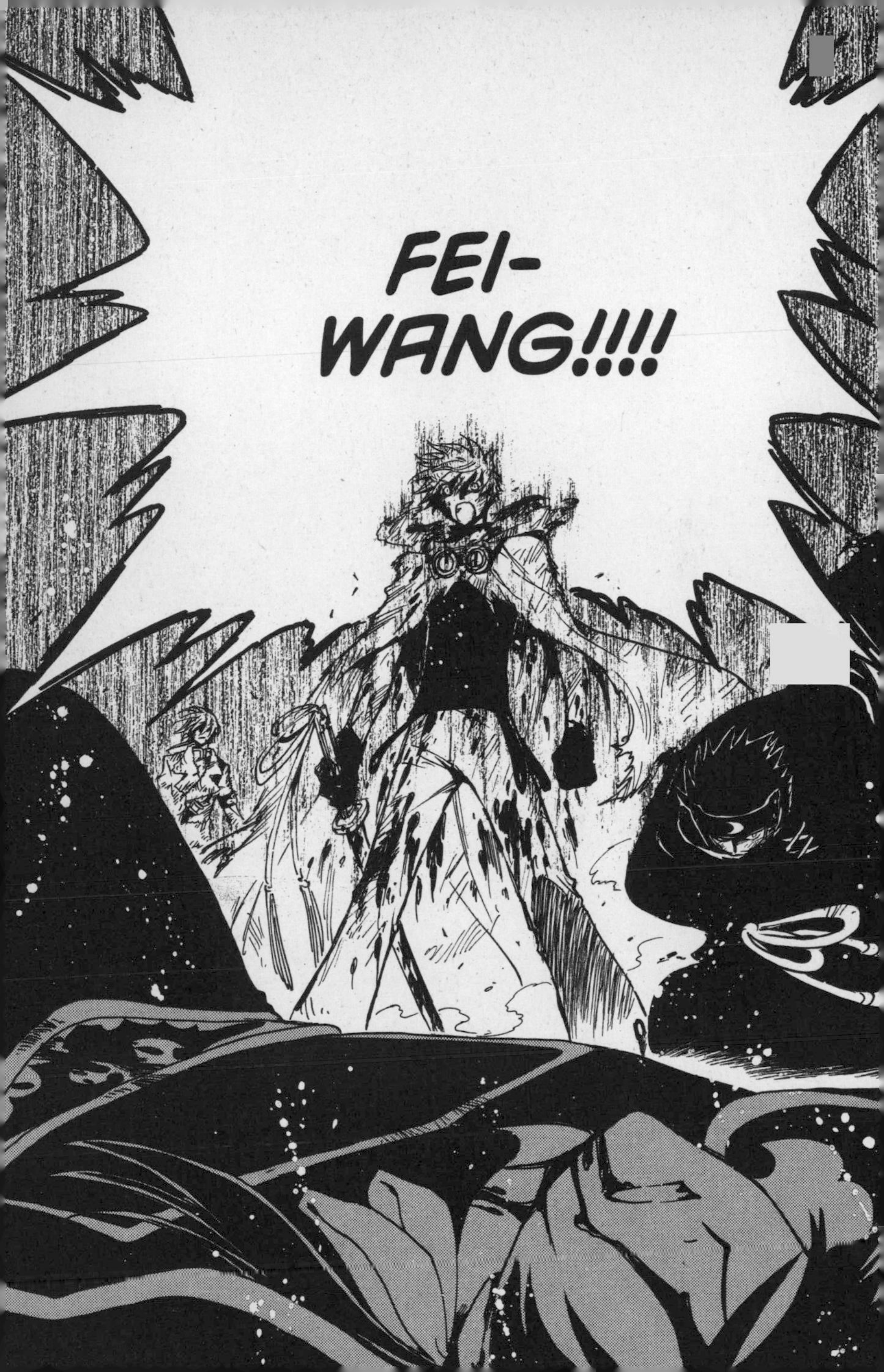
FEI-
WANG!!!!

ツバサ
RESERVoir CHRoNiCLE

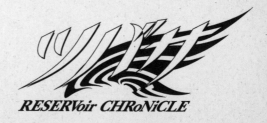

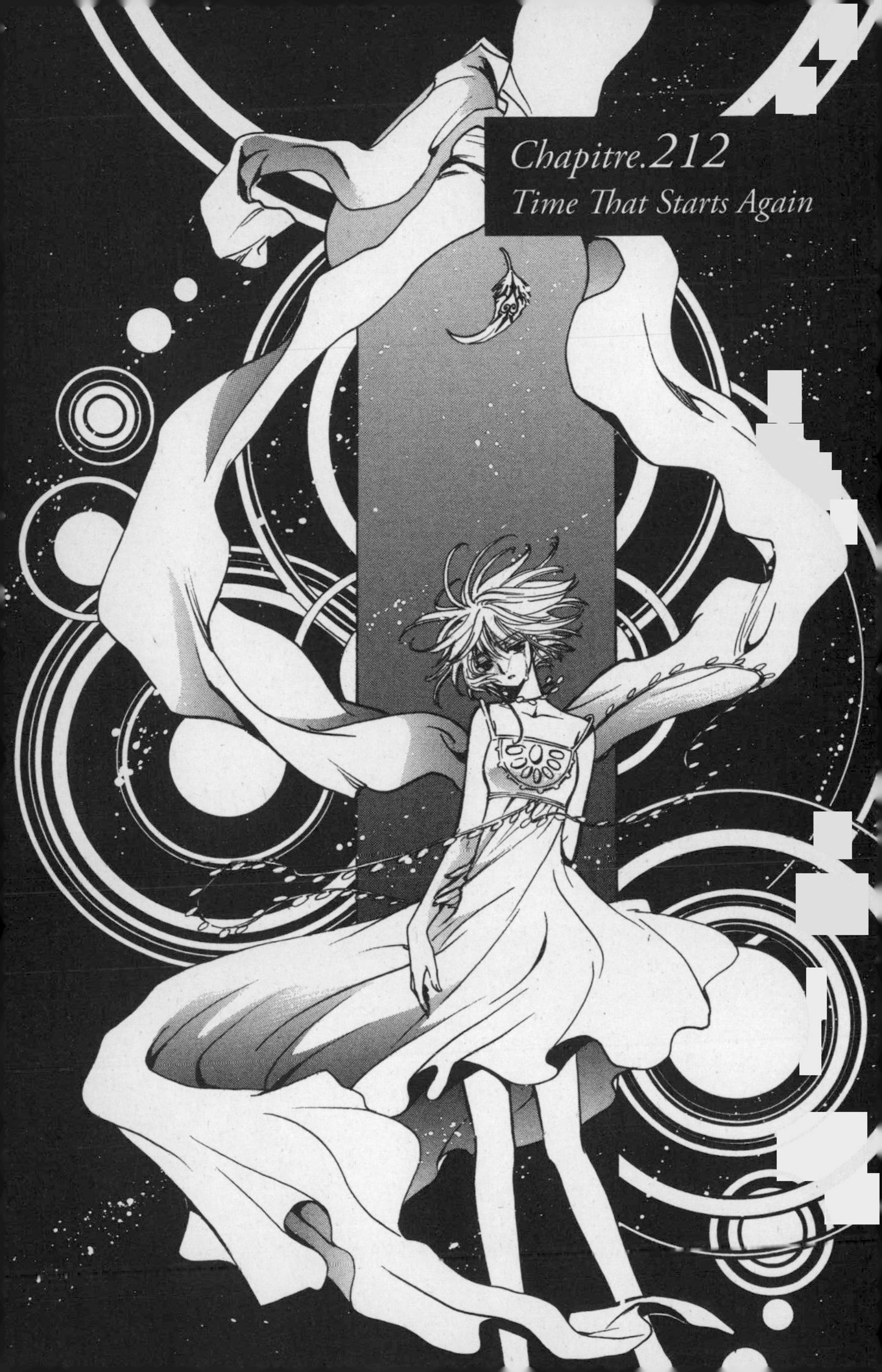
Chapitre.212
Time That Starts Again

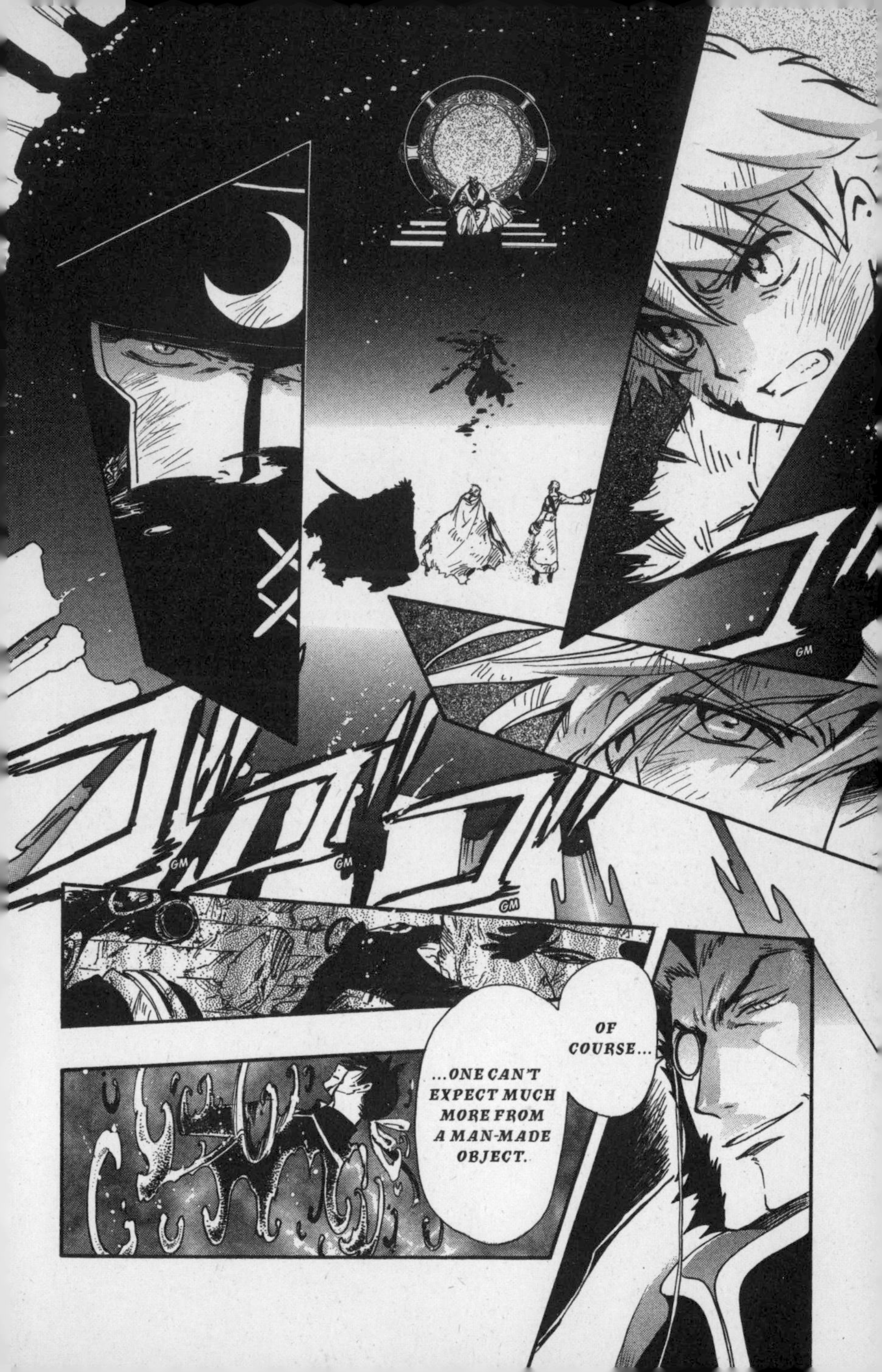
OF COURSE...
...ONE CAN'T EXPECT MUCH MORE FROM A MAN-MADE OBJECT.

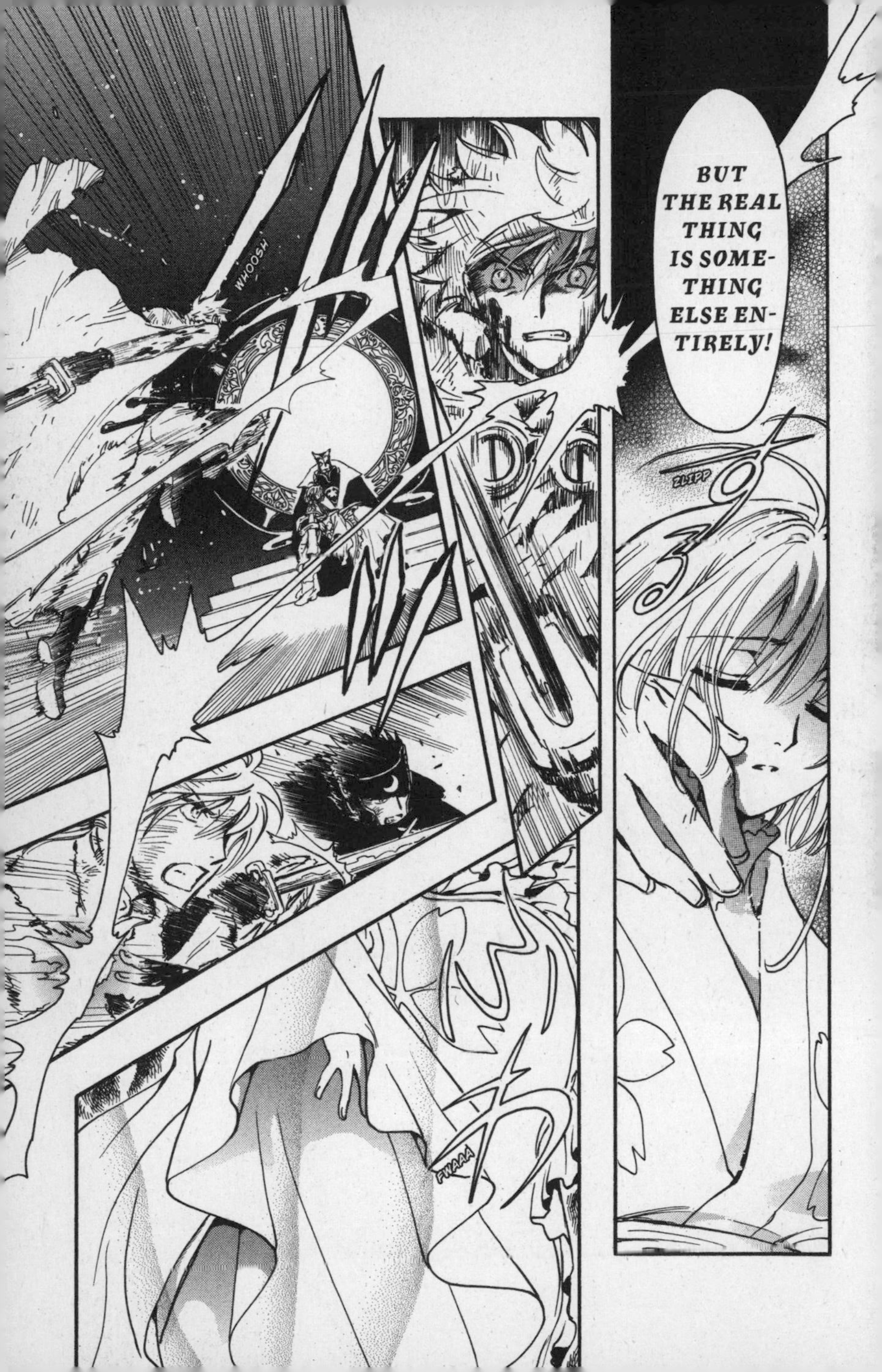
BUT THE REAL THING IS SOME-THING ELSE EN-TIRELY!
ZLIPP
WHOOSH
FWAAA

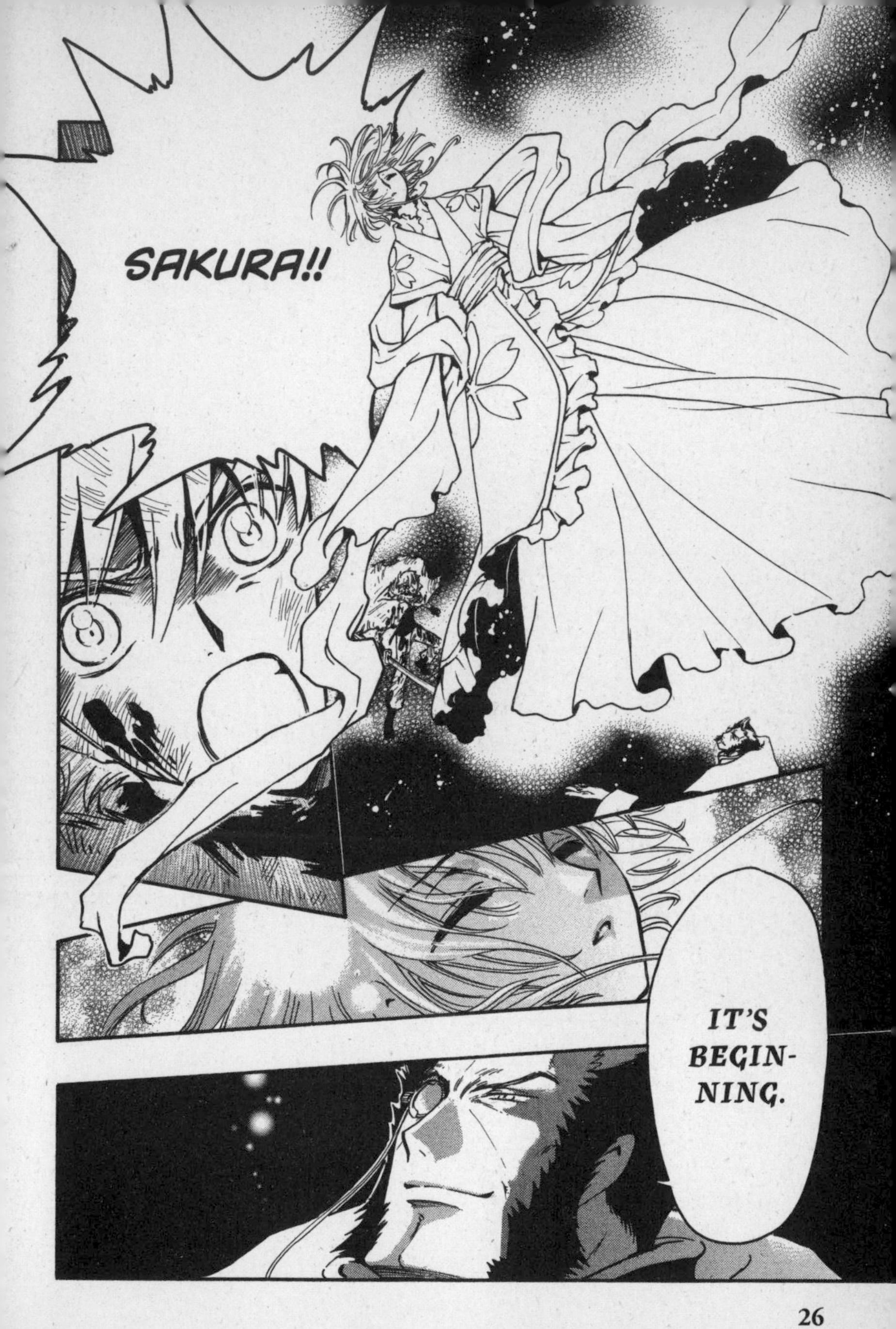
SAKURA!!
IT'S BEGIN-NING.

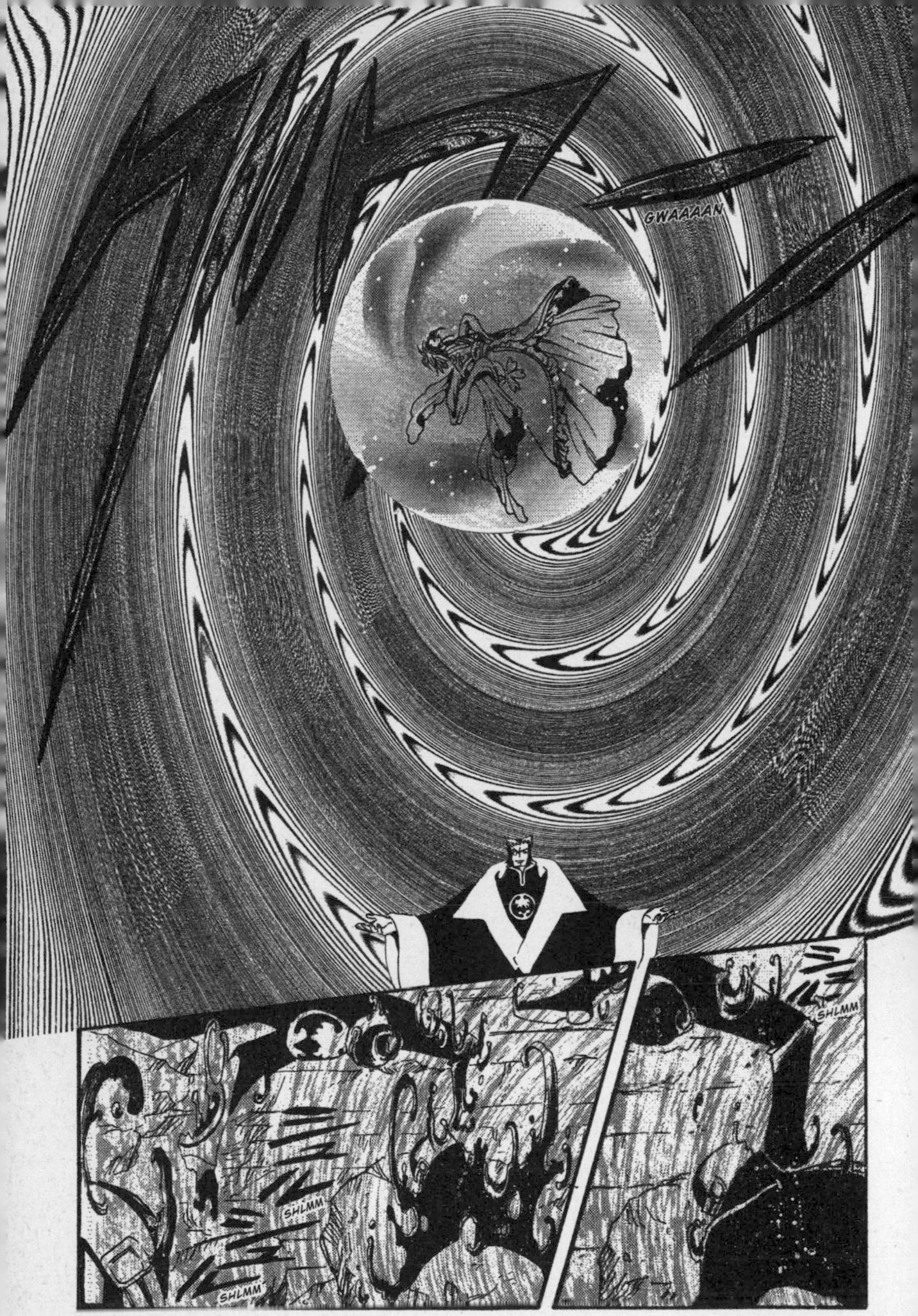
GWAAAAN
SHLMM
SHLMM
SHLMM

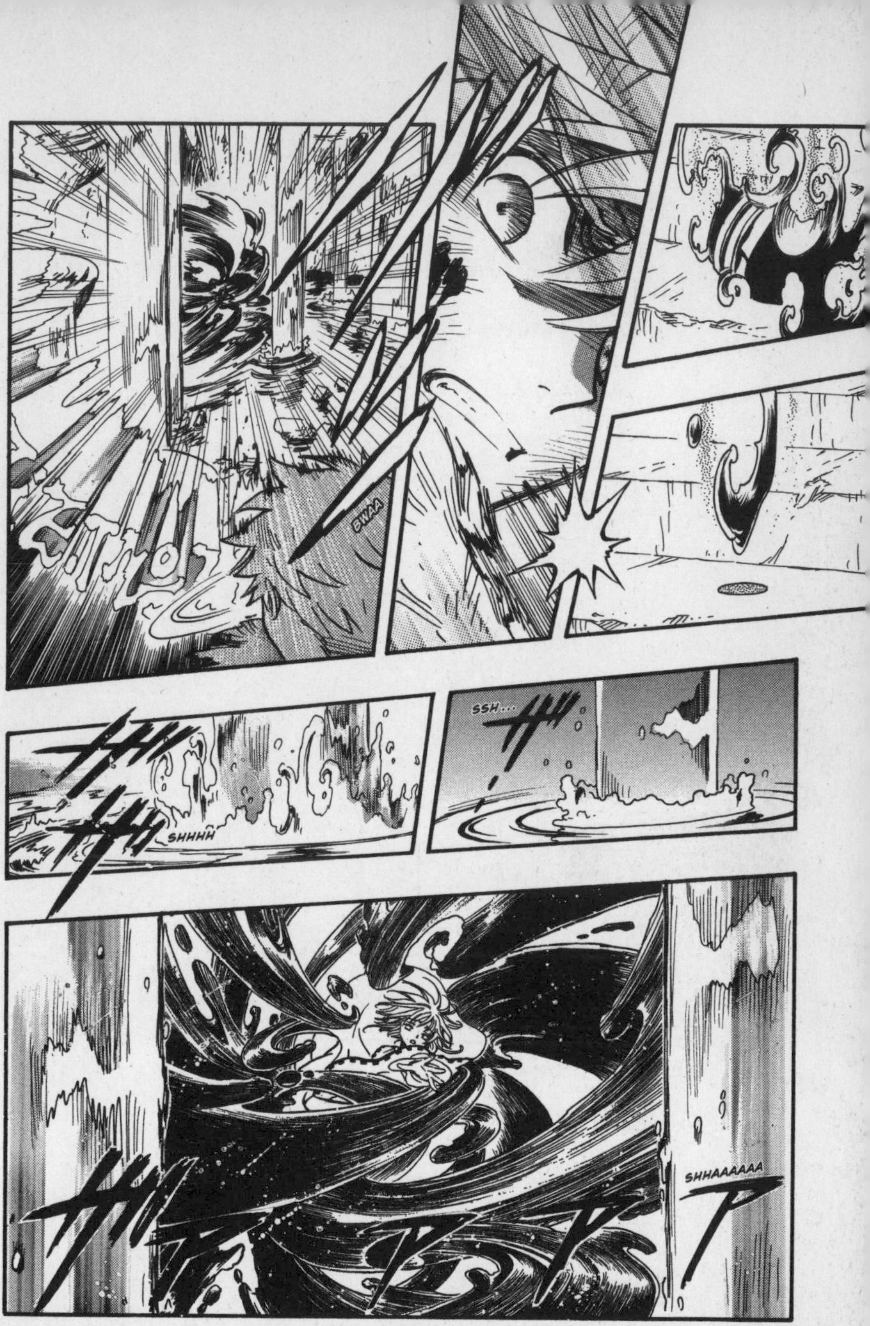
BWAA
SSH...
SHHHH
SHHAAAAAA

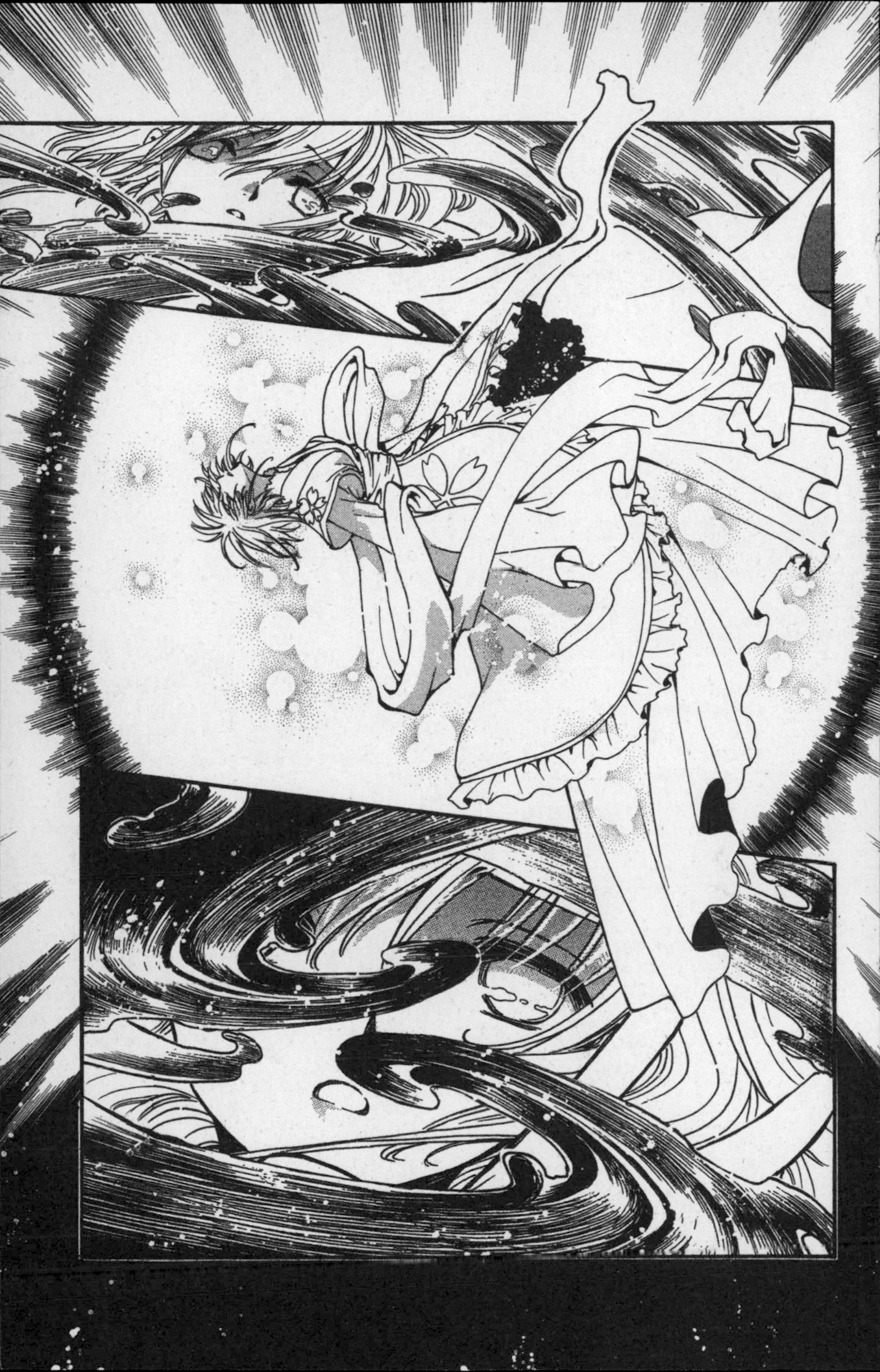

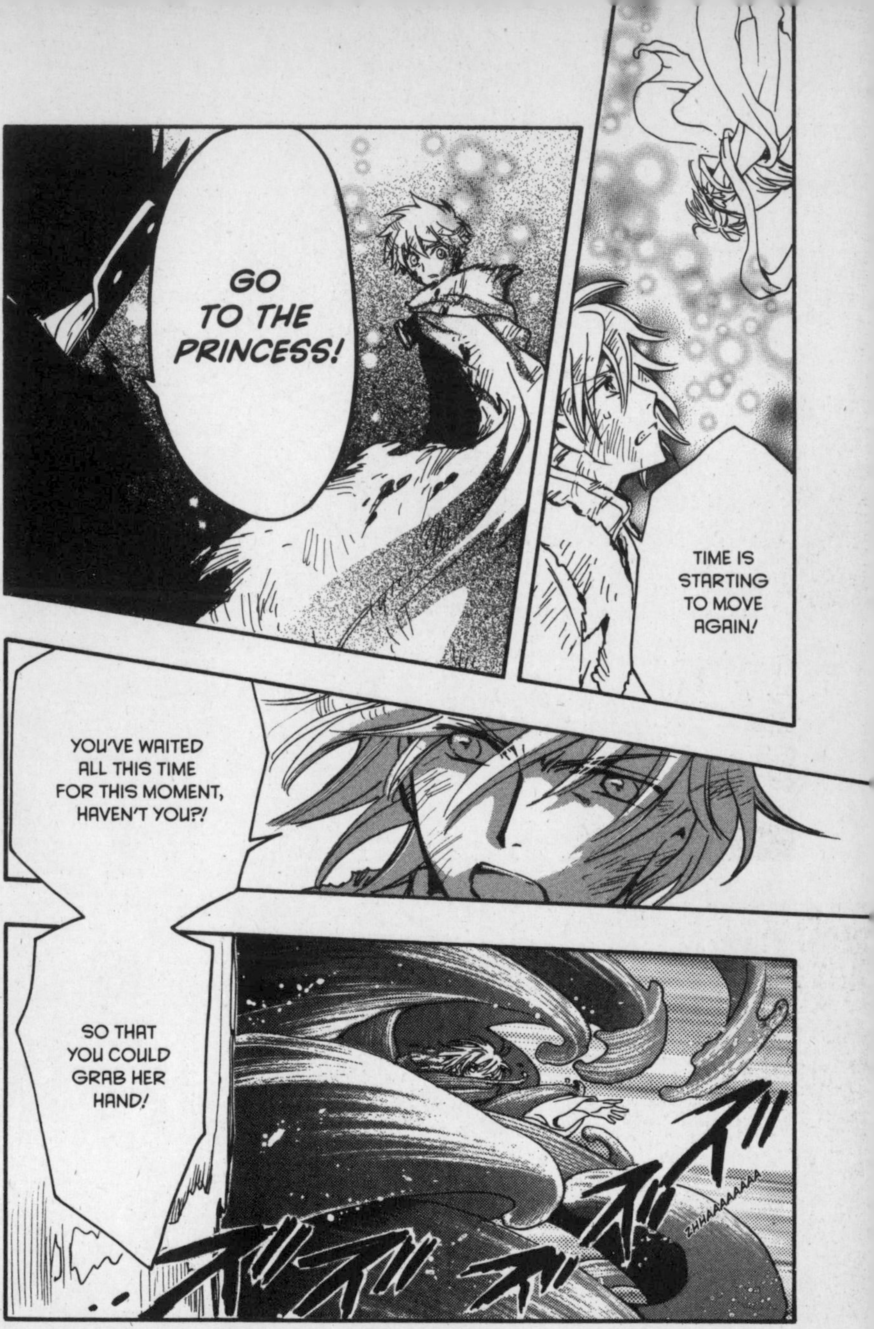
TIME IS STARTING TO MOVE AGAIN!
GO TO THE PRINCESS!
YOU'VE WAITED ALL THIS TIME FOR THIS MOMENT, HAVEN'T YOU?!
SO THAT YOU COULD GRAB HER HAND!
ZHHAAAAAAAAA

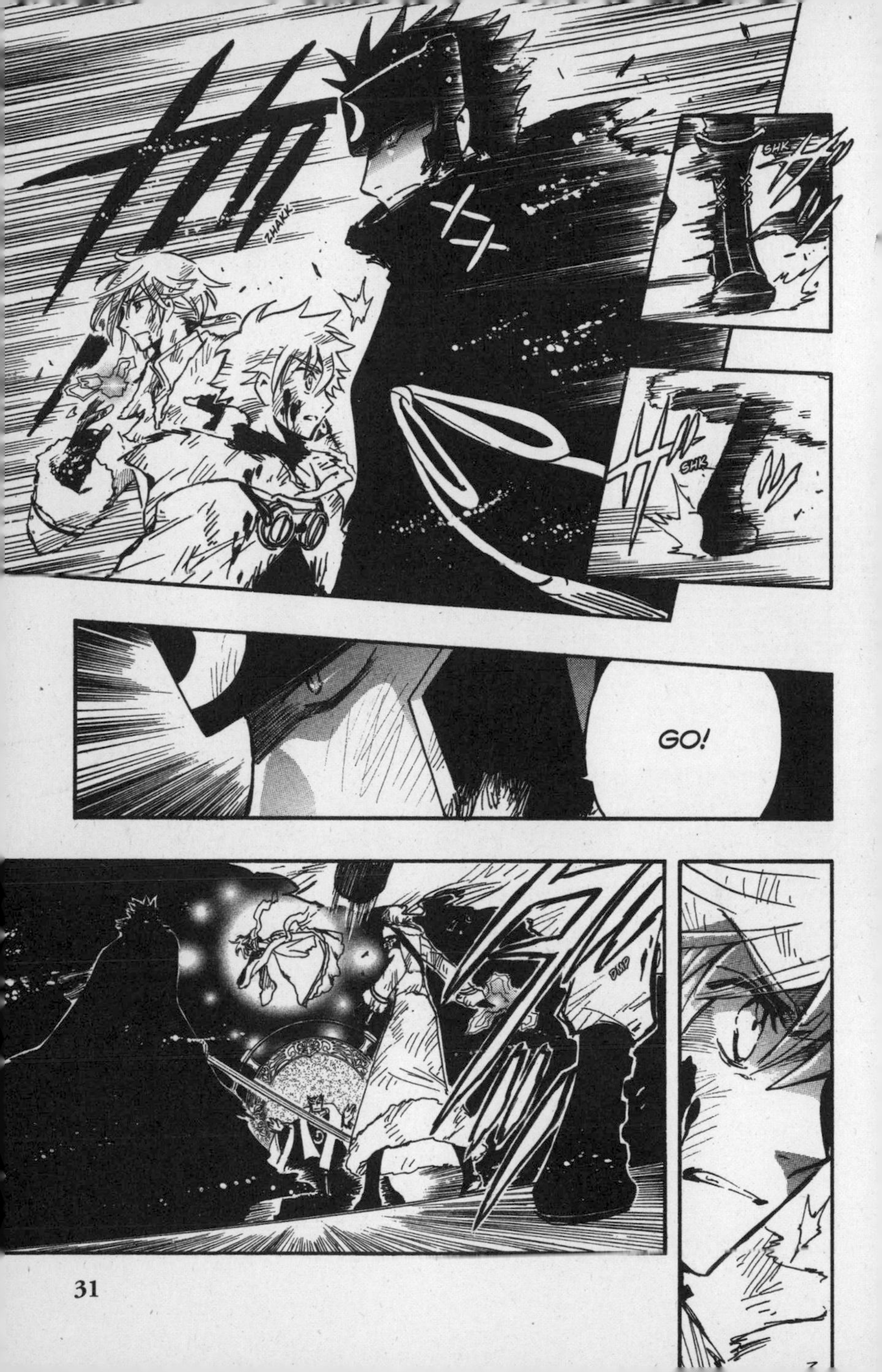
SHK
SHK
ZHAKK
GO!
DMP

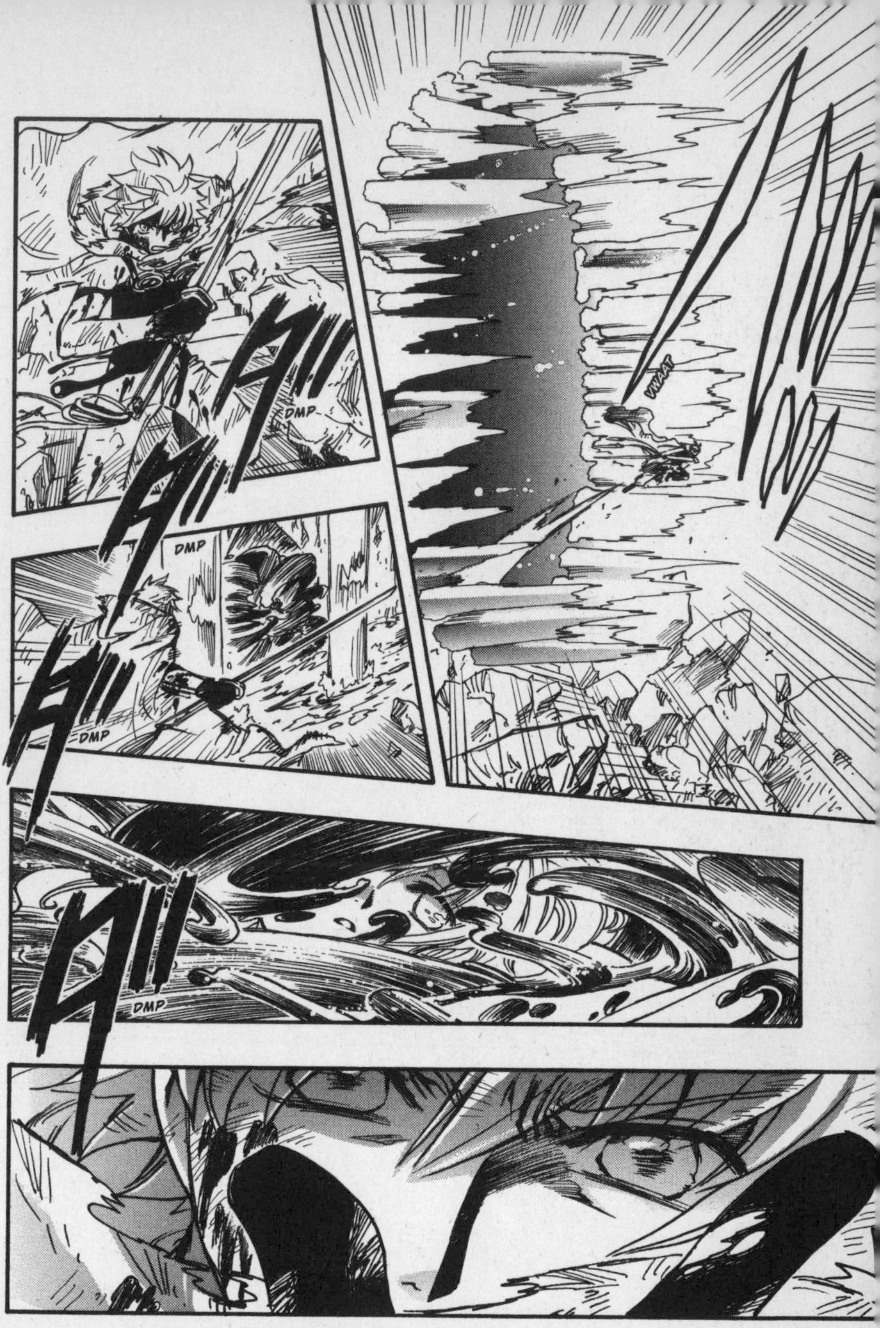
VWAAT
DMP
DMP
DMP
DMP

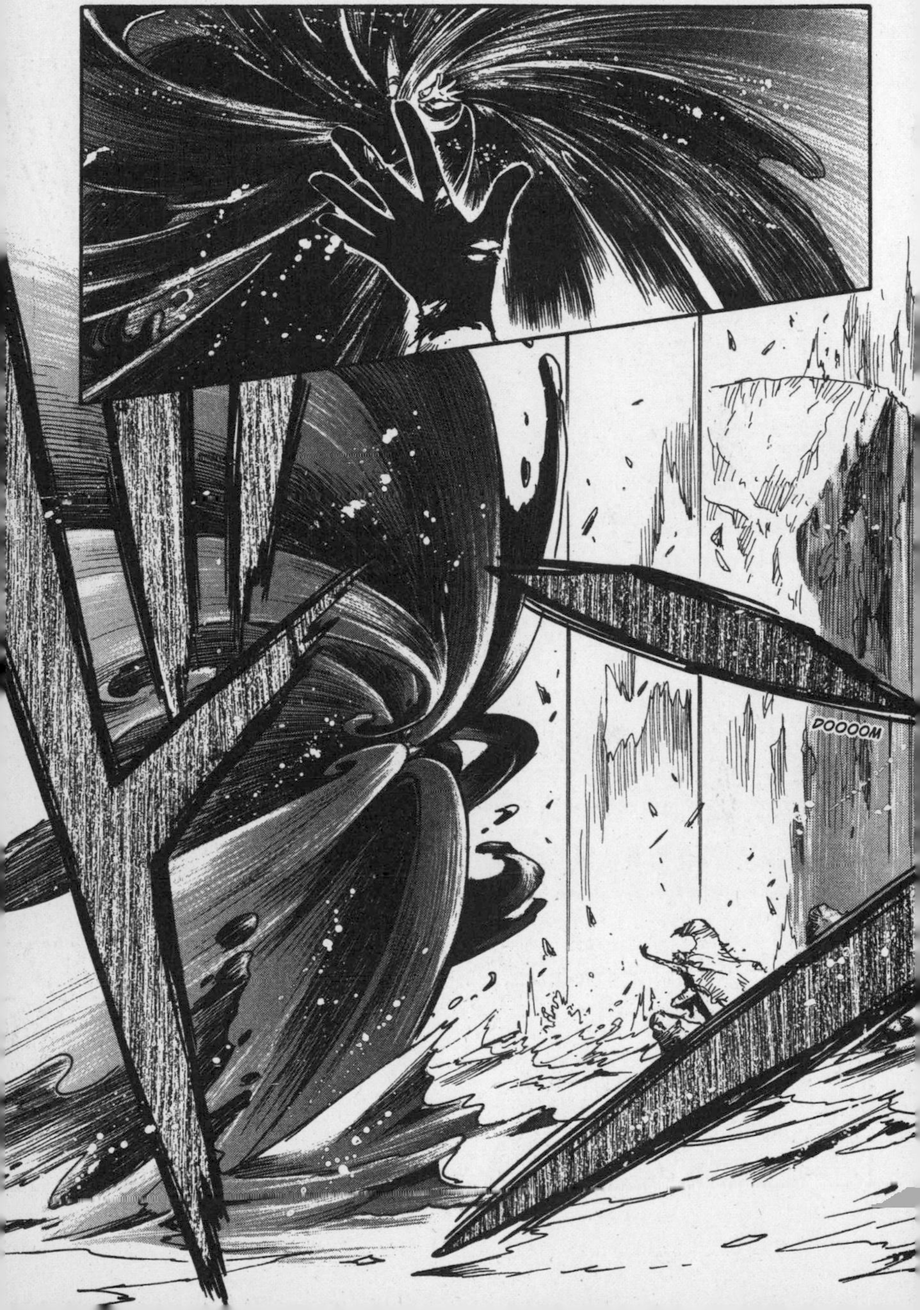
DOOOOM

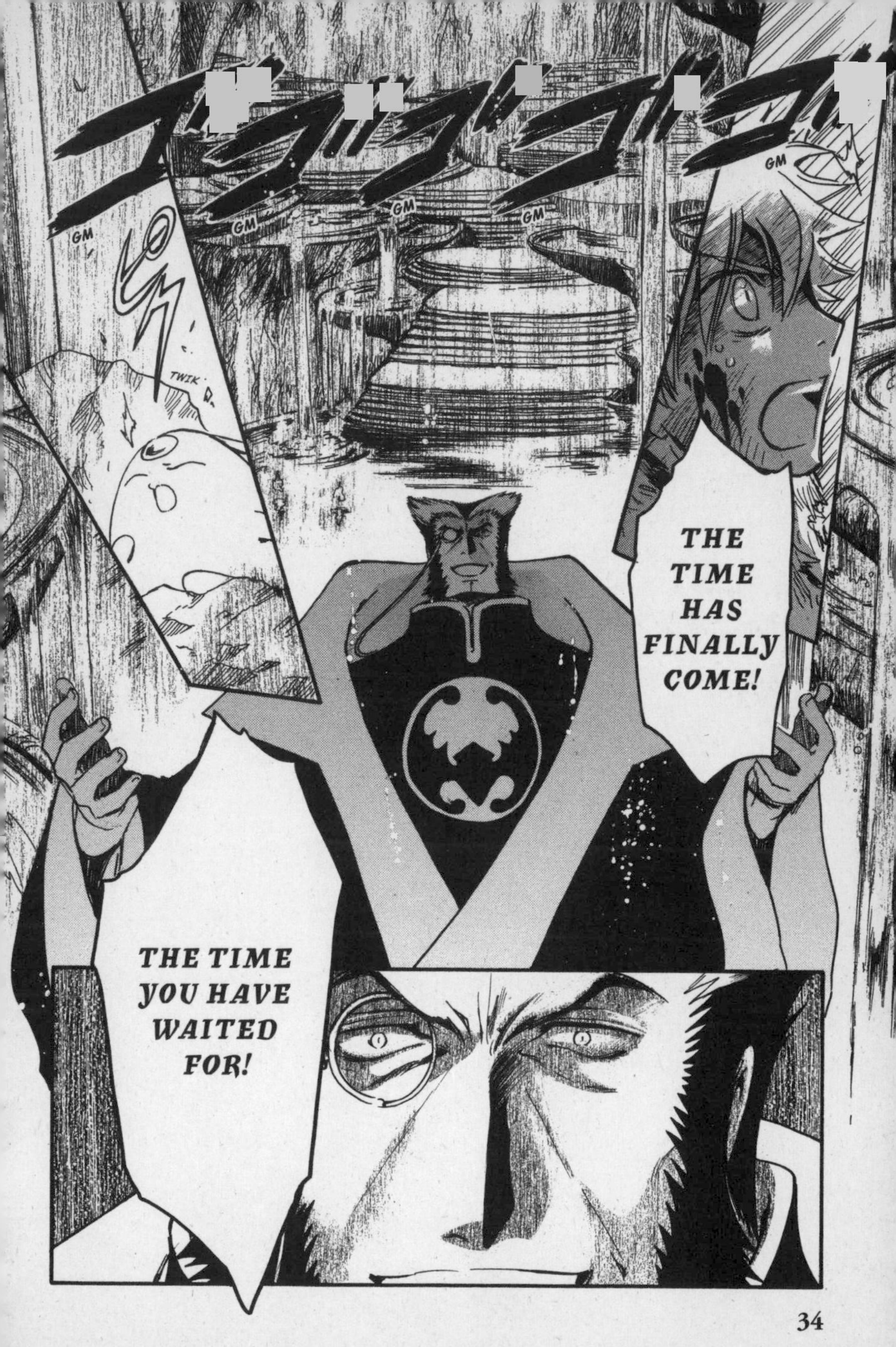
GM
GM
GM
GM
GM
TWIK
THE TIME HAS FINALLY COME!
THE TIME YOU HAVE WAITED FOR!

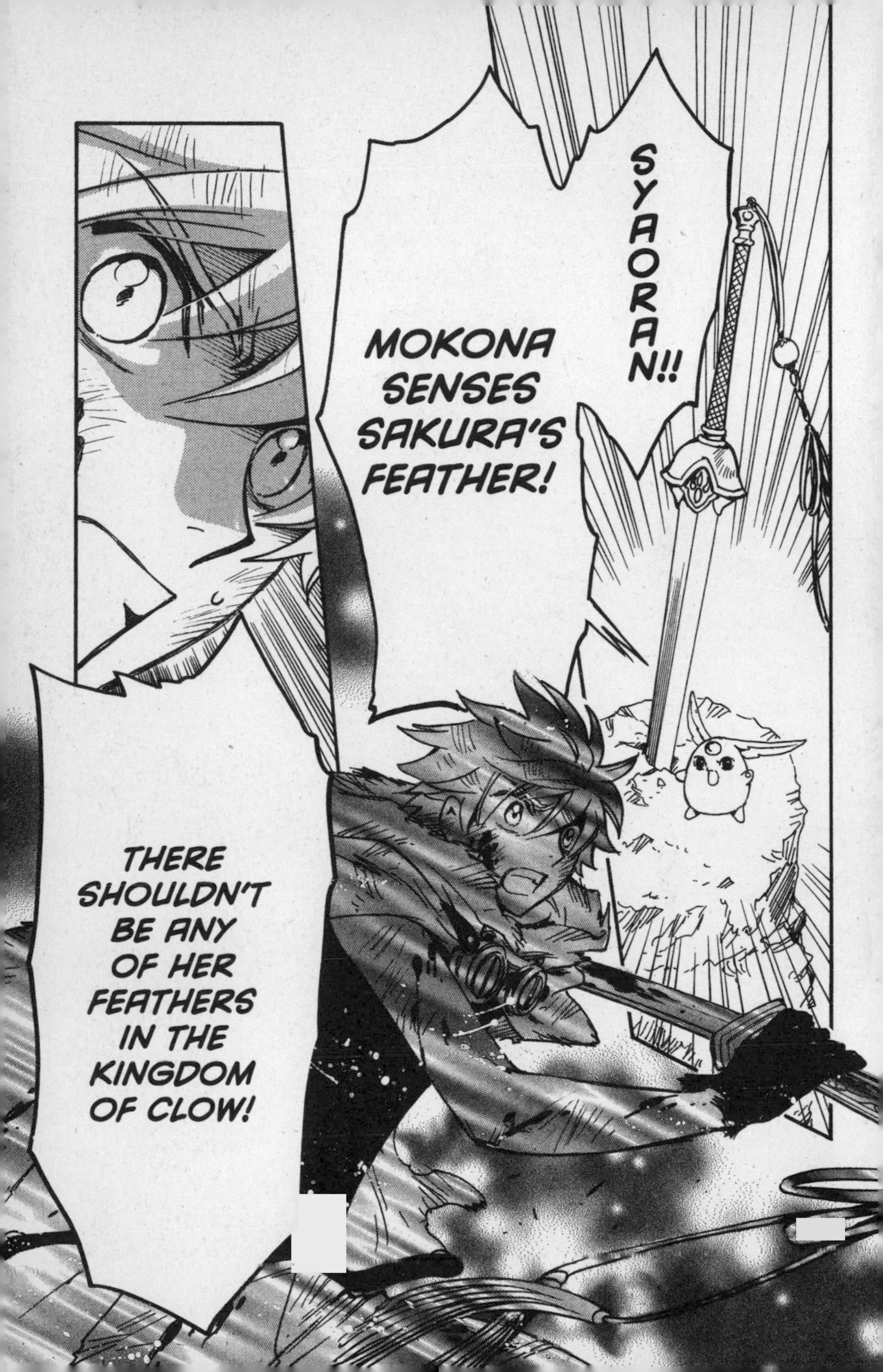
SYAORAN!!
MOKONA SENSES SAKURA'S FEATHER!
THERE SHOULDN'T BE ANY OF HER FEATHERS IN THE KINGDOM OF CLOW!

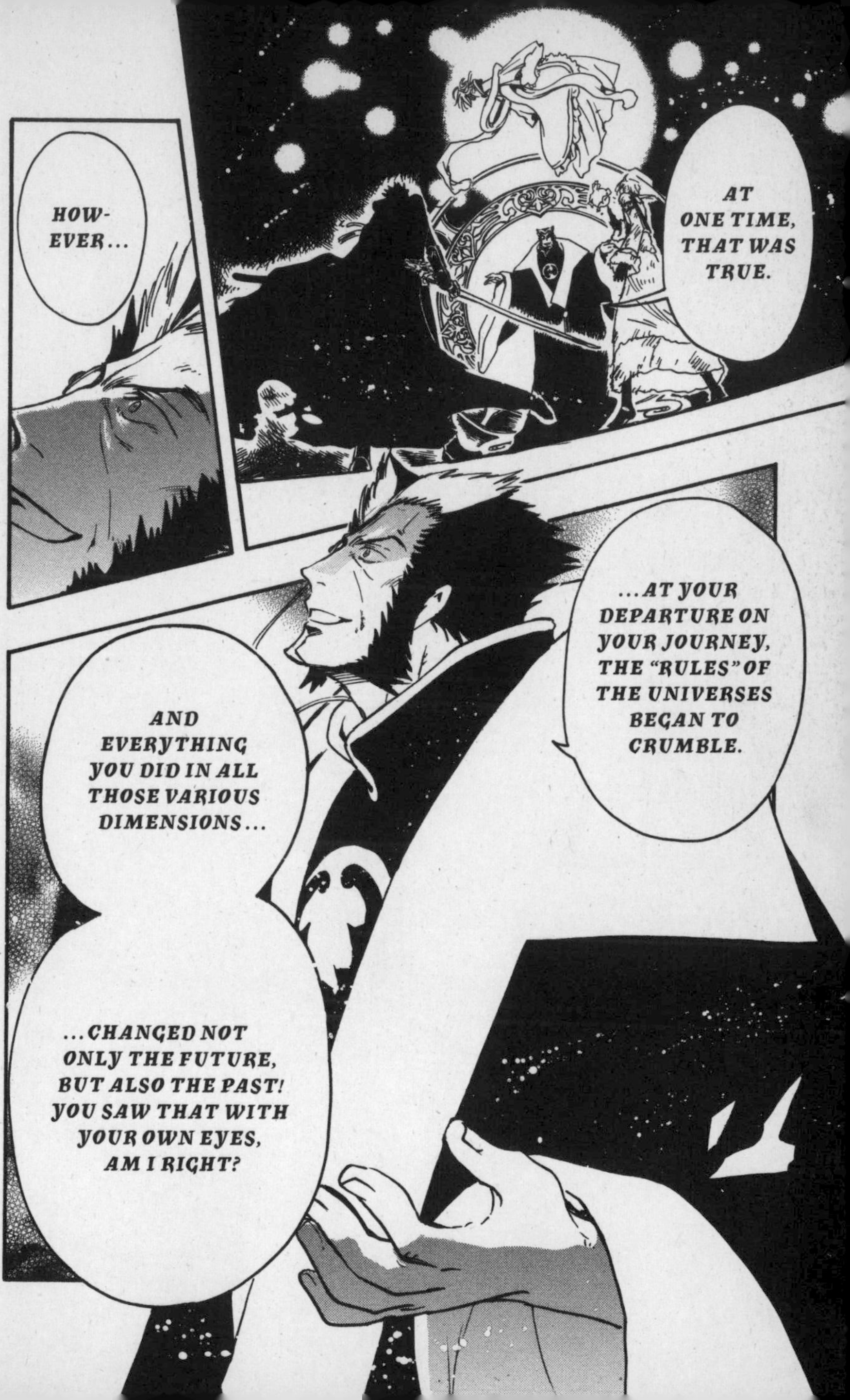
AT ONE TIME, THAT WAS TRUE.
HOW-EVER...
...AT YOUR DEPARTURE ON YOUR JOURNEY, THE "RULES" OF THE UNIVERSES BEGAN TO CRUMBLE.
AND EVERYTHING YOU DID IN ALL THOSE VARIOUS DIMENSIONS...
...CHANGED NOT ONLY THE FUTURE, BUT ALSO THE PAST! YOU SAW THAT WITH YOUR OWN EYES, AM I RIGHT?

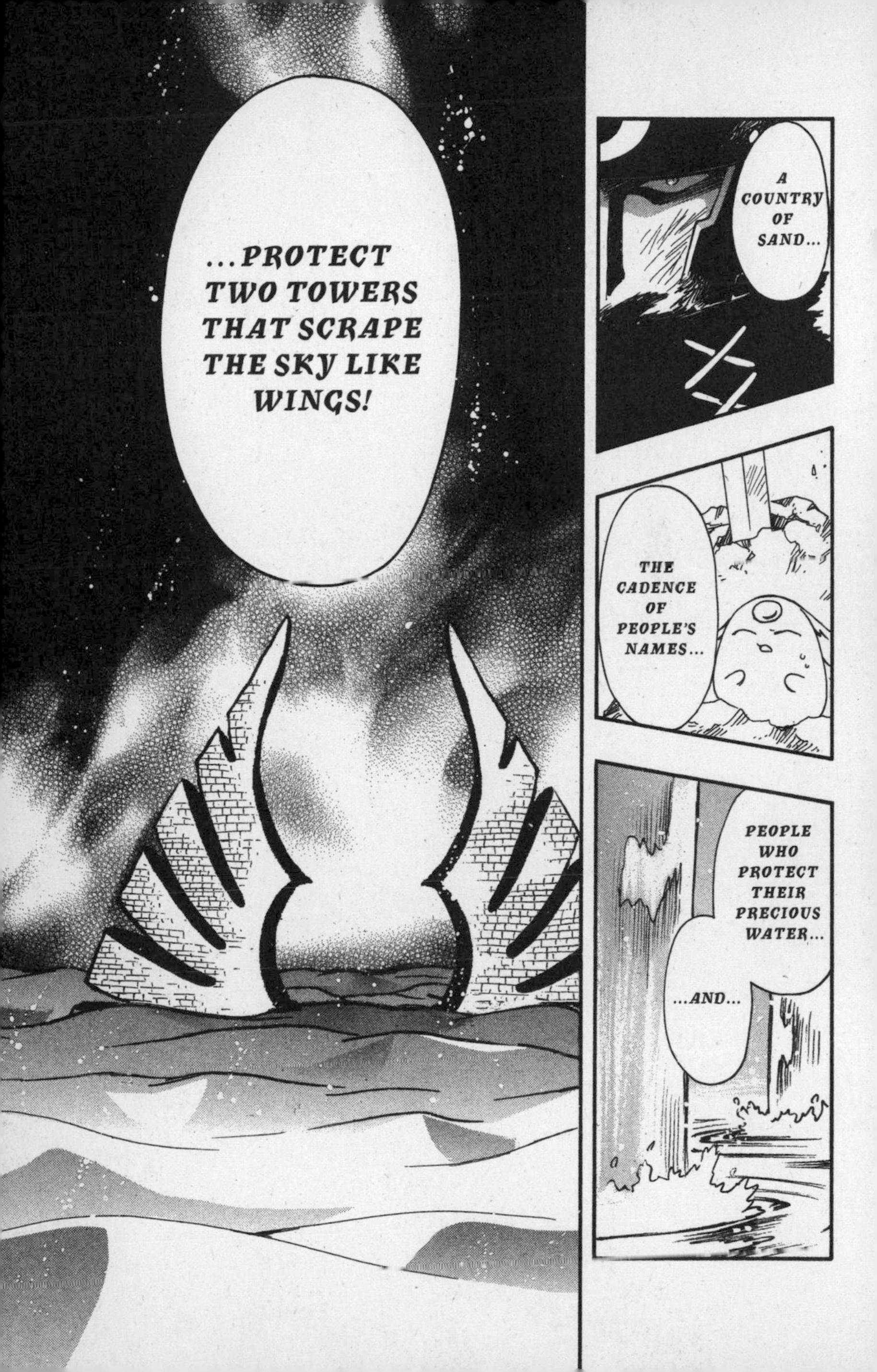
A COUNTRY OF SAND...
THE CADENCE OF PEOPLE'S NAMES...
PEOPLE WHO PROTECT THEIR PRECIOUS WATER...
...AND...
...PROTECT TWO TOWERS THAT SCRAPE THE SKY LIKE WINGS!

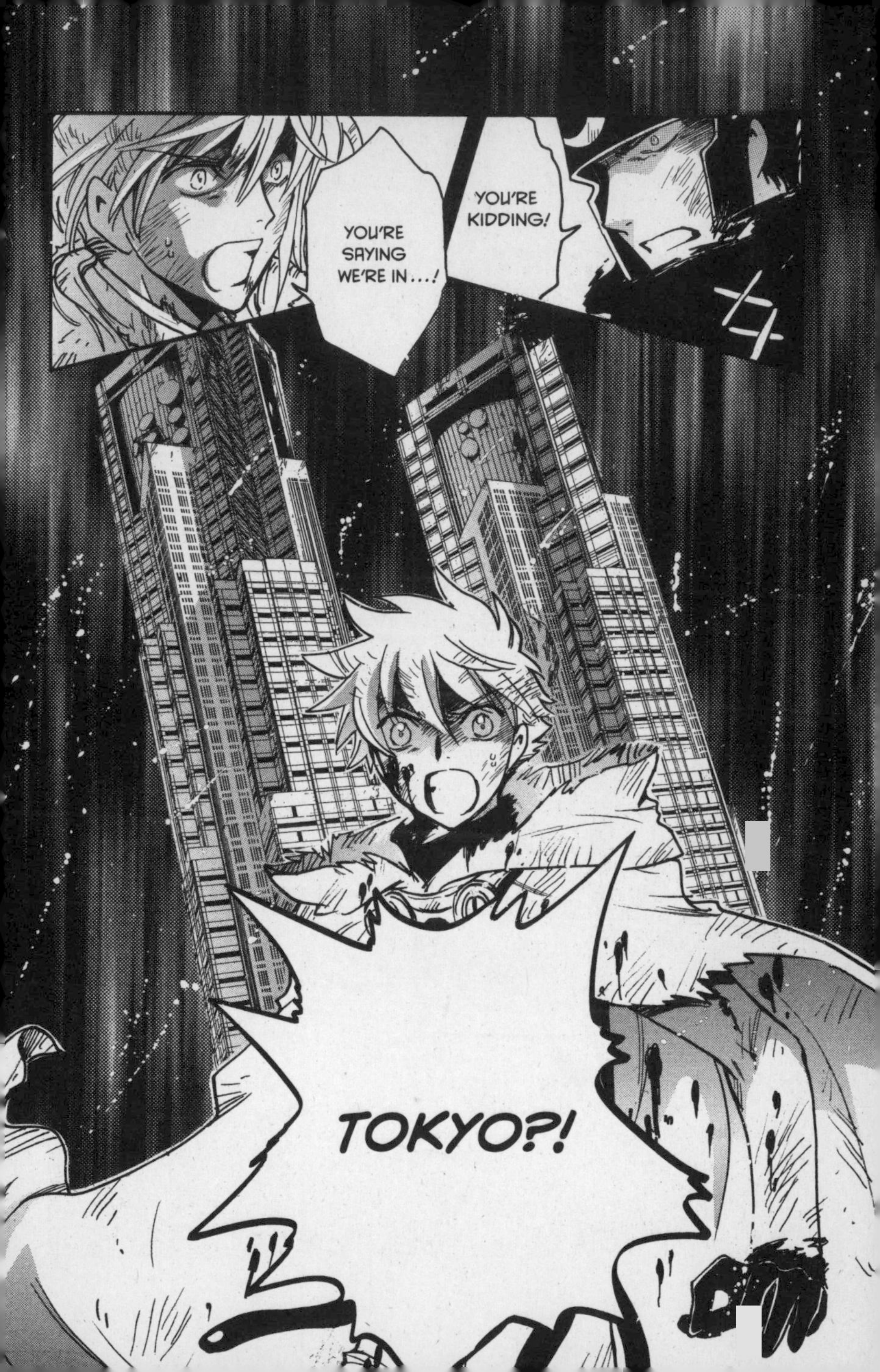
YOU'RE KIDDING!
YOU'RE SAYING WE'RE IN...!
TOKYO?!

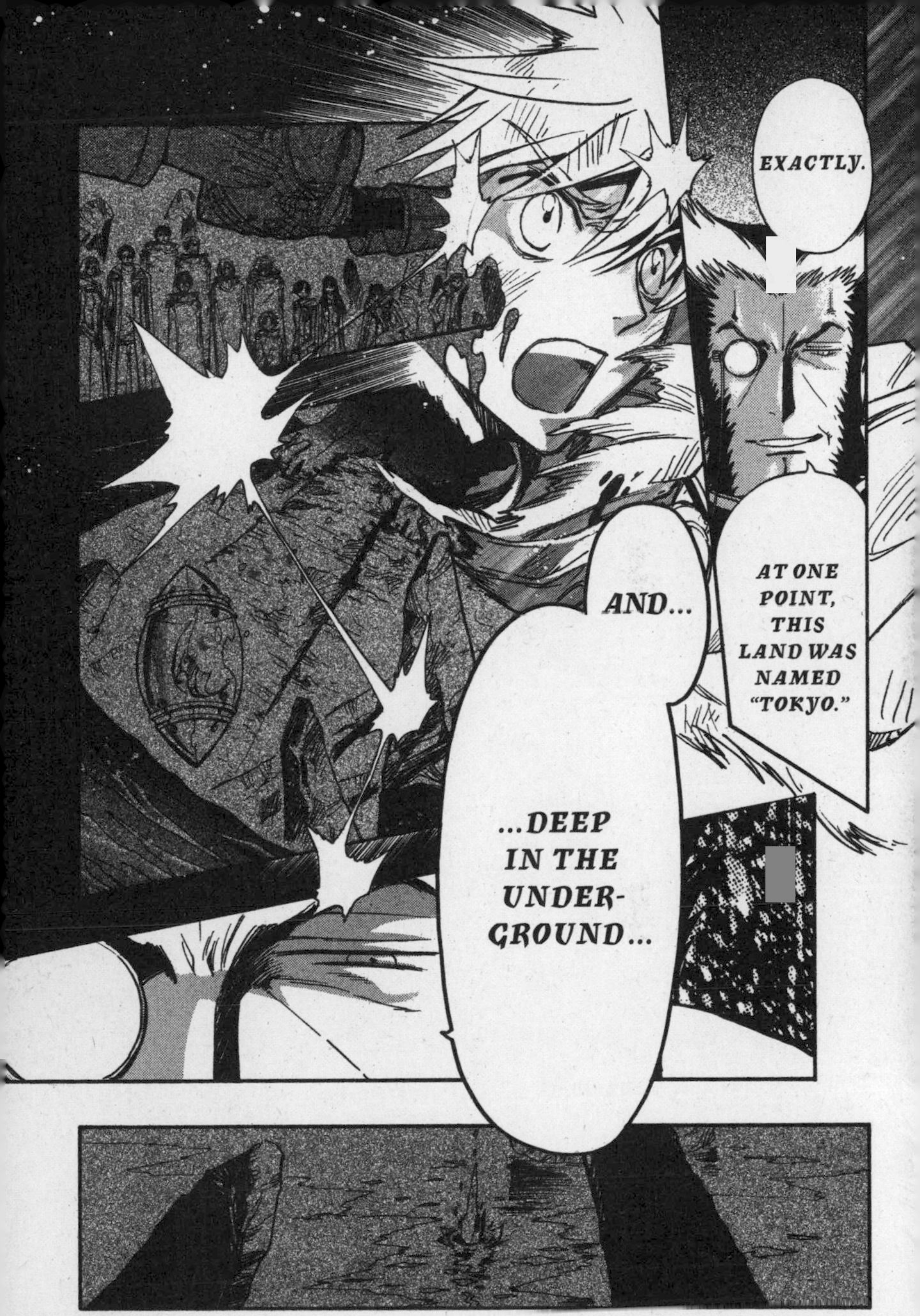
EXACTLY.
AT ONE POINT, THIS LAND WAS NAMED "TOKYO."
AND...
...DEEP IN THE UNDER-GROUND...

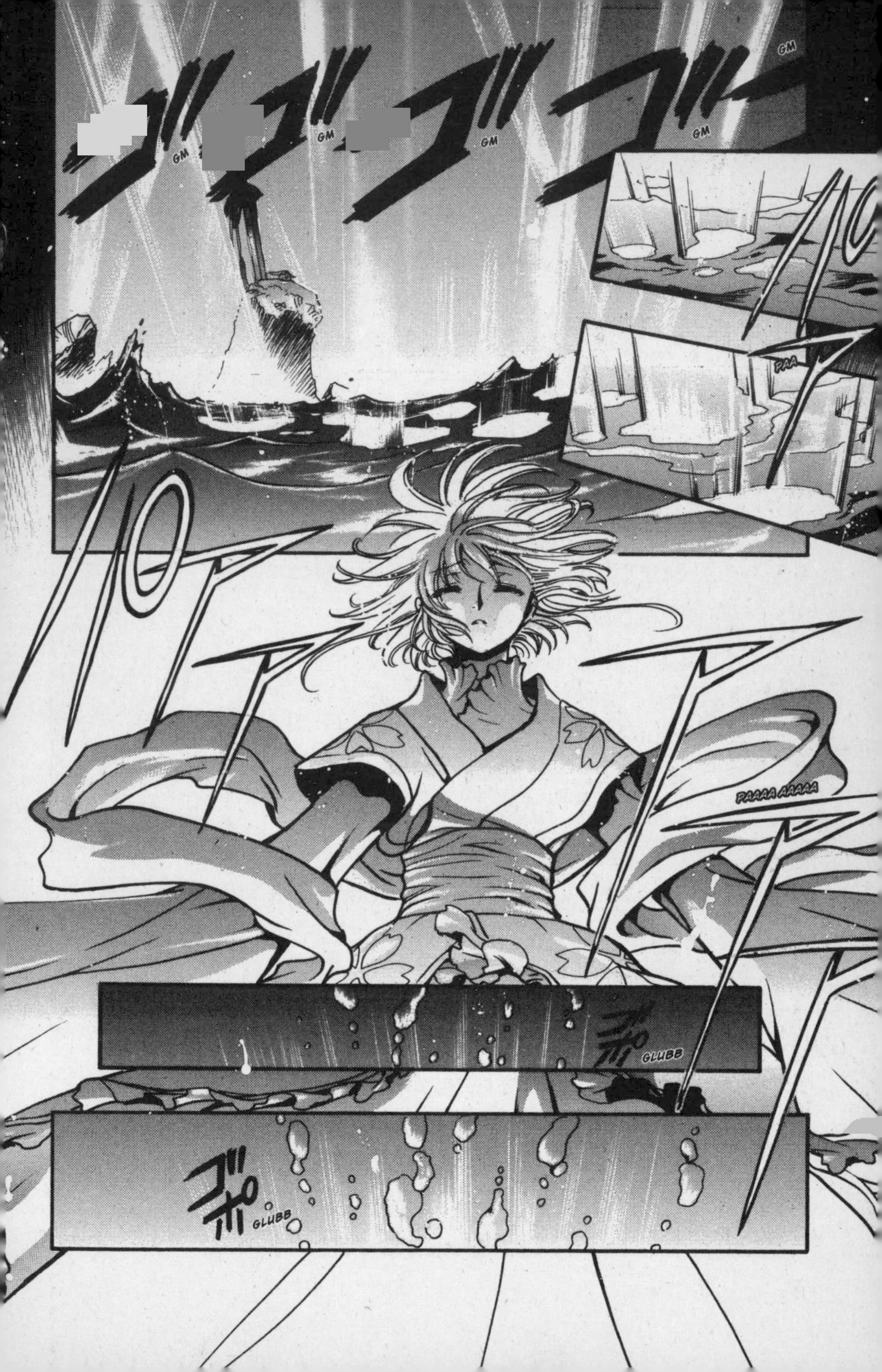
GM
GM
GM
GM
GM
PAA
PAAAA AAAAA
GLUBB
GLUBB

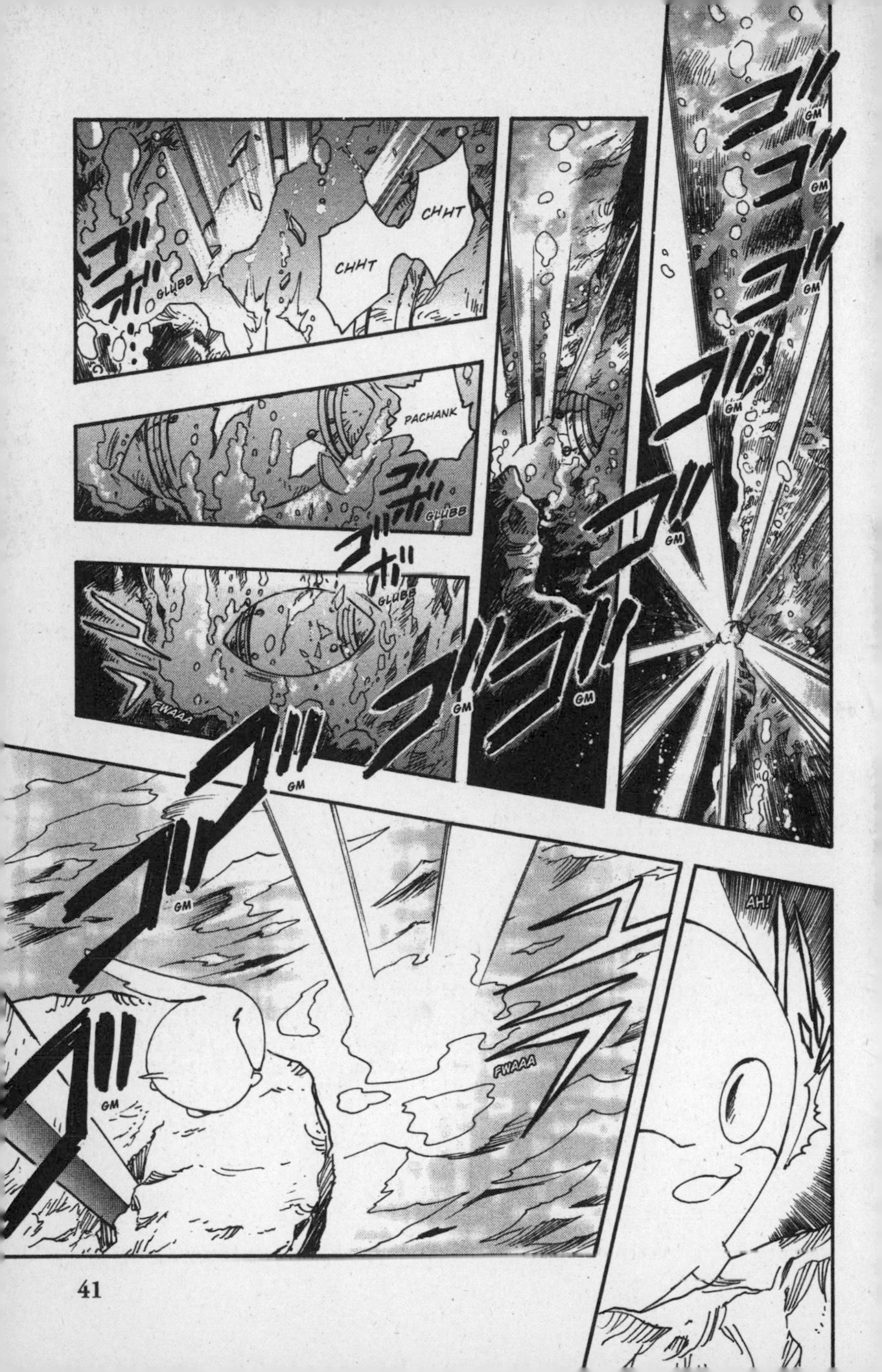
GM
GM
GM
GM
GM
GM
GM
CHHT
CHHT
GLUBB
PACHANK
GLUBB
GLUBB
FWAAA
GM
GM
GM
AH!
FWAAA

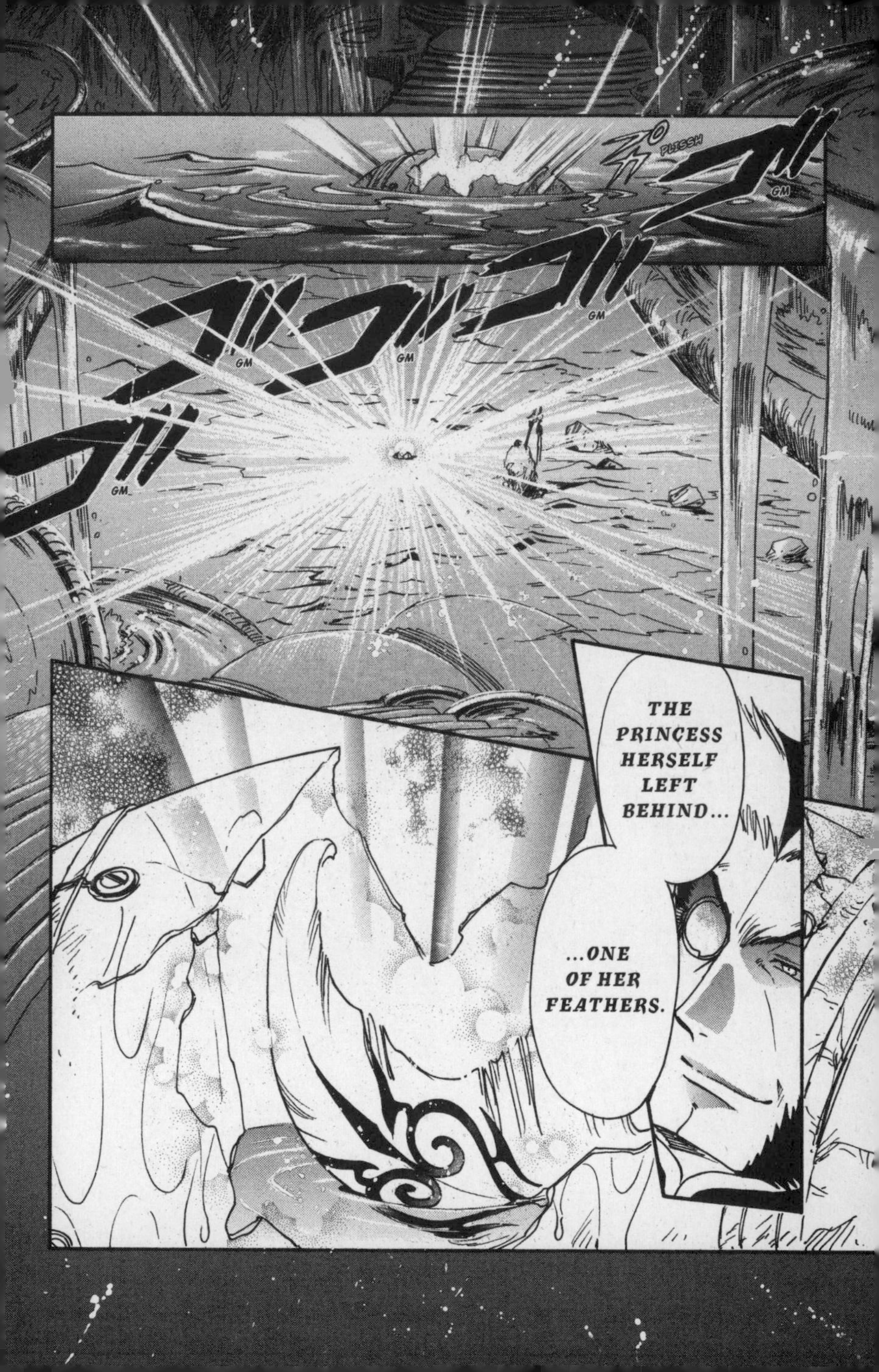
PLISSH
GM
GM
GM
GM
GM
THE PRINCESS HERSELF LEFT BEHIND...
...ONE OF HER FEATHERS.

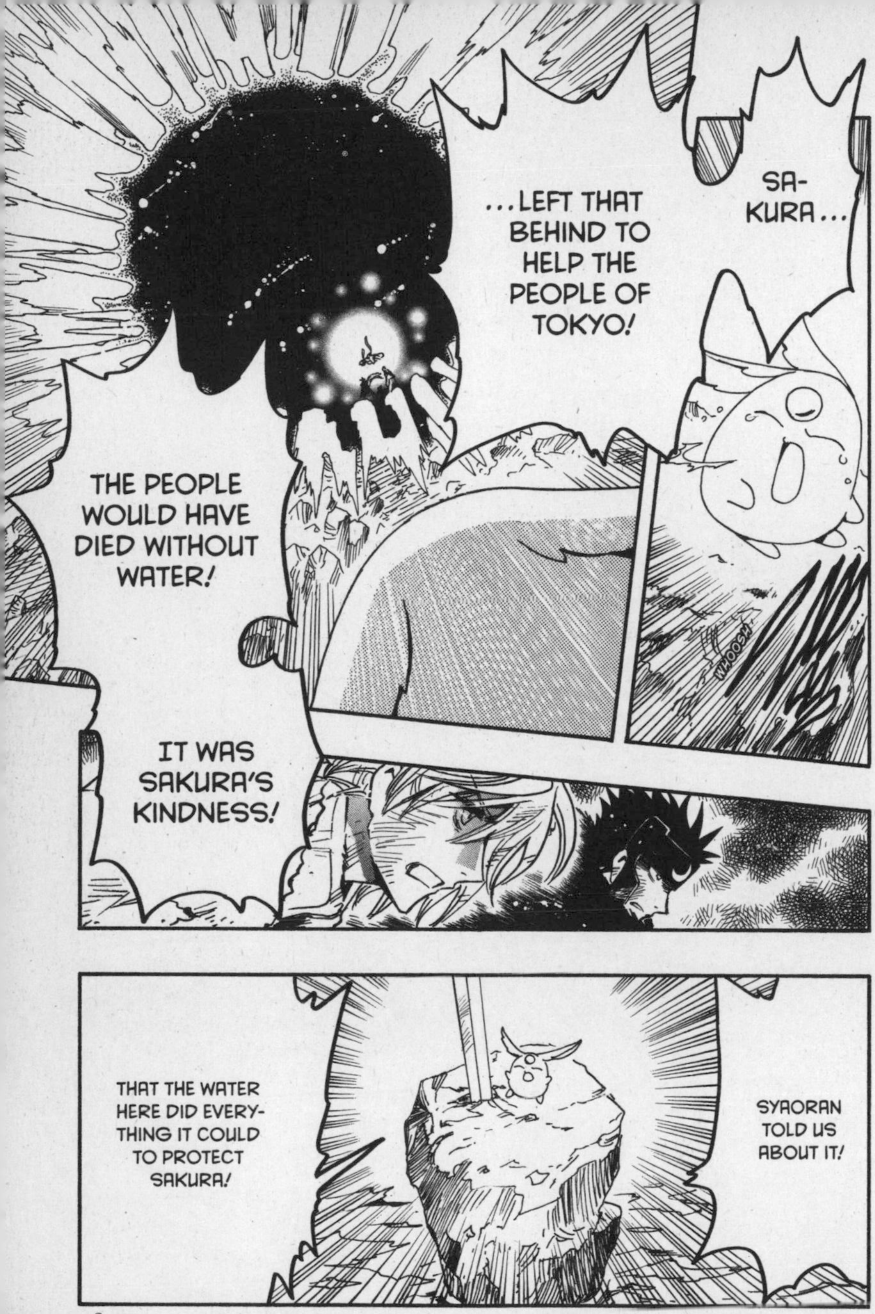
SA-KURA...
...LEFT THAT BEHIND TO HELP THE PEOPLE OF TOKYO!
THE PEOPLE WOULD HAVE DIED WITHOUT WATER!
WHOOSH
IT WAS SAKURA'S KINDNESS!
SYAORAN TOLD US ABOUT IT!
THAT THE WATER HERE DID EVERY-THING IT COULD TO PROTECT SAKURA!

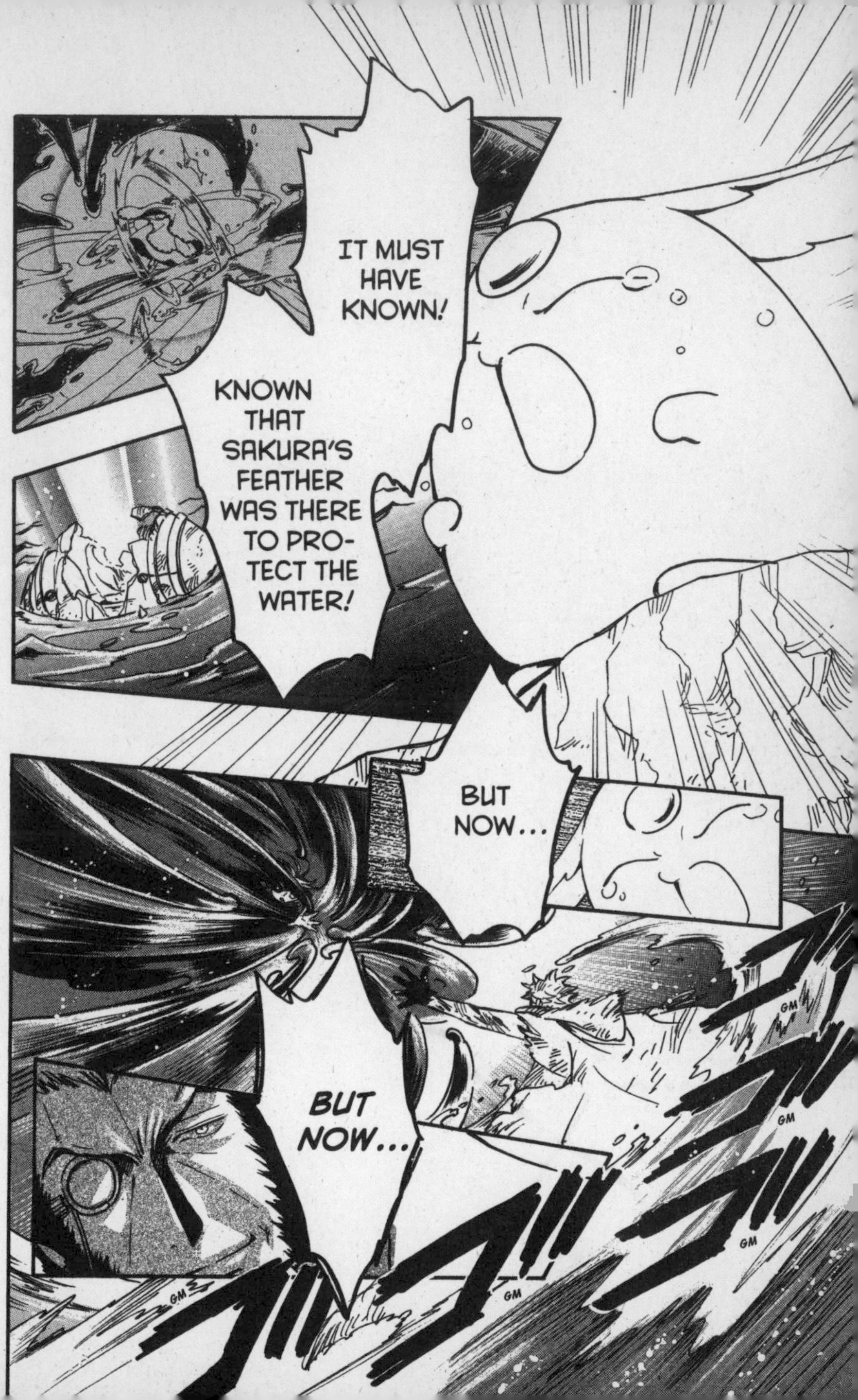
IT MUST HAVE KNOWN!
KNOWN THAT SAKURA'S FEATHER WAS THERE TO PRO-TECT THE WATER!
BUT NOW...
BUT NOW...
GM
GM
GM
GM
GM

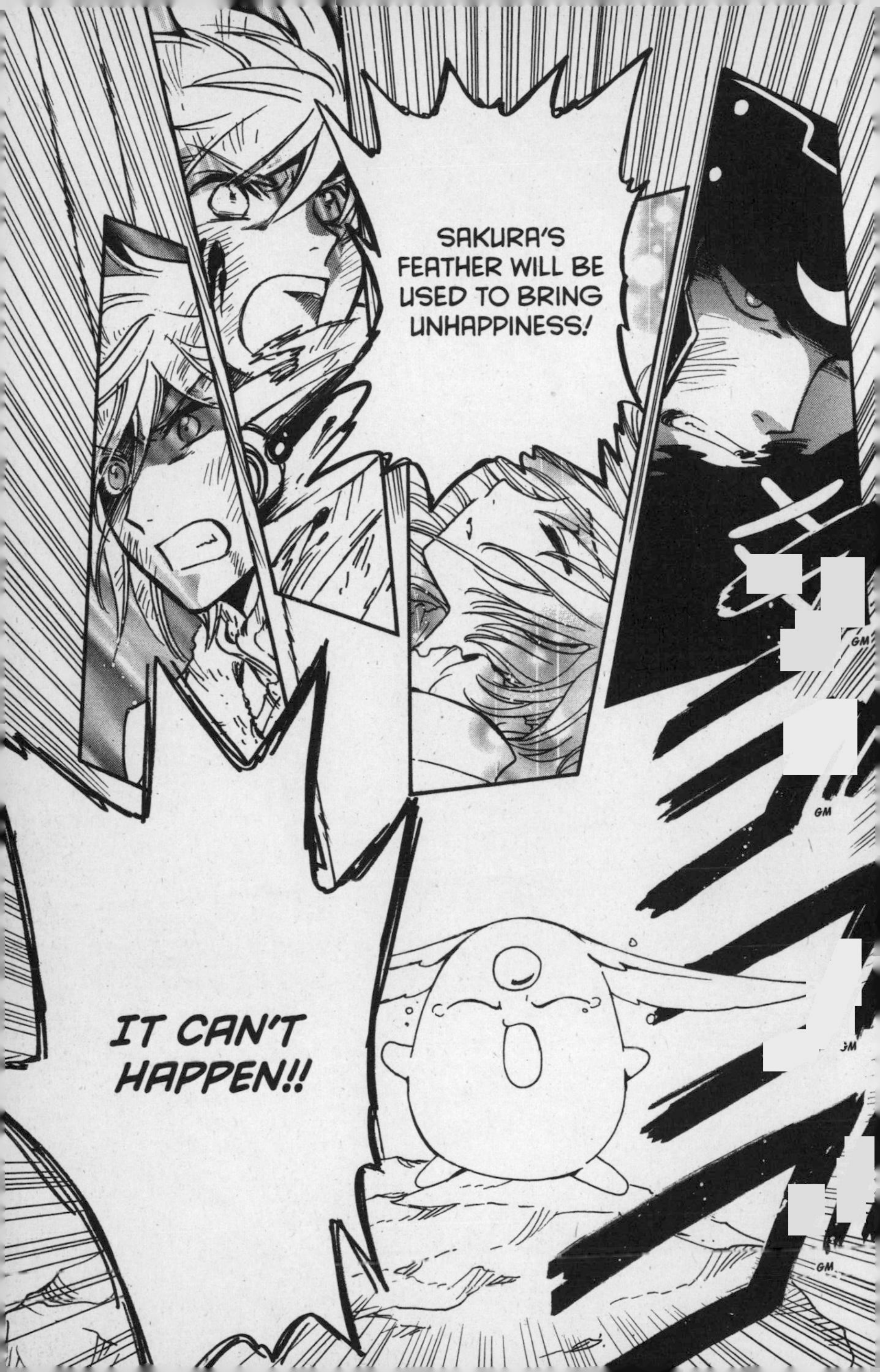
SAKURA'S FEATHER WILL BE USED TO BRING UNHAPPINESS!
GM
GM
GM
GM
IT CAN'T HAPPEN!!

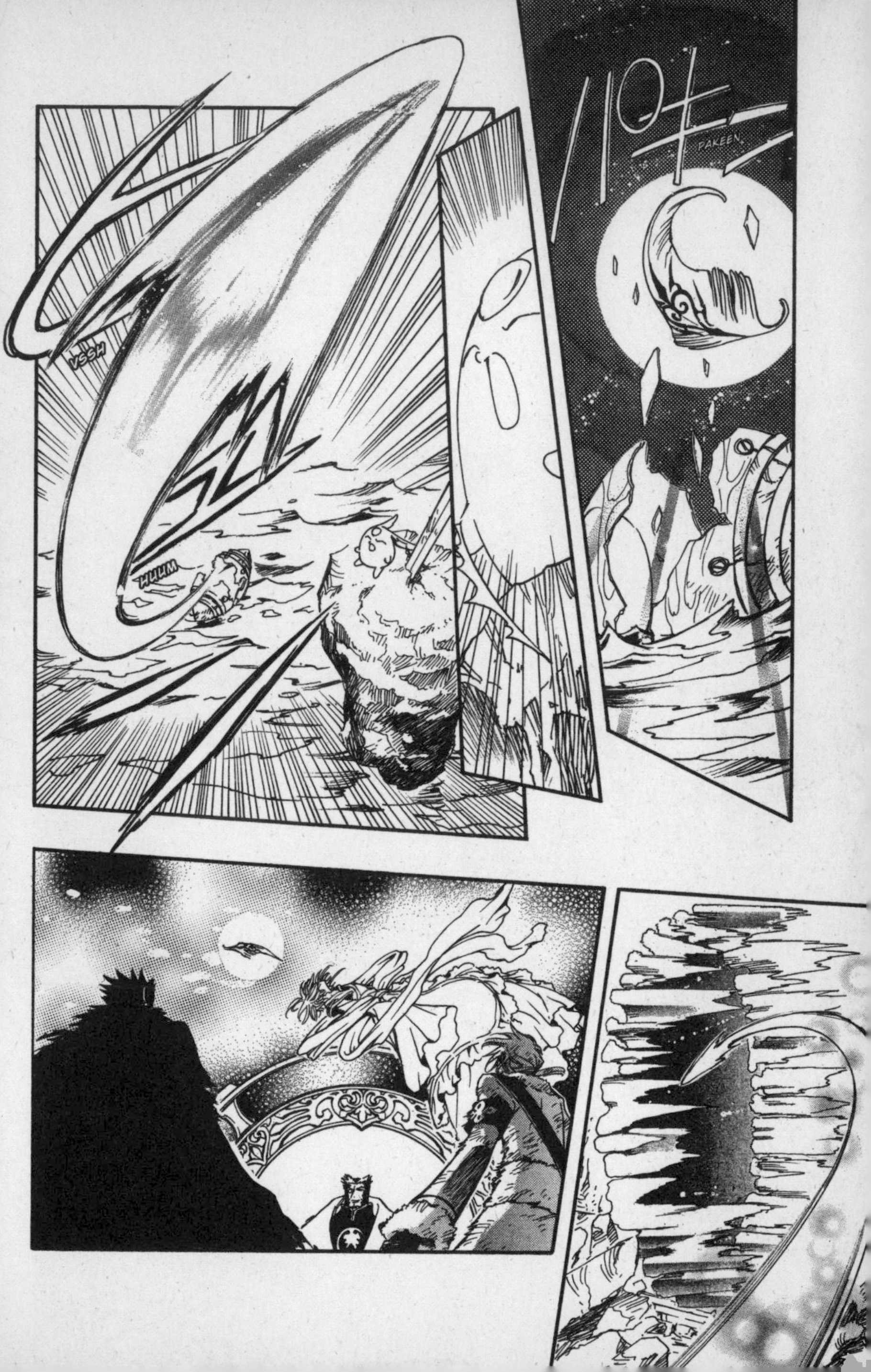
PAKEEN
VSSH
HUUM

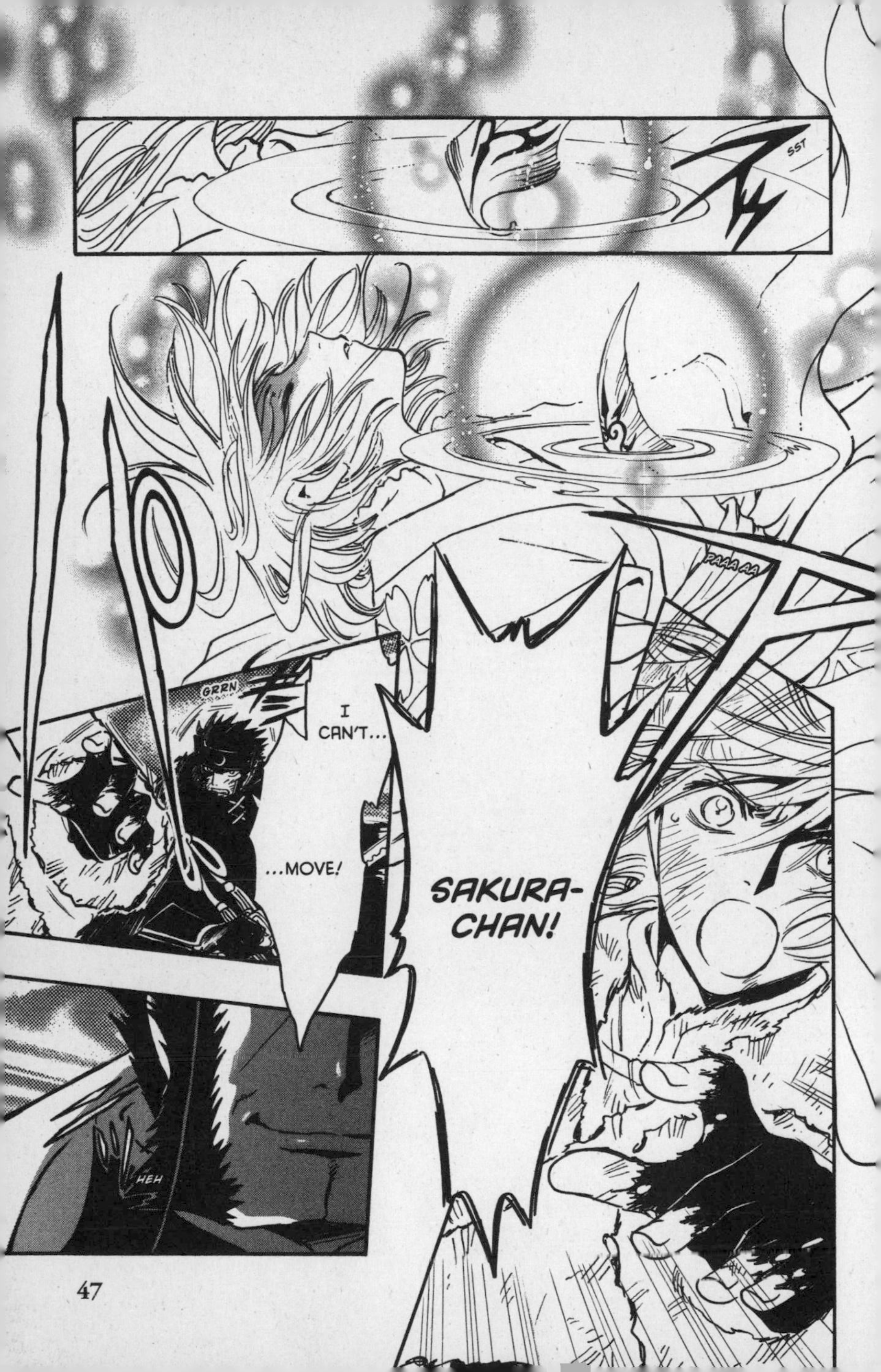
SST
PAAA AA
SAKURA-CHAN!
GRRN
I CAN'T...
...MOVE!
HEH

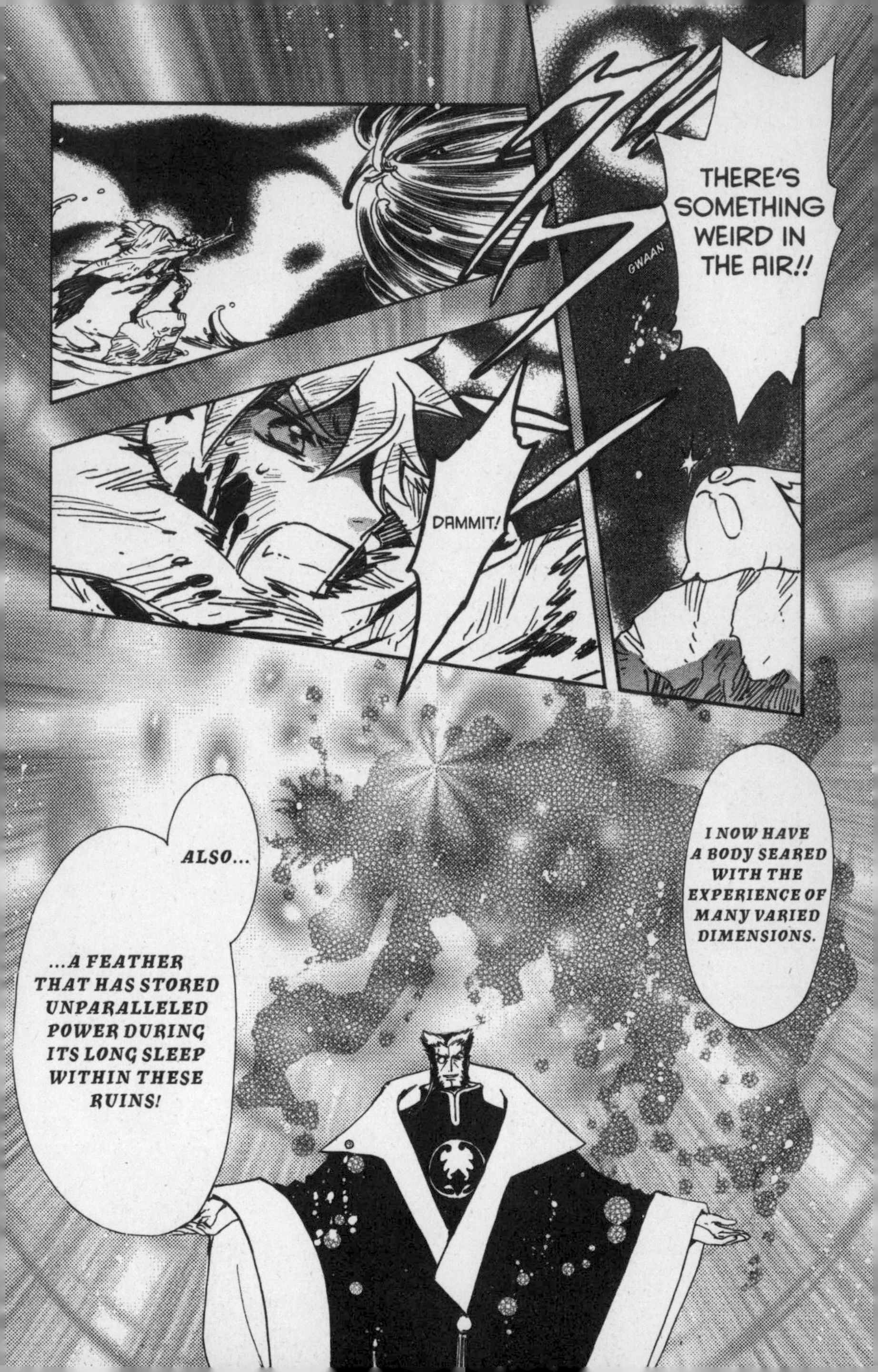
THERE'S SOMETHING WEIRD IN THE AIR!!
GWAAN
DAMMIT!
I NOW HAVE A BODY SEARED WITH THE EXPERIENCE OF MANY VARIED DIMENSIONS.
ALSO...
...A FEATHER THAT HAS STORED UNPARALLELED POWER DURING ITS LONG SLEEP WITHIN THESE RUINS!

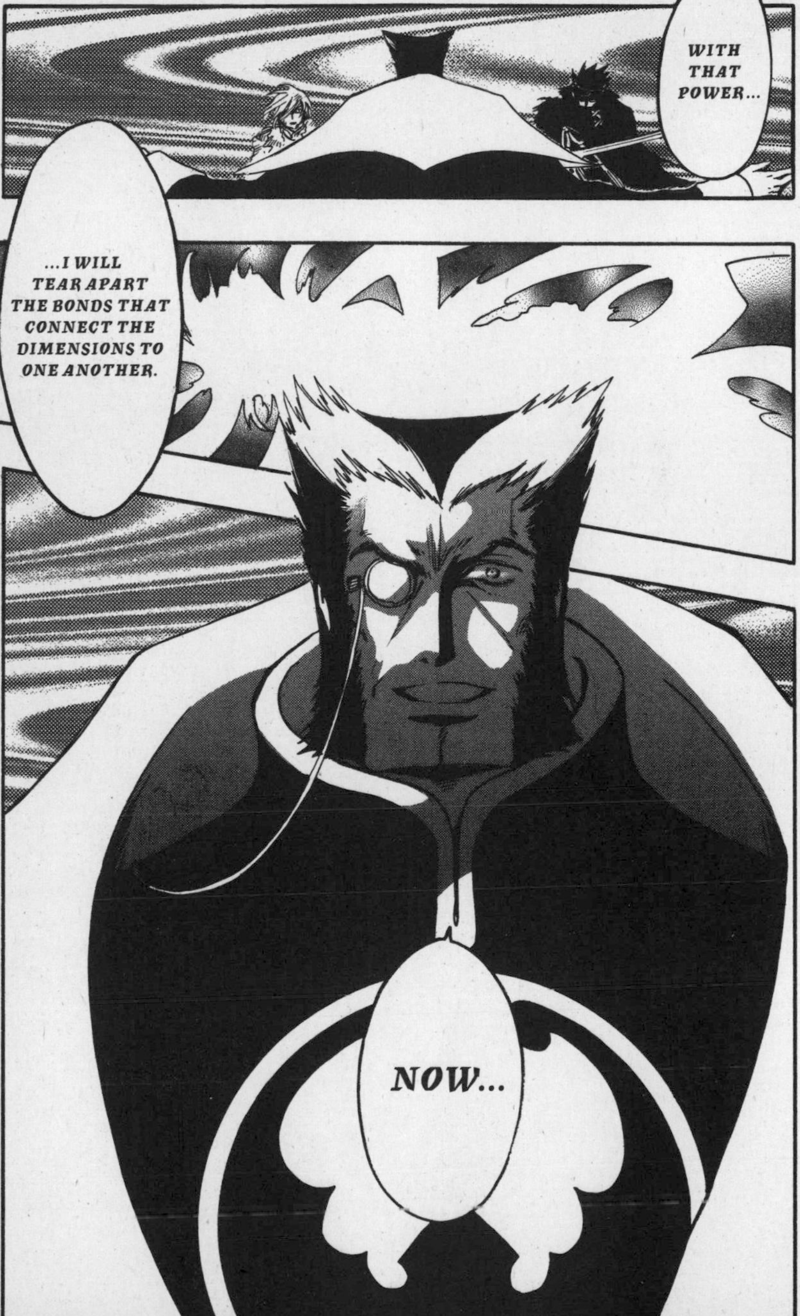
WITH THAT POWER...
...I WILL TEAR APART THE BONDS THAT CONNECT THE DIMENSIONS TO ONE ANOTHER.
NOW...

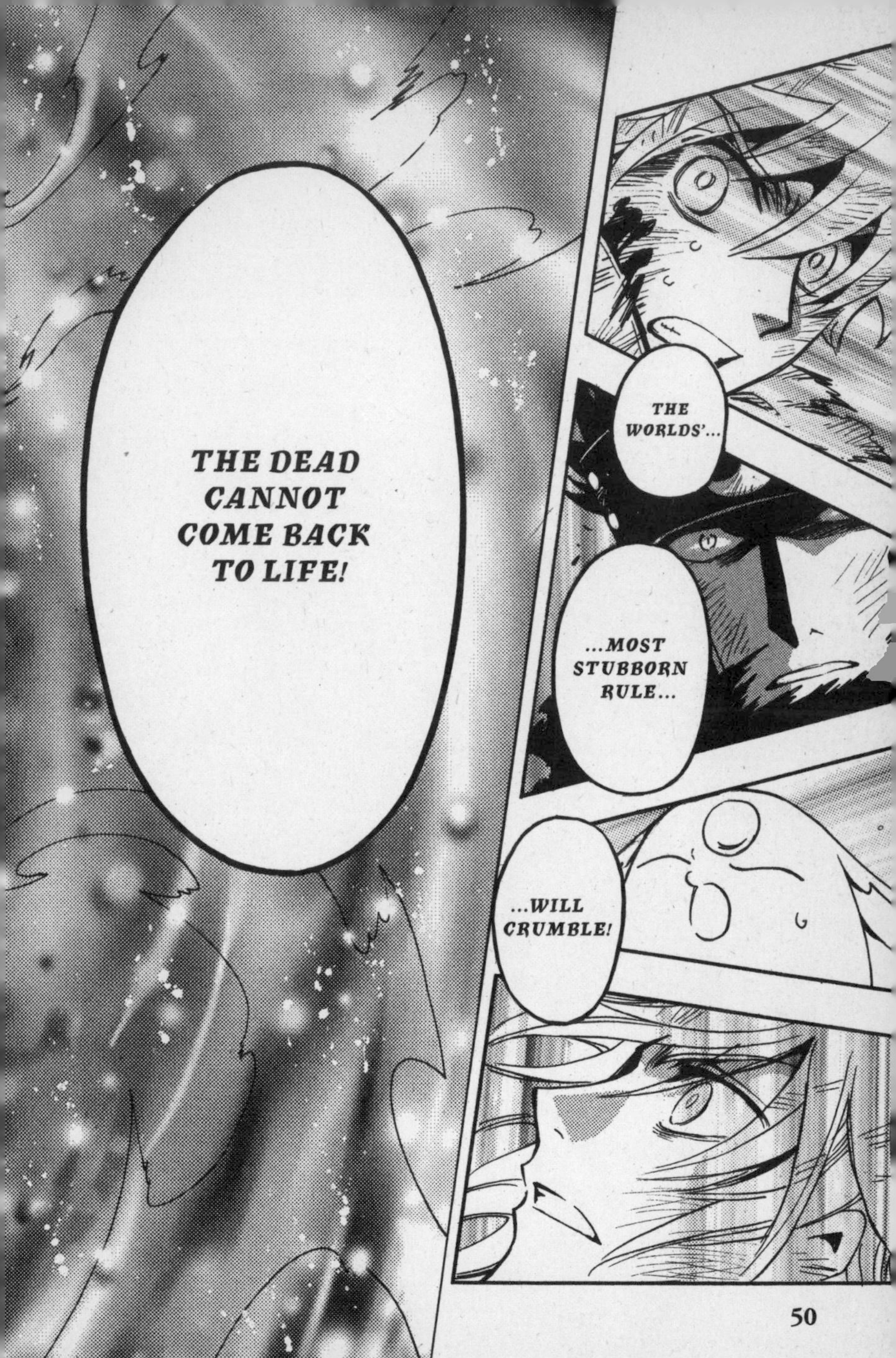
THE WORLDS'...
...MOST STUBBORN RULE...
...WILL CRUMBLE!
THE DEAD CANNOT COME BACK TO LIFE!

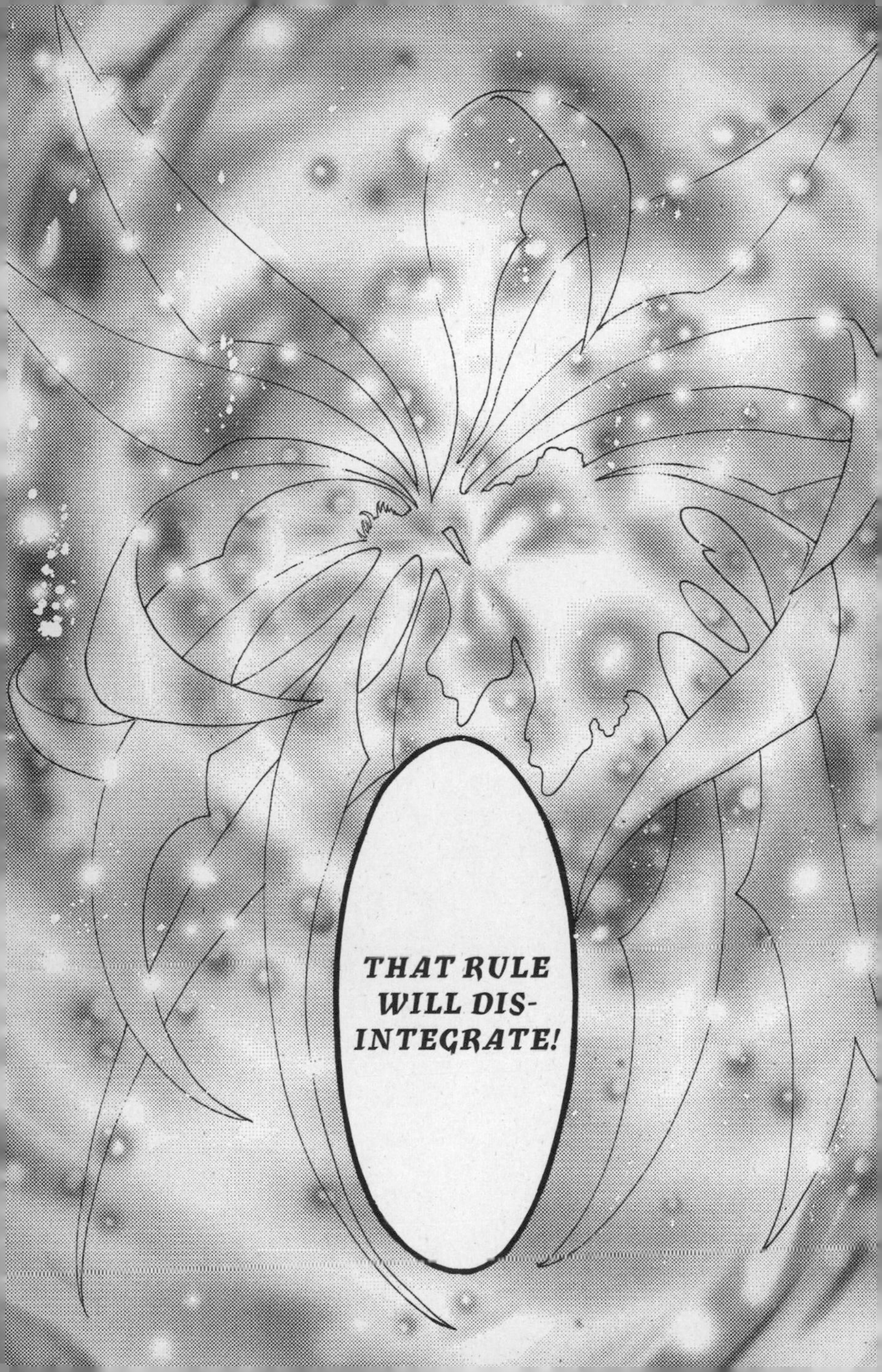
THAT RULE WILL DIS-INTEGRATE!

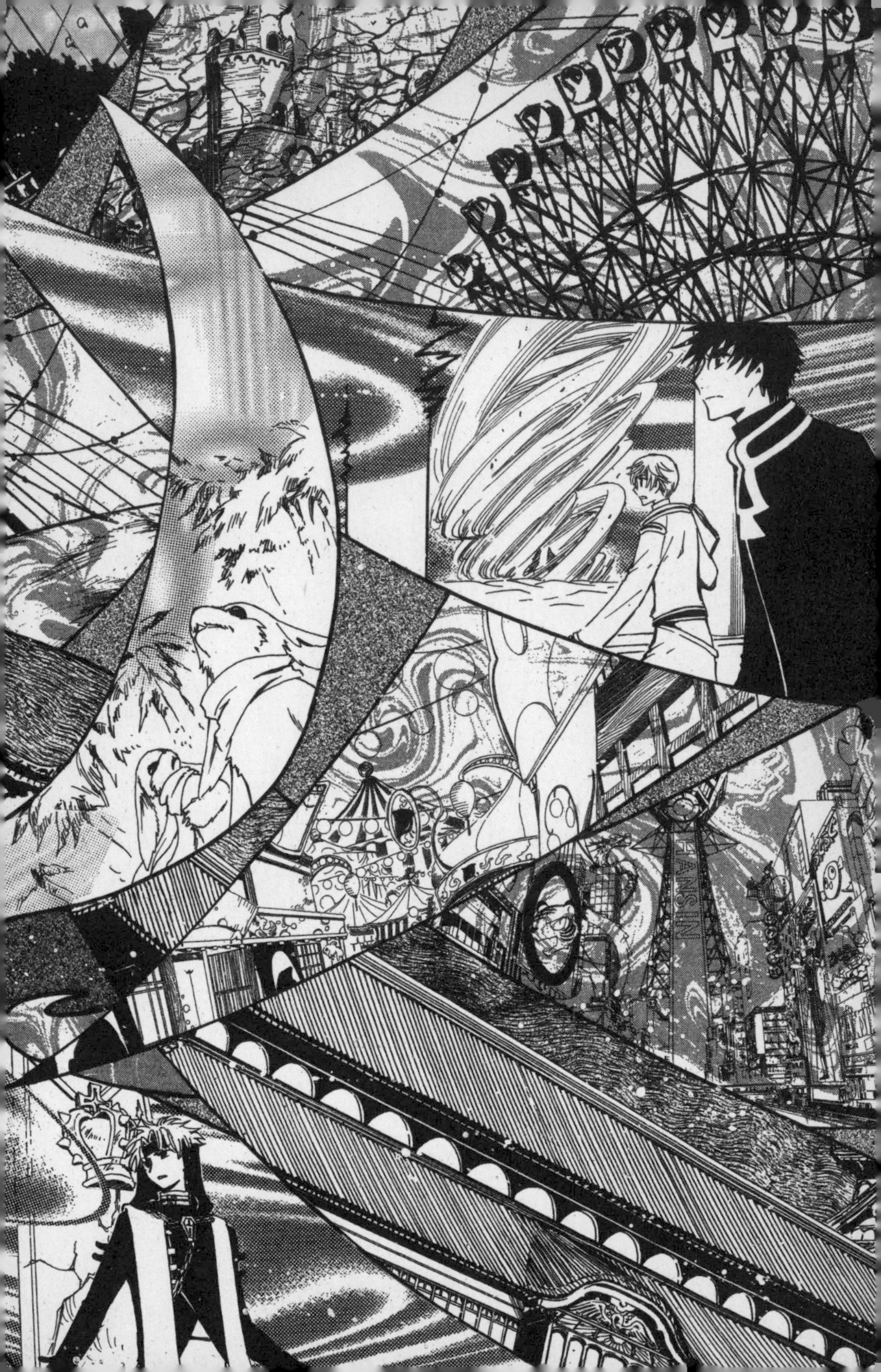
HANSIN

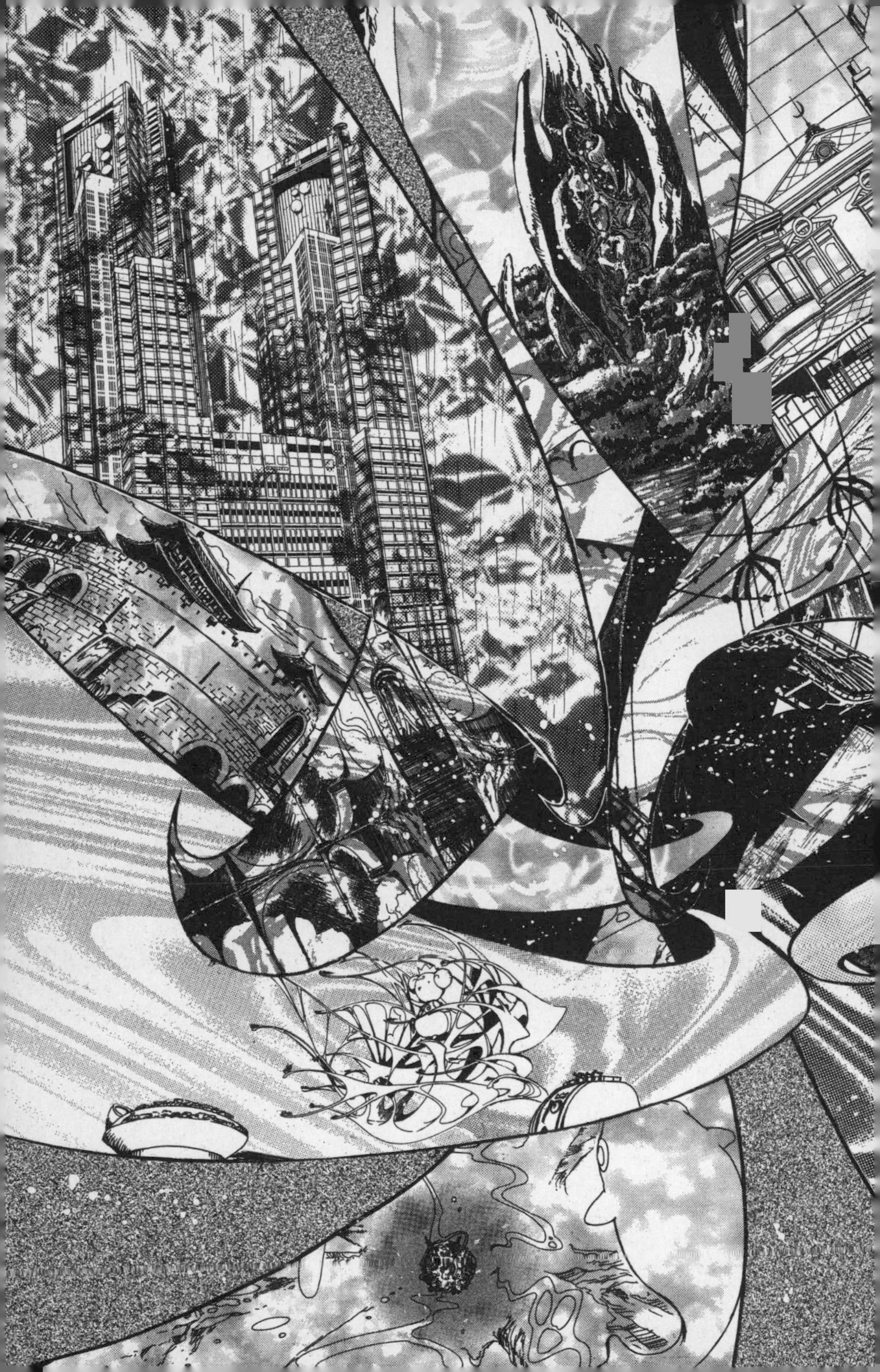

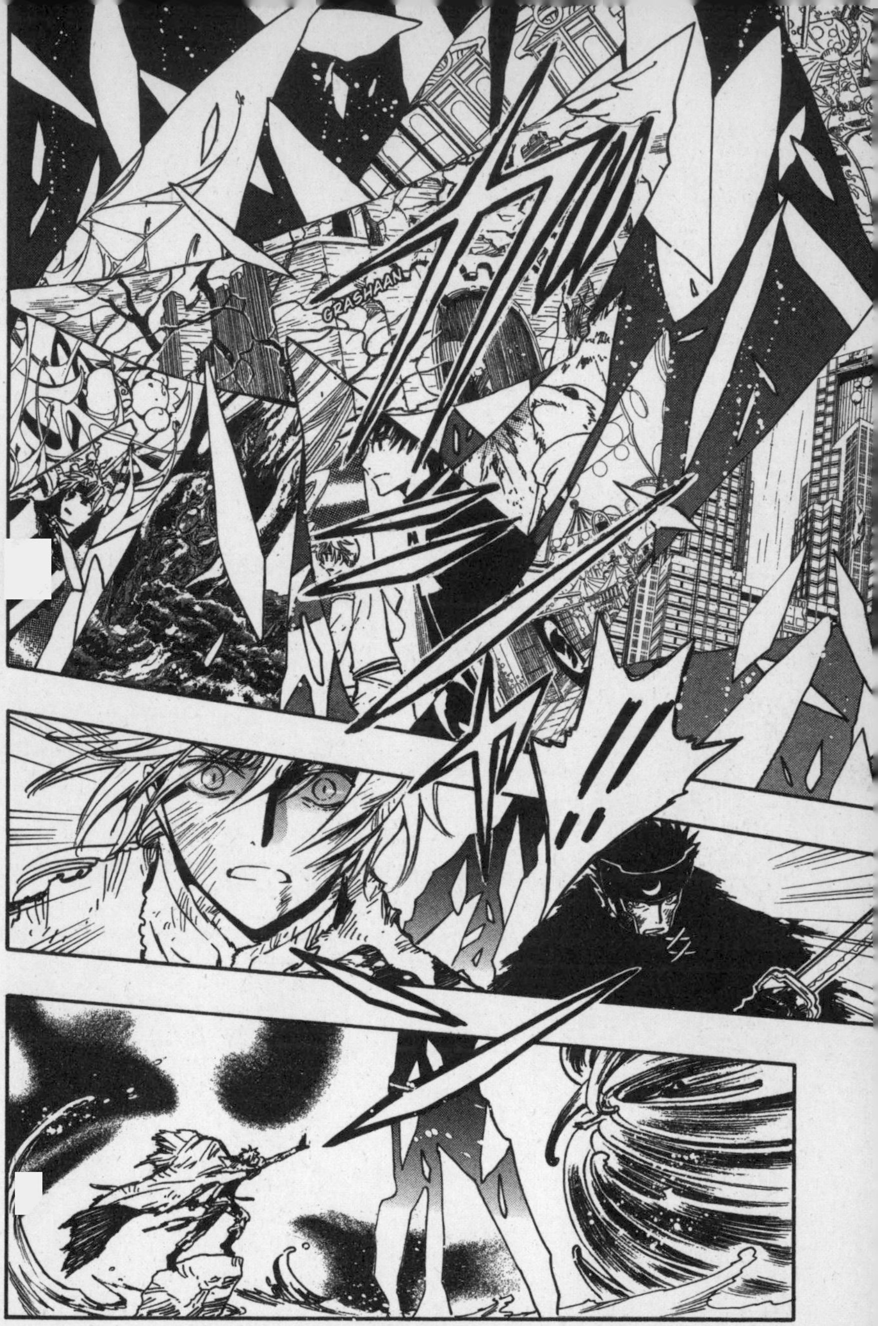
CRASHAAN

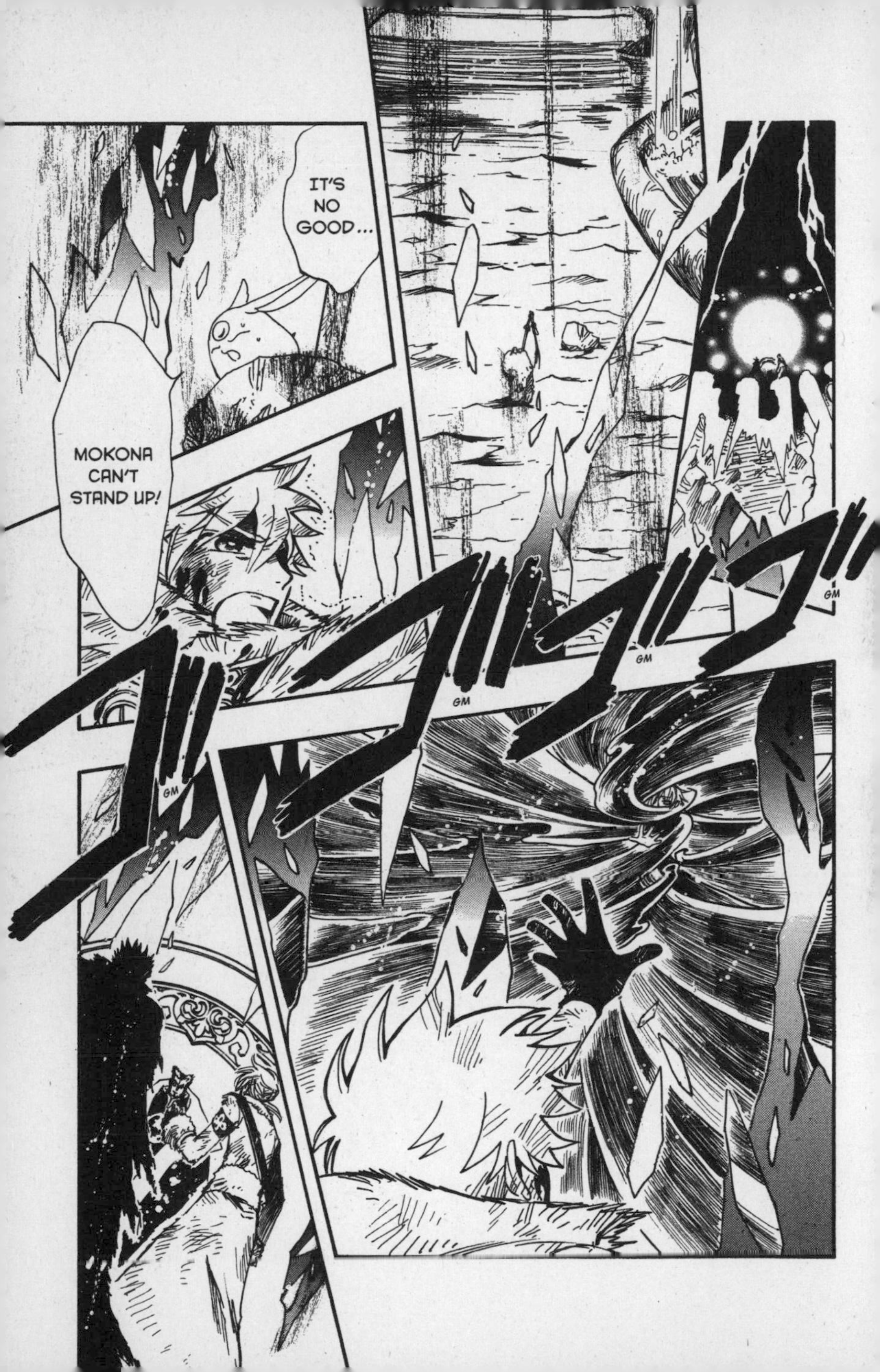
IT'S NO GOOD...
MOKONA CAN'T STAND UP!
GM
GM
GM
GM

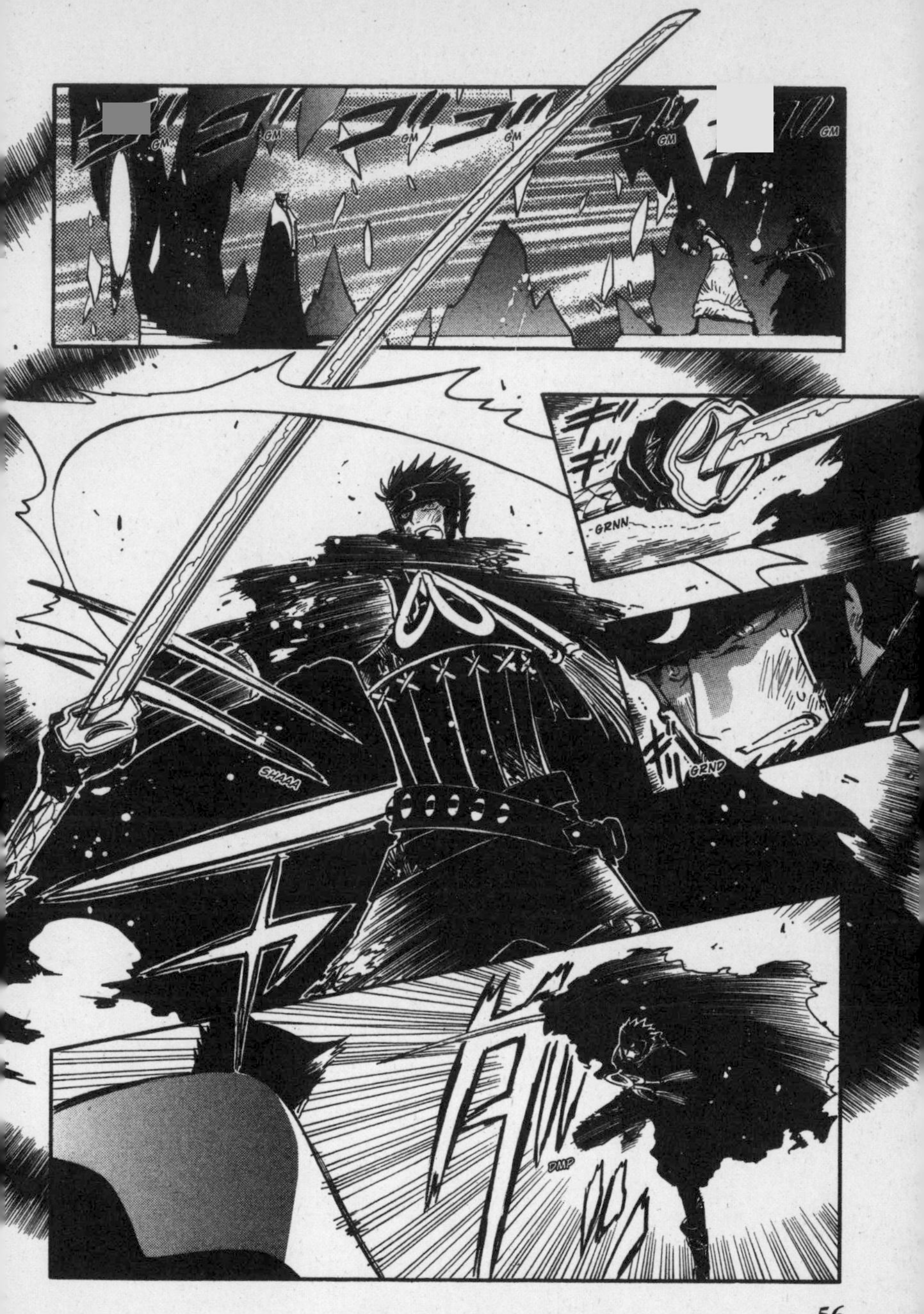
GM
GM
GM
GM
GM
GM
GRNN
GRND
SHAAA
DMP

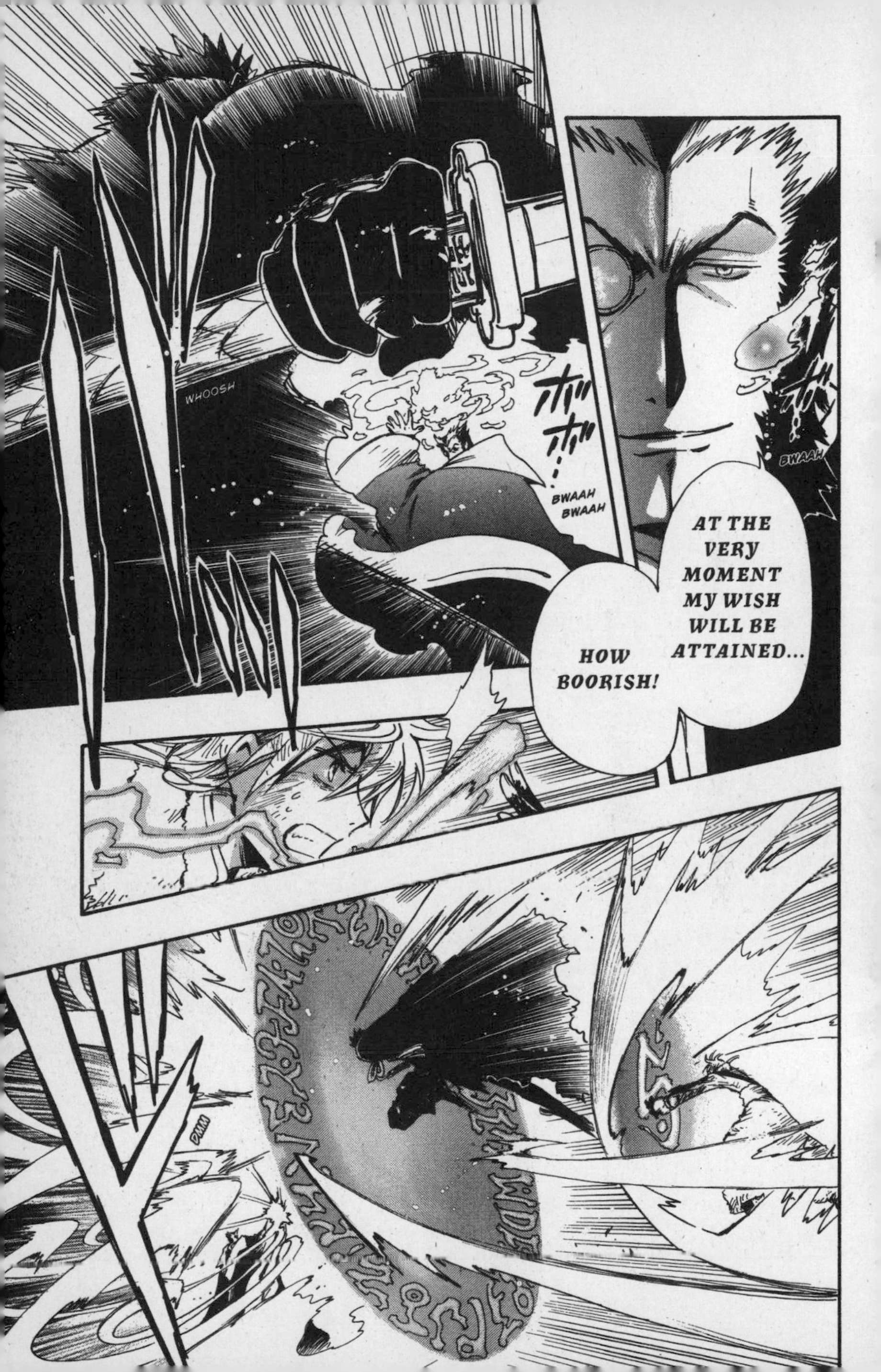
BWAAH
AT THE VERY MOMENT MY WISH WILL BE ATTAINED...
HOW BOORISH!
BWAAH BWAAH
WHOOSH

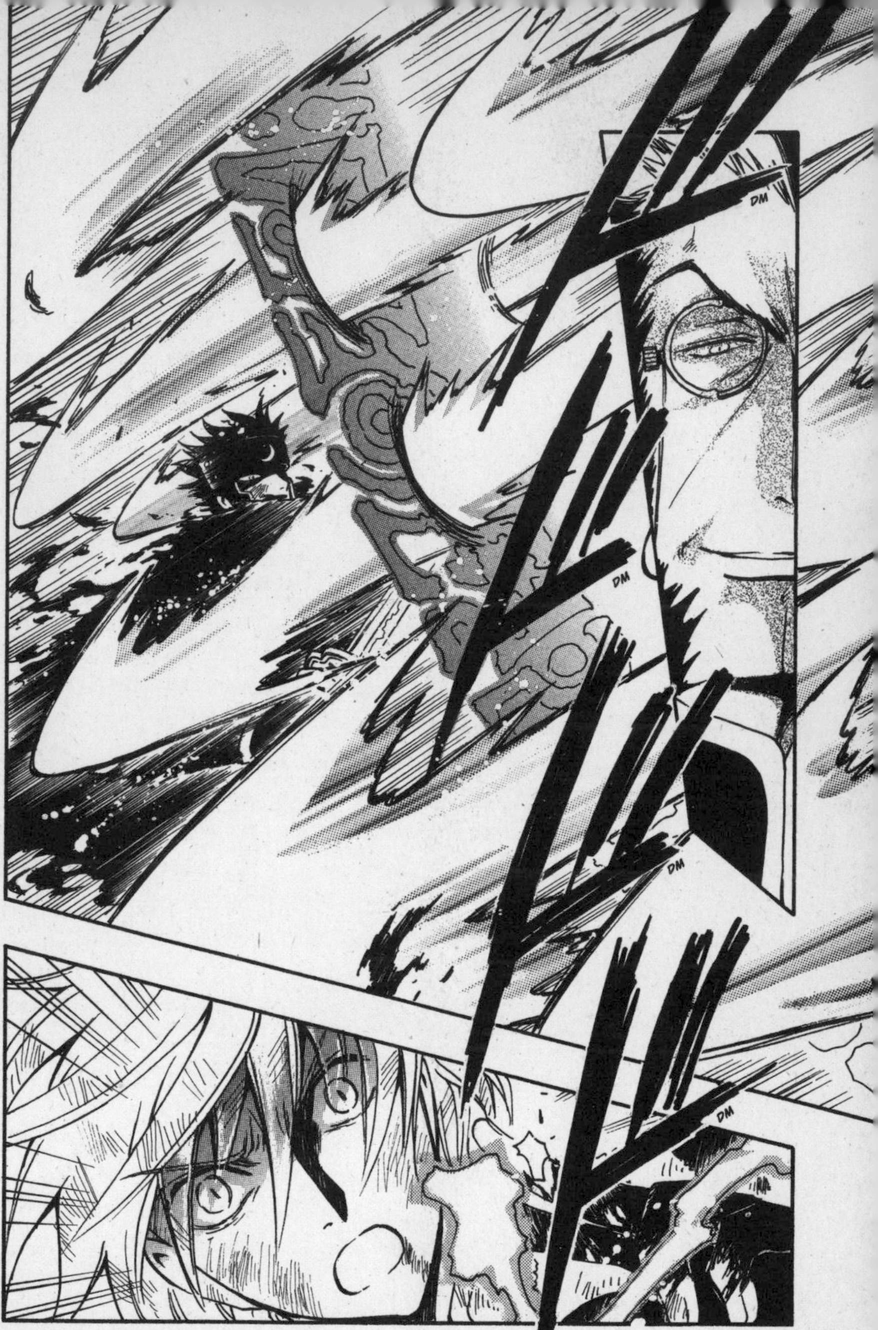
DM
DM
DM
DM

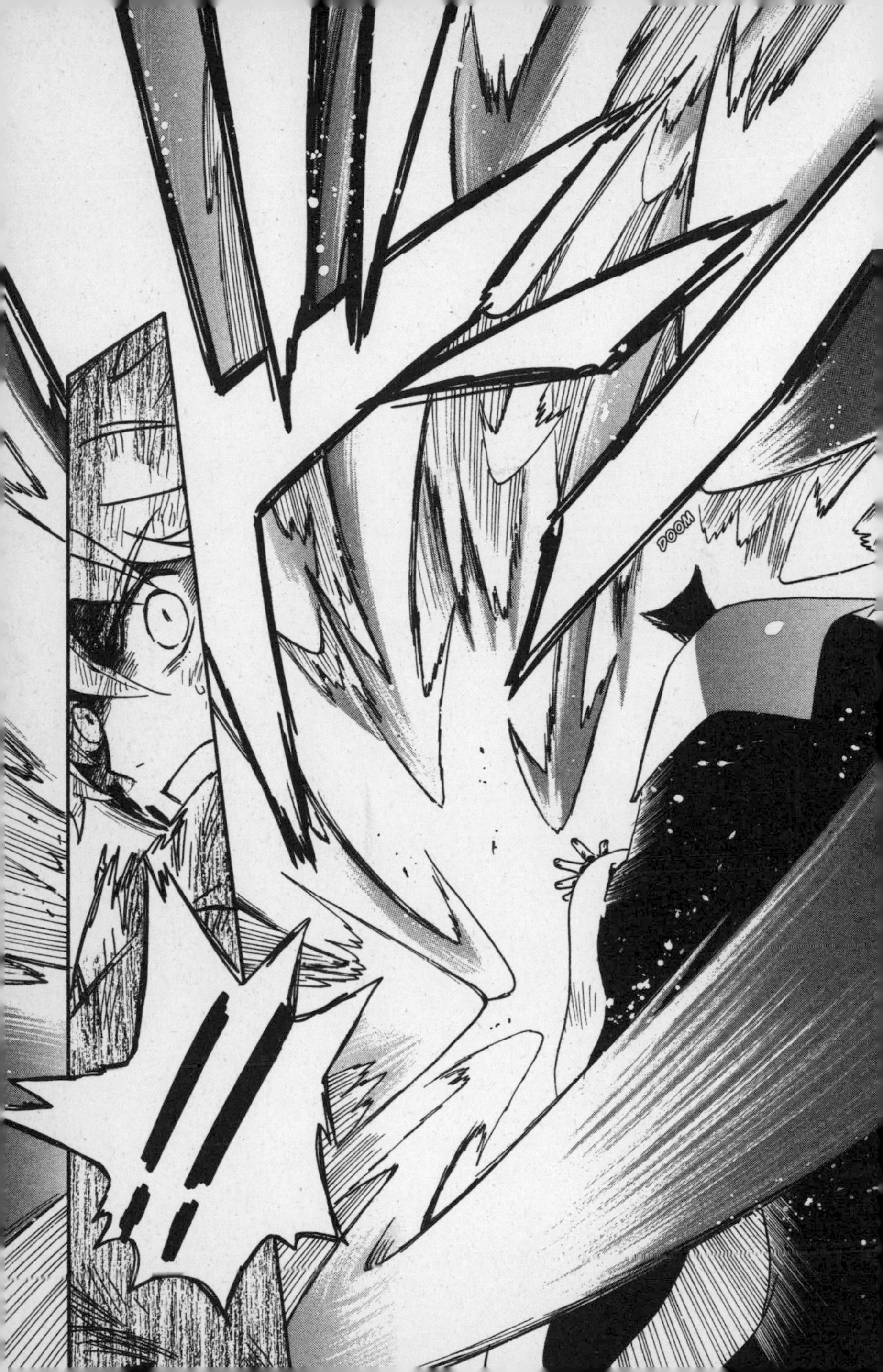
DOOM
!!

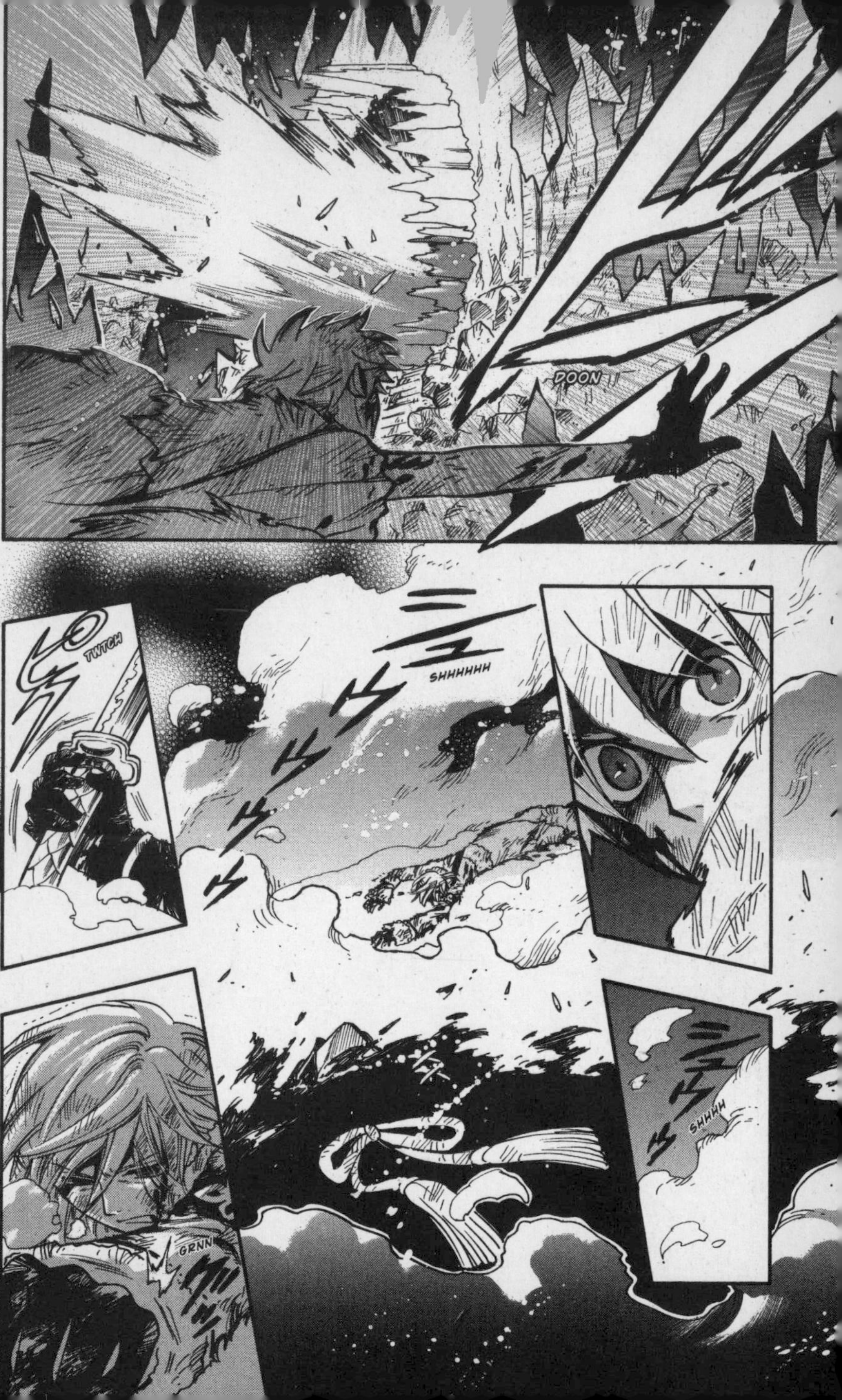
DOON
SHHHHHH
TWTCH
SHHHH
GRNN

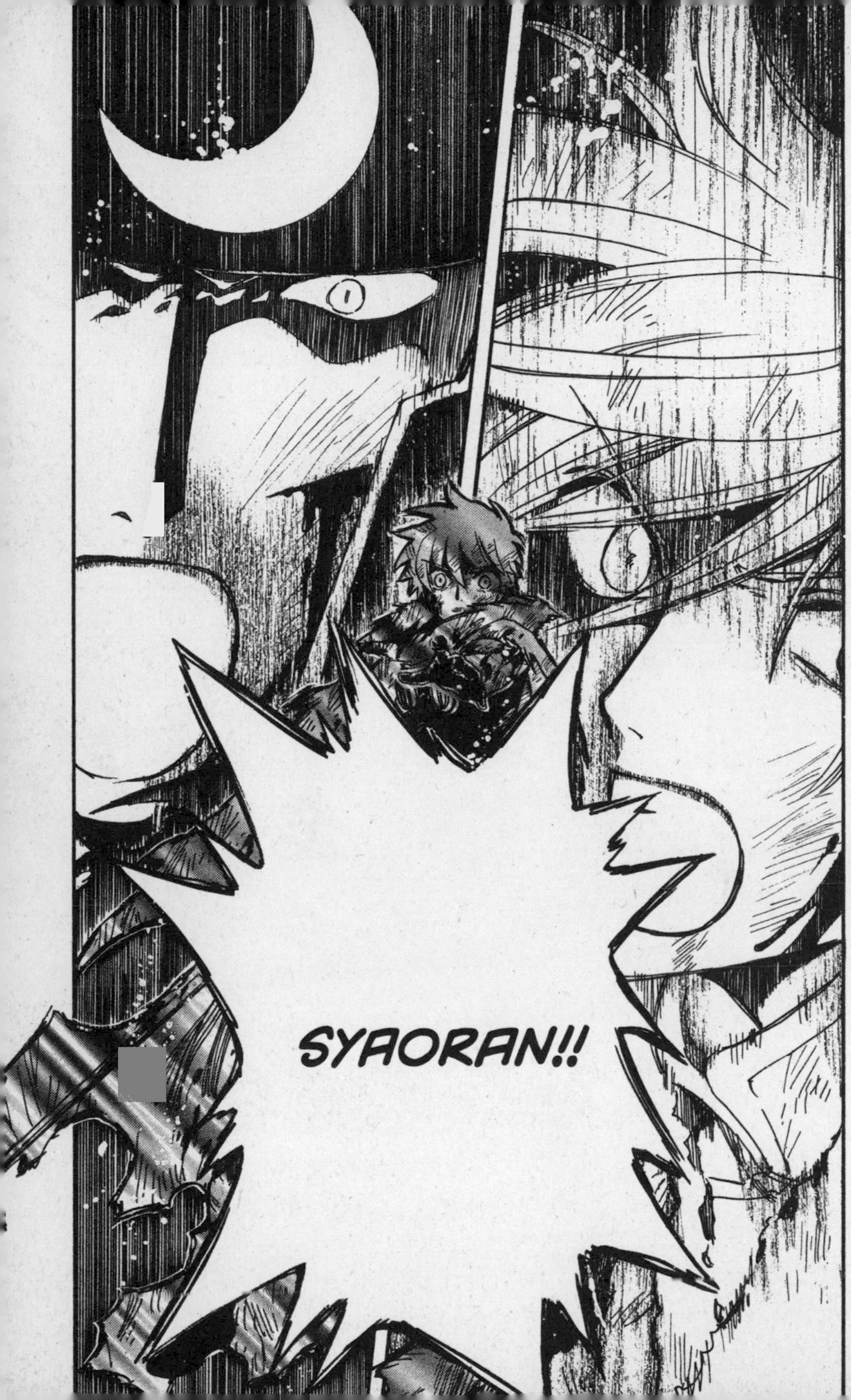
SYAORAN!!

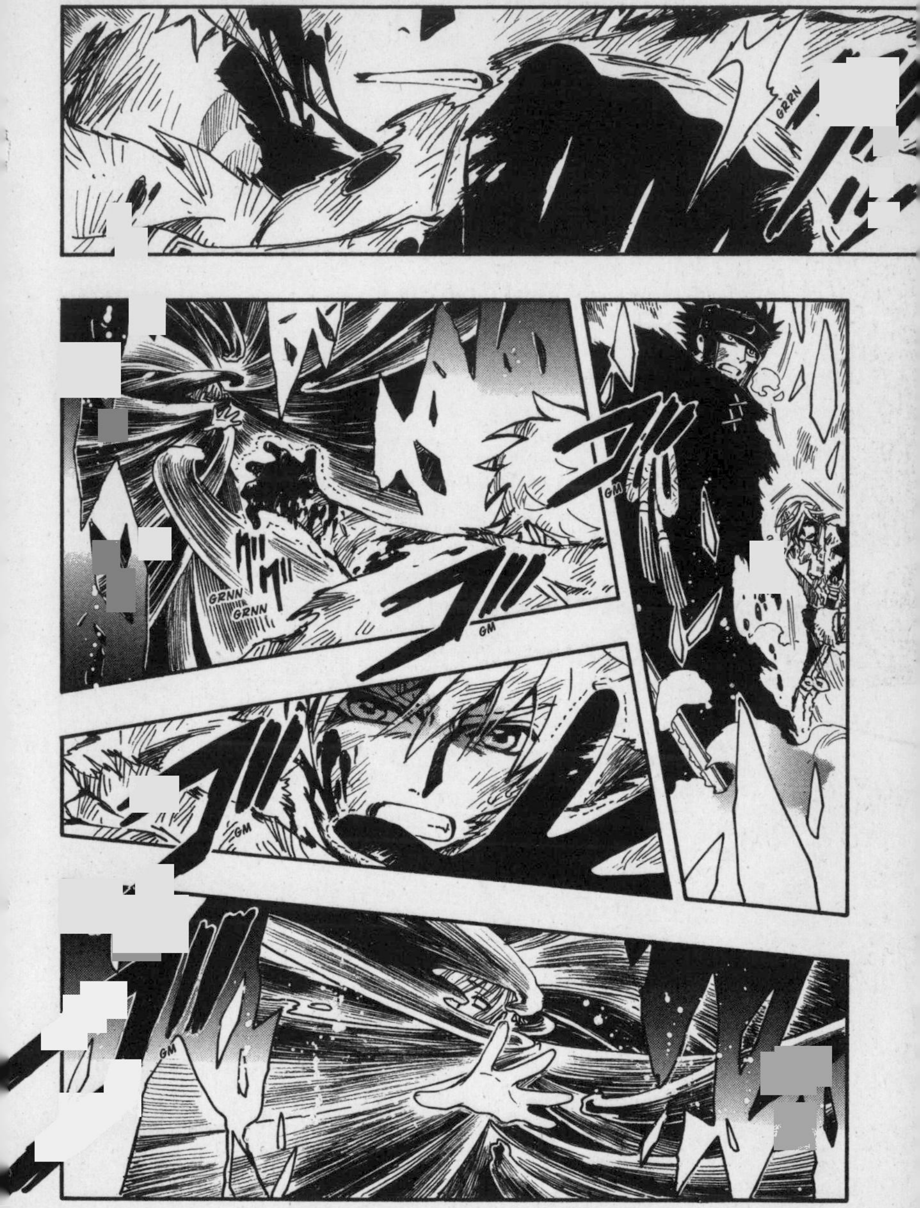
GRRN
GM
GRNN GRNN
GM
GM
GM

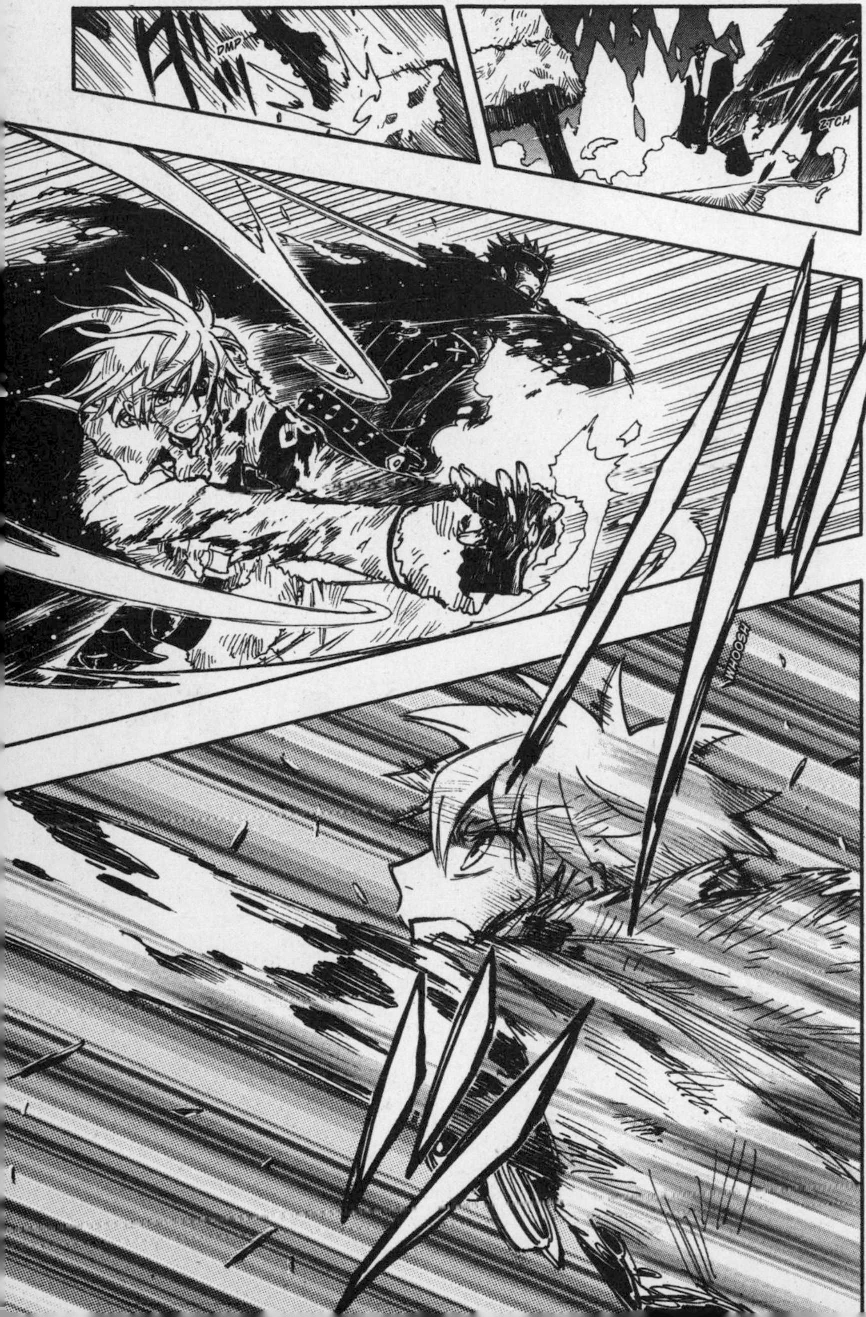
ZTCH
DMP
WHOOSH

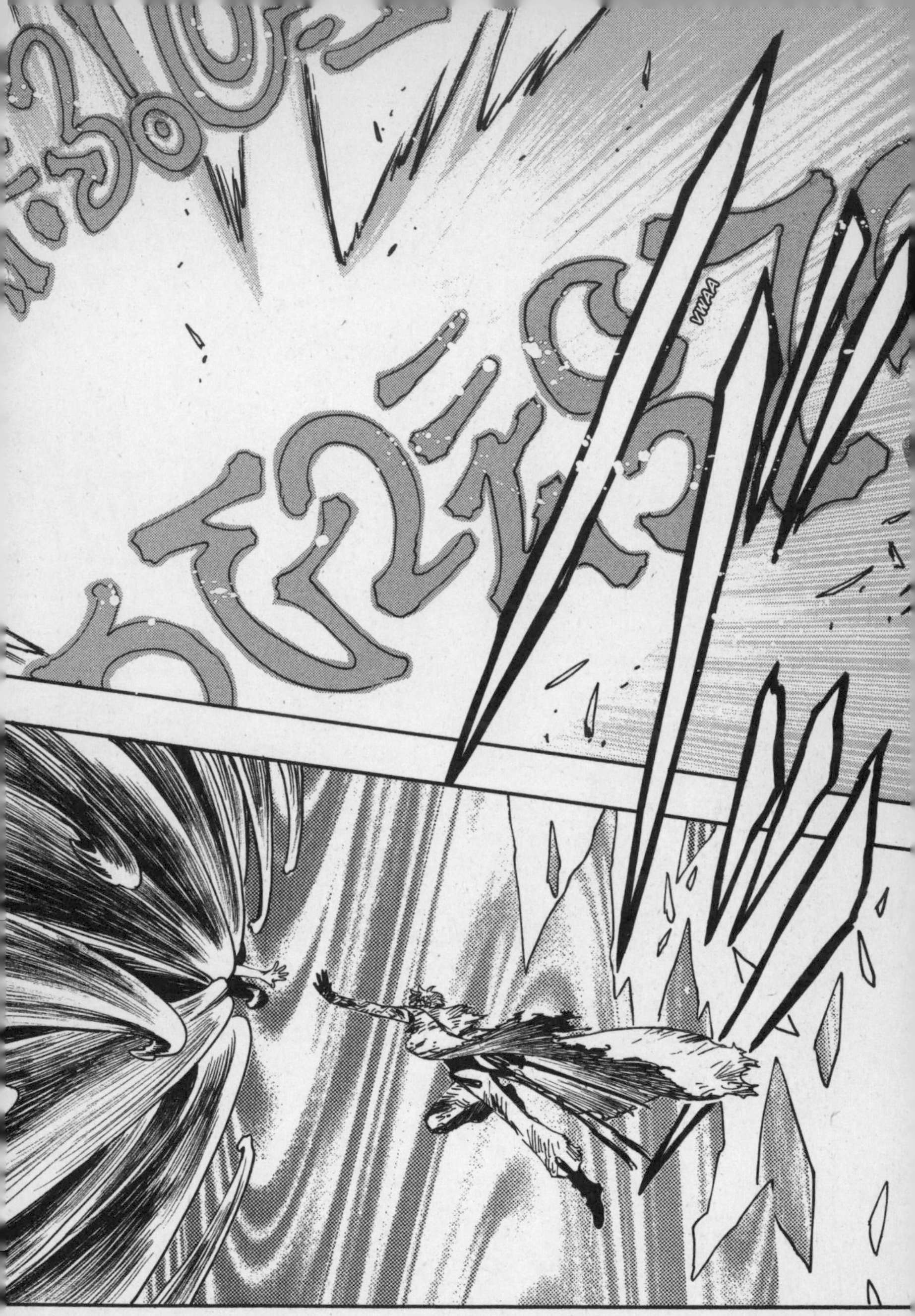
VWAA

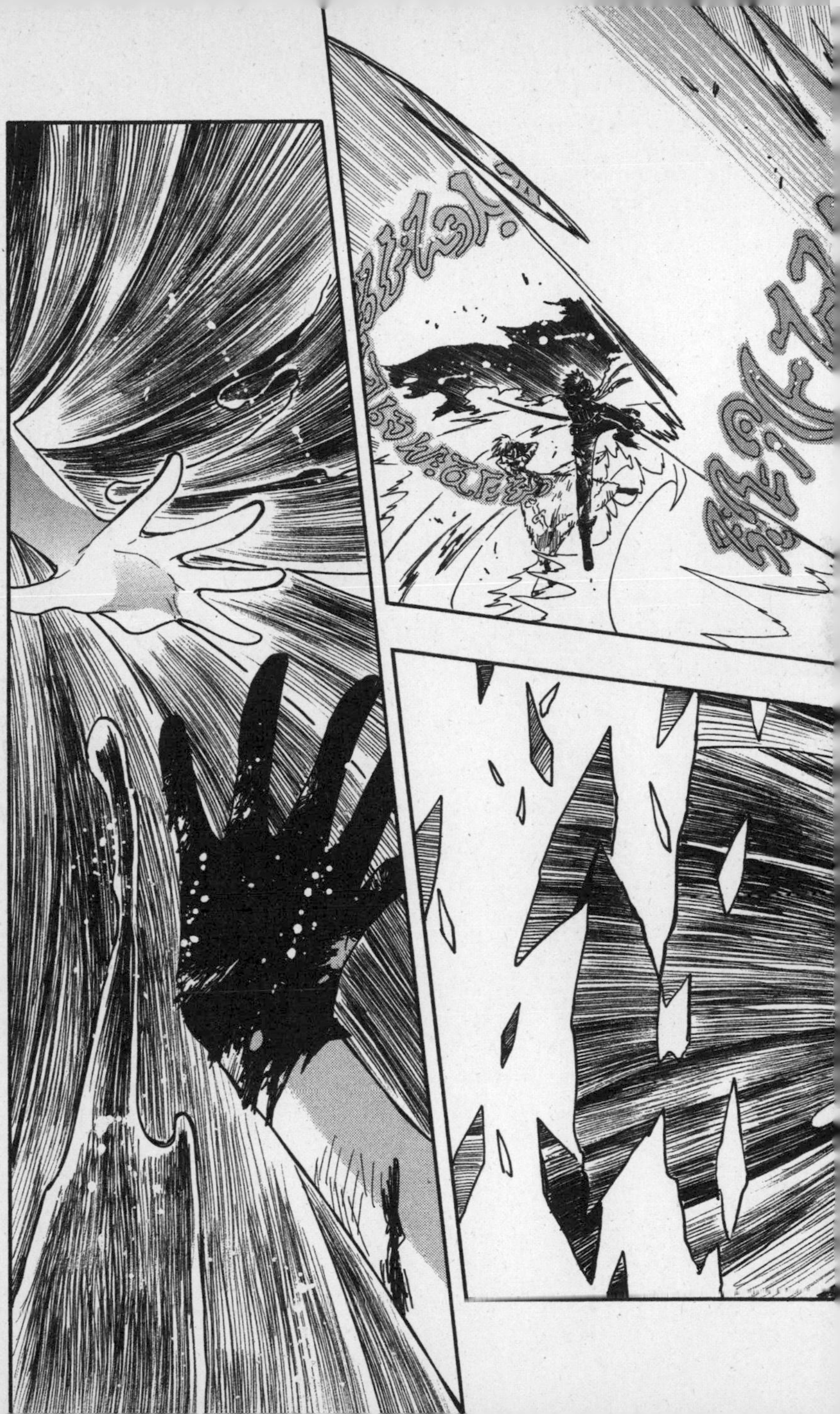

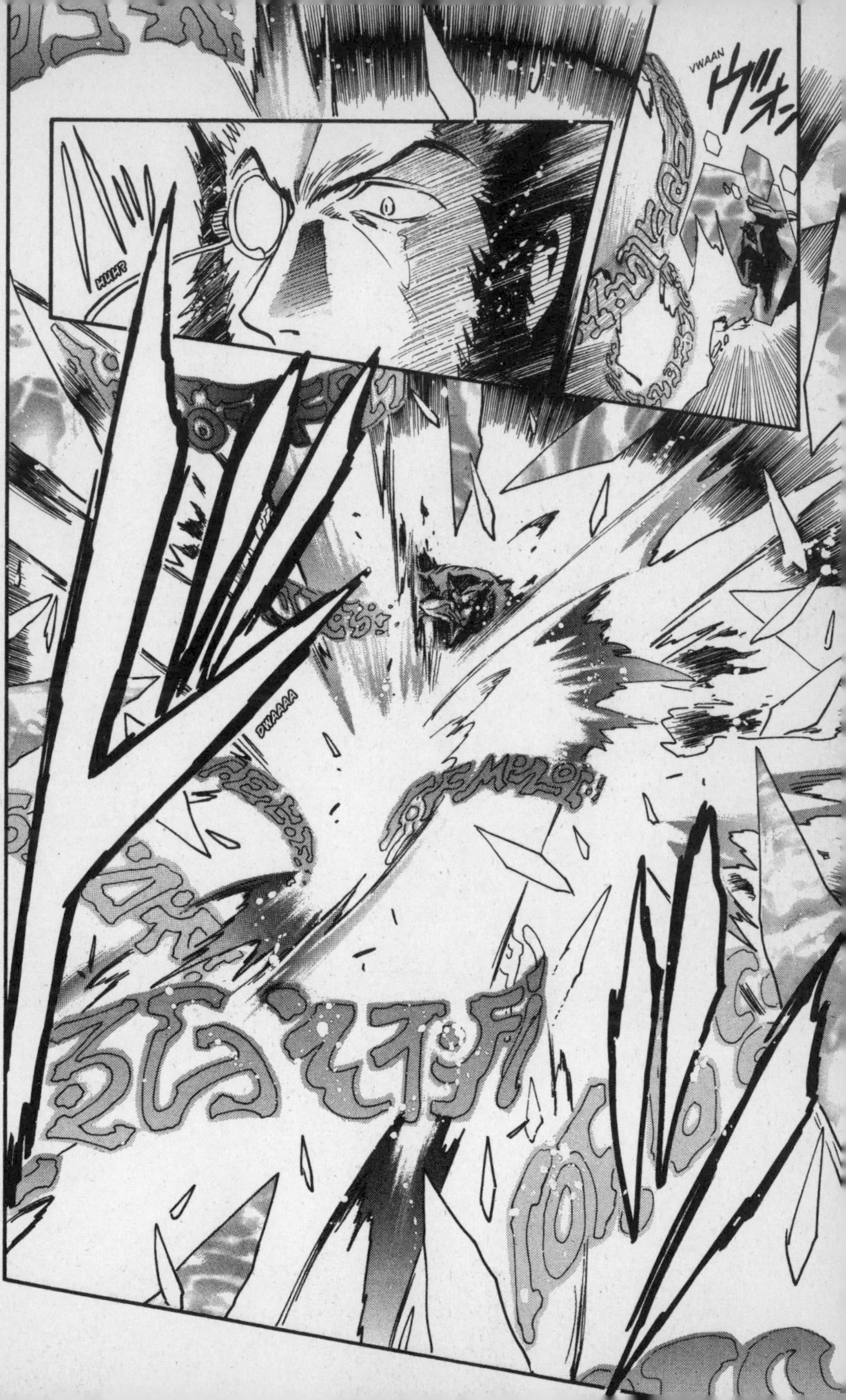
VWAAN
HUH?
DWAAAA

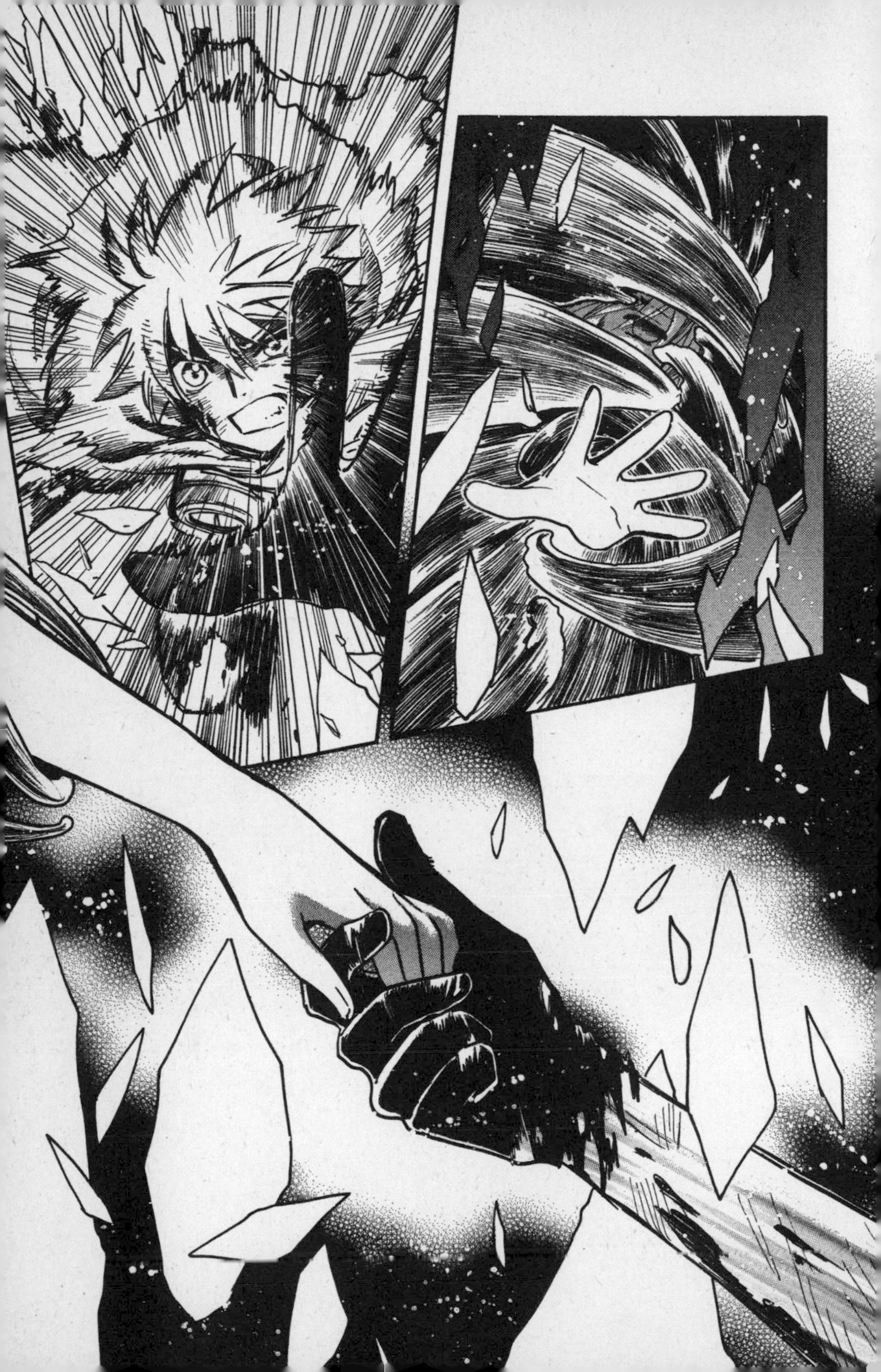

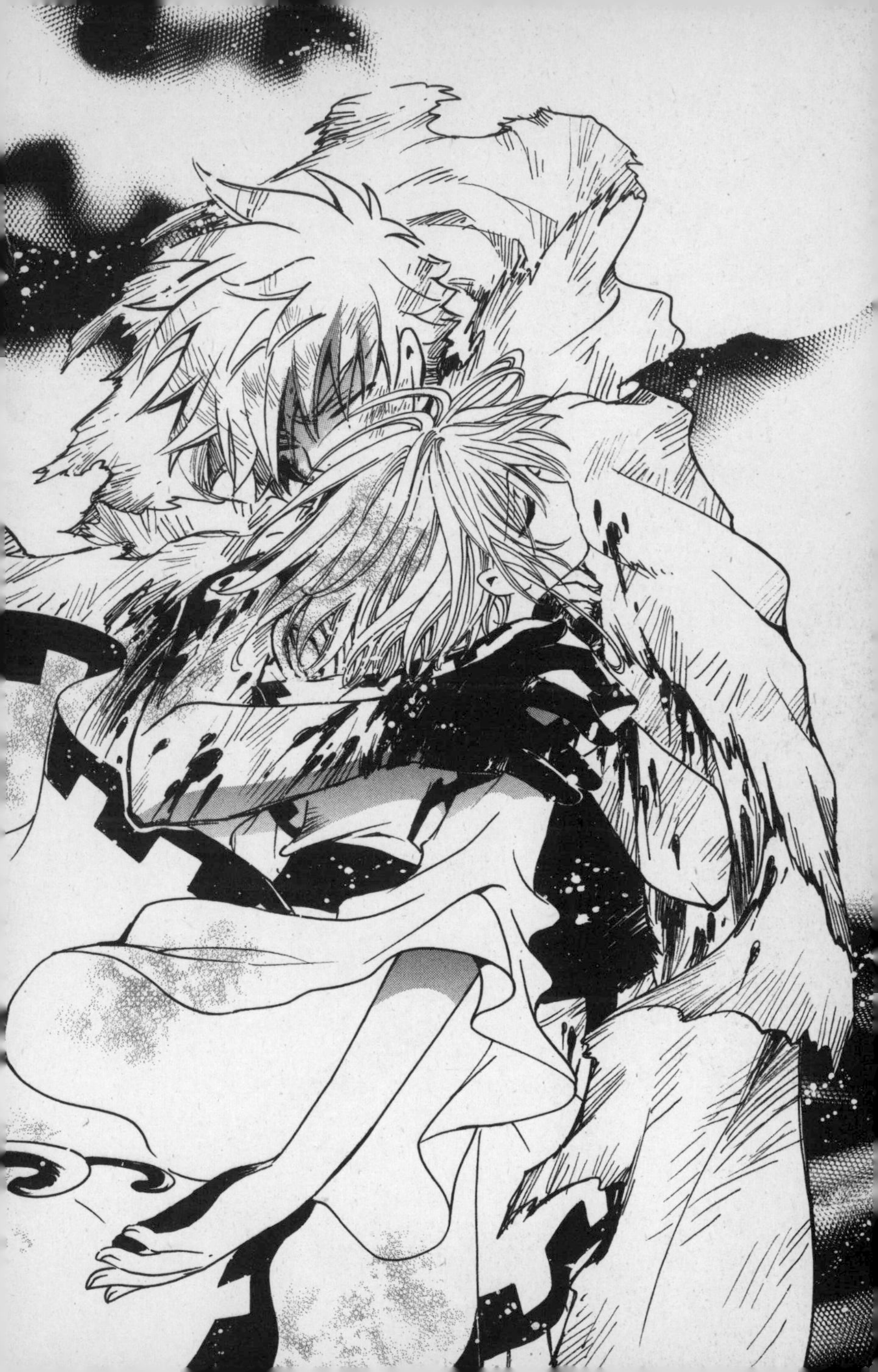

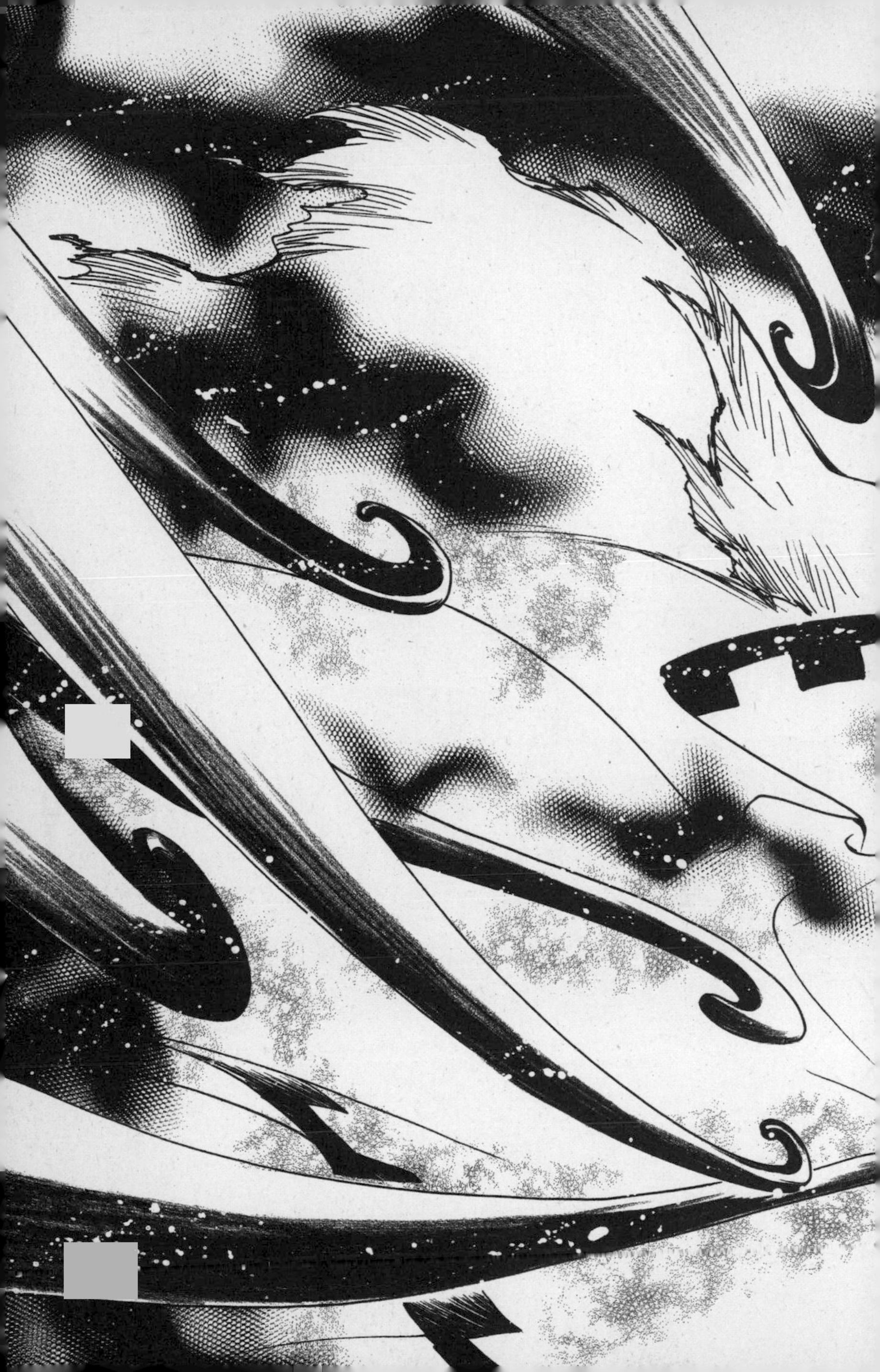

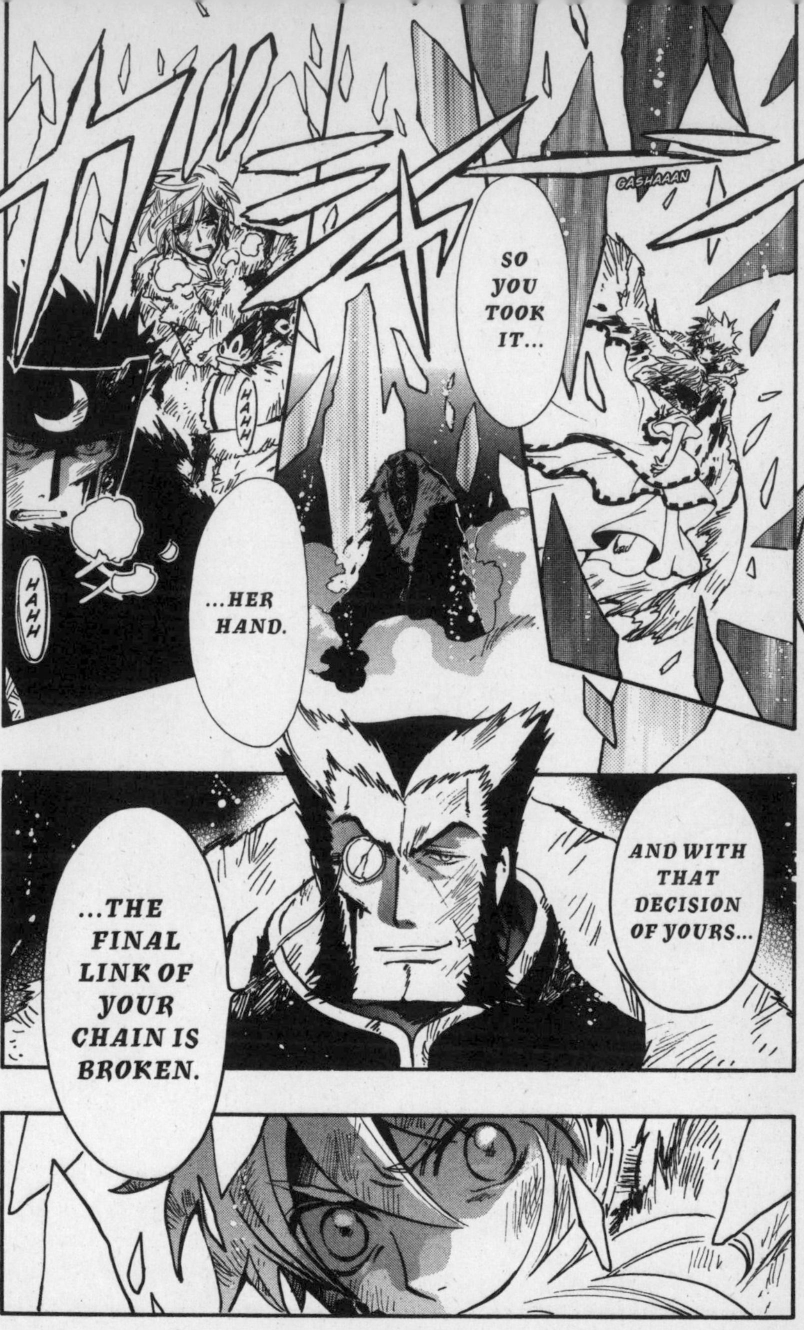
GASHAAAN
SO YOU TOOK IT...
HAHH
HAHH
...HER HAND.
AND WITH THAT DECISION OF YOURS...
...THE FINAL LINK OF YOUR CHAIN IS BROKEN.

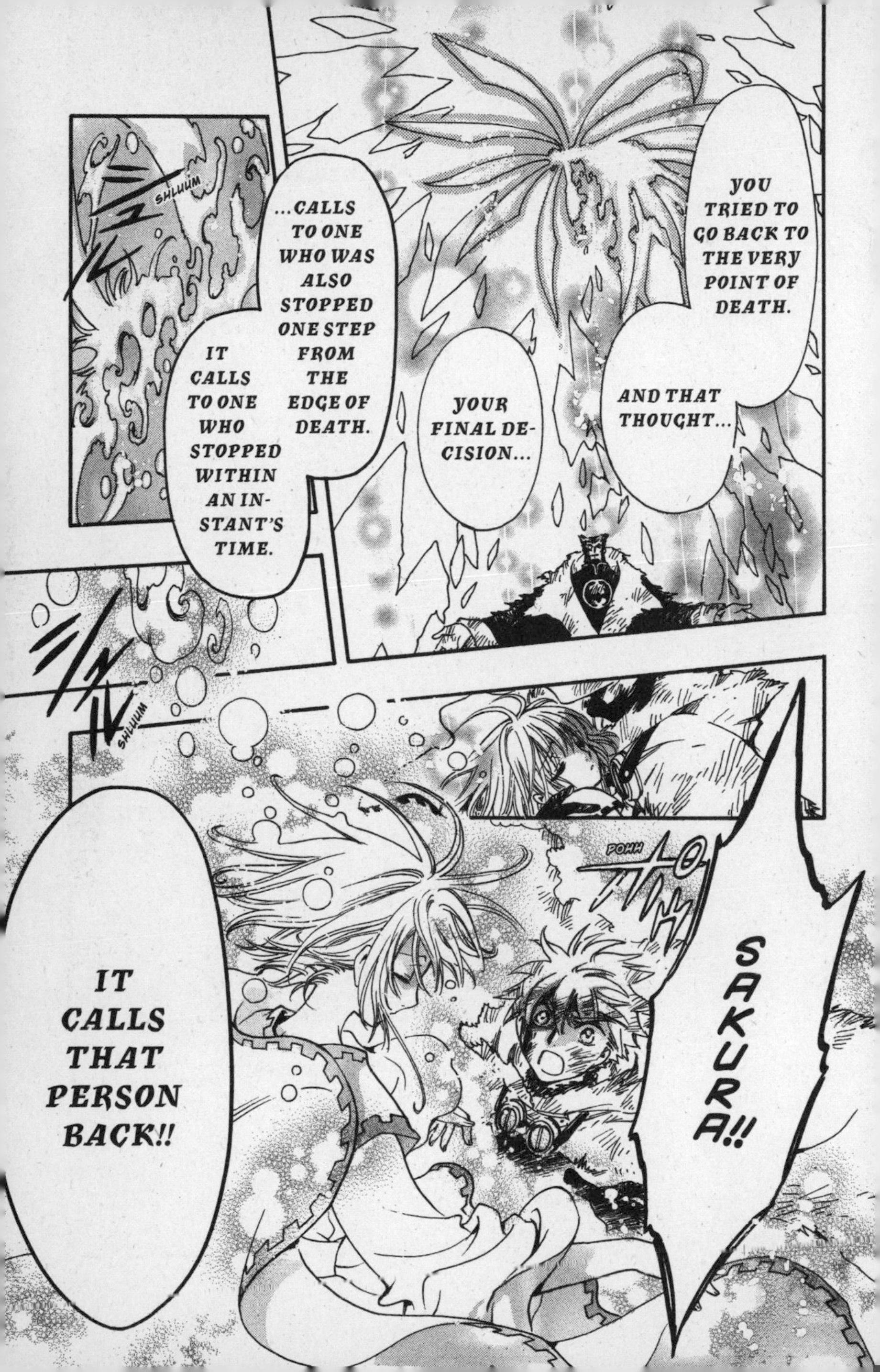
YOU TRIED TO GO BACK TO THE VERY POINT OF DEATH.
AND THAT THOUGHT...
YOUR FINAL DE-CISION...
...CALLS TO ONE WHO WAS ALSO STOPPED ONE STEP FROM THE EDGE OF DEATH.
SHLUUM
IT CALLS TO ONE WHO STOPPED WITHIN AN IN-STANT'S TIME.
SHLUUM
POHH
SAKURA!!
IT CALLS THAT PERSON BACK!!

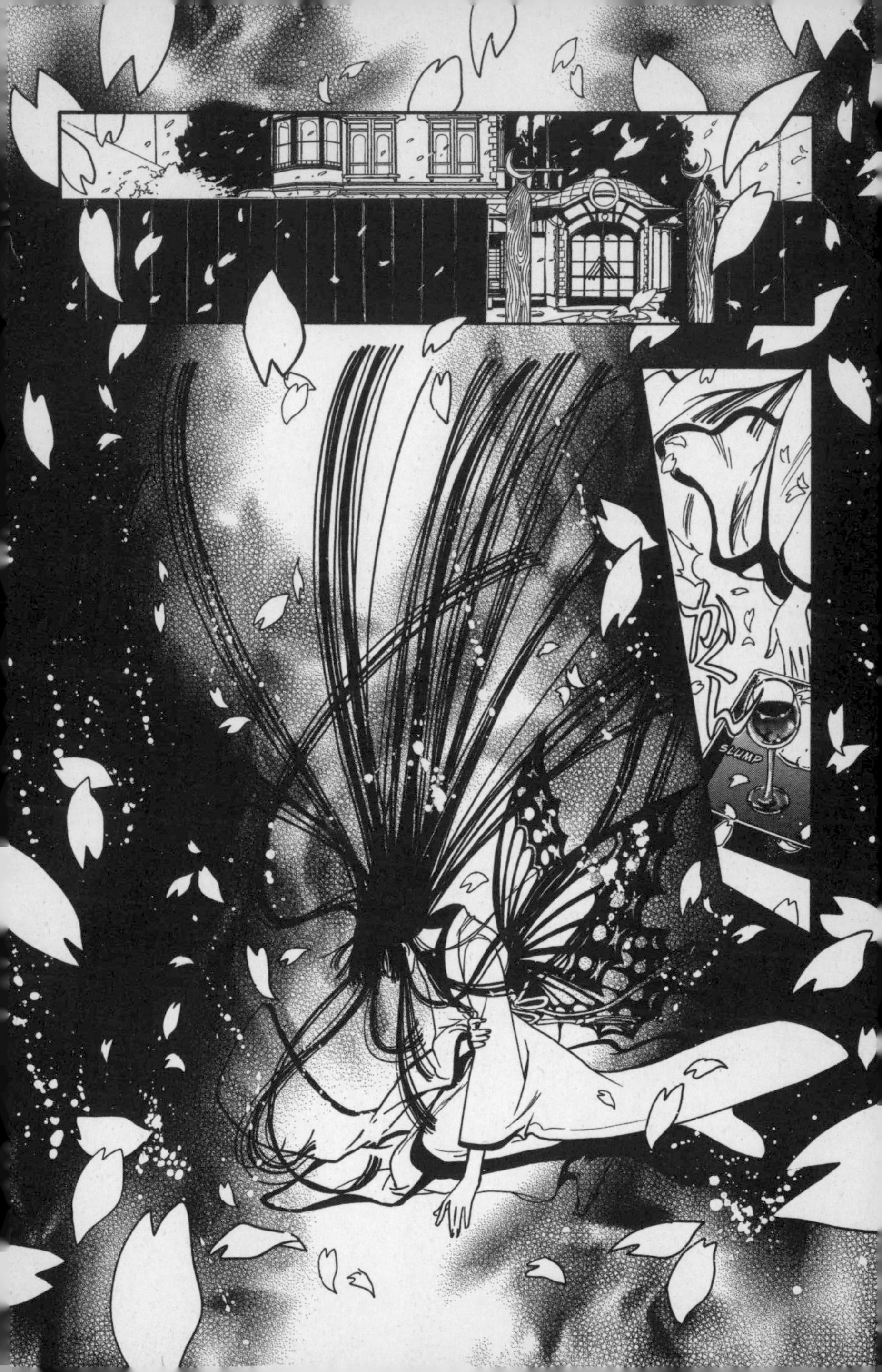
SLUMP

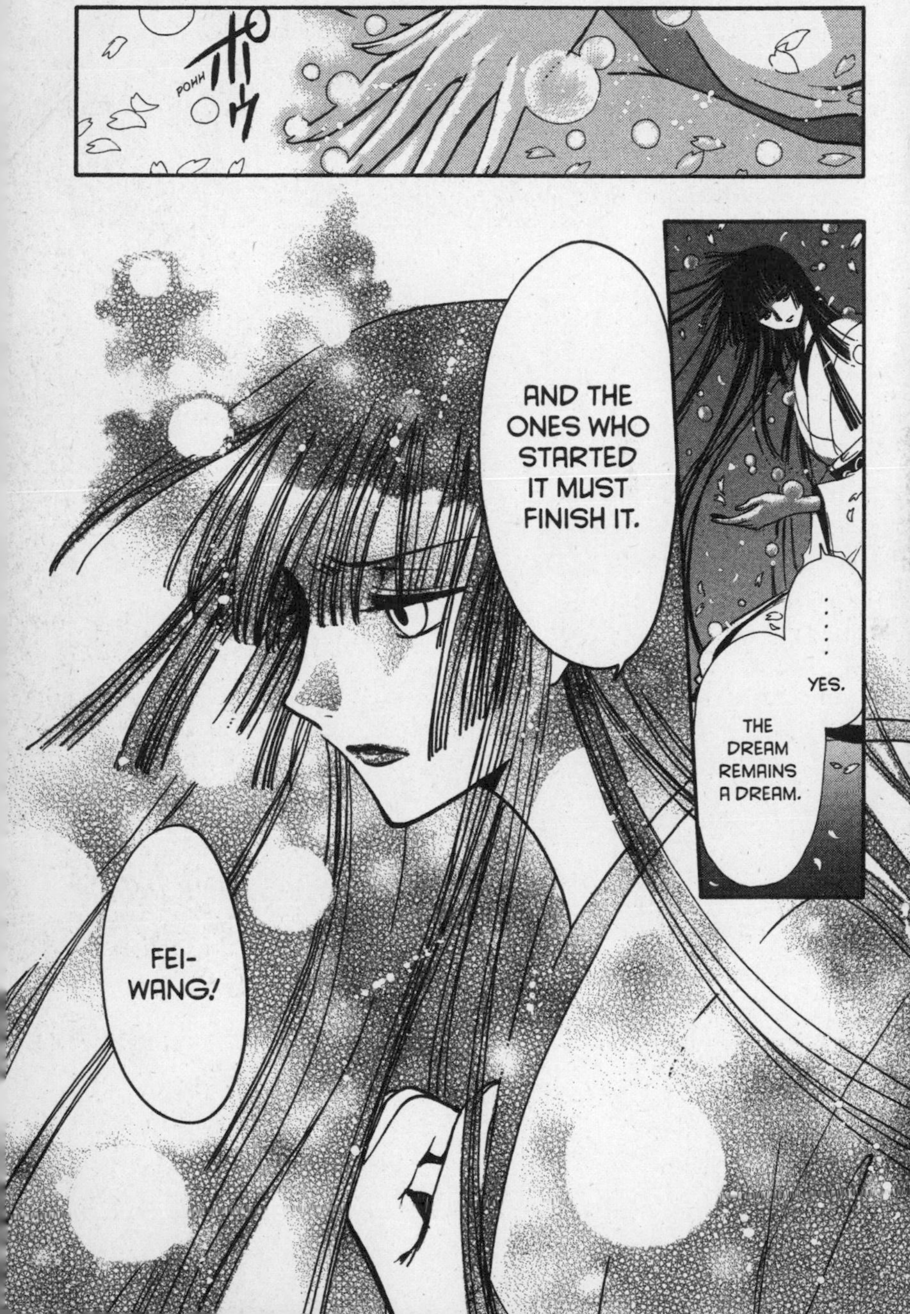
ポウ
POHH
AND THE ONES WHO STARTED IT MUST FINISH IT.
.....
YES.
THE DREAM REMAINS A DREAM.
FEI-WANG!

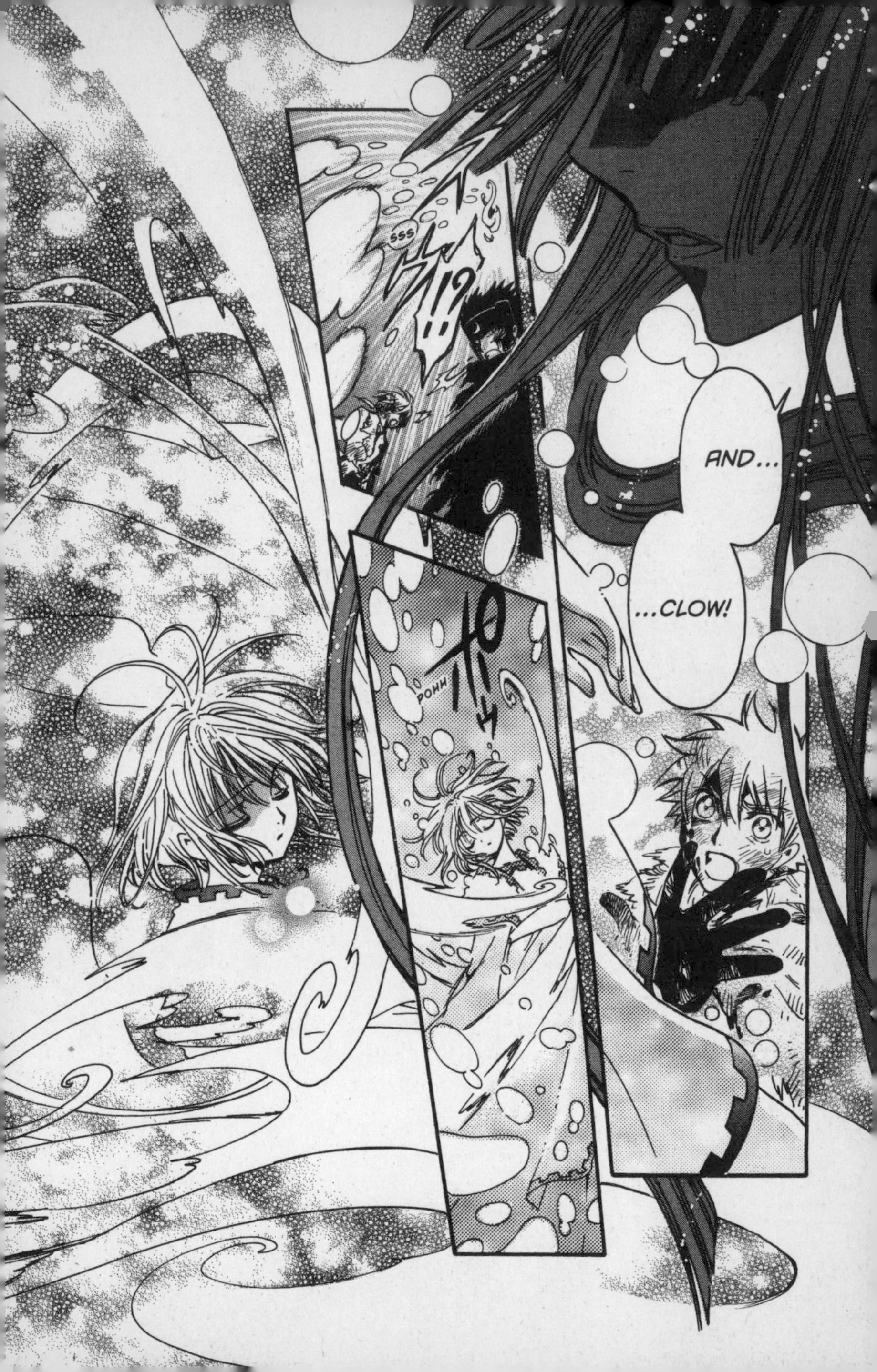
SSS
AND...
...CLOW!
POHH

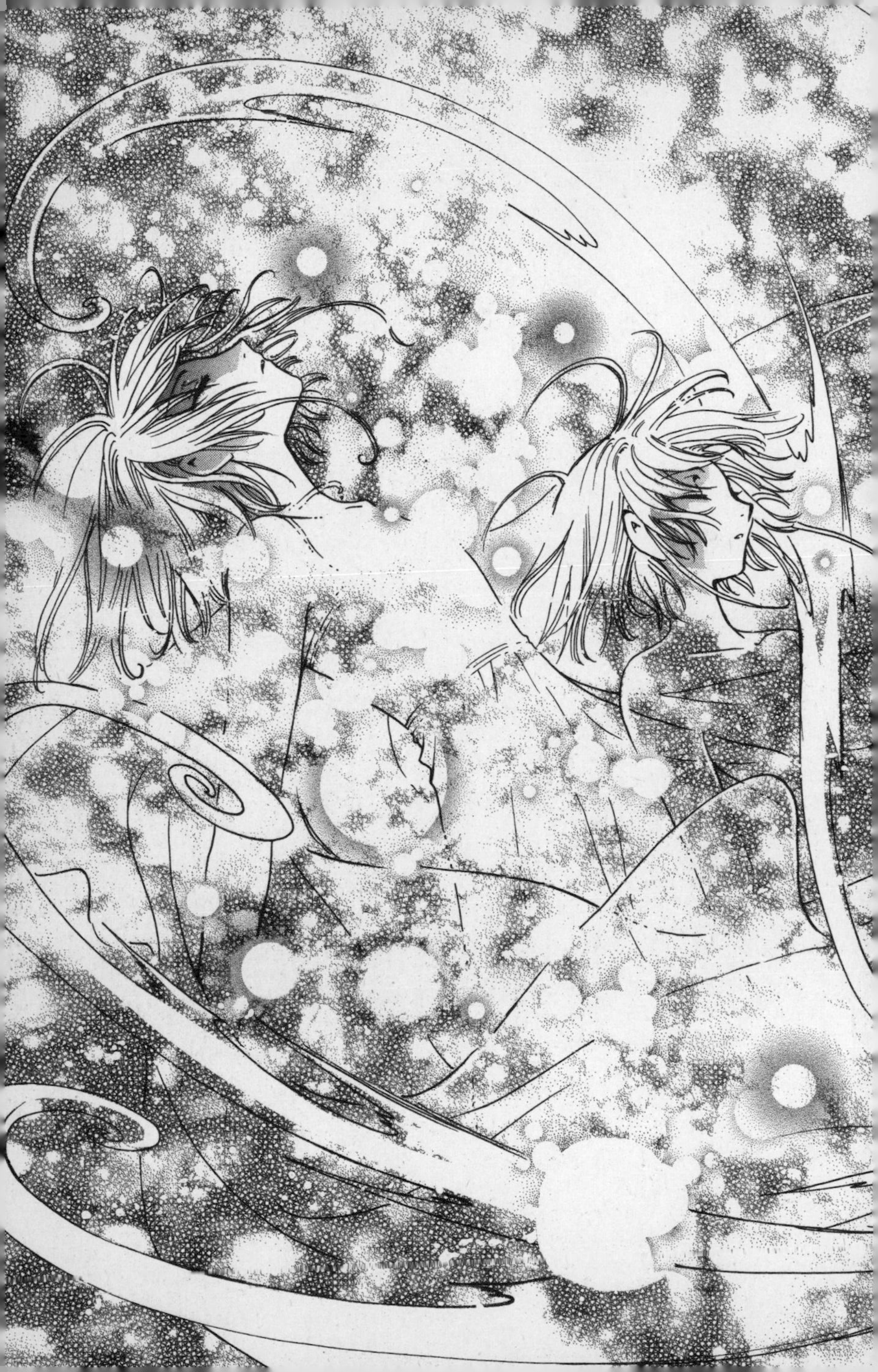

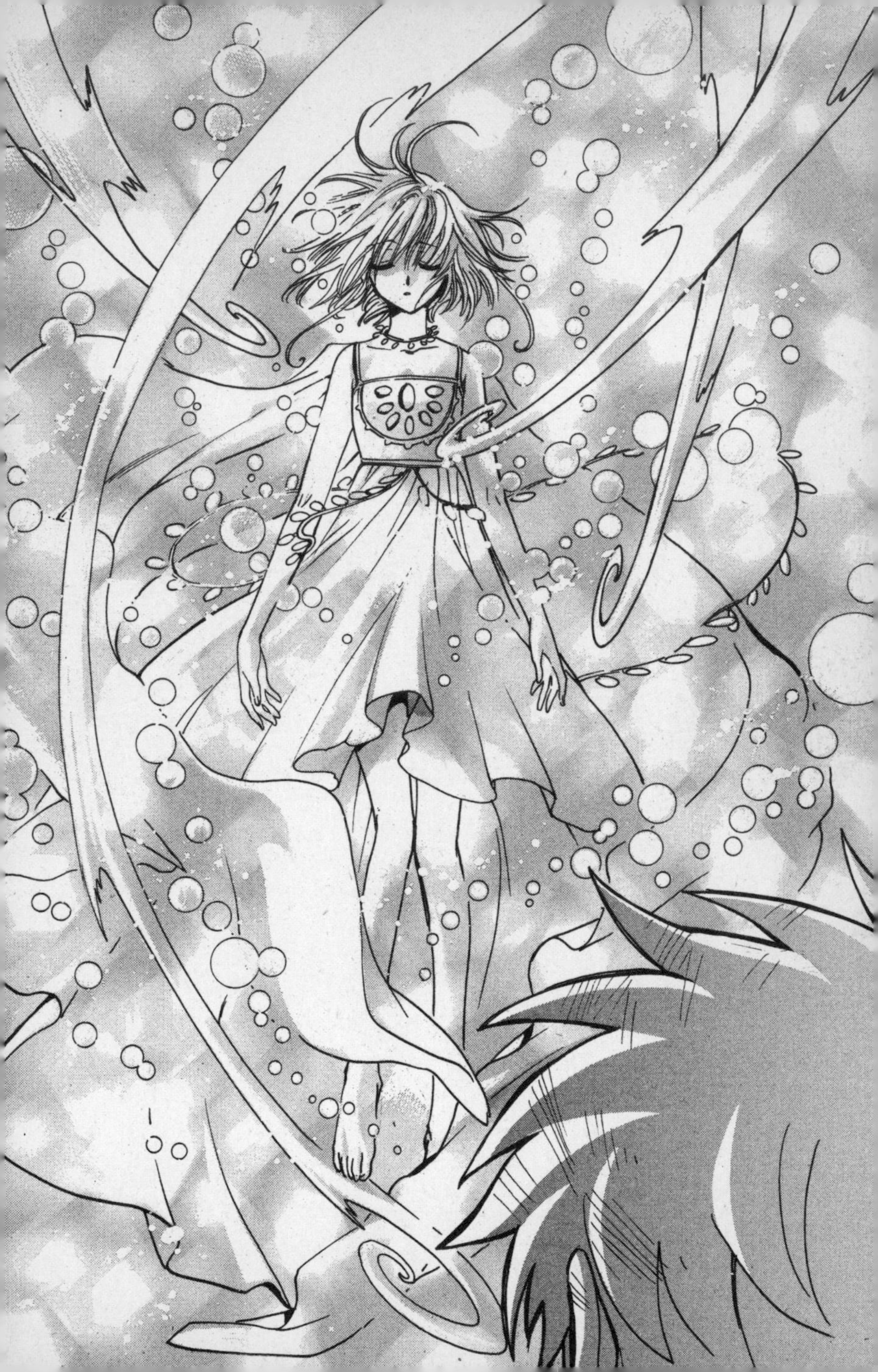

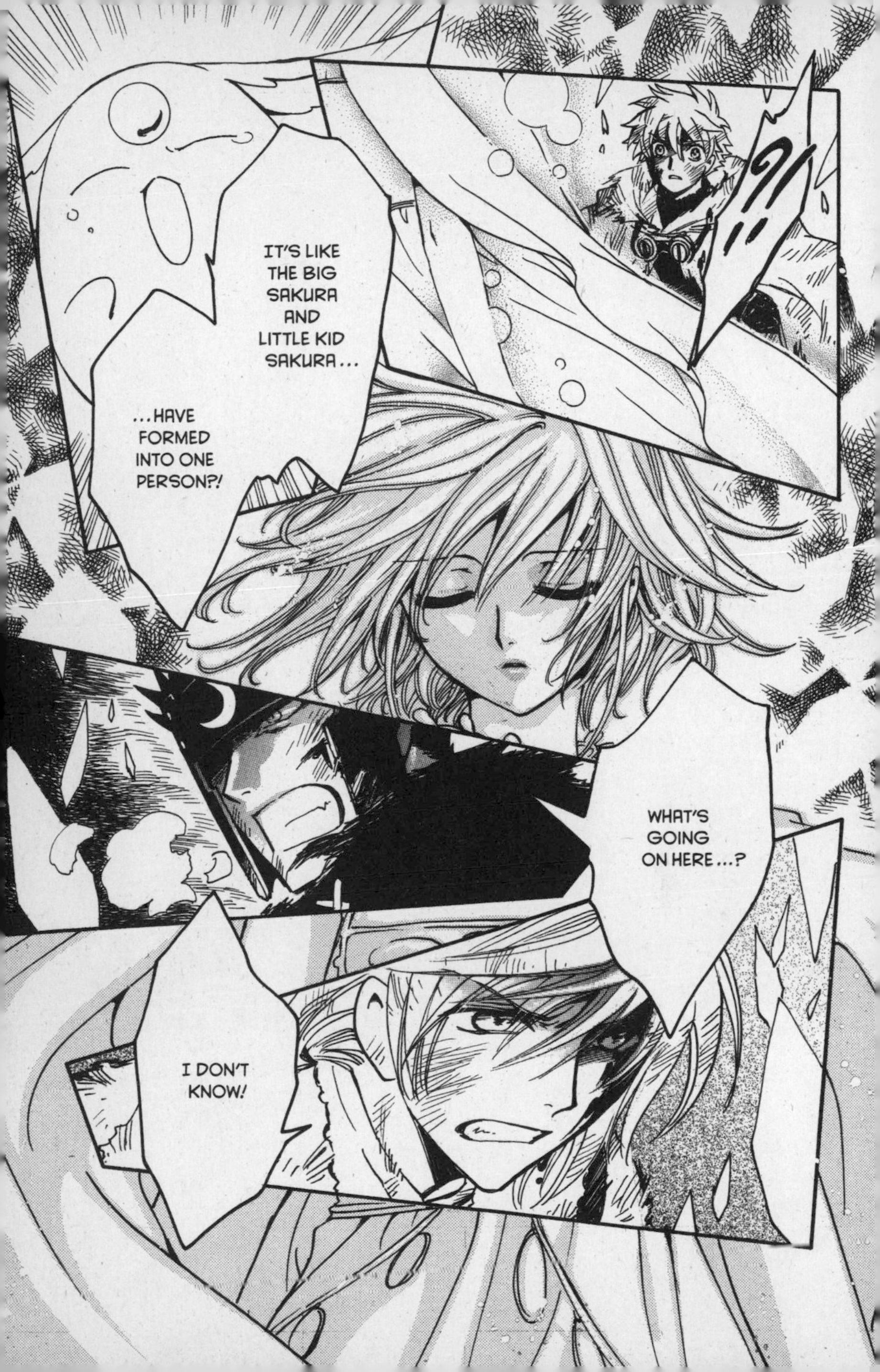
?!
IT'S LIKE THE BIG SAKURA AND LITTLE KID SAKURA...
...HAVE FORMED INTO ONE PERSON?!
WHAT'S GOING ON HERE...?
I DON'T KNOW!

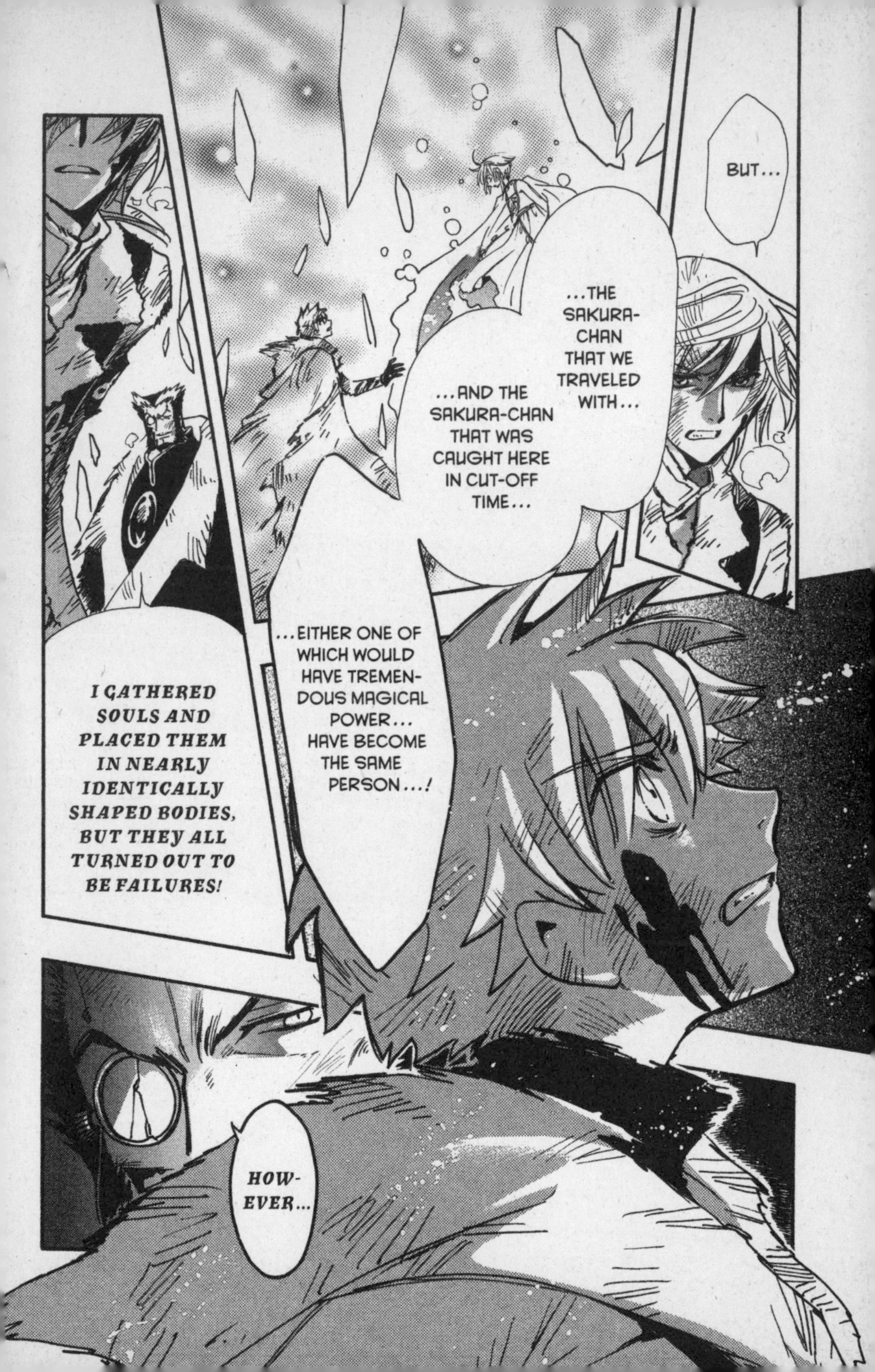
BUT...
...THE SAKURA-CHAN THAT WE TRAVELED WITH...
...AND THE SAKURA-CHAN THAT WAS CAUGHT HERE IN CUT-OFF TIME...
...EITHER ONE OF WHICH WOULD HAVE TREMEN-DOUS MAGICAL POWER... HAVE BECOME THE SAME PERSON...!
I GATHERED SOULS AND PLACED THEM IN NEARLY IDENTICALLY SHAPED BODIES, BUT THEY ALL TURNED OUT TO BE FAILURES!
HOW-EVER...

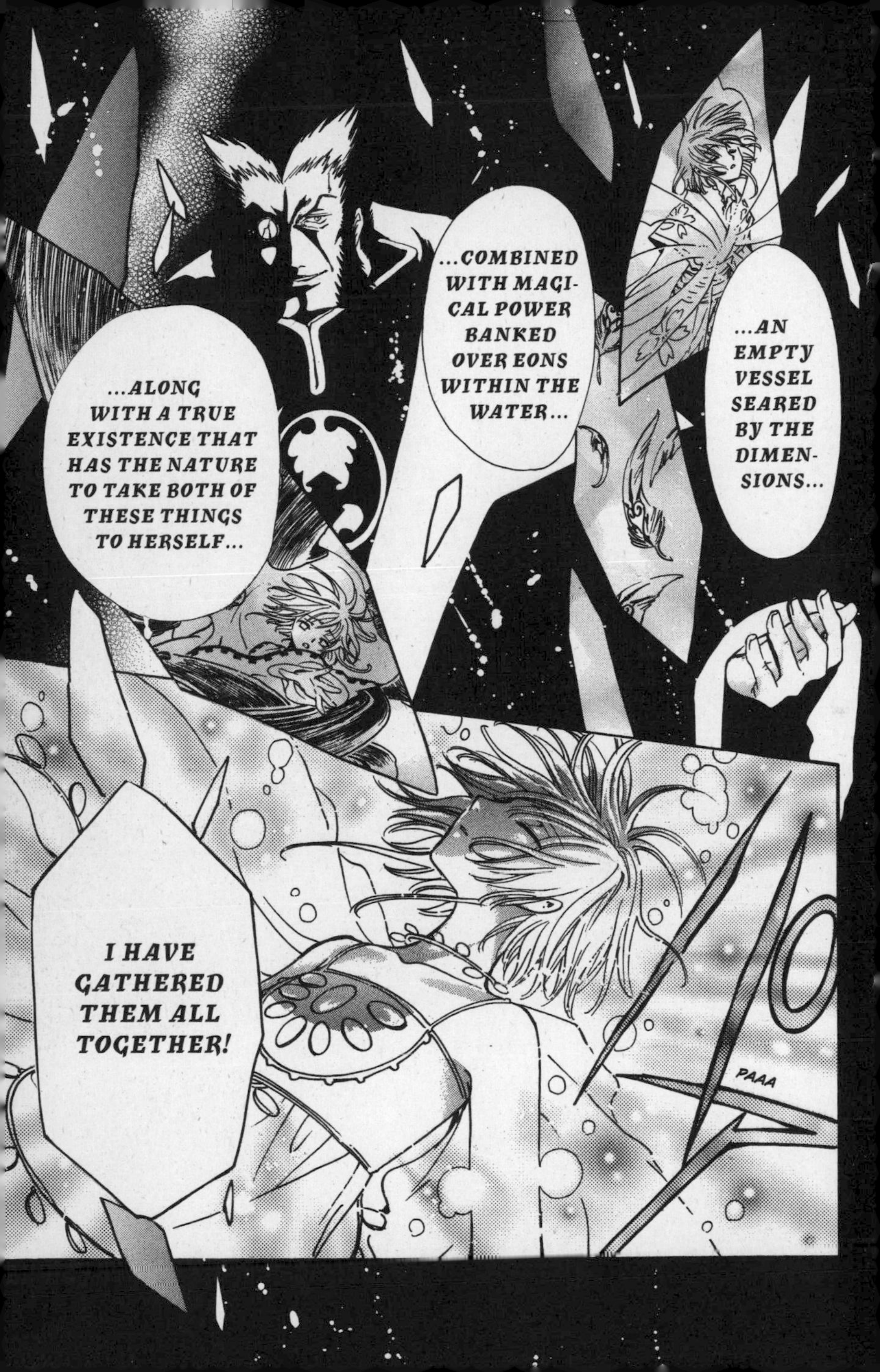
...AN EMPTY VESSEL SEARED BY THE DIMENSIONS...
...COMBINED WITH MAGICAL POWER BANKED OVER EONS WITHIN THE WATER...
...ALONG WITH A TRUE EXISTENCE THAT HAS THE NATURE TO TAKE BOTH OF THESE THINGS TO HERSELF...
PAAA
I HAVE GATHERED THEM ALL TOGETHER!

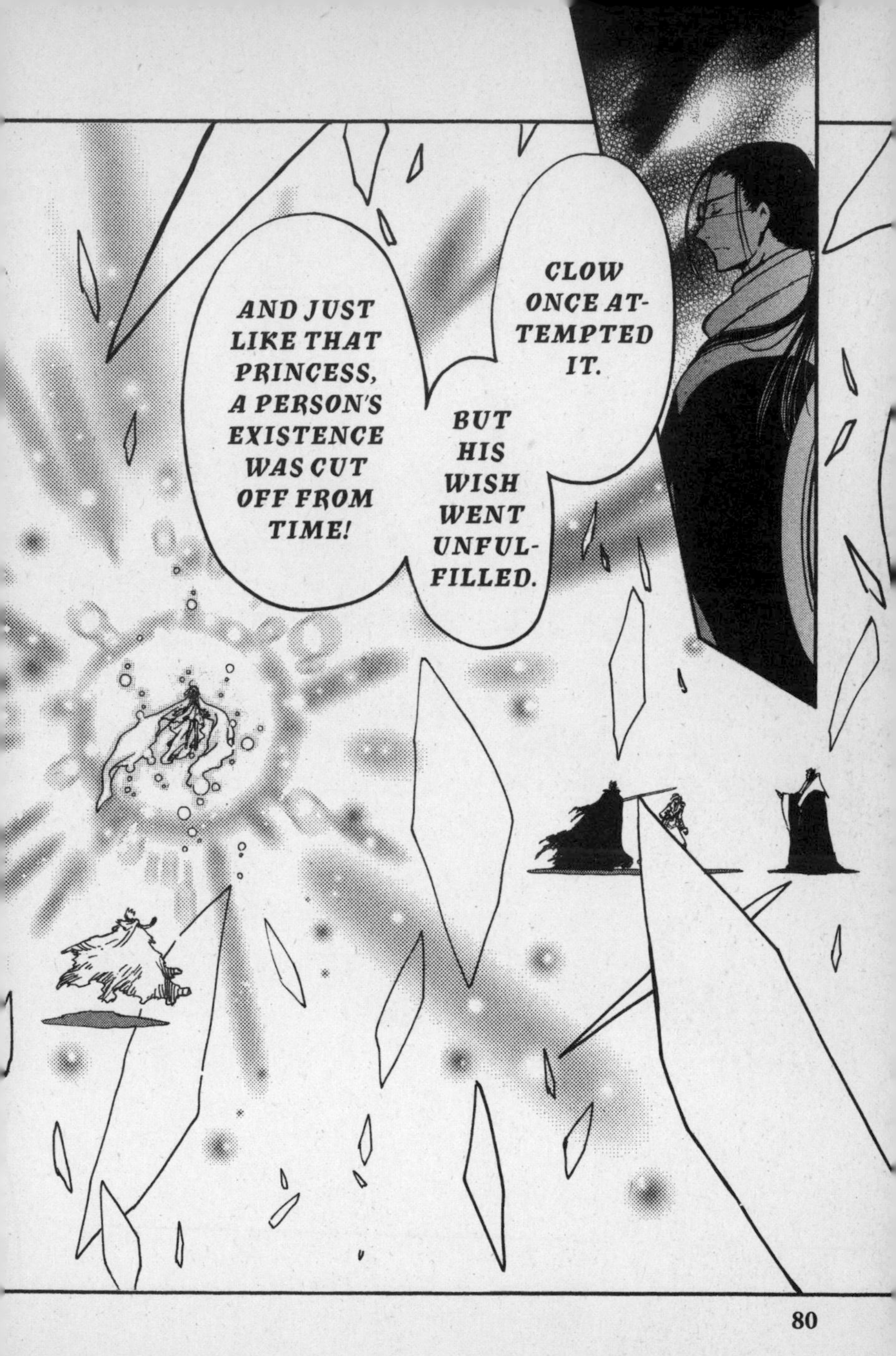
CLOW ONCE ATTEMPTED IT.
BUT HIS WISH WENT UNFULFILLED.
AND JUST LIKE THAT PRINCESS, A PERSON'S EXISTENCE WAS CUT OFF FROM TIME!

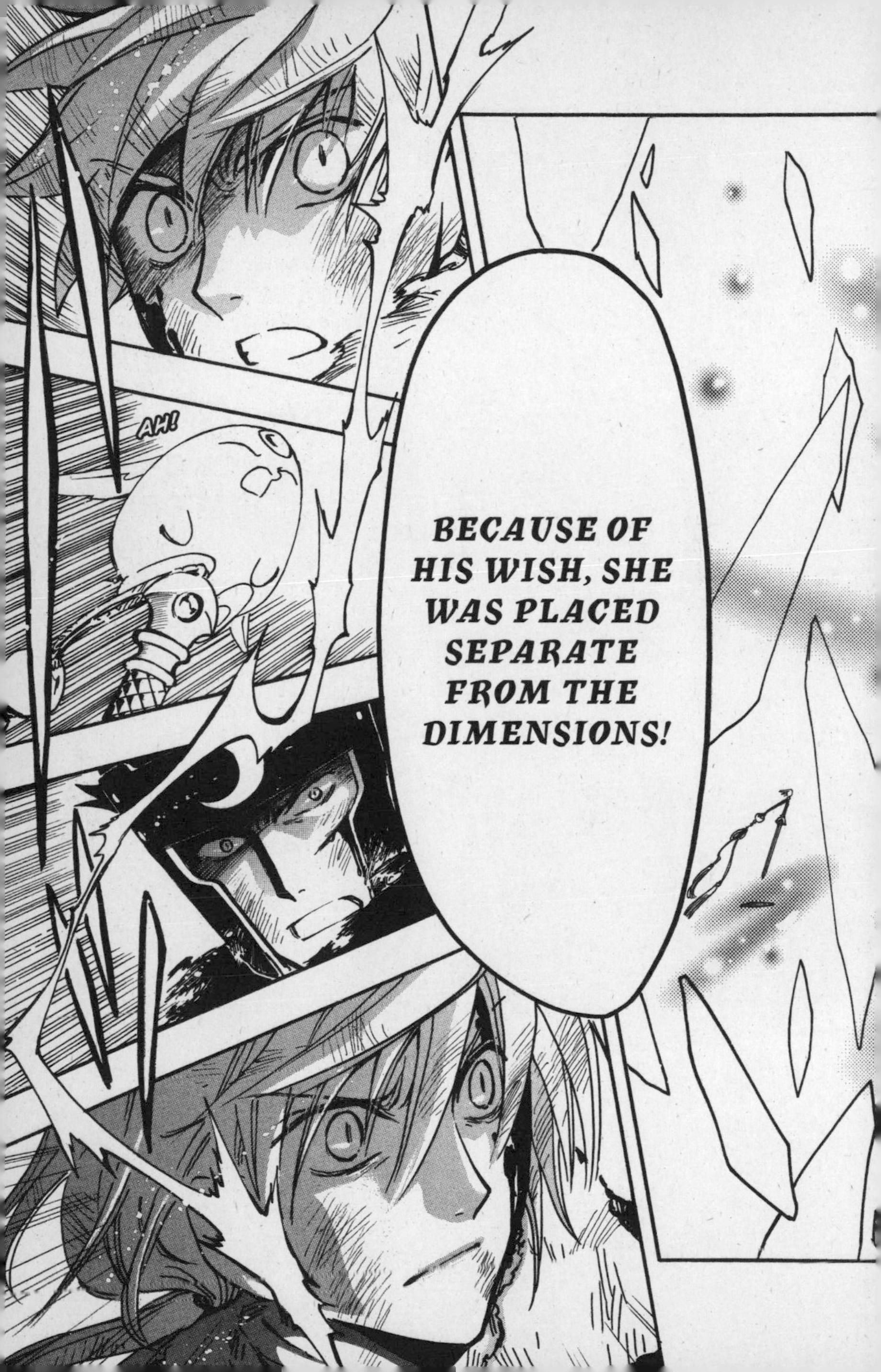
AH!
BECAUSE OF HIS WISH, SHE WAS PLACED SEPARATE FROM THE DIMENSIONS!

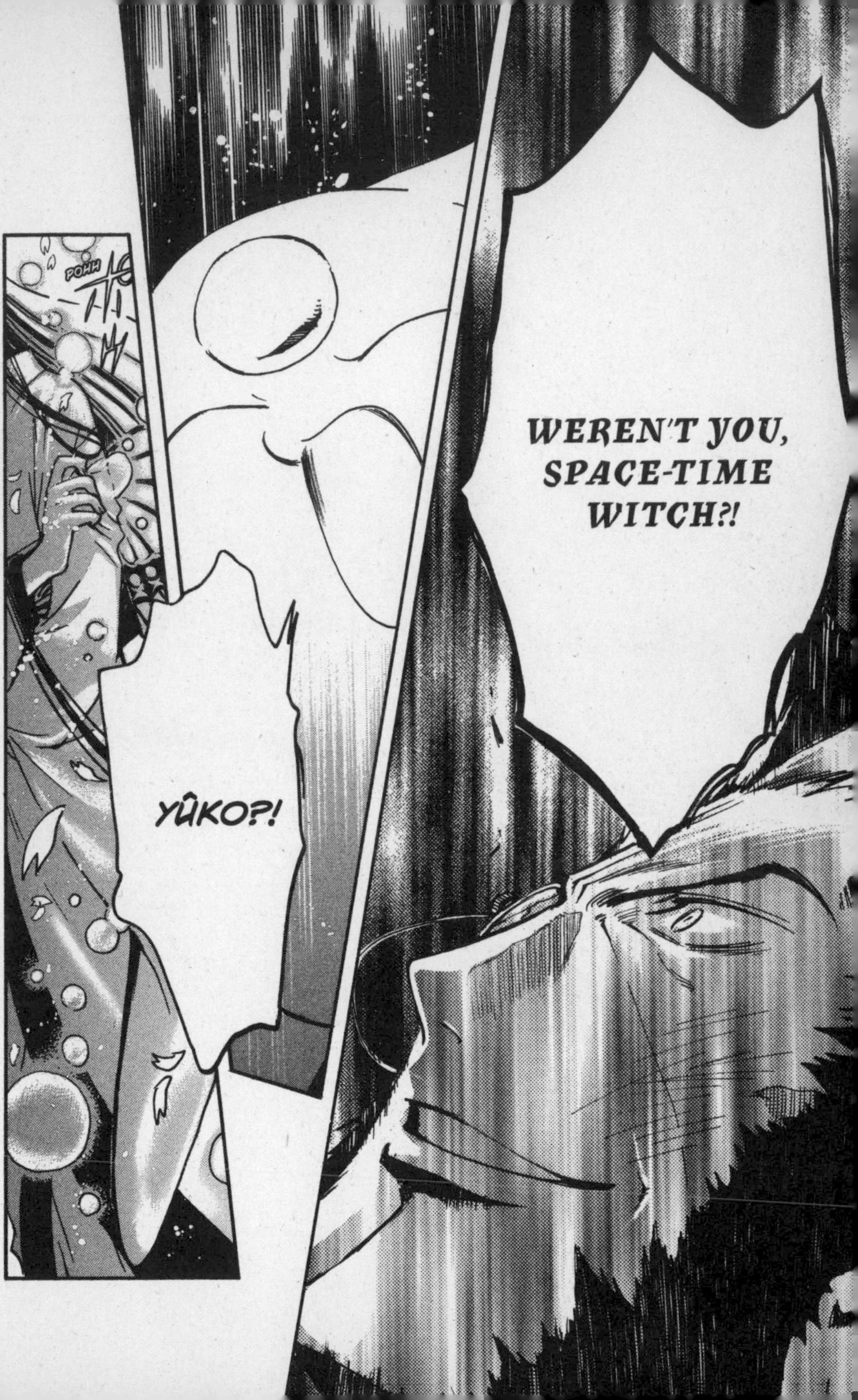
WEREN'T YOU, SPACE-TIME WITCH?!
YÛKO?!
POHH

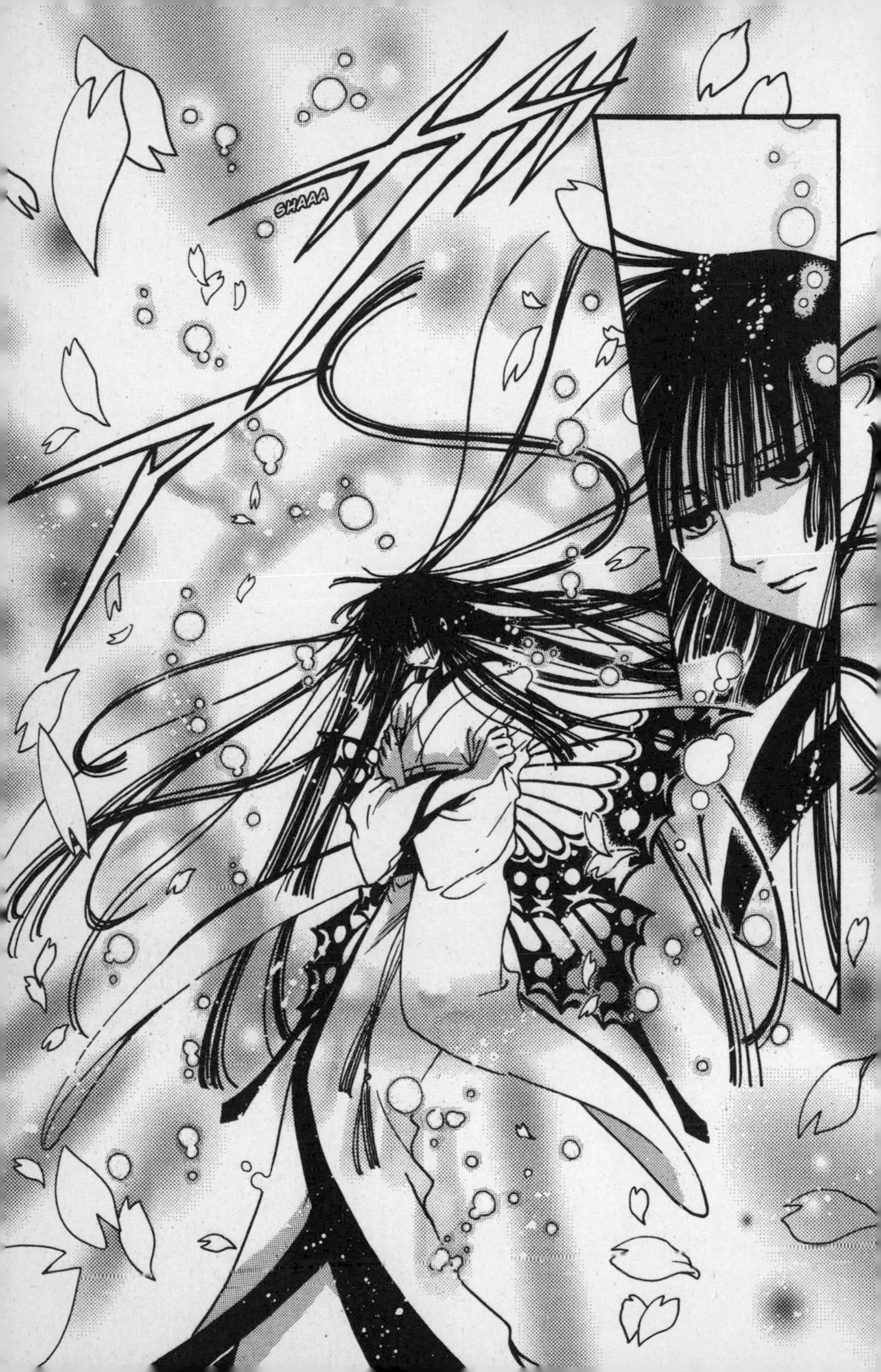
SHAAA

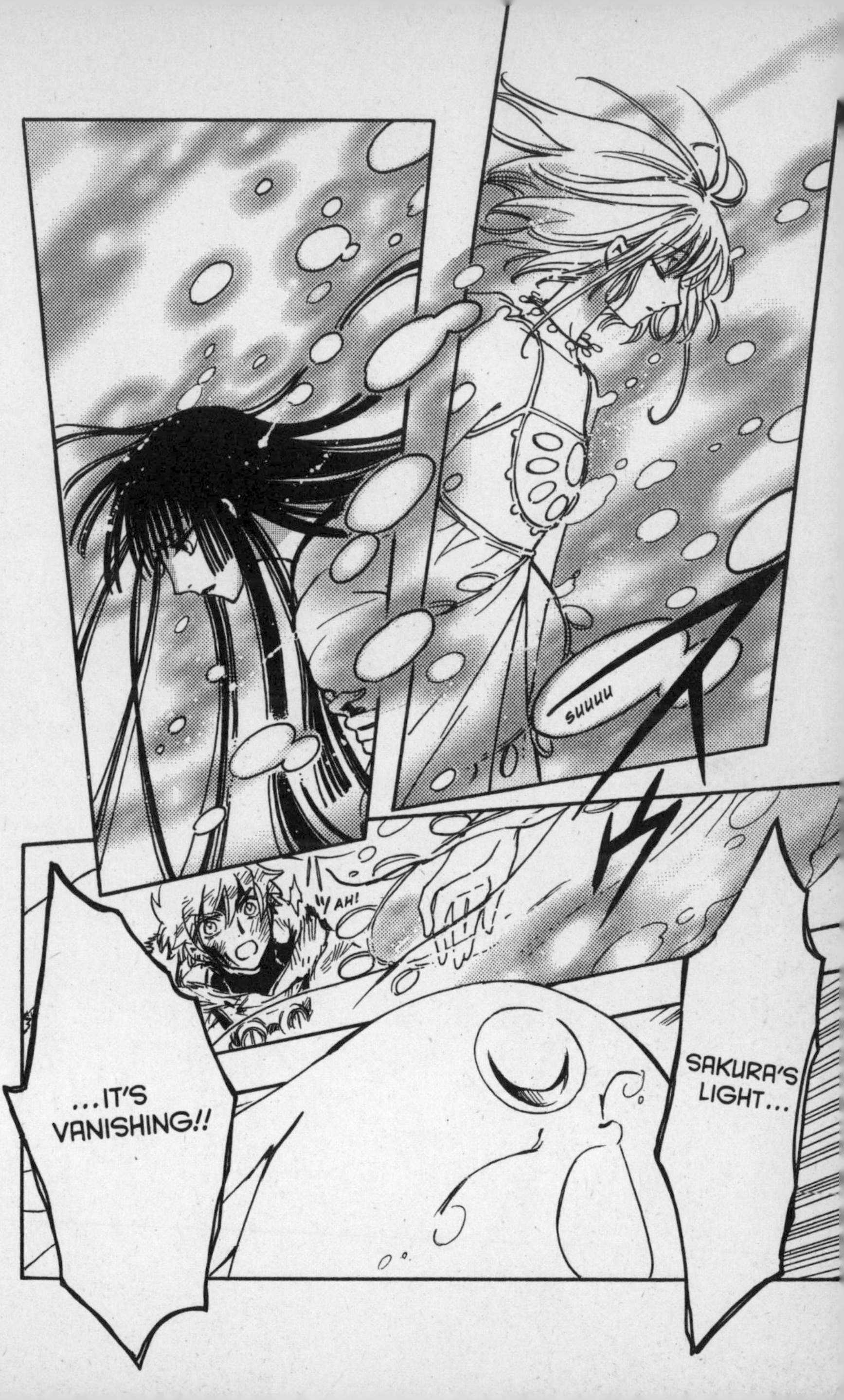
SUUUU
AH!
SAKURA'S LIGHT...
...IT'S VANISHING!!

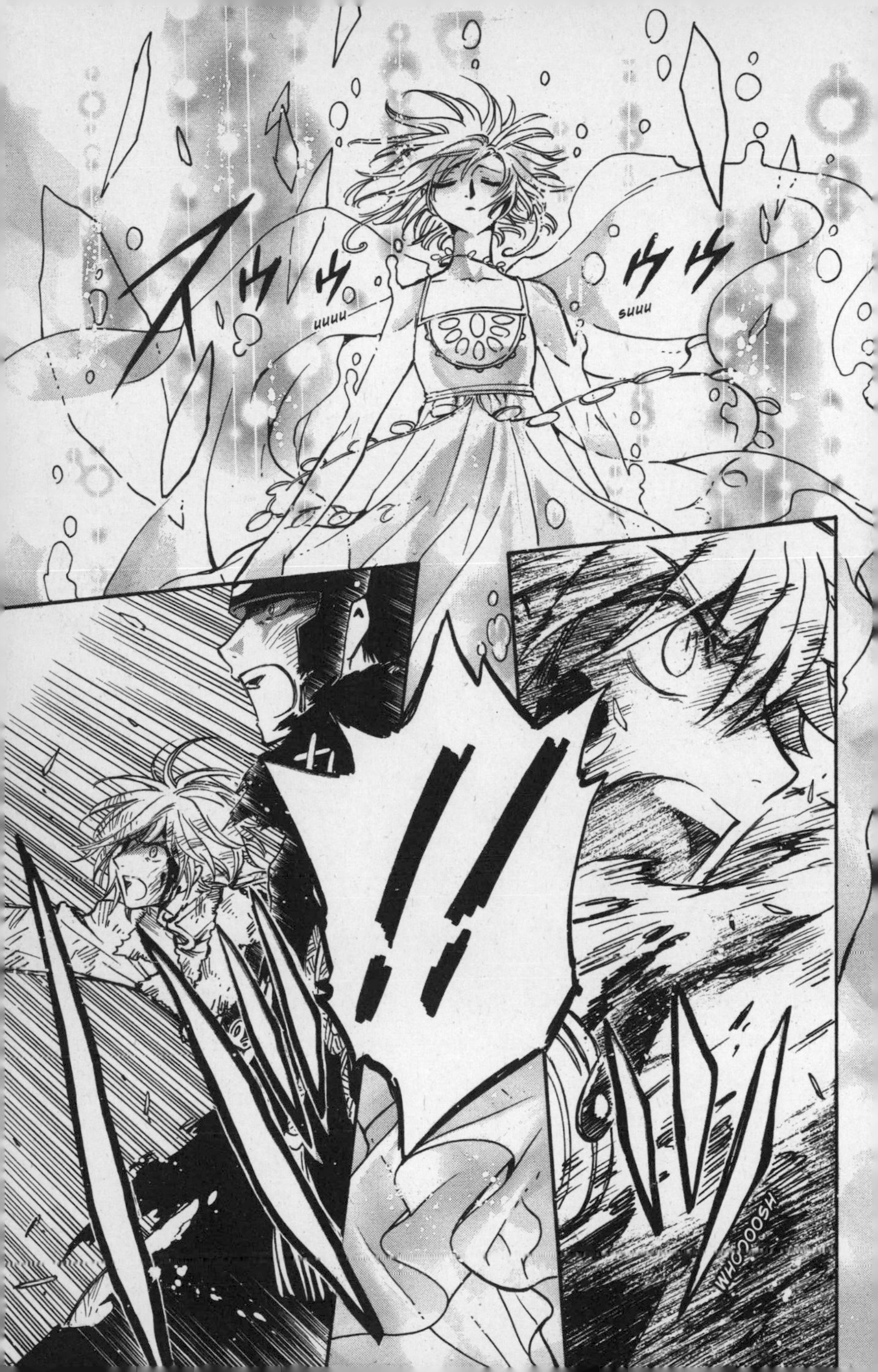
suuu
uuuu
!!
WHOOOOSH

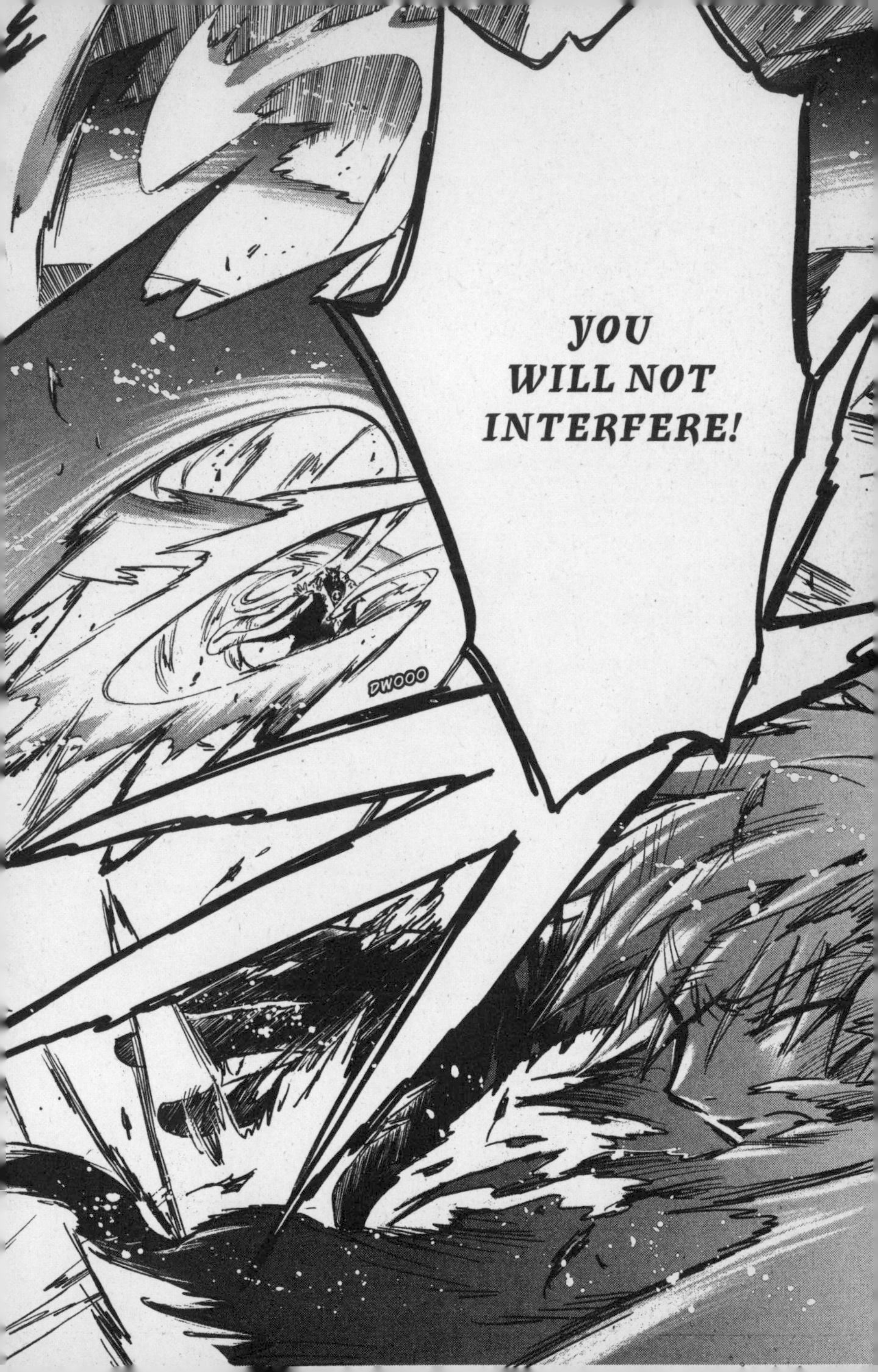
YOU WILL NOT INTERFERE!
DWOOO

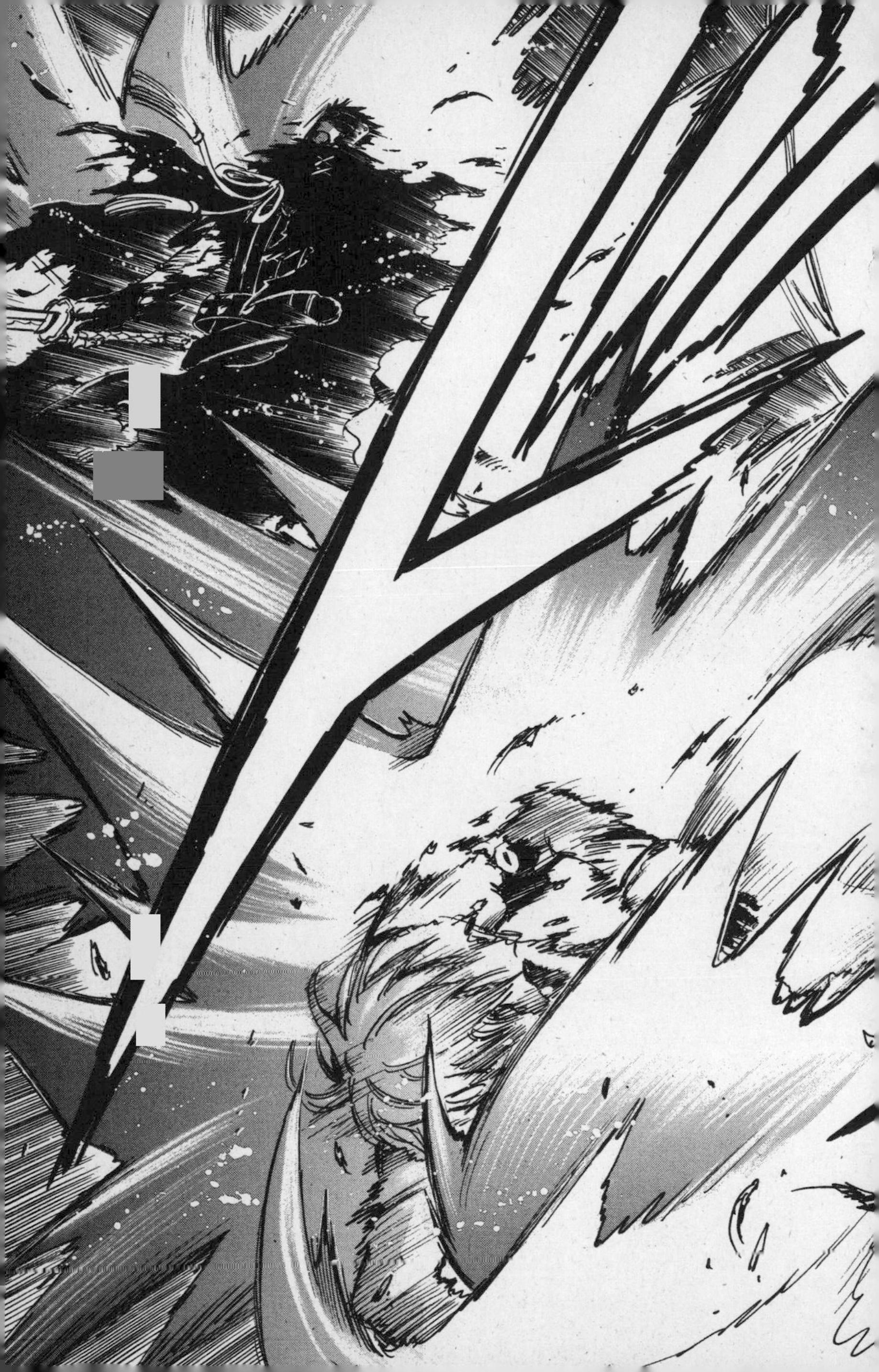

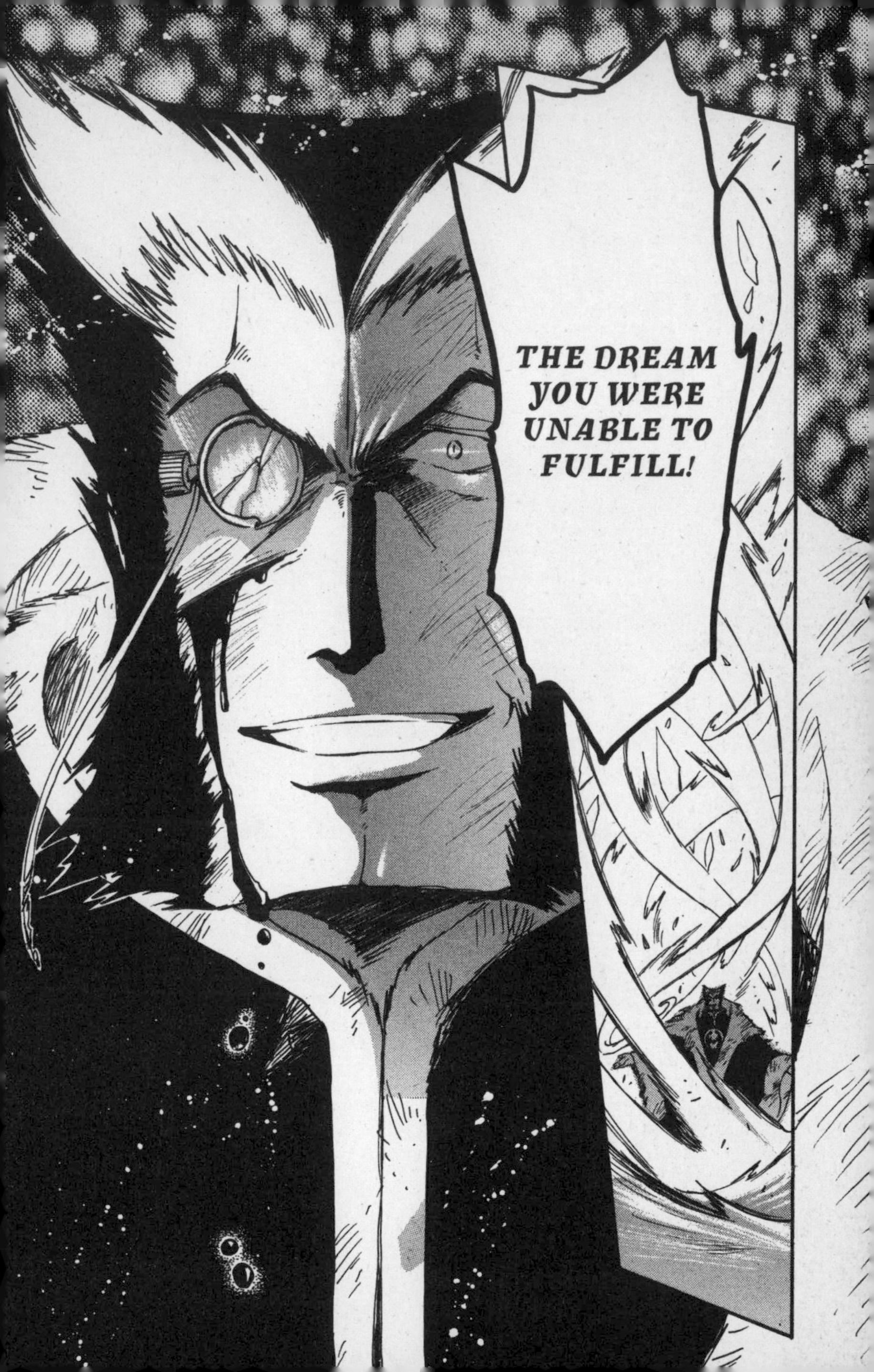
THE DREAM YOU WERE UNABLE TO FULFILL!

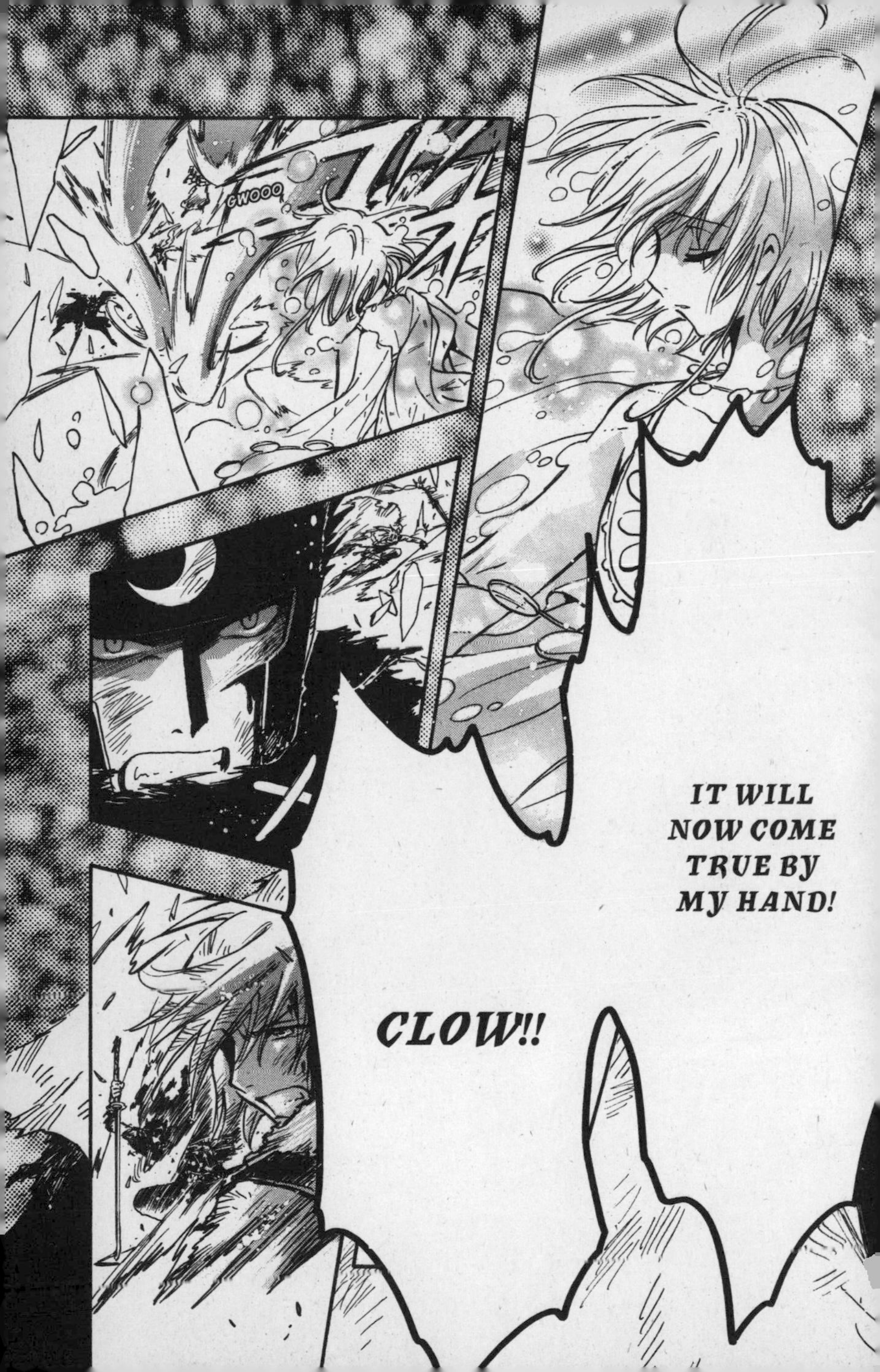
GWOOO
IT WILL NOW COME TRUE BY MY HAND!
CLOW!!

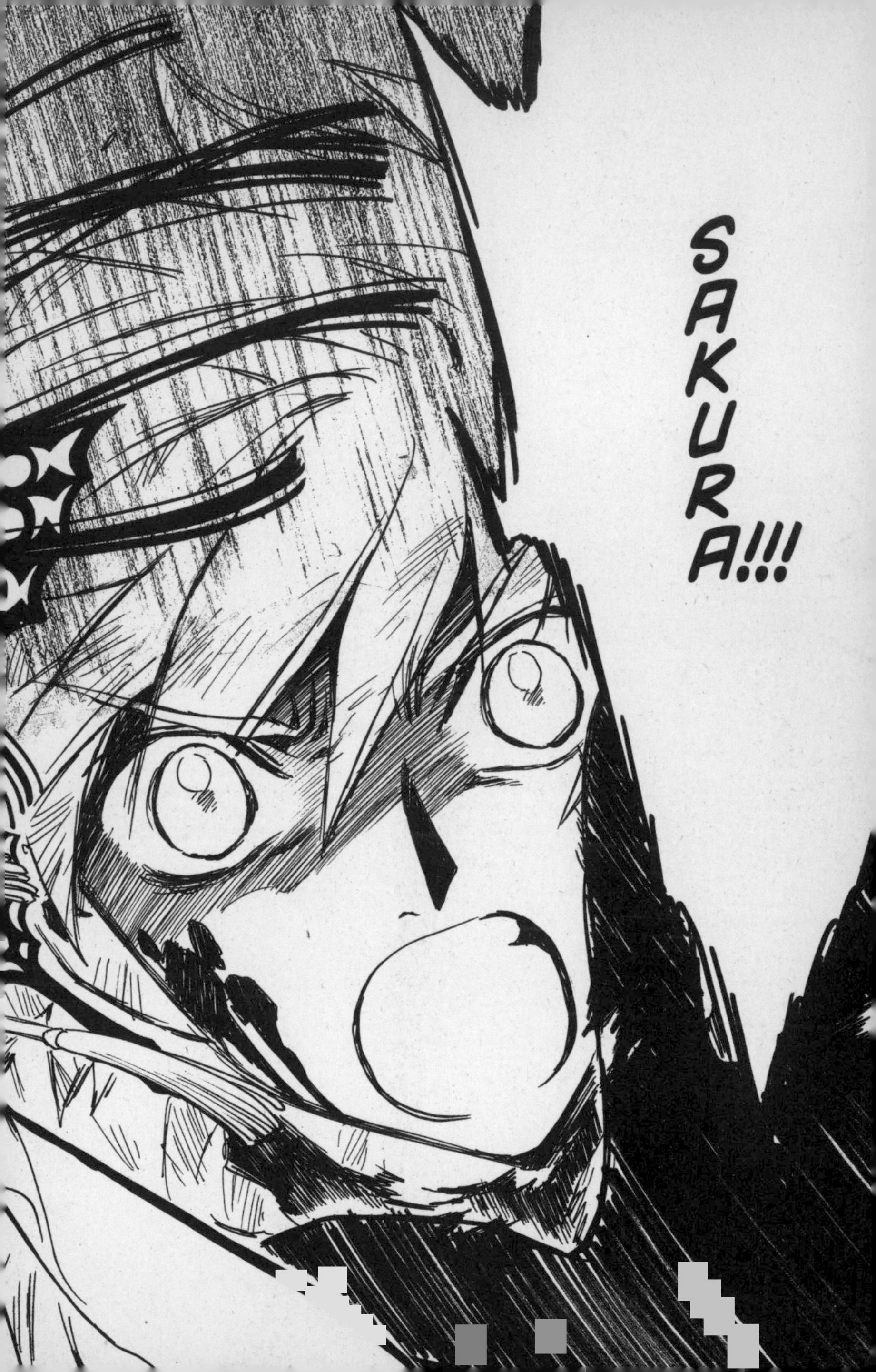
SAKURA!!!

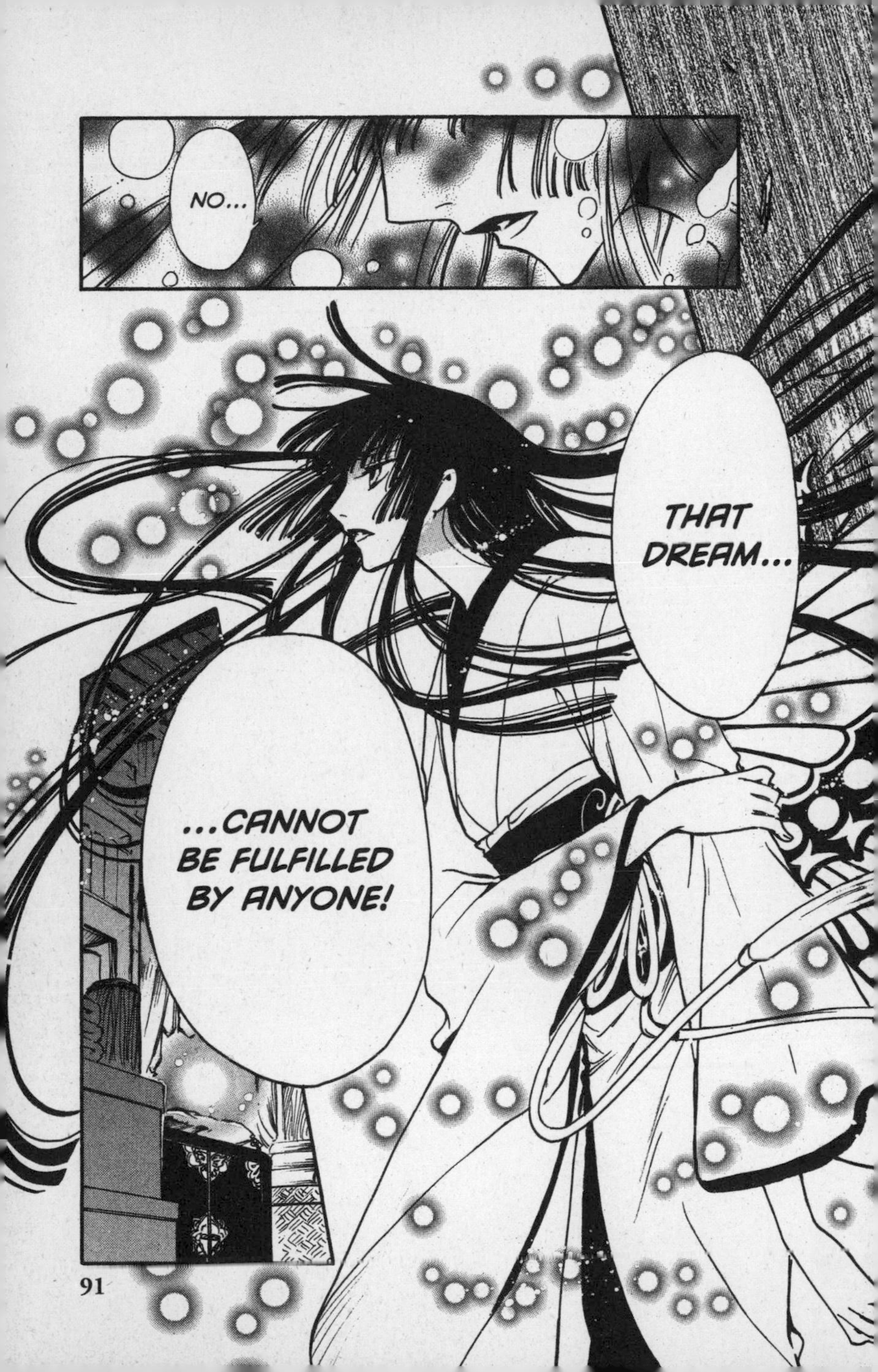
NO...
THAT DREAM...
...CANNOT BE FULFILLED BY ANYONE!

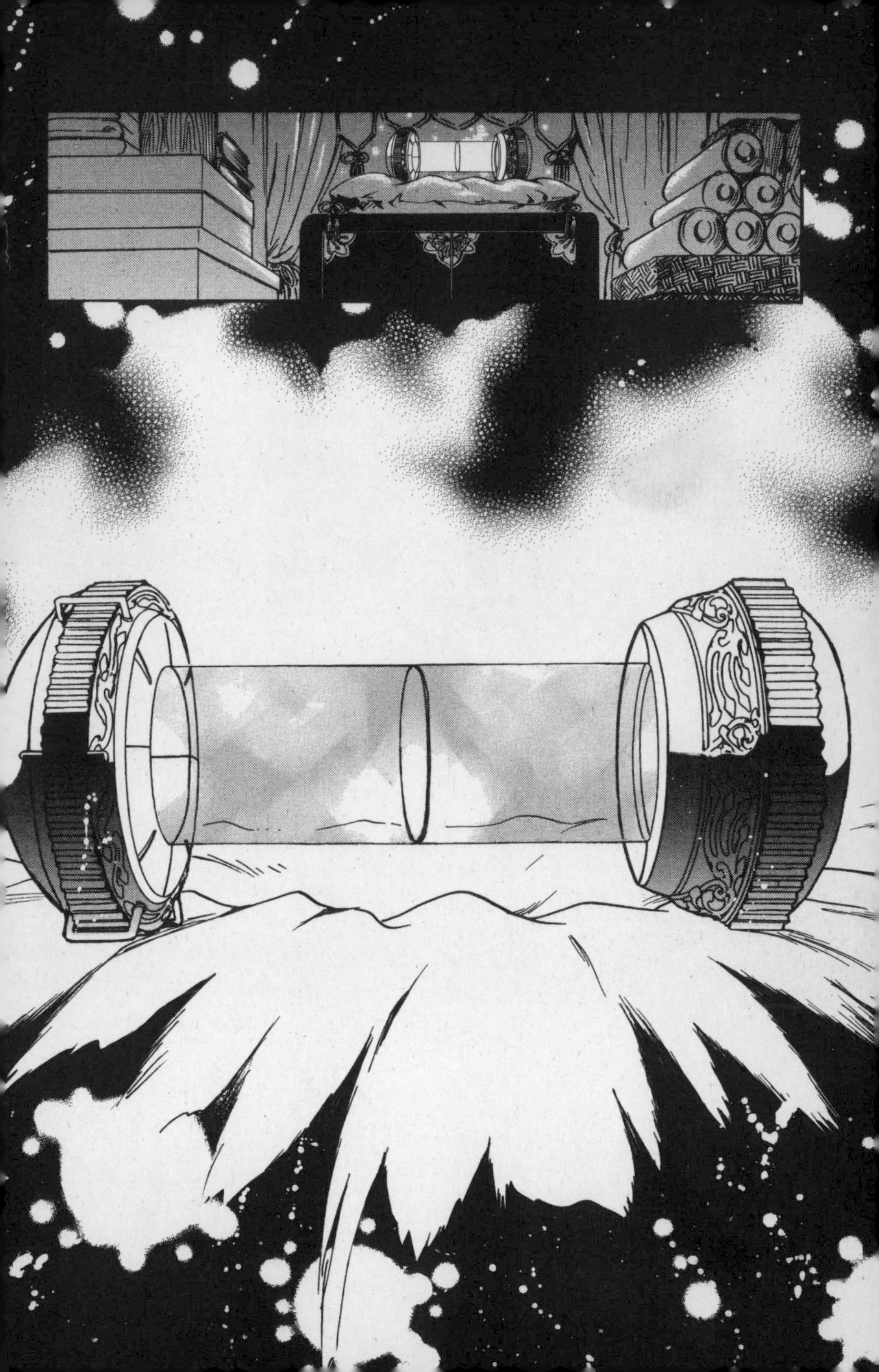

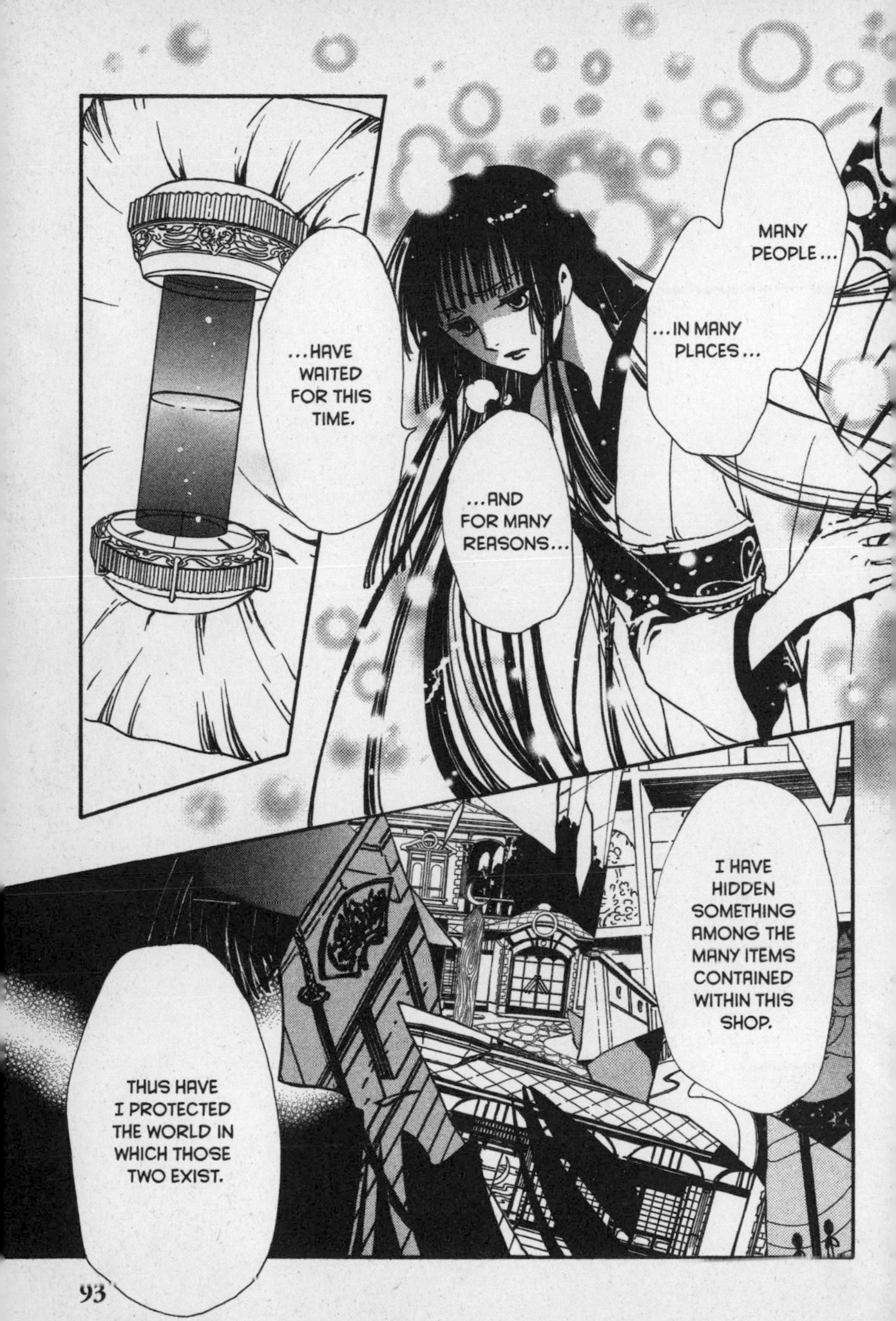
MANY PEOPLE...
...IN MANY PLACES...
...AND FOR MANY REASONS...
...HAVE WAITED FOR THIS TIME.
I HAVE HIDDEN SOMETHING AMONG THE MANY ITEMS CONTAINED WITHIN THIS SHOP.
THUS HAVE I PROTECTED THE WORLD IN WHICH THOSE TWO EXIST.

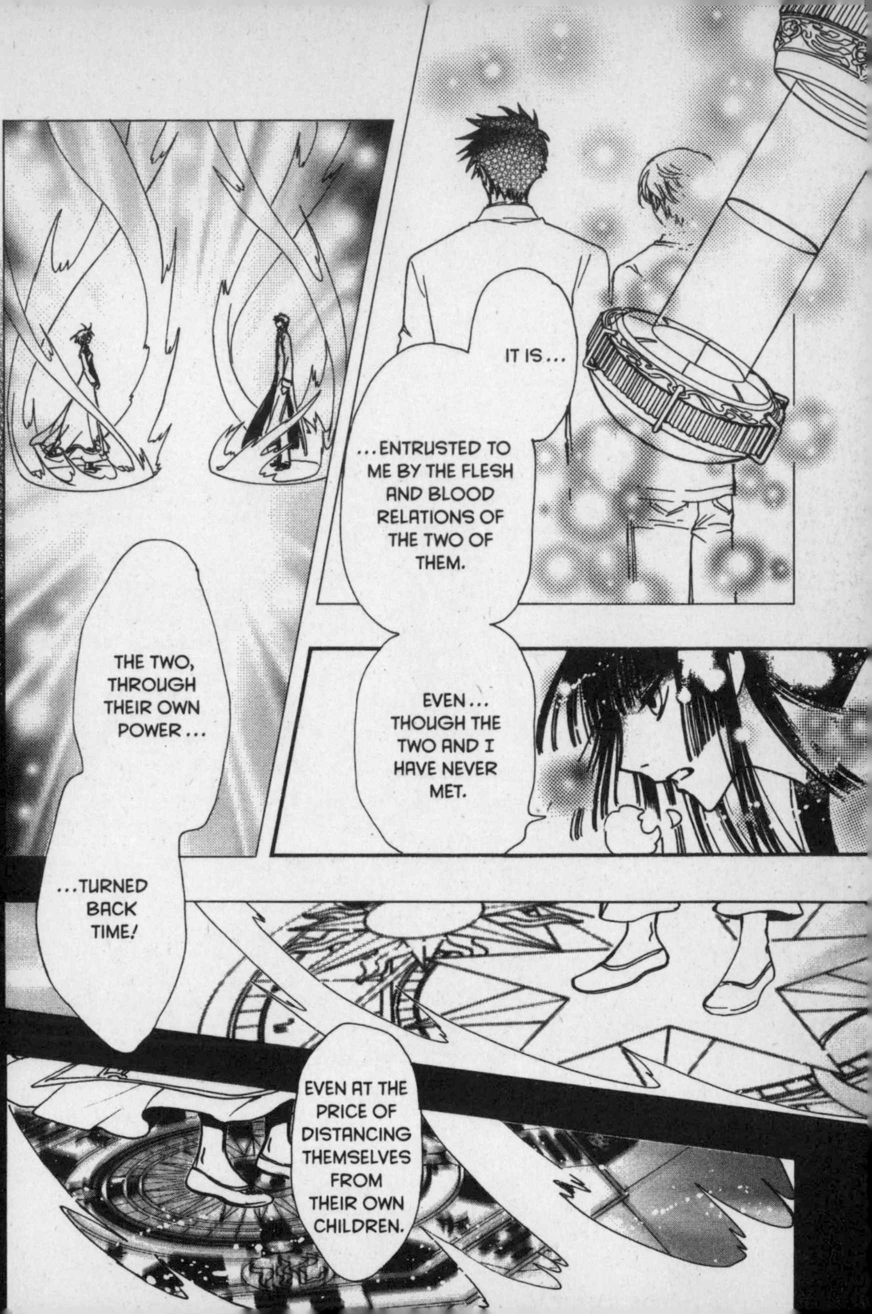
IT IS...
...ENTRUSTED TO ME BY THE FLESH AND BLOOD RELATIONS OF THE TWO OF THEM.
EVEN... THOUGH THE TWO AND I HAVE NEVER MET.
THE TWO, THROUGH THEIR OWN POWER...
...TURNED BACK TIME!
EVEN AT THE PRICE OF DISTANCING THEMSELVES FROM THEIR OWN CHILDREN.

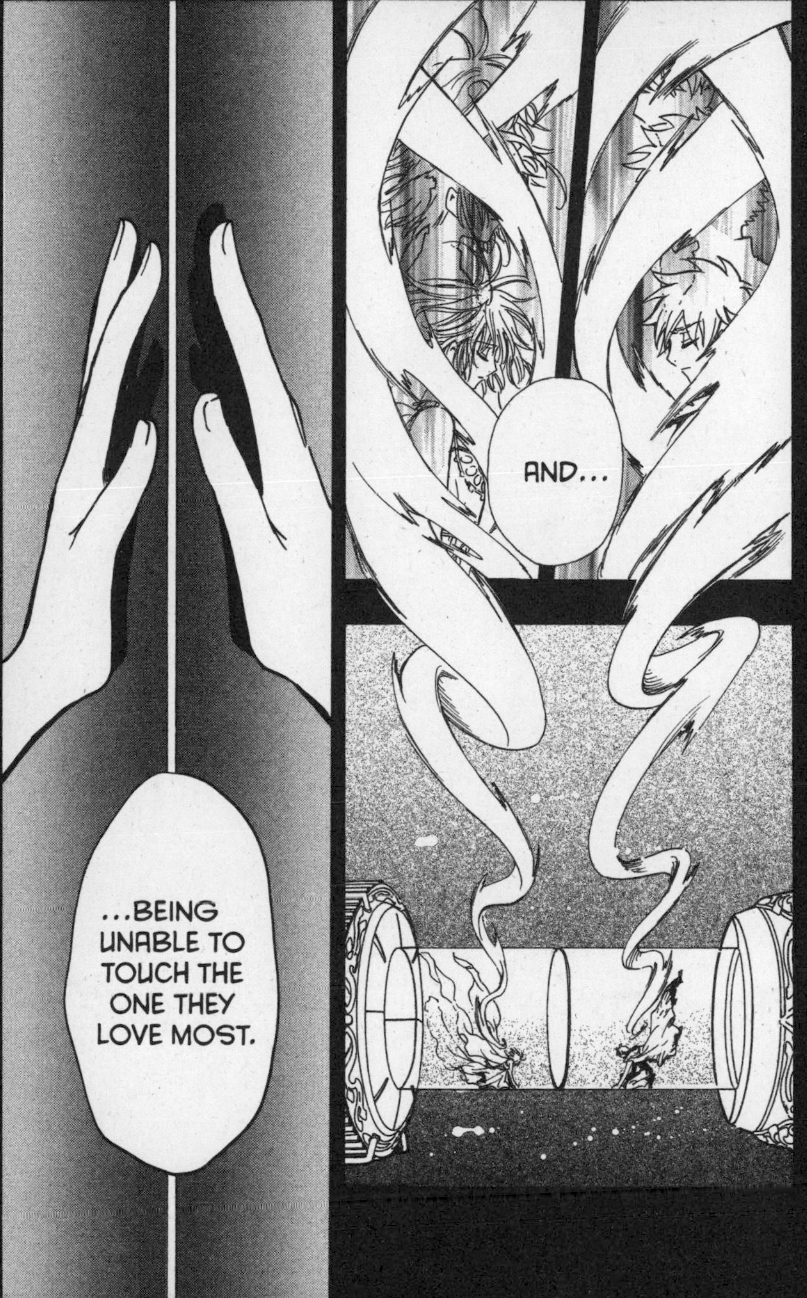
AND...
...BEING UNABLE TO TOUCH THE ONE THEY LOVE MOST.

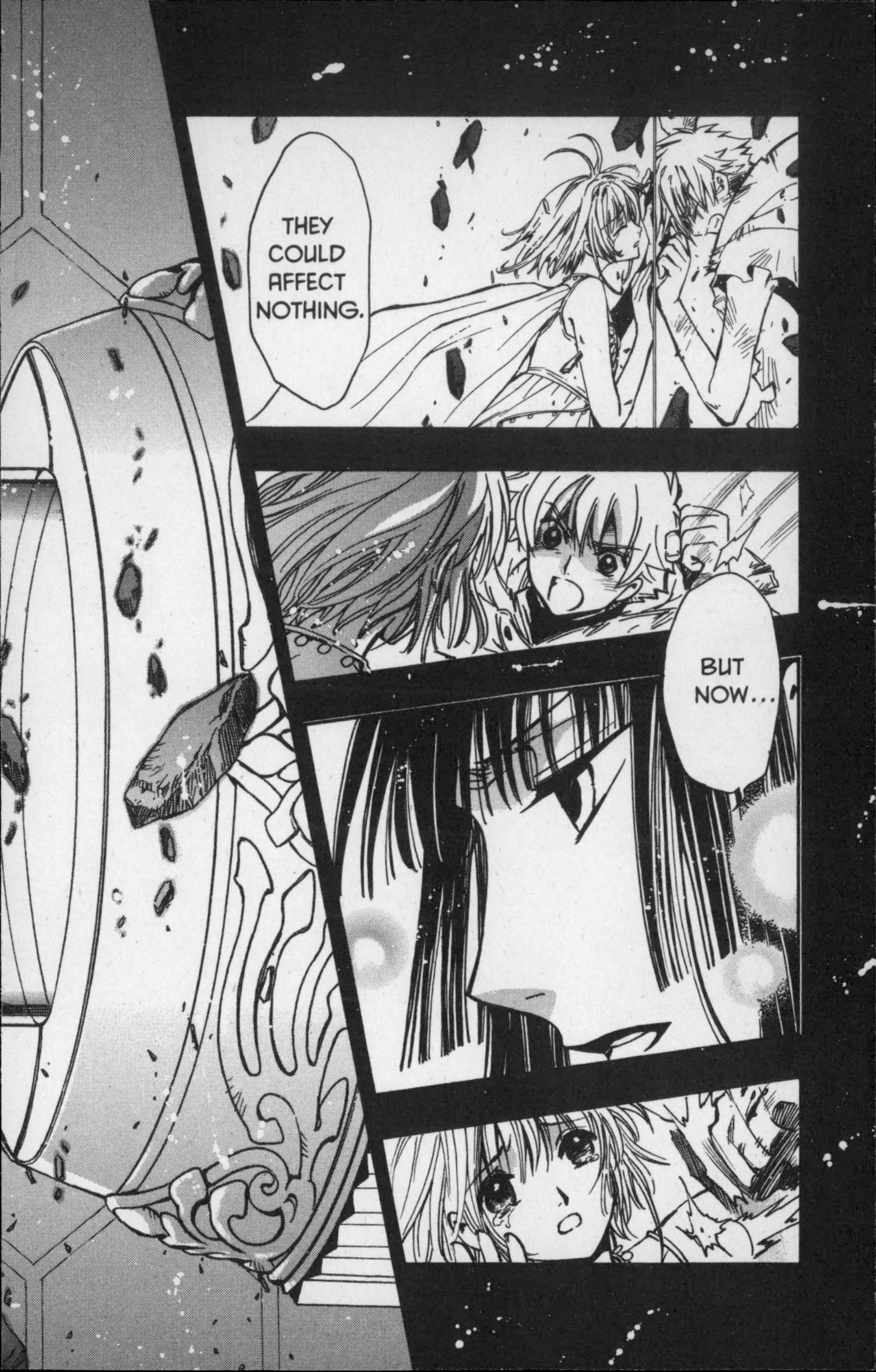
THEY COULD AFFECT NOTHING.
BUT NOW...

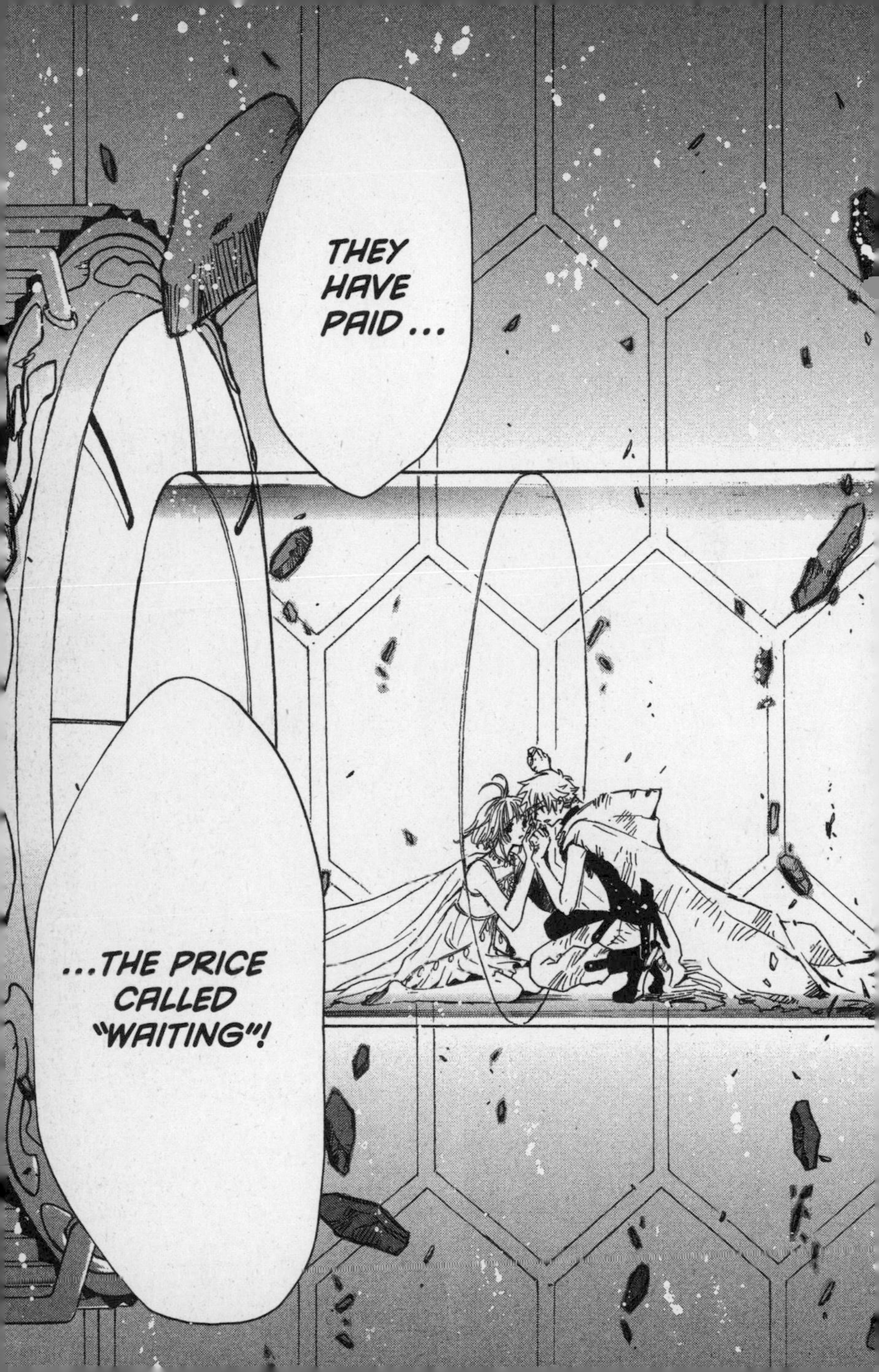
THEY HAVE PAID...
...THE PRICE CALLED "WAITING"!

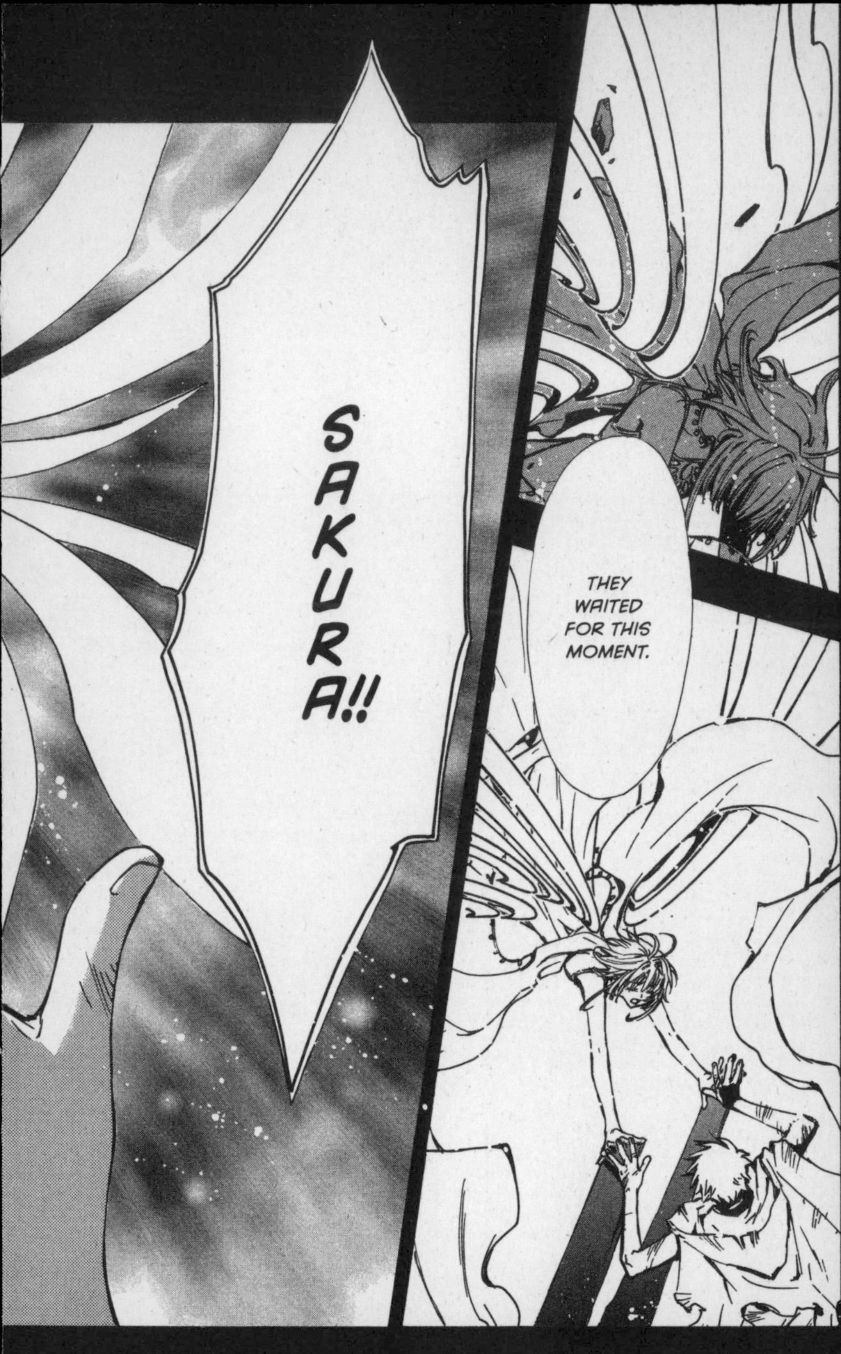
THEY WAITED FOR THIS MOMENT.
SAKURA!!

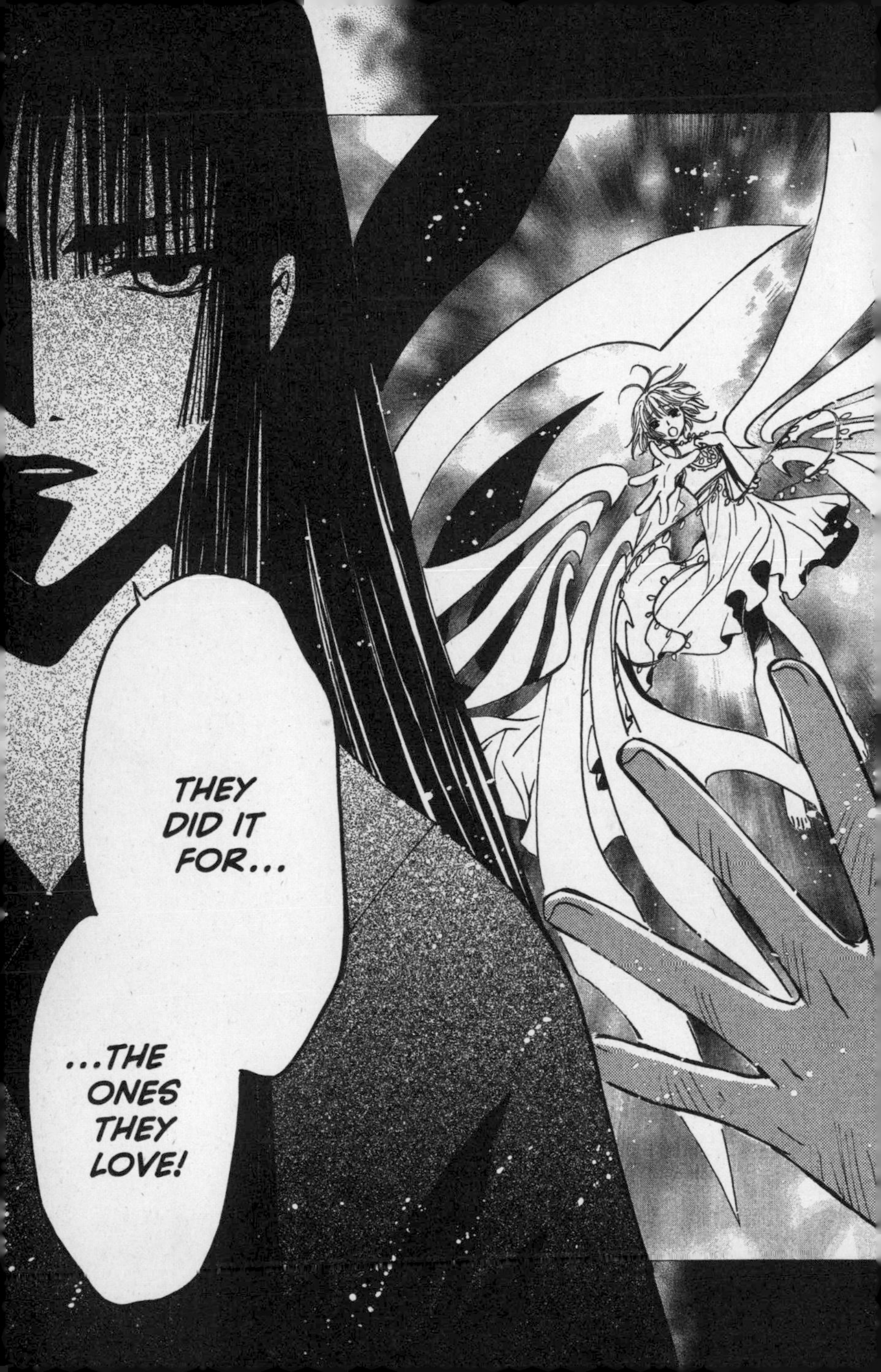
THEY DID IT FOR...
...THE ONES THEY LOVE!

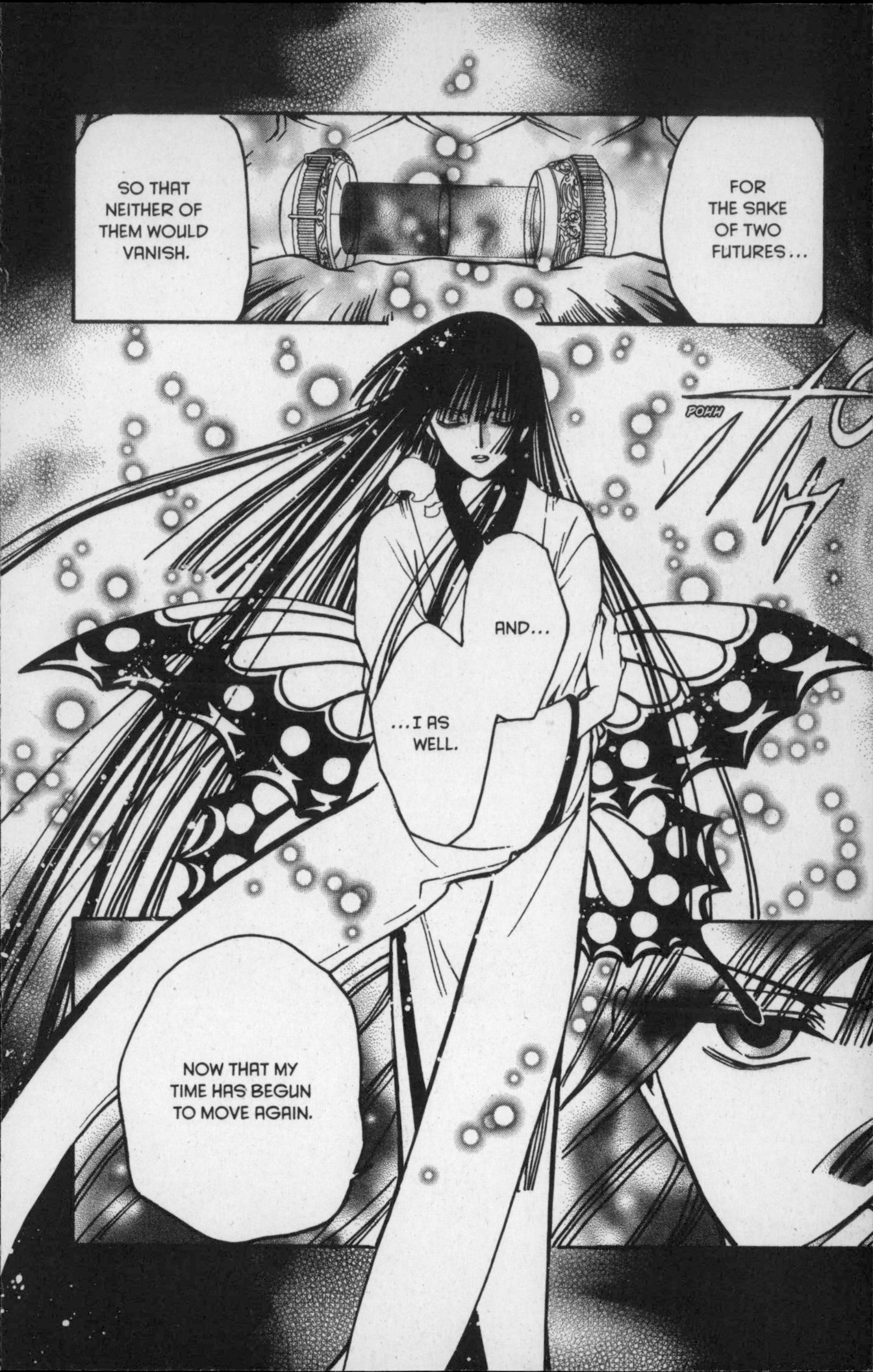
FOR THE SAKE OF TWO FUTURES...
SO THAT NEITHER OF THEM WOULD VANISH.
POHH
AND...
...I AS WELL.
NOW THAT MY TIME HAS BEGUN TO MOVE AGAIN.

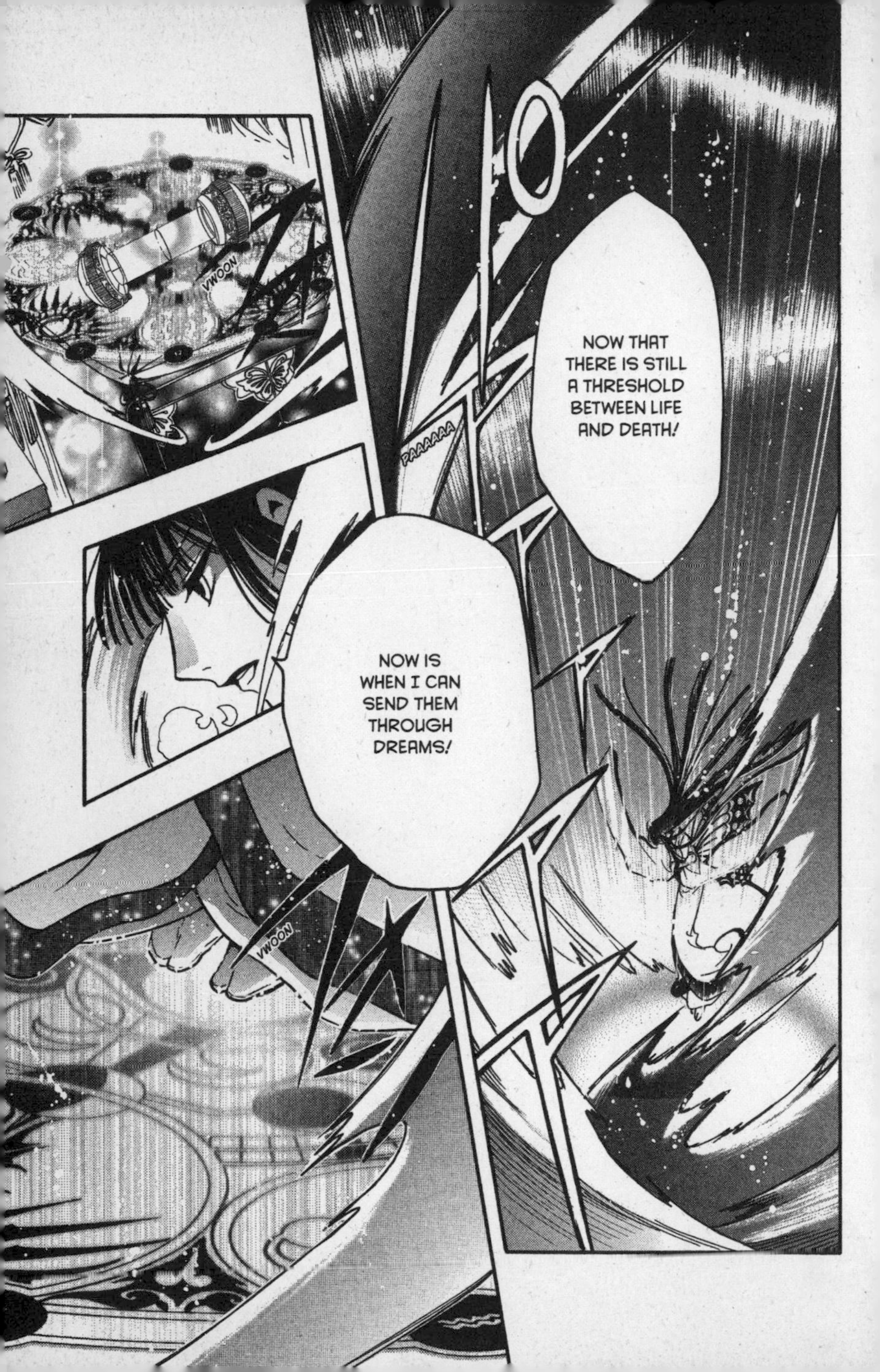
VWOON
NOW THAT THERE IS STILL A THRESHOLD BETWEEN LIFE AND DEATH!
PAAAAAA
NOW IS WHEN I CAN SEND THEM THROUGH DREAMS!
VWOON

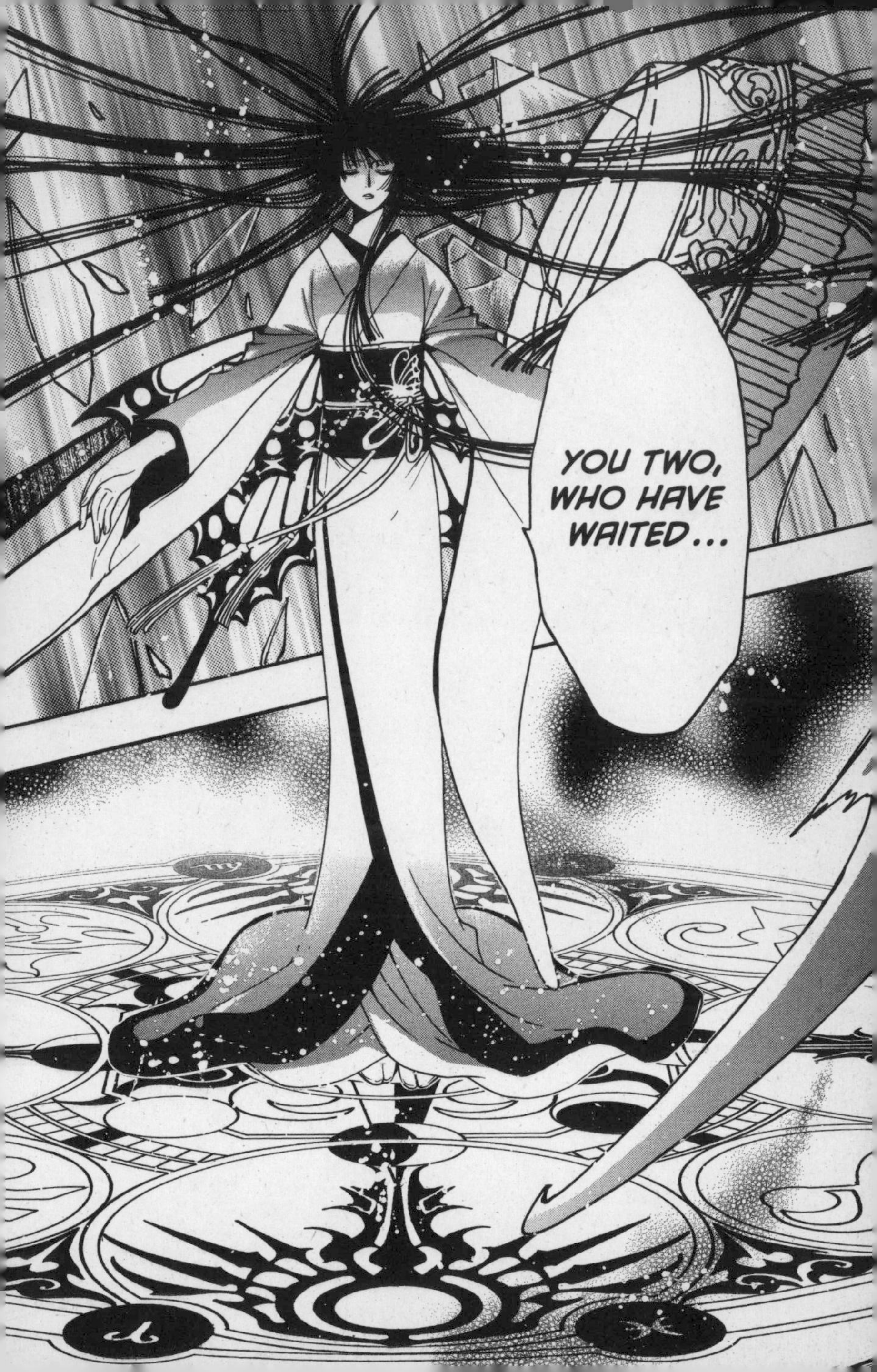
YOU TWO, WHO HAVE WAITED...

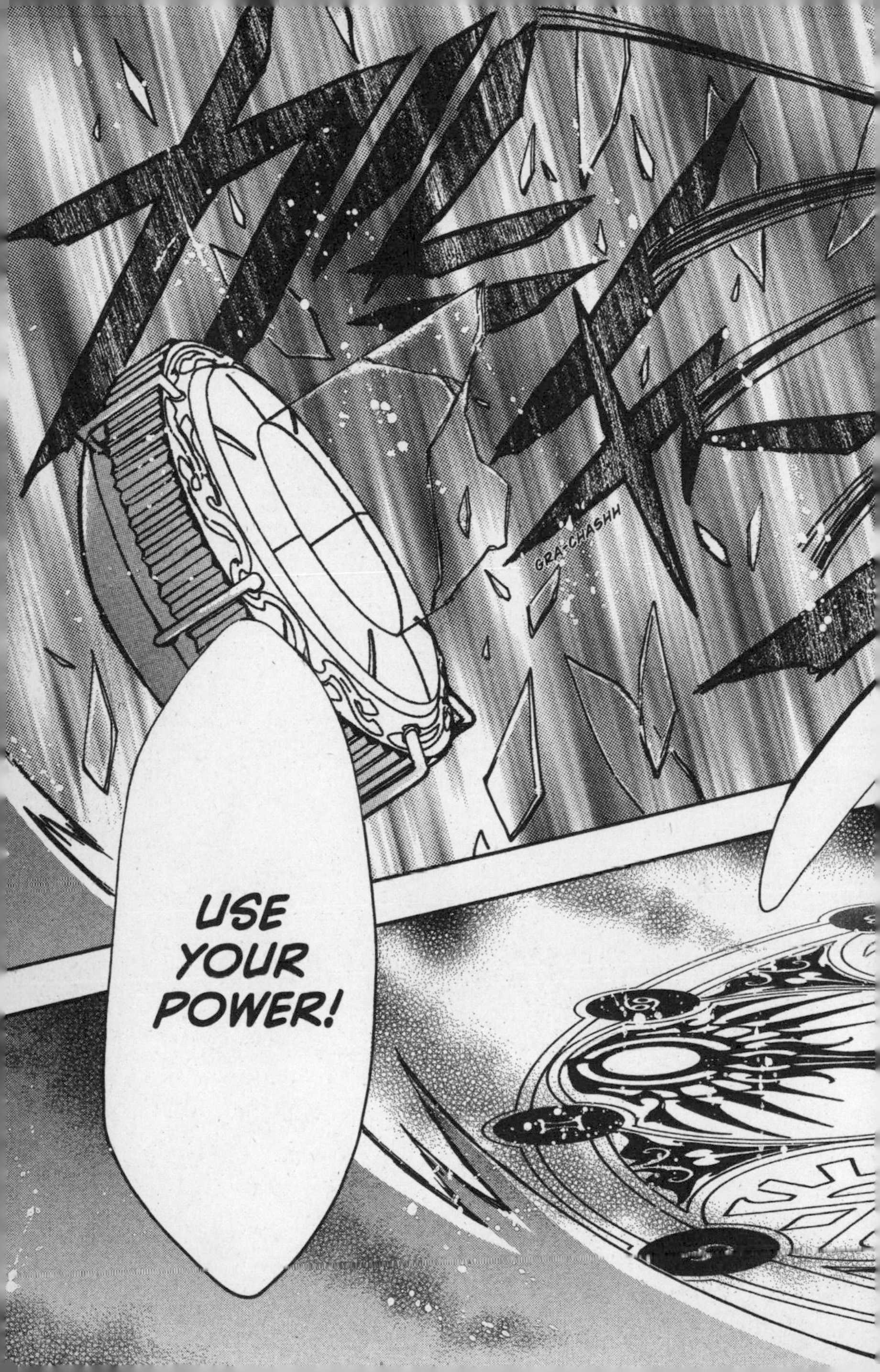
GRA-CHASHH
USE YOUR POWER!

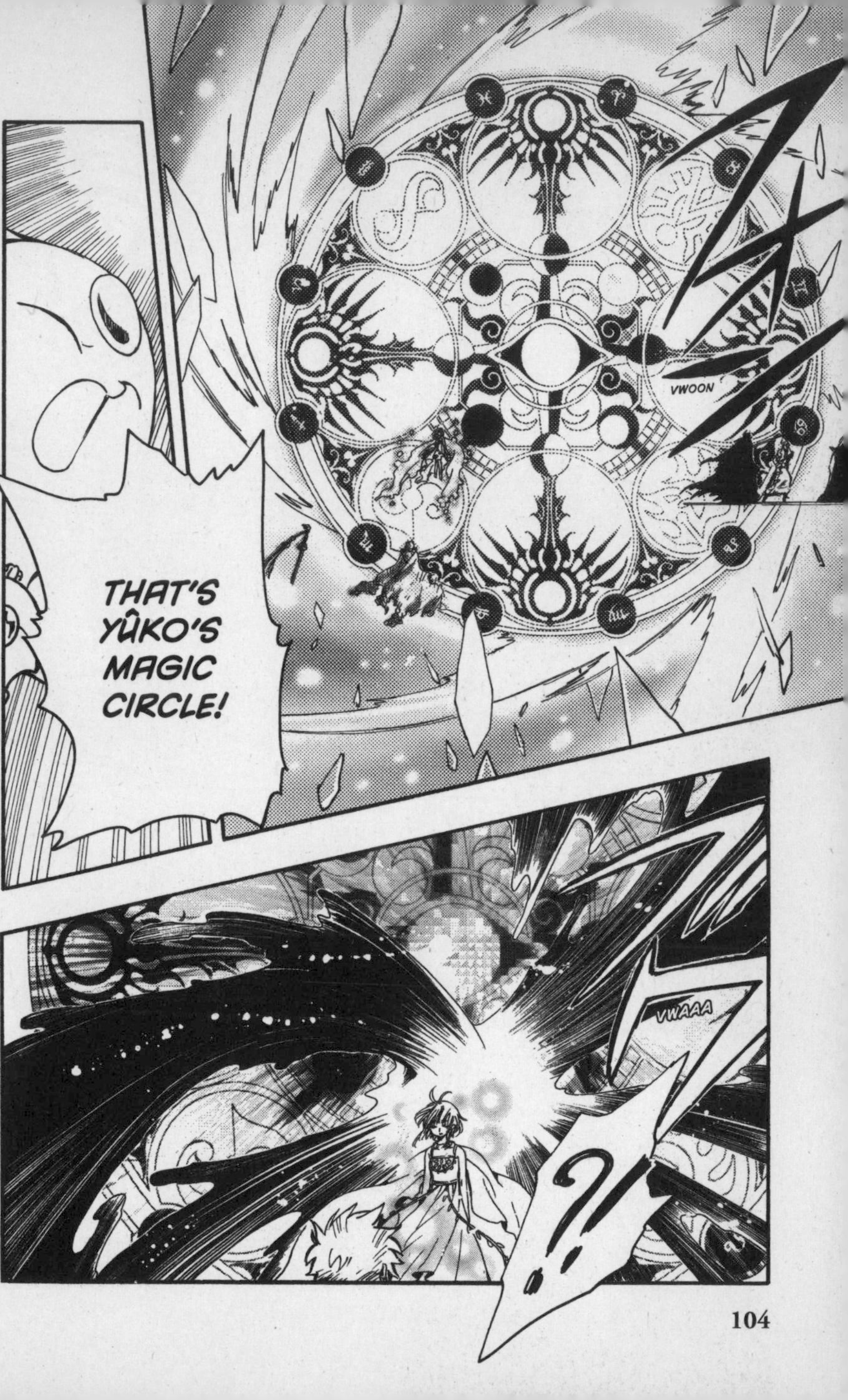
VWOON
THAT'S YÛKO'S MAGIC CIRCLE!
VWAAA
?!

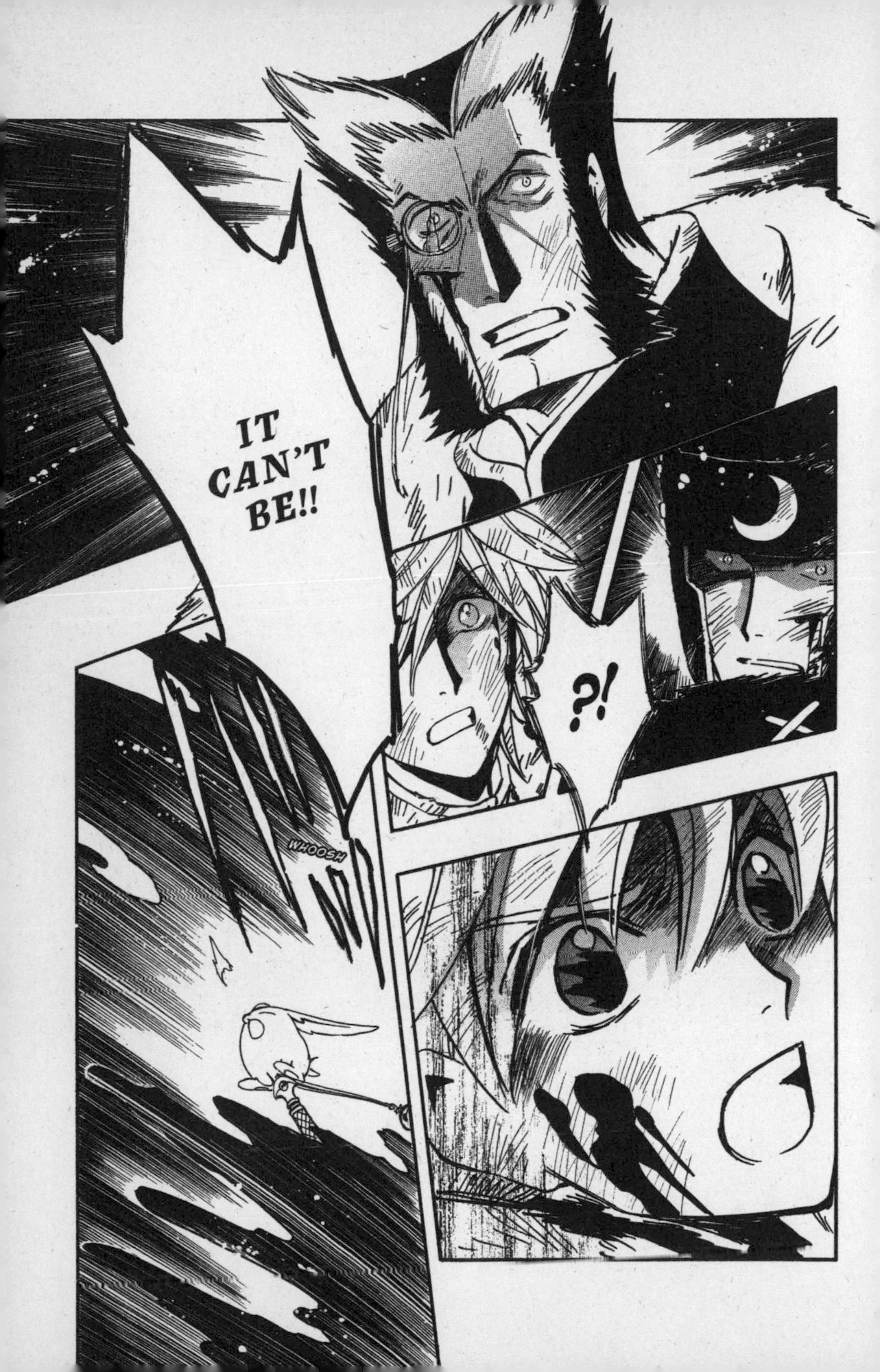
IT CAN'T BE!!
?!
WHOOSH

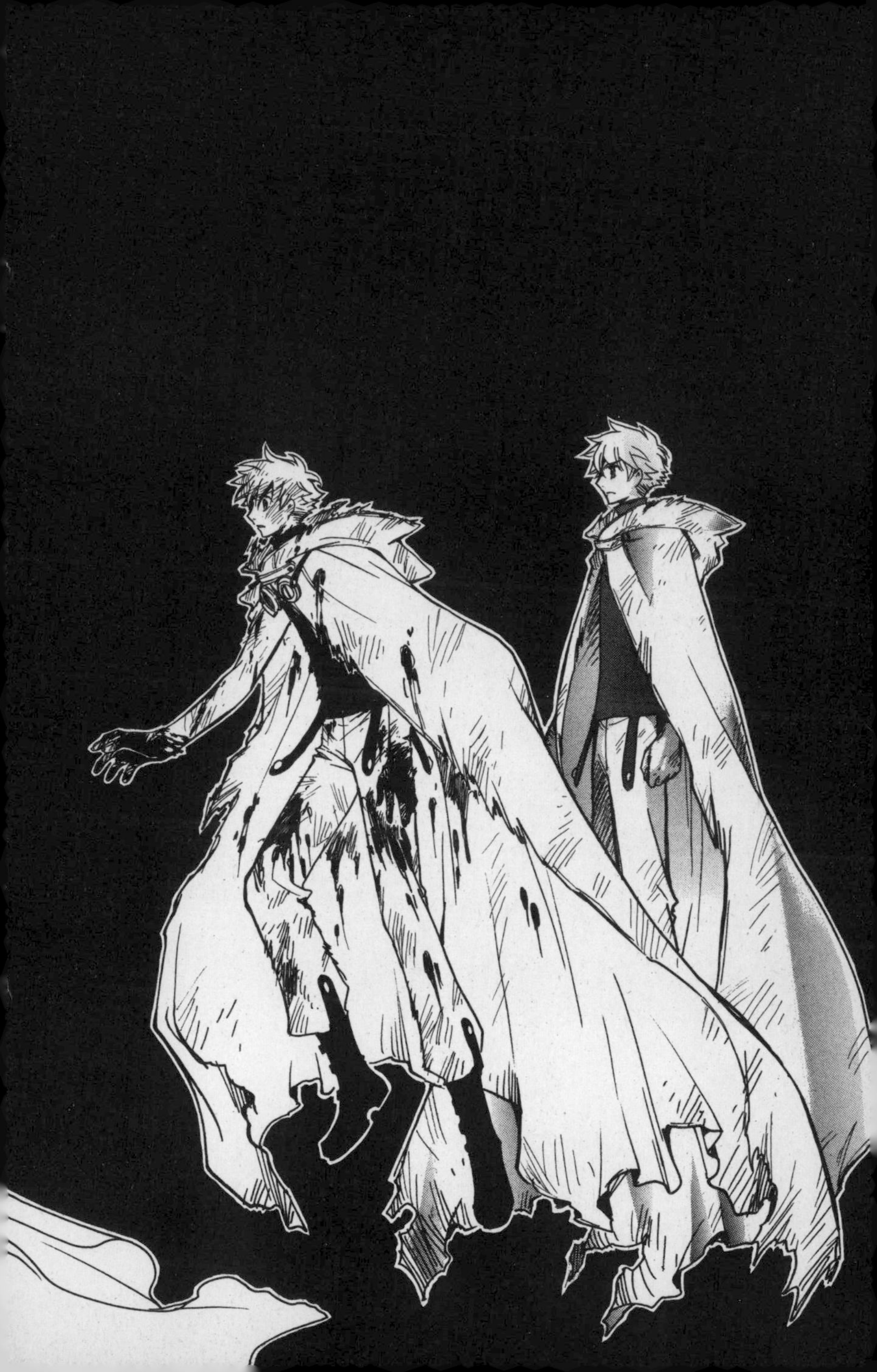

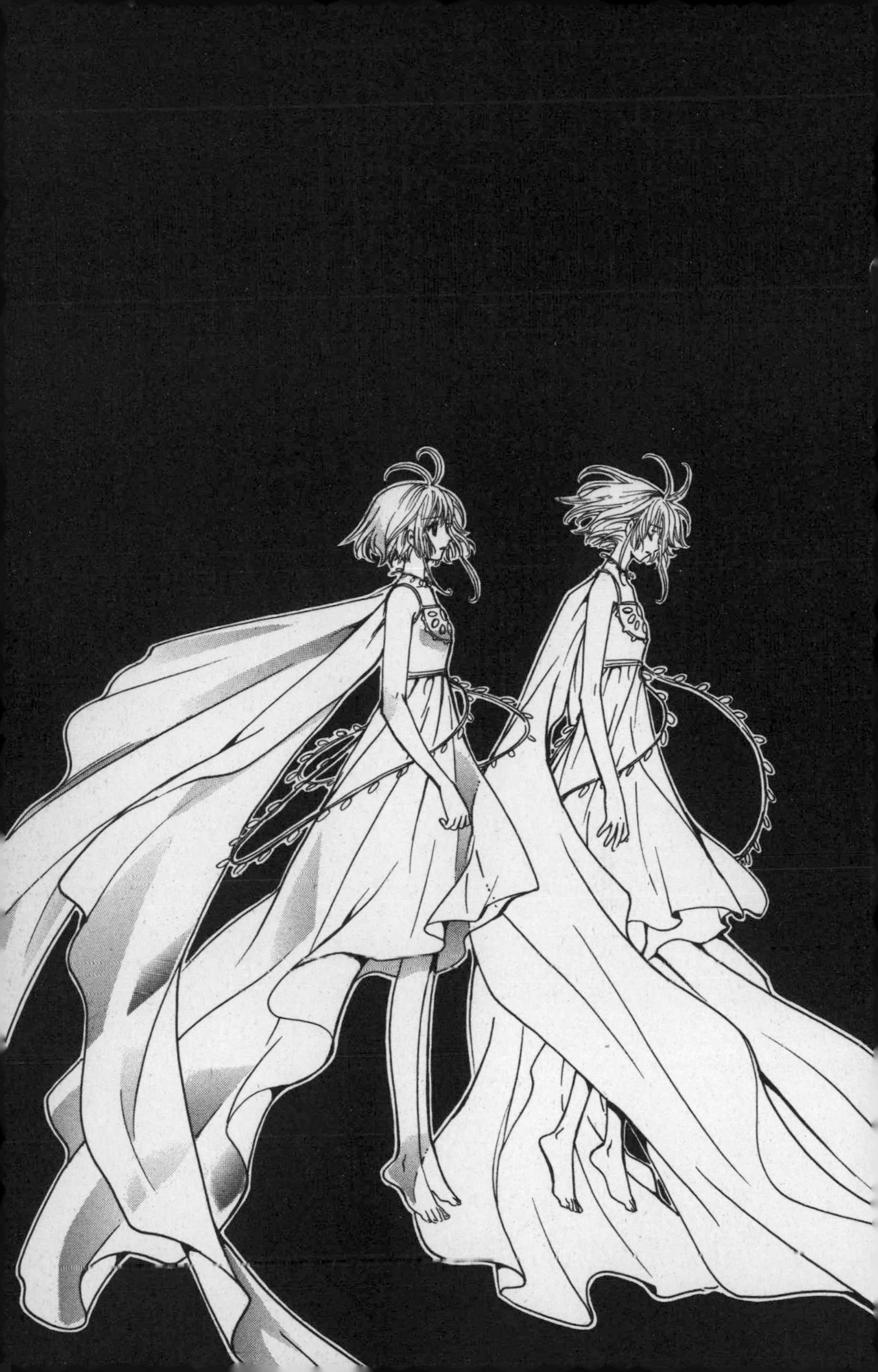

ツバサ

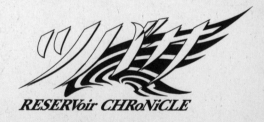

RESERVoir CHRoNiCLE

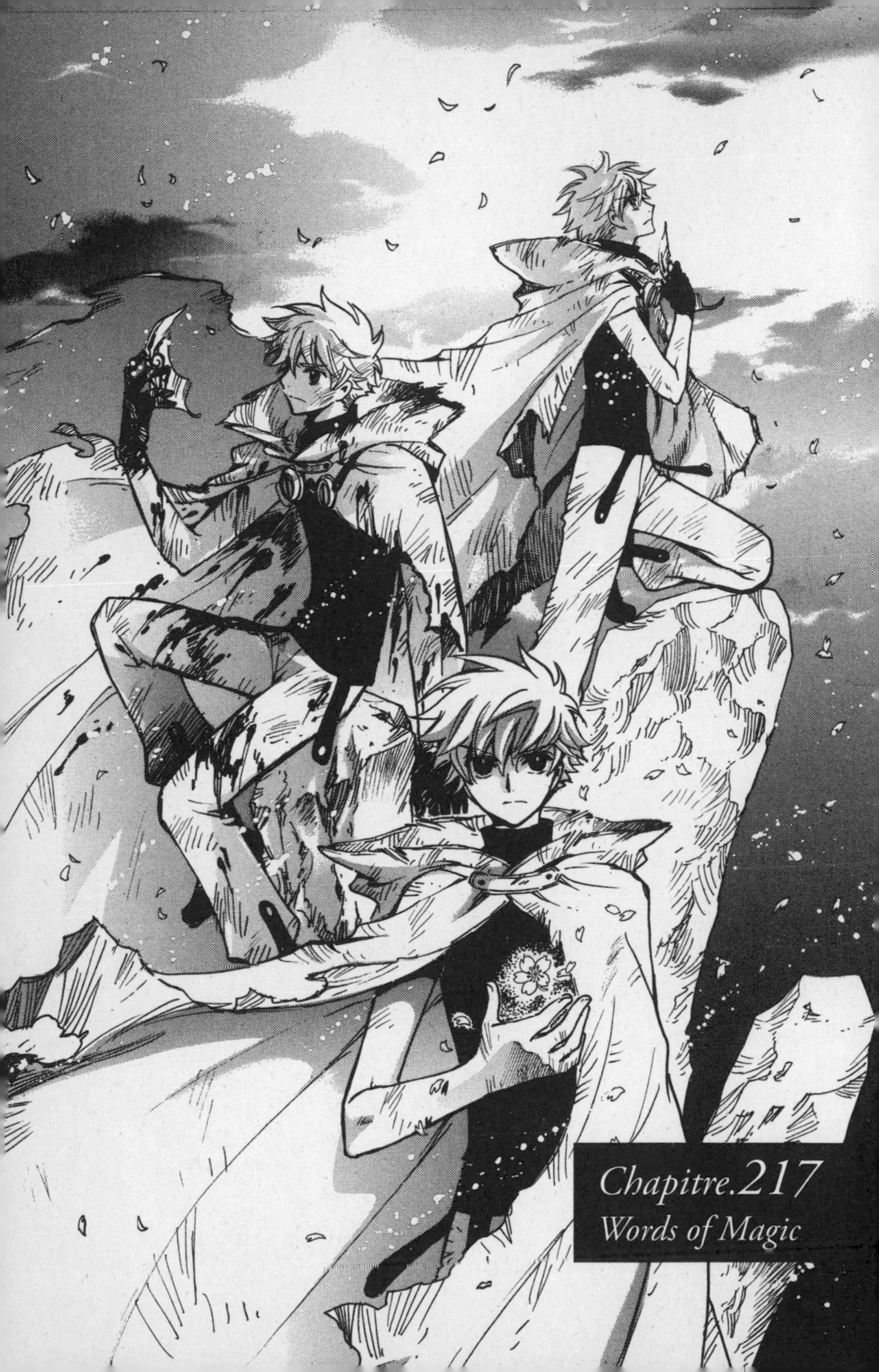
Chapitre.217
Words of Magic

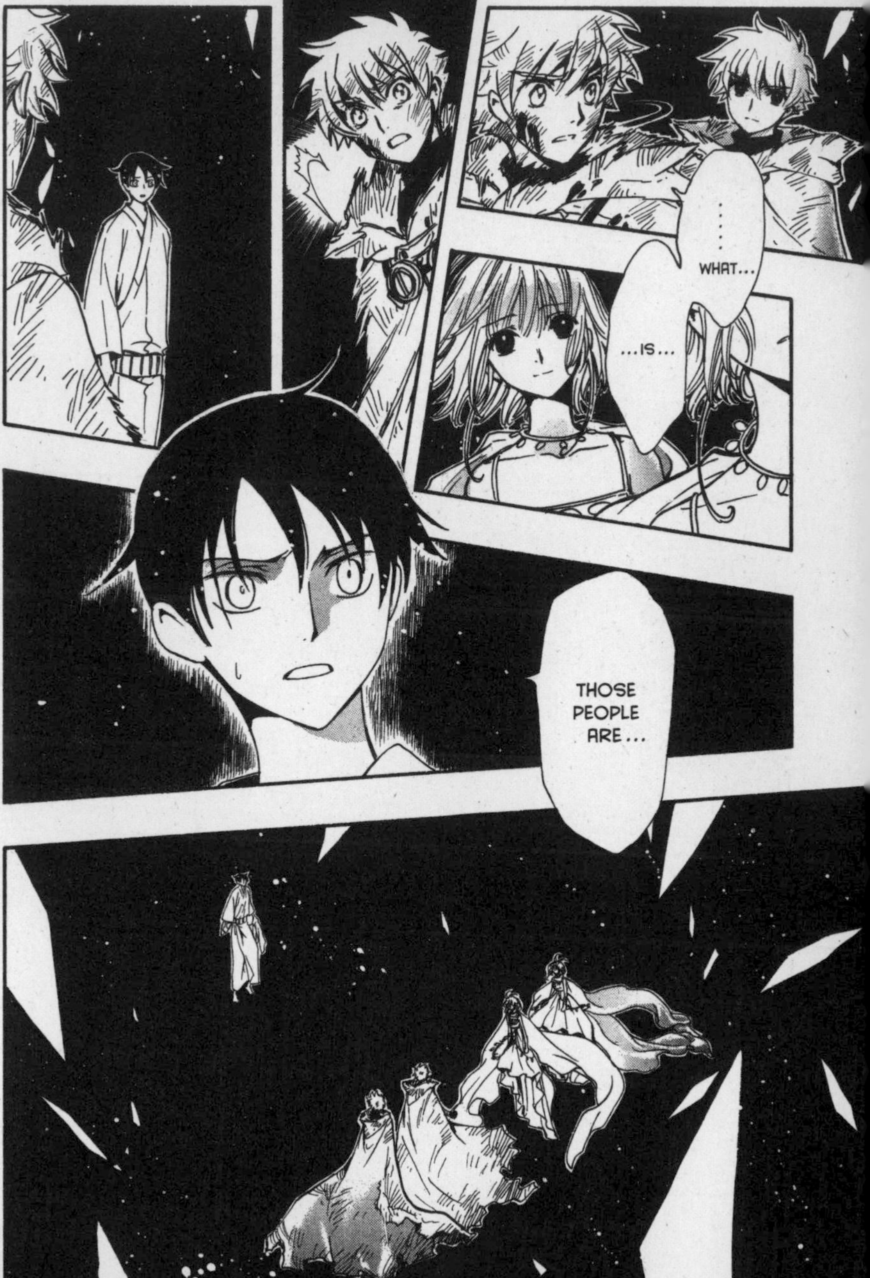
. . . . WHAT...
...IS...
THOSE PEOPLE ARE...

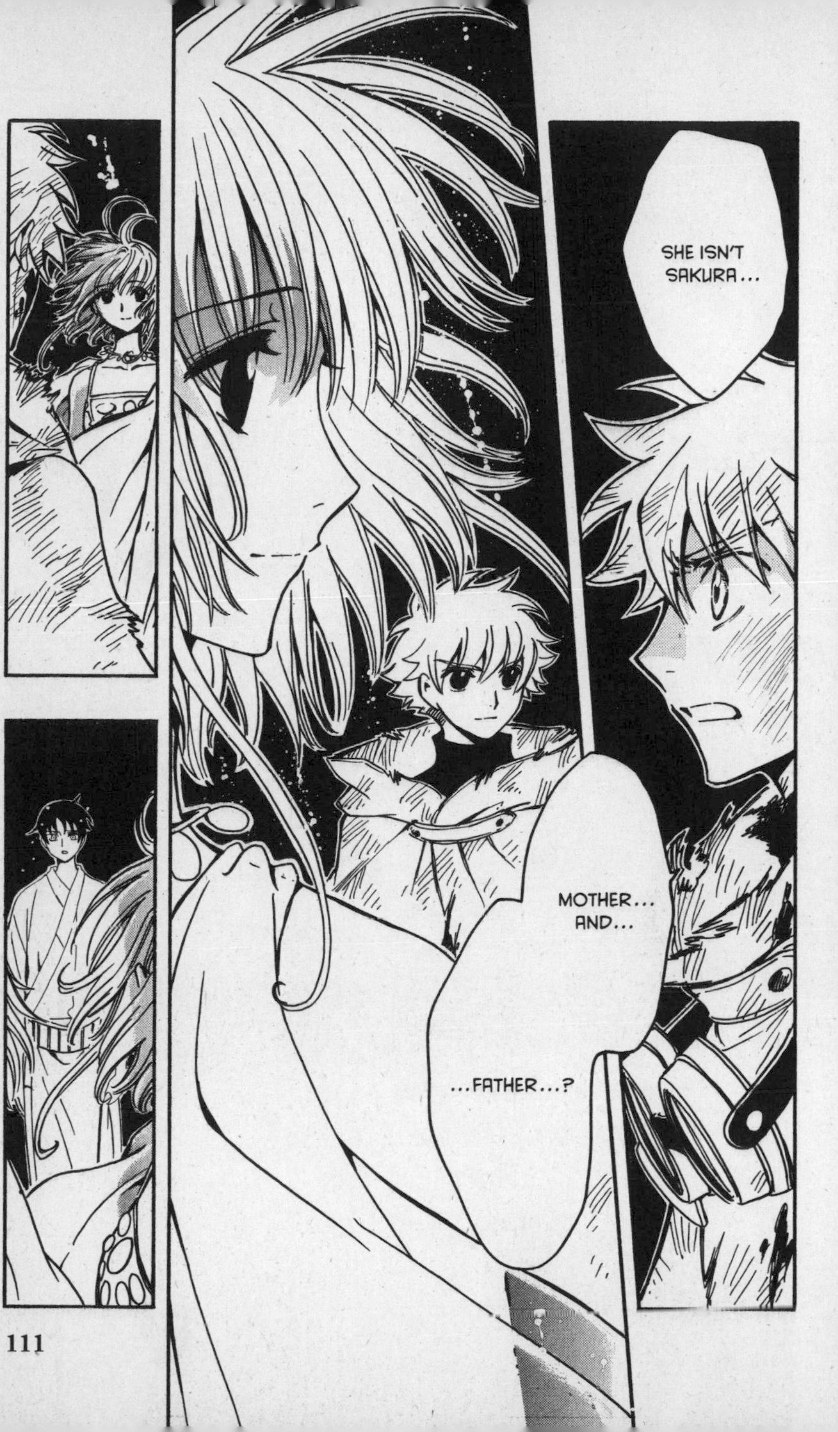
SHE ISN'T SAKURA...
MOTHER... AND...
...FATHER...?

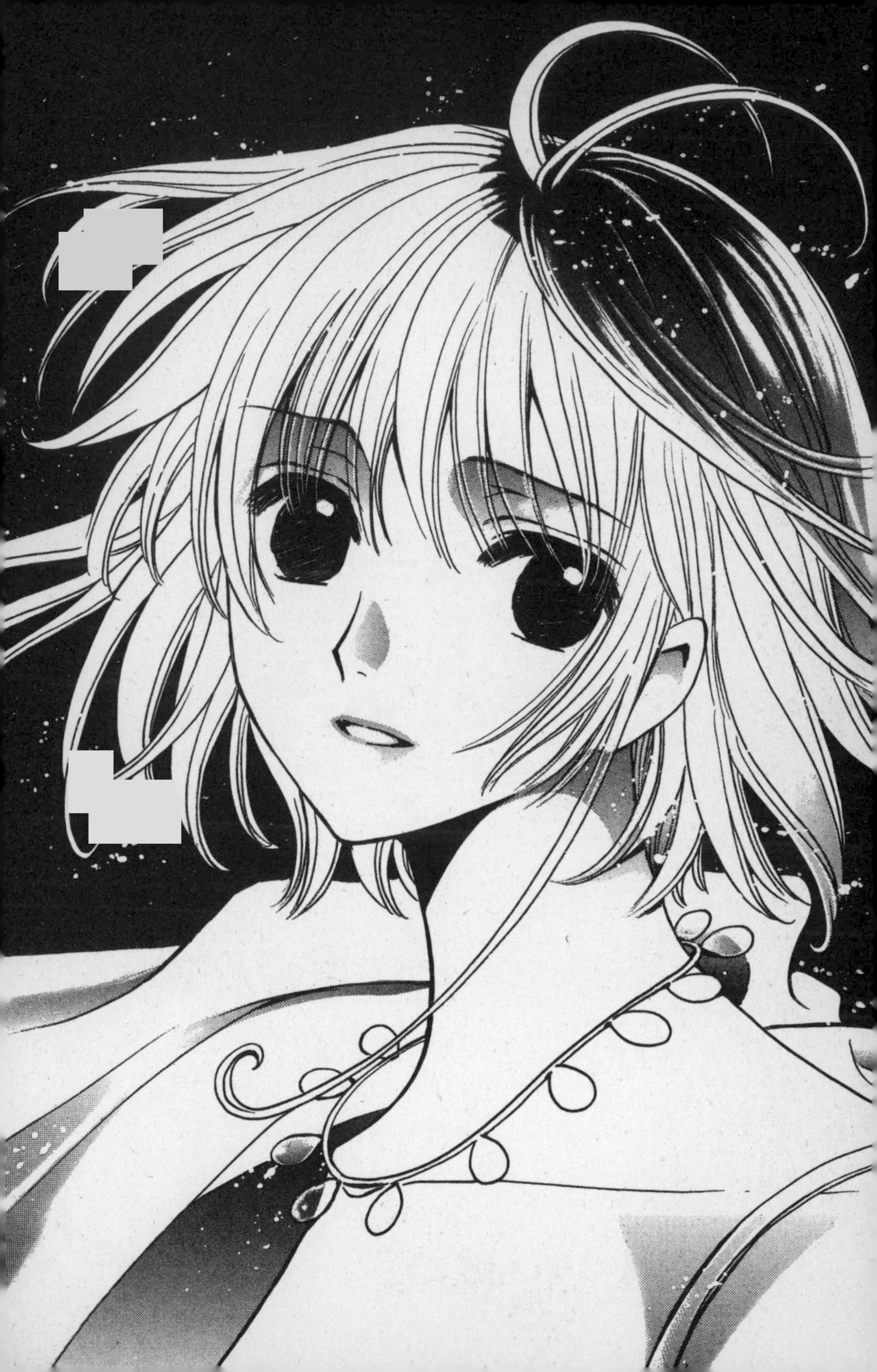

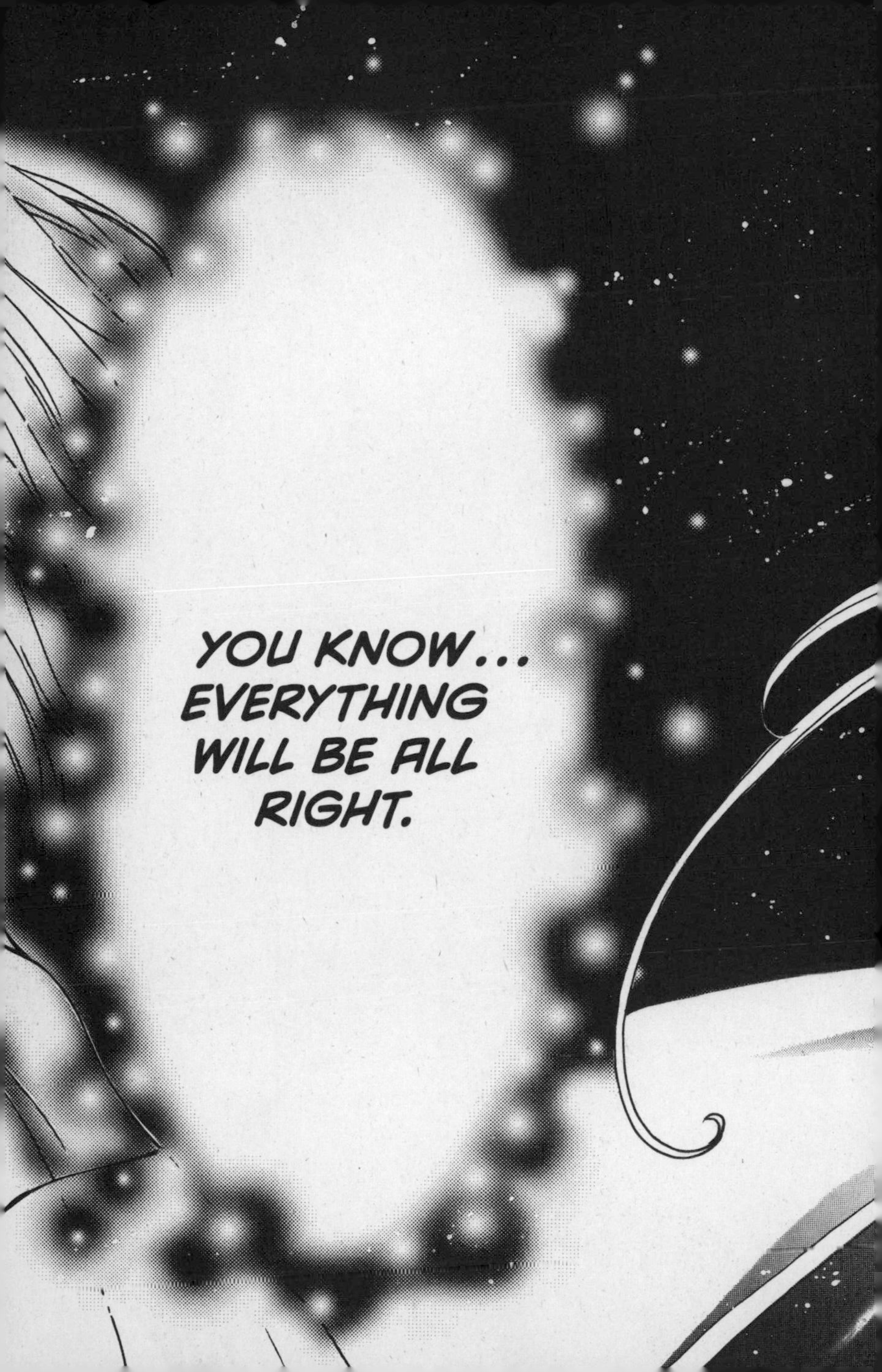
YOU KNOW... EVERYTHING WILL BE ALL RIGHT.

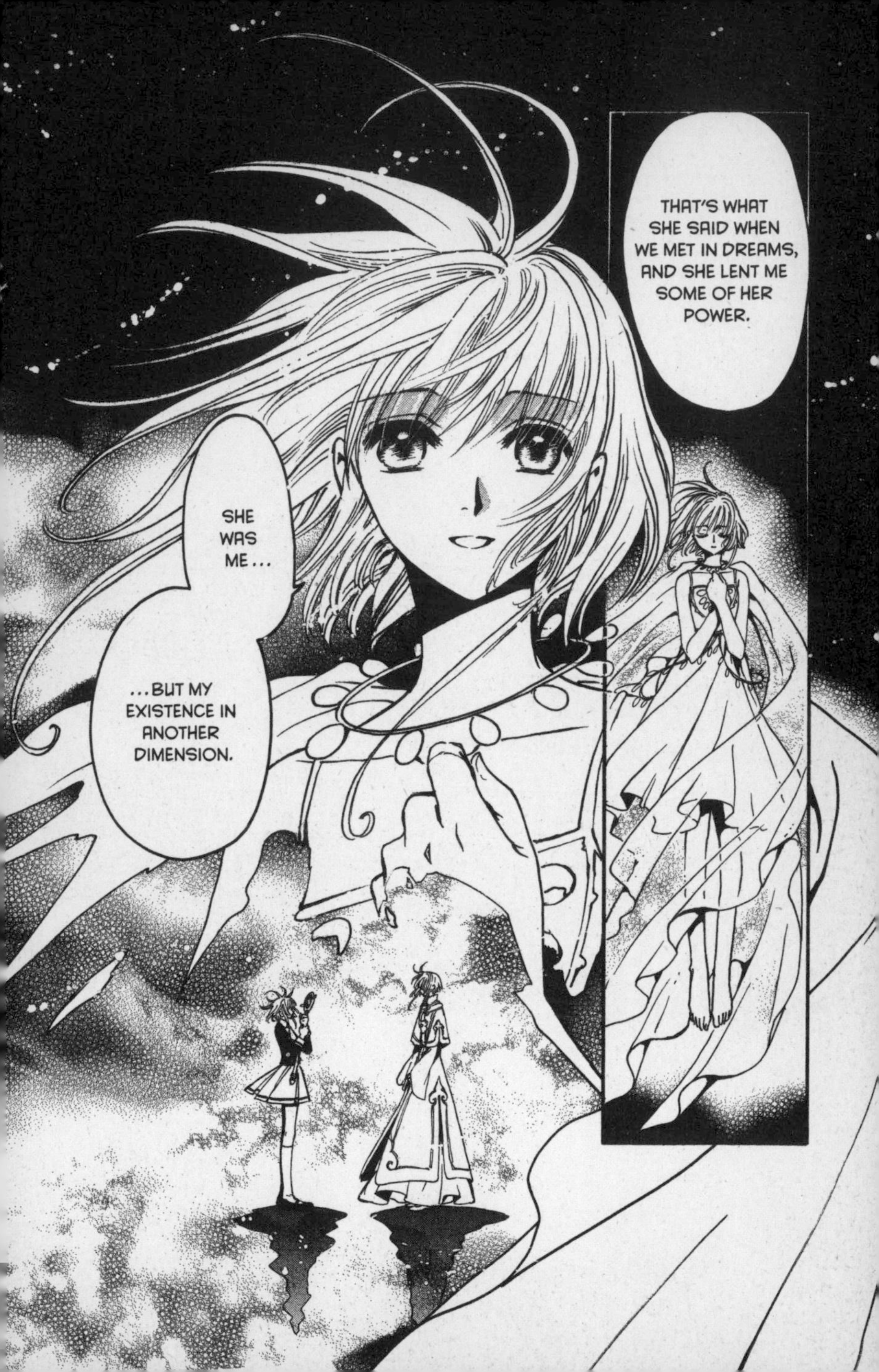
SHE WAS ME...
...BUT MY EXISTENCE IN ANOTHER DIMENSION.
THAT'S WHAT SHE SAID WHEN WE MET IN DREAMS, AND SHE LENT ME SOME OF HER POWER.

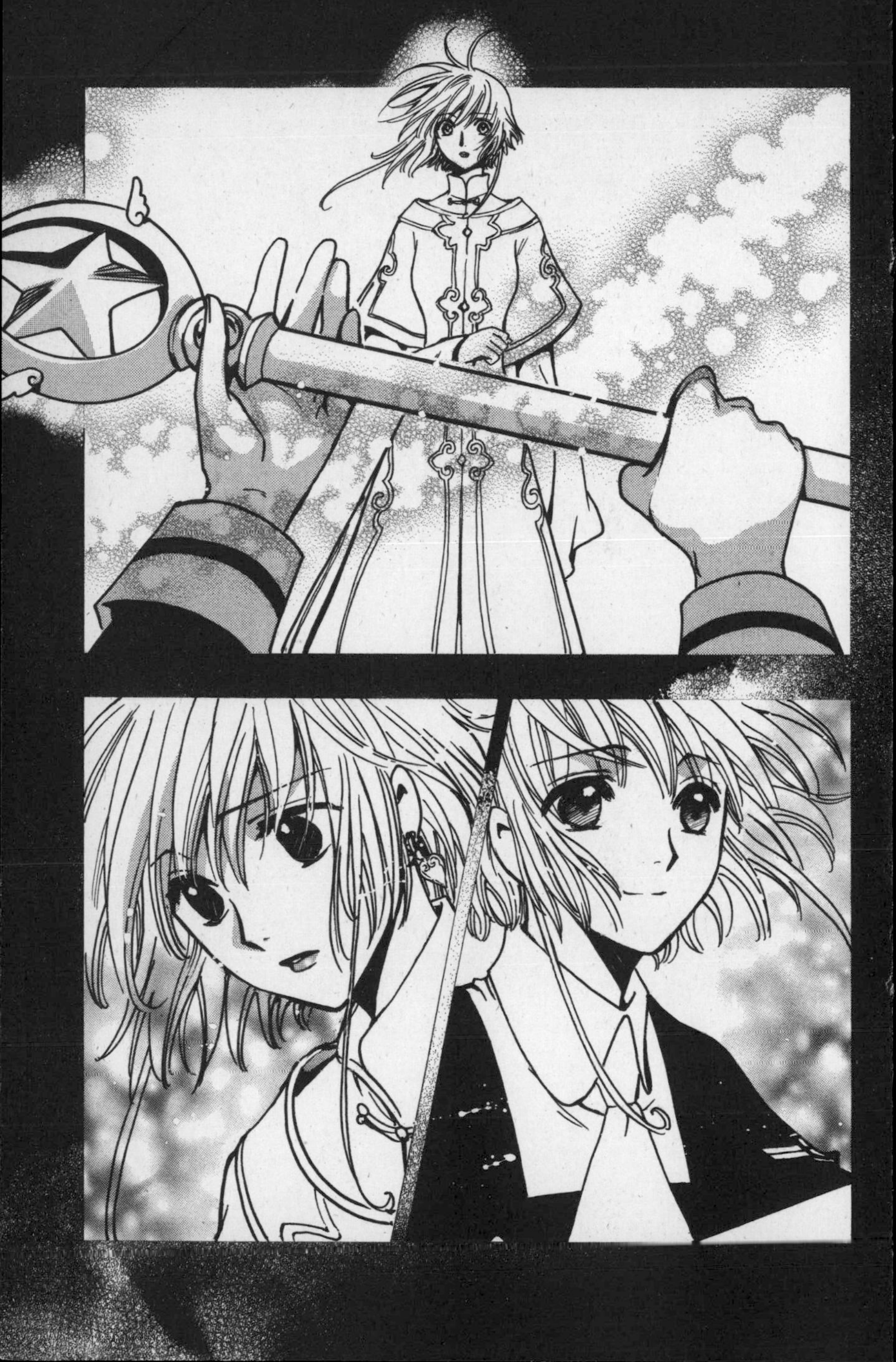

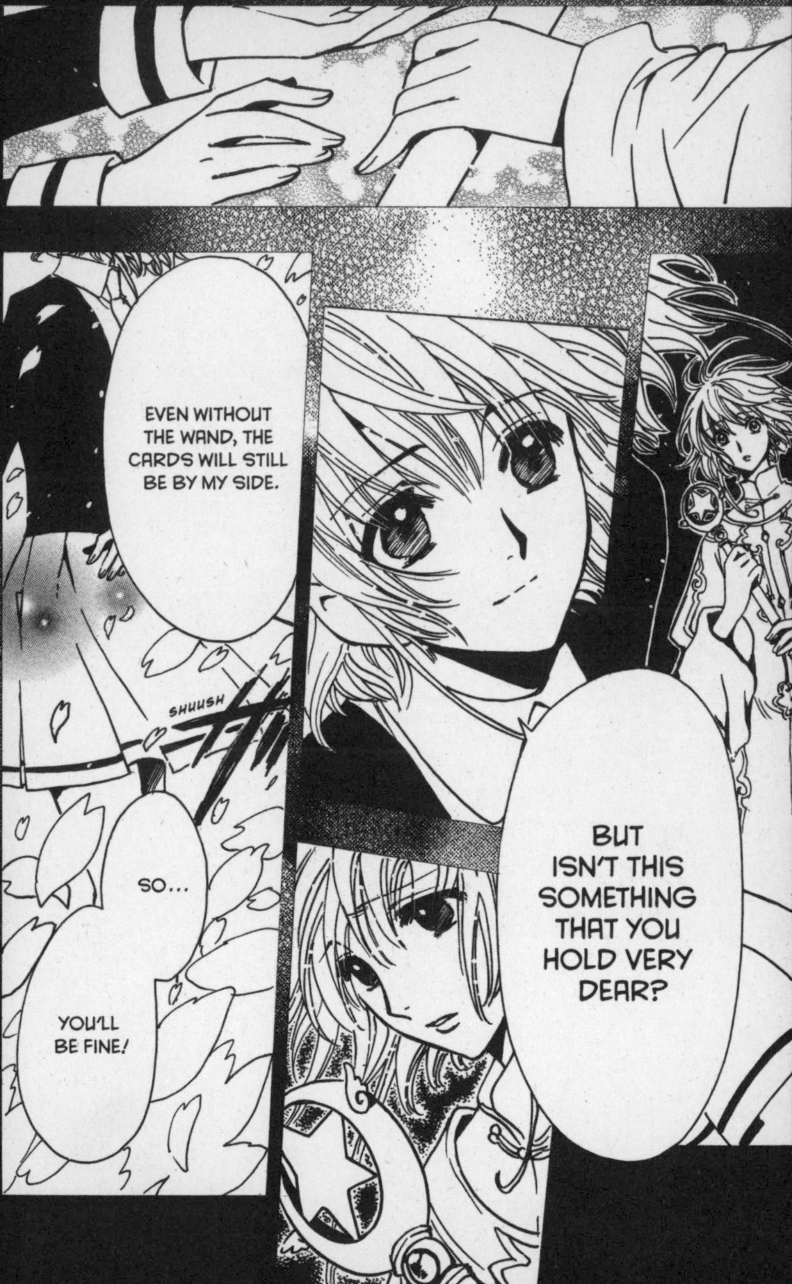
BUT ISN'T THIS SOMETHING THAT YOU HOLD VERY DEAR?
EVEN WITHOUT THE WAND, THE CARDS WILL STILL BE BY MY SIDE.
SHUUSH
SO...
YOU'LL BE FINE!

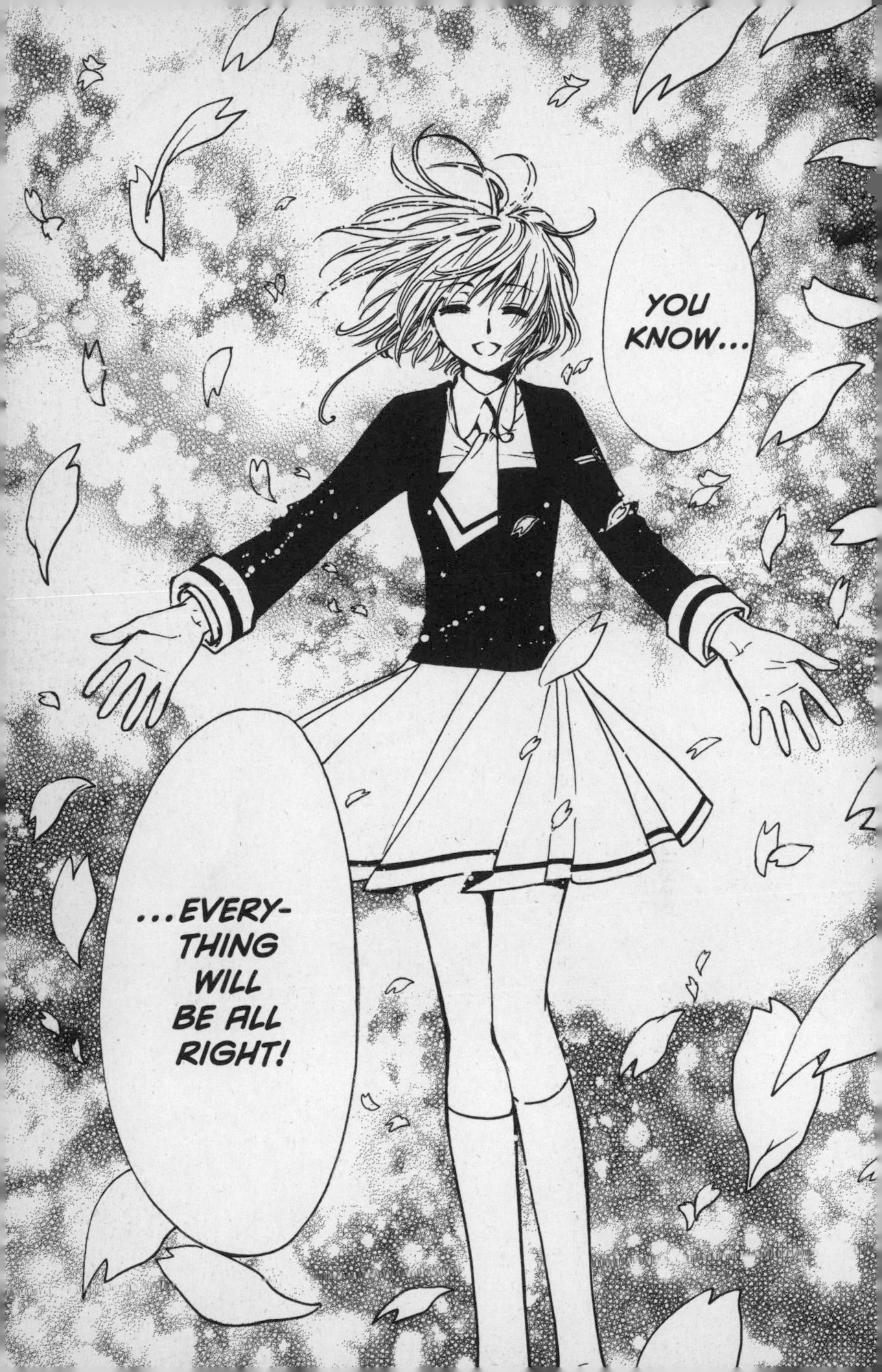
YOU KNOW...
...EVERYTHING WILL BE ALL RIGHT!

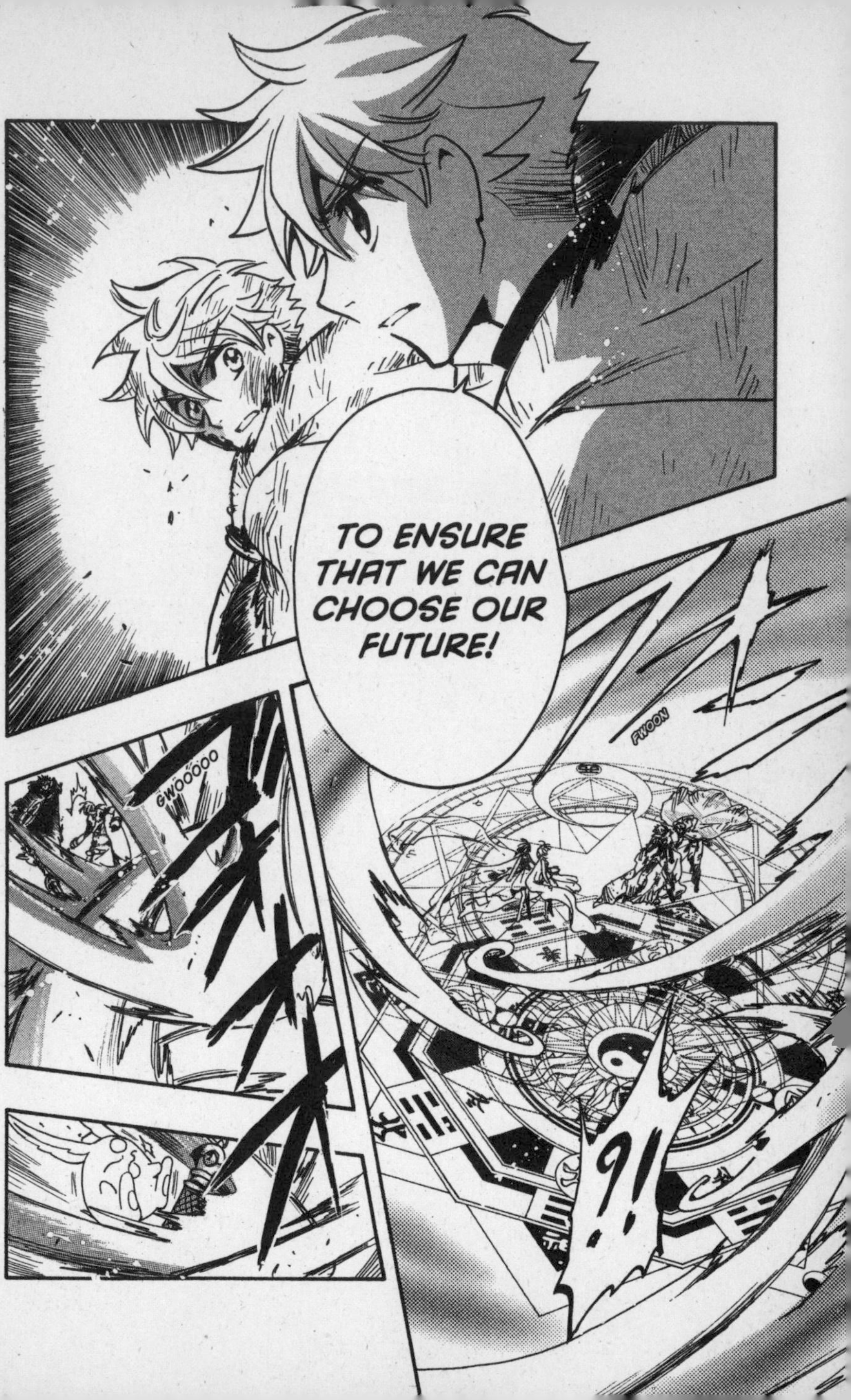
TO ENSURE THAT WE CAN CHOOSE OUR FUTURE!
FWOON
GWOOOOO
?!

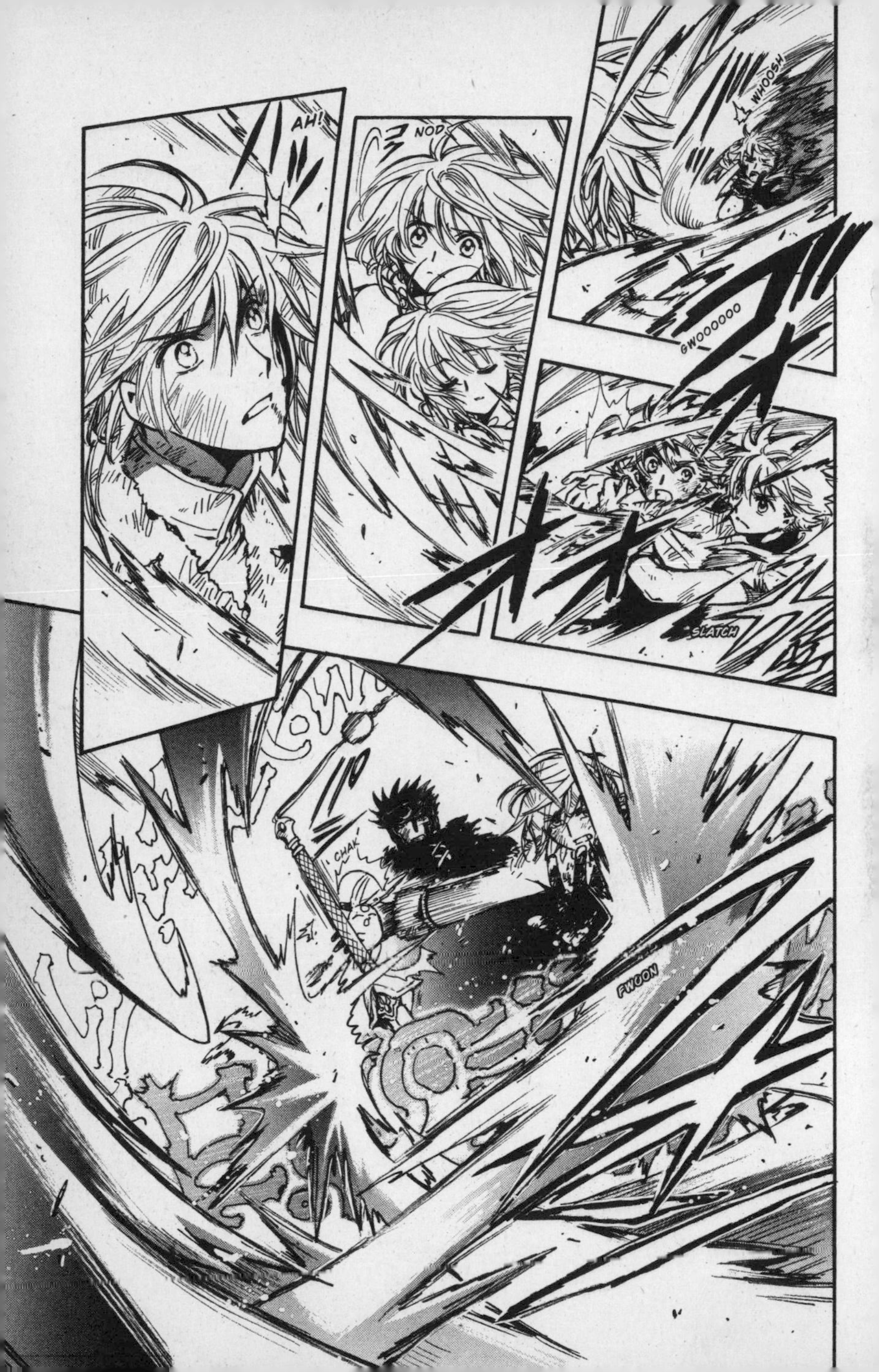

WHOOSH
GWOOOOOO
SLATCH
NOD
AH!
CHAK
FWOON

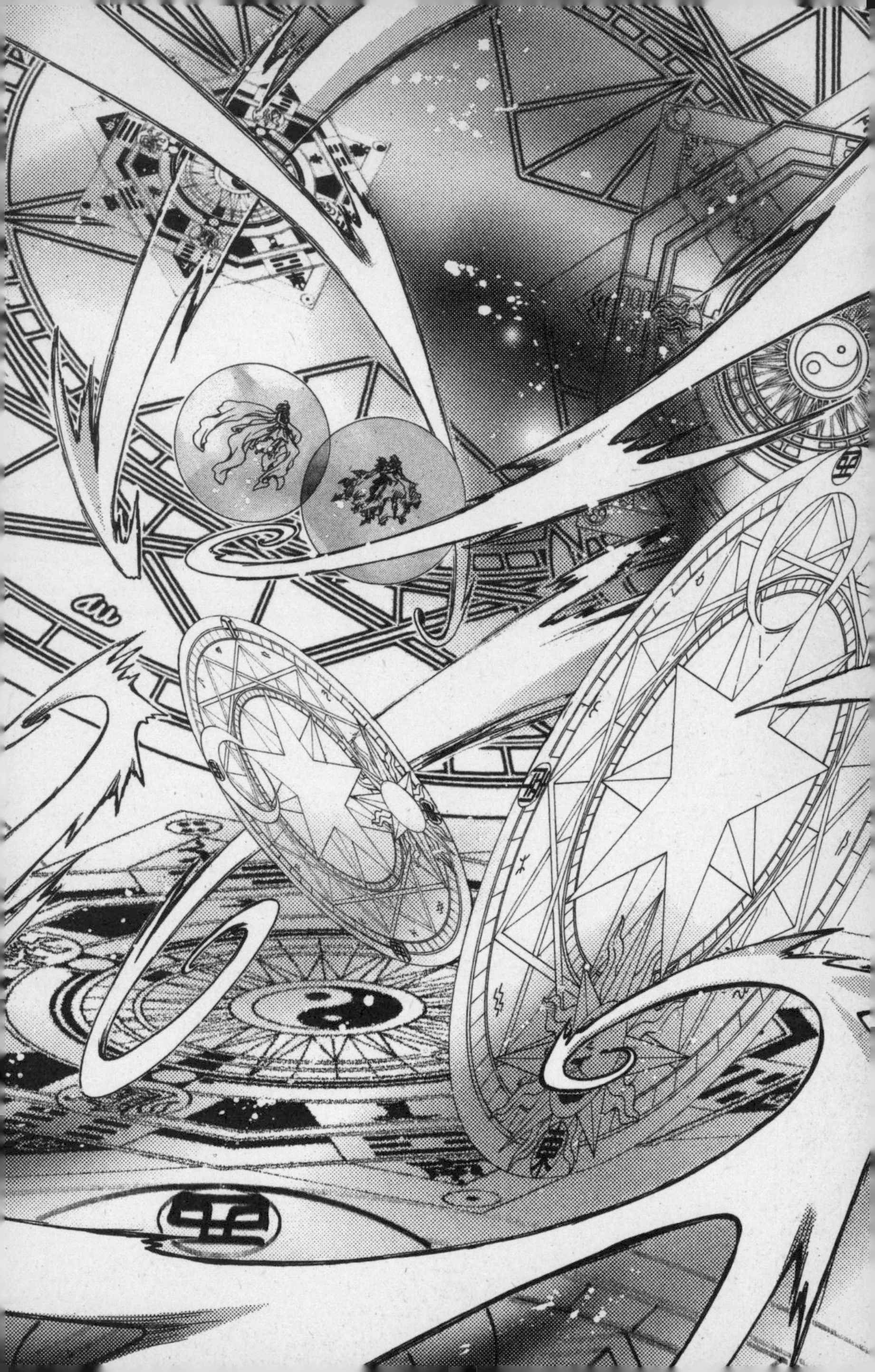

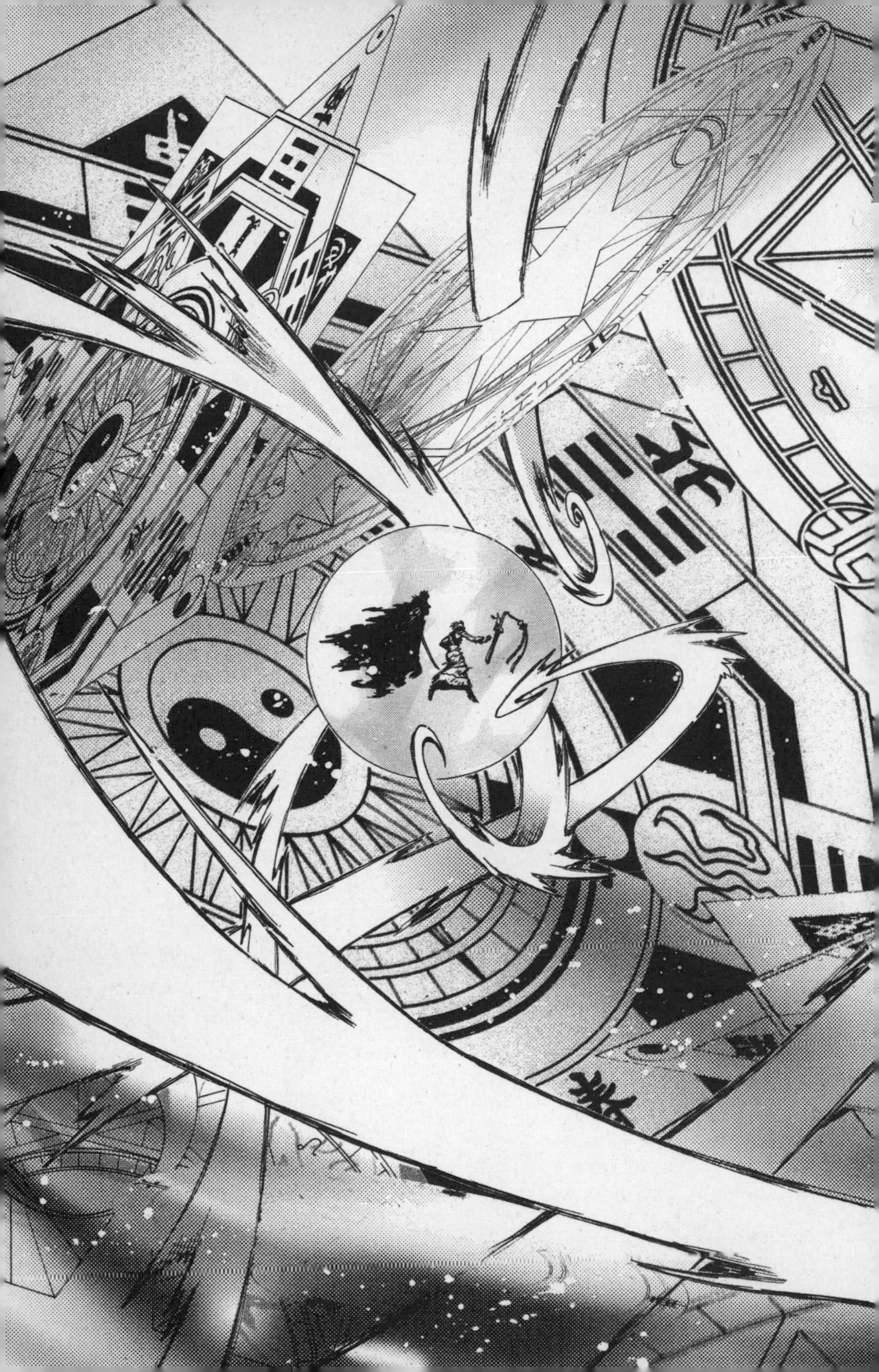

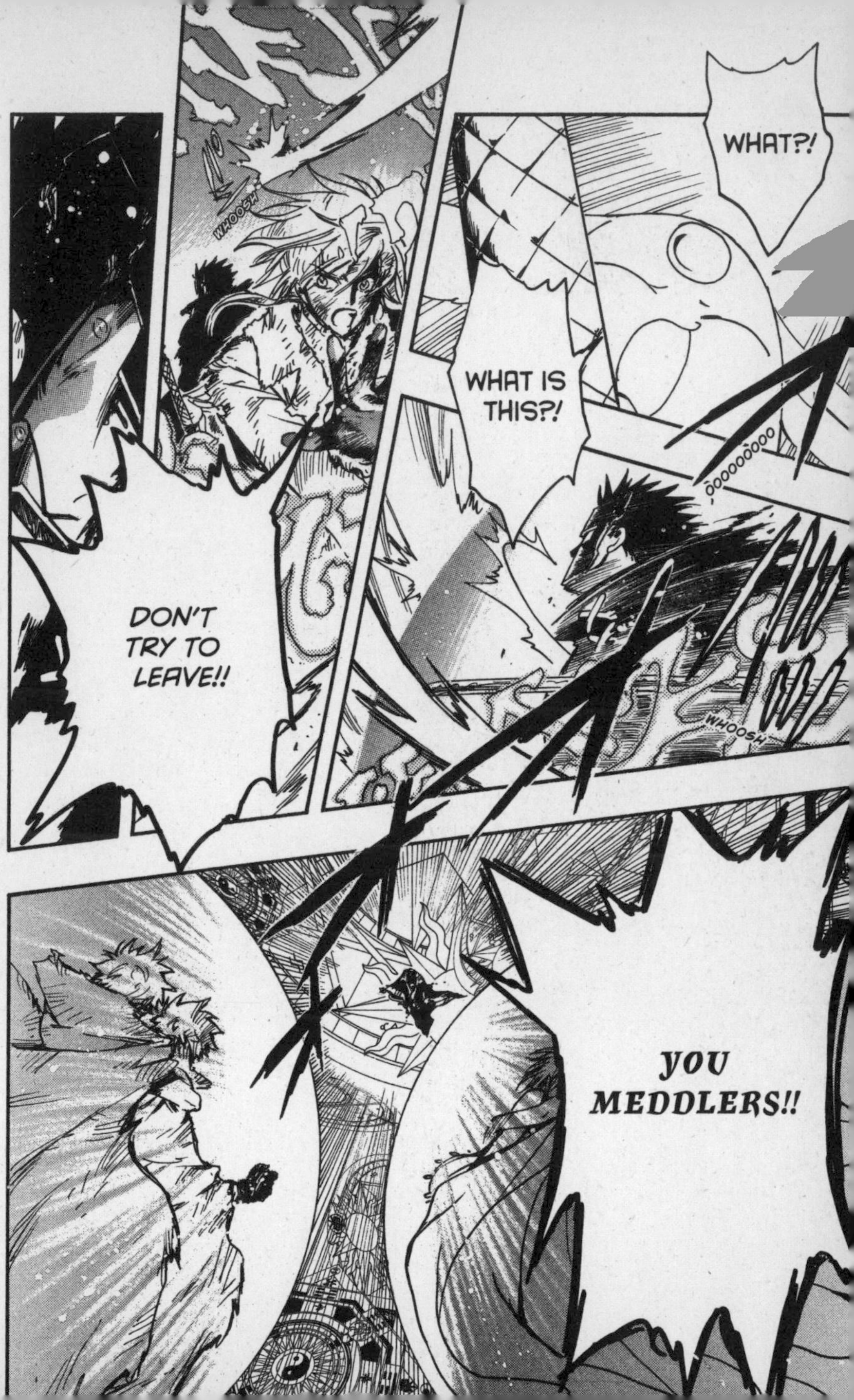
WHAT?!
WHAT IS THIS?!
OOOOOOOOO
WHOOSH
WHOOSH
DON'T TRY TO LEAVE!!
YOU MEDDLERS!!

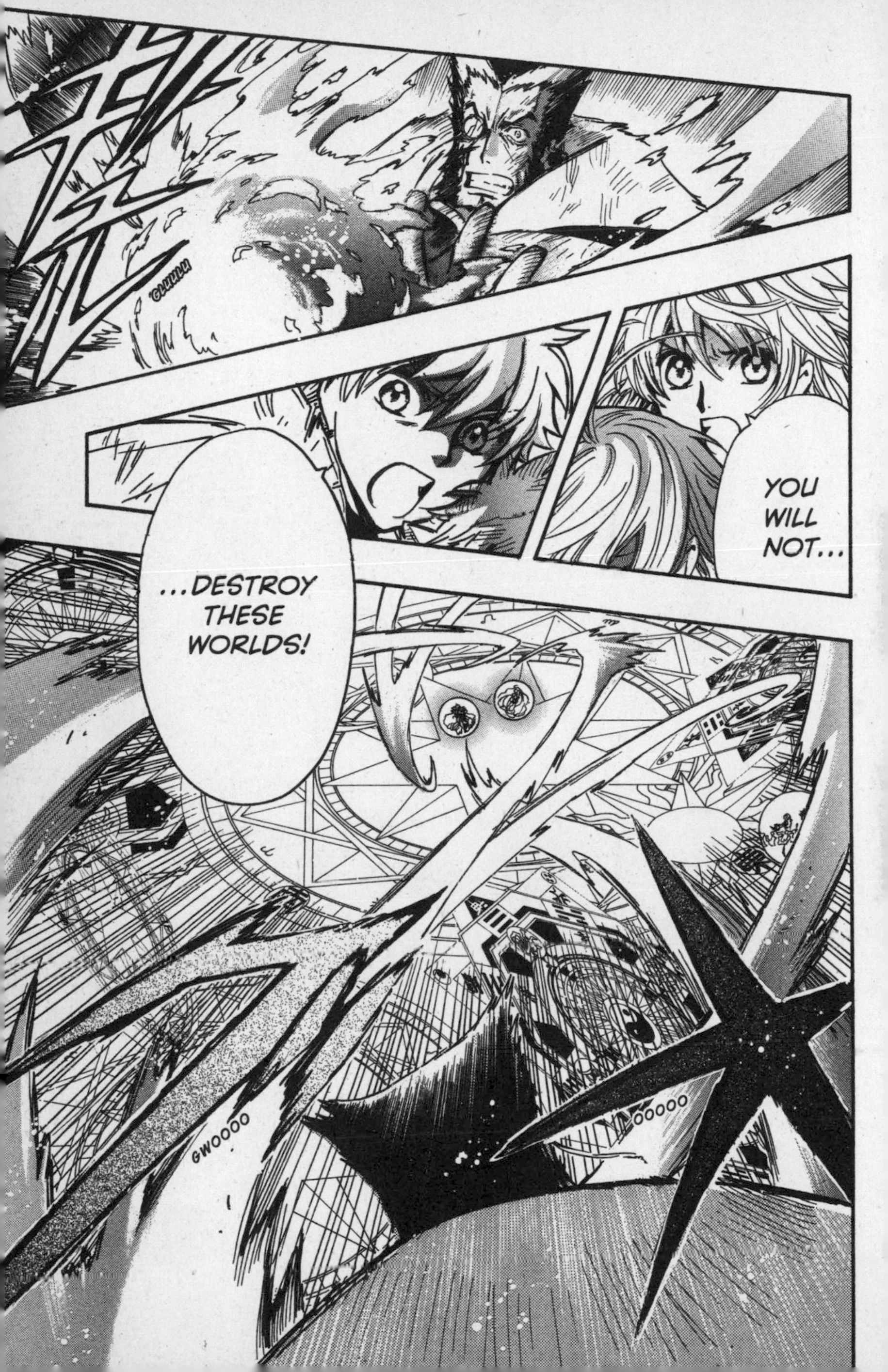
GLUULU
YOU WILL NOT...
...DESTROY THESE WORLDS!
OOOOO
GWOOOO

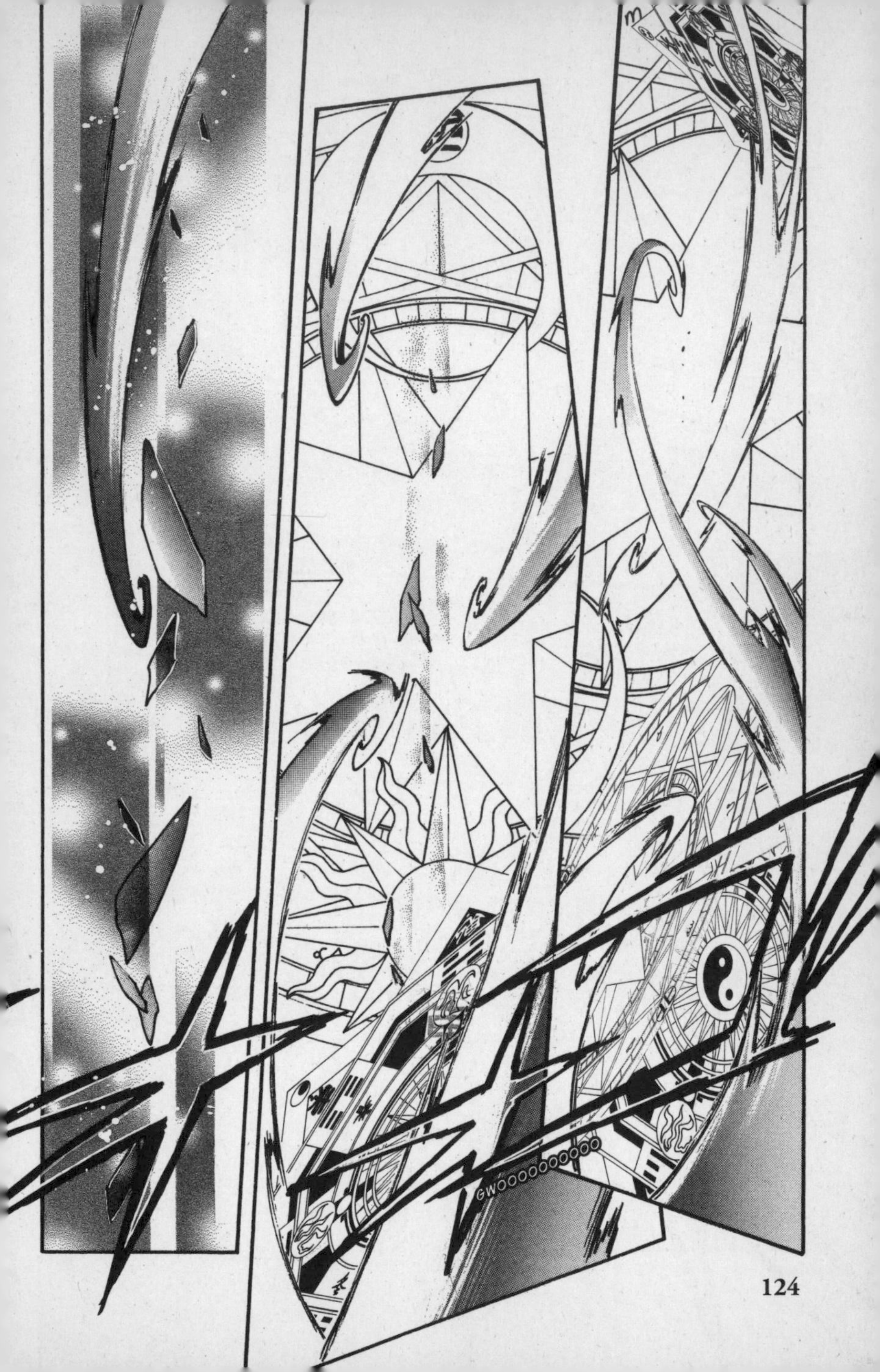
GWOOOOOOOOOO

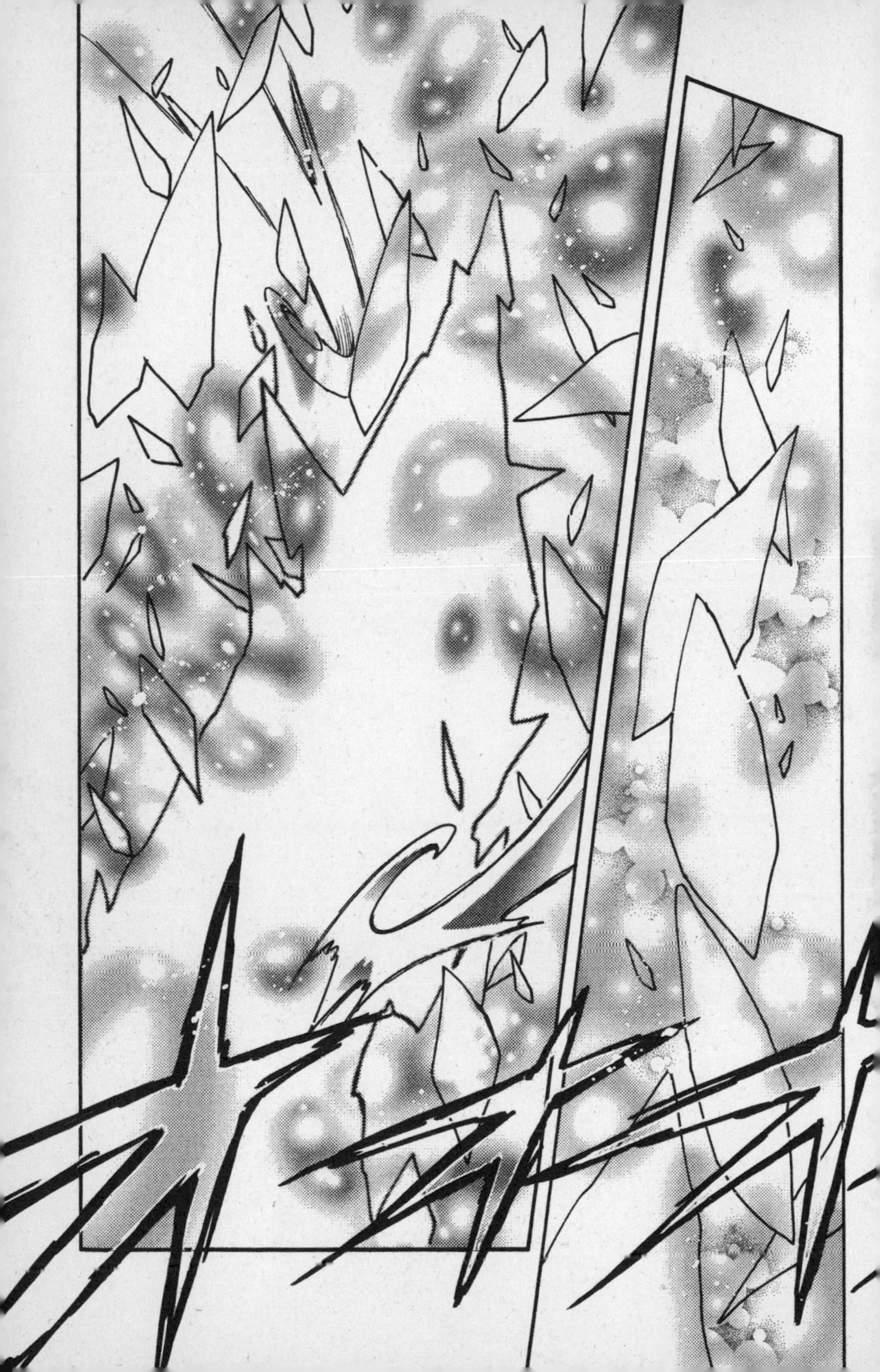

ツバサ
RESERVoir CHRoNiCLE

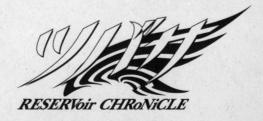

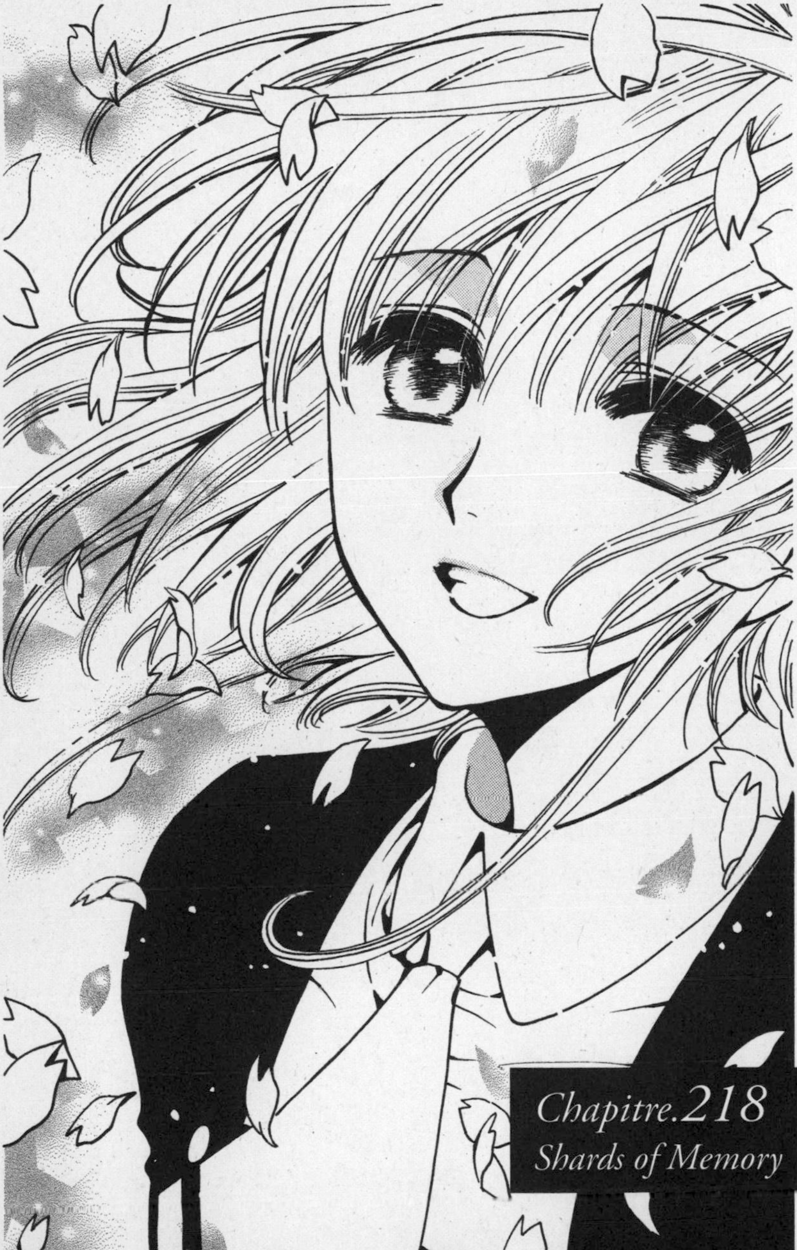
Chapitre.218
Shards of Memory

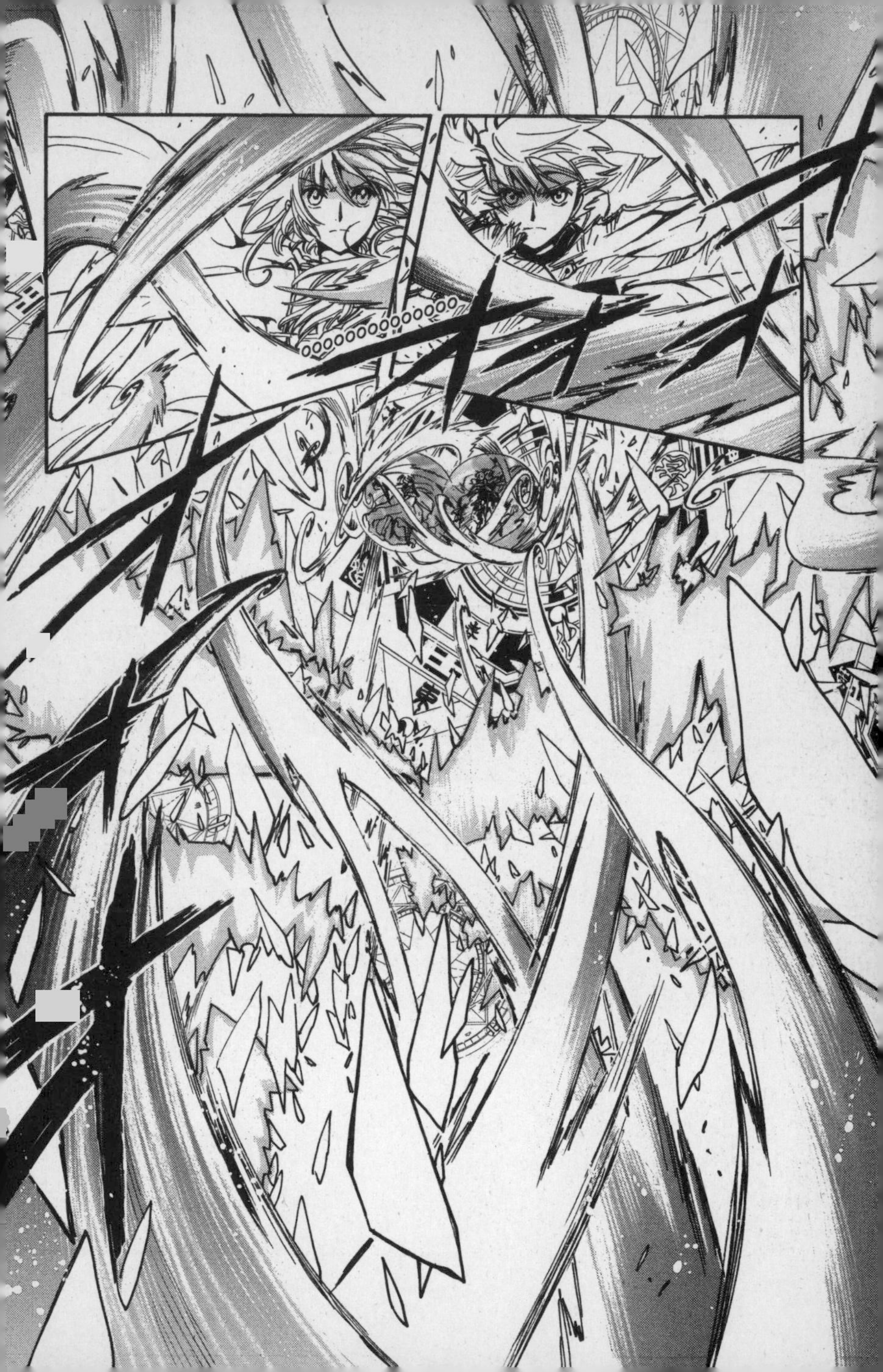
OOOOOOOOOOOOOO

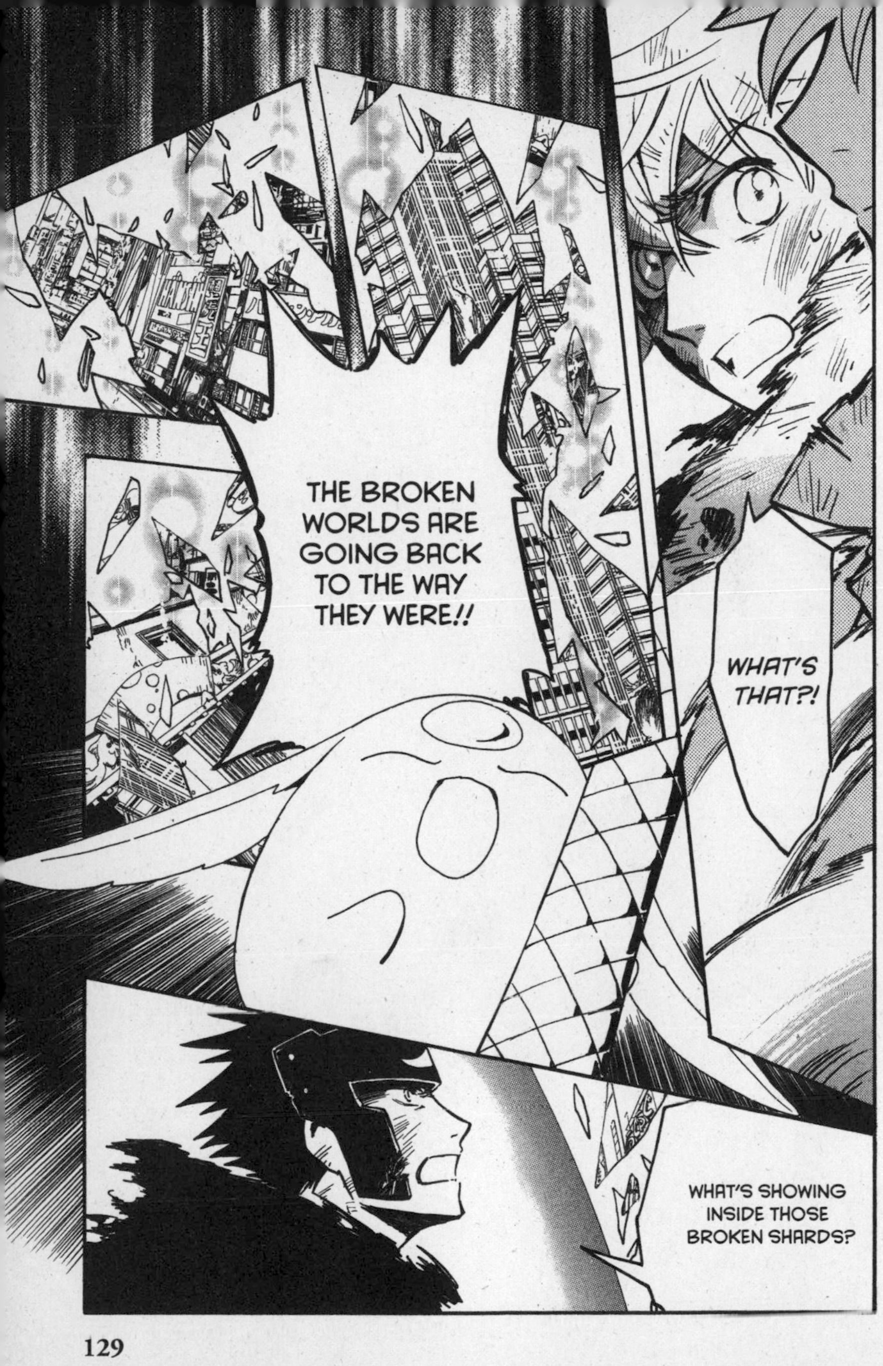
WHAT'S THAT?!
THE BROKEN WORLDS ARE GOING BACK TO THE WAY THEY WERE!!
WHAT'S SHOWING INSIDE THOSE BROKEN SHARDS?

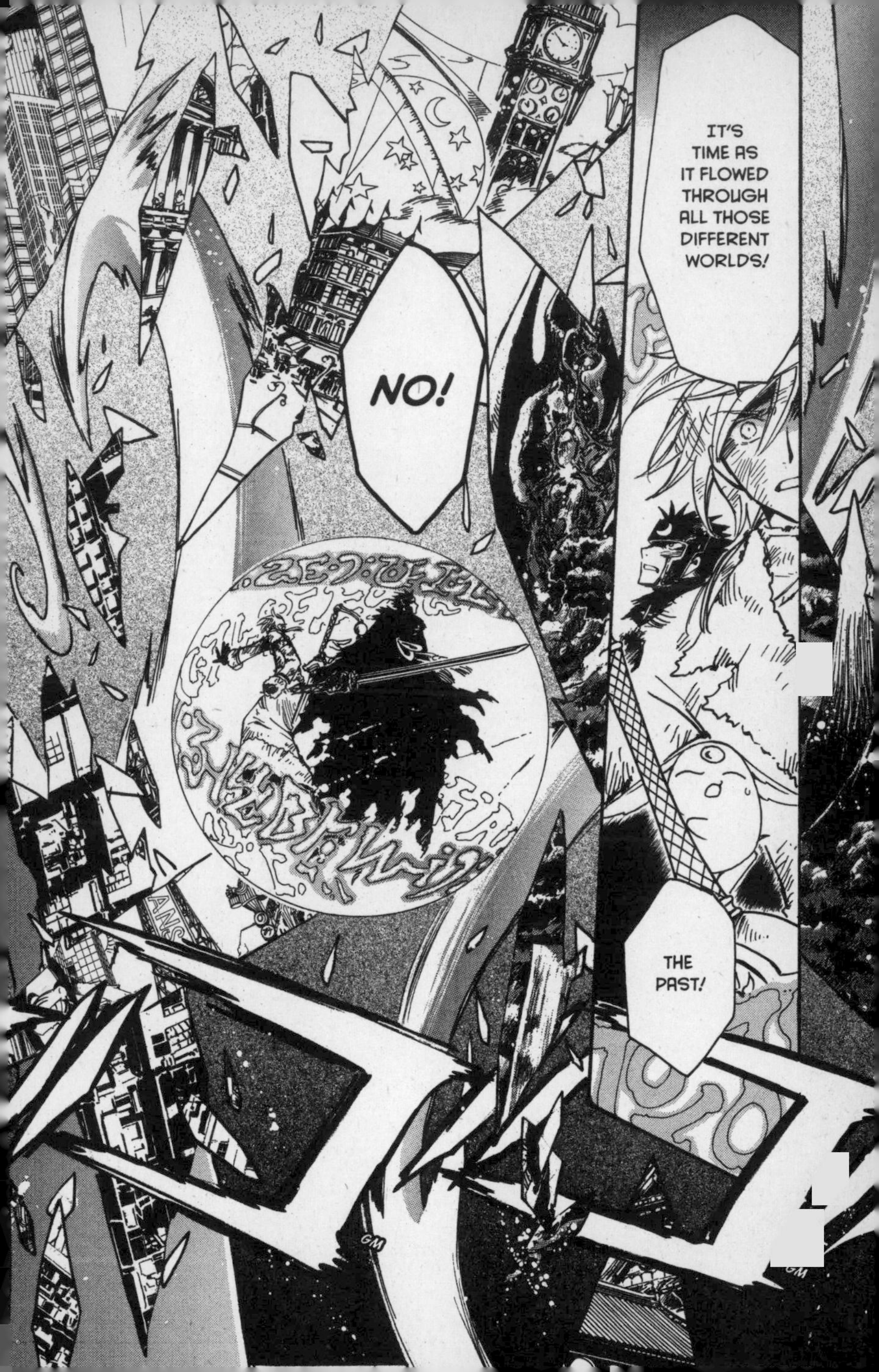
IT'S TIME AS IT FLOWED THROUGH ALL THOSE DIFFERENT WORLDS!
THE PAST!
NO!

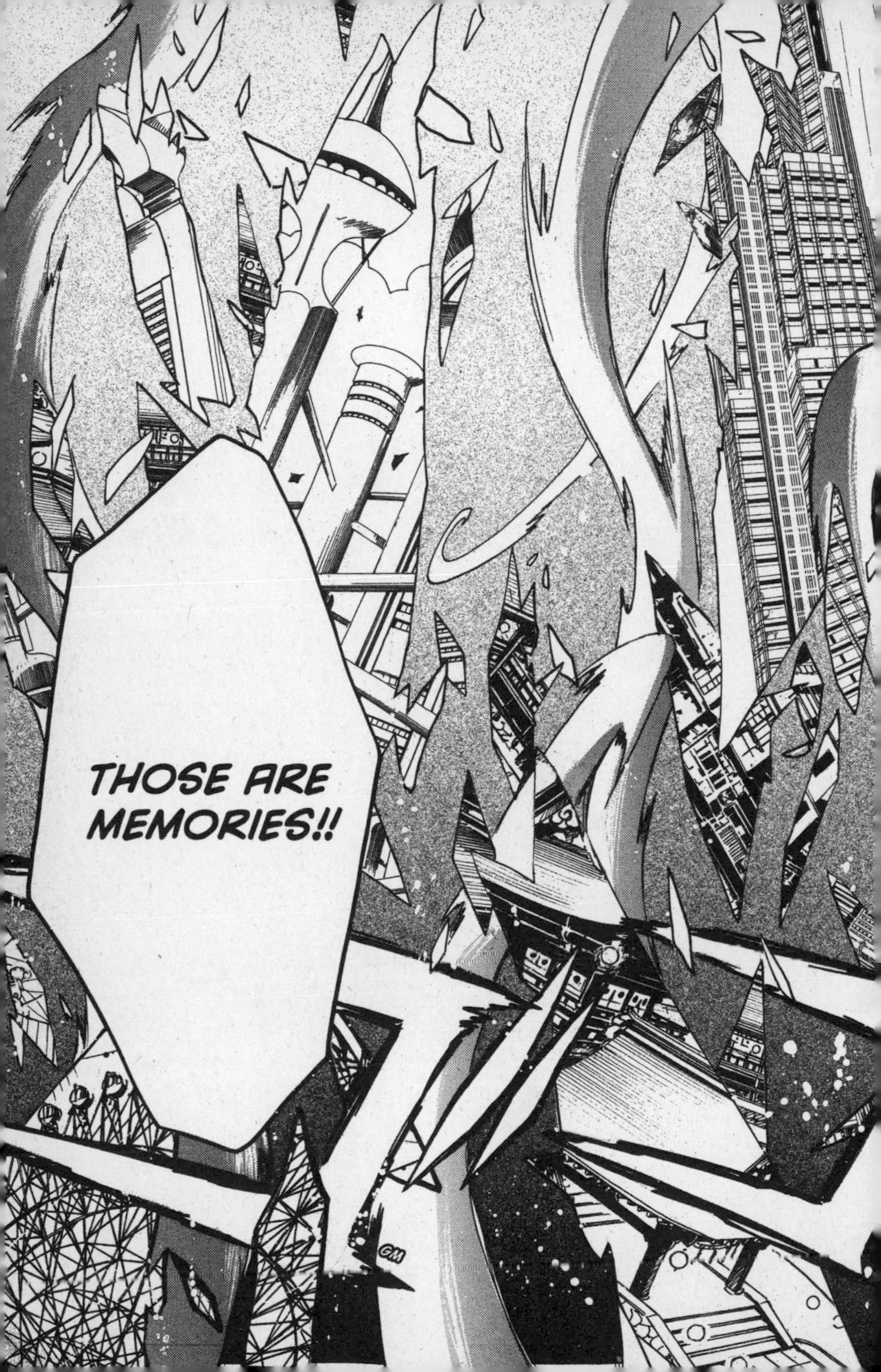
THOSE ARE MEMORIES!!

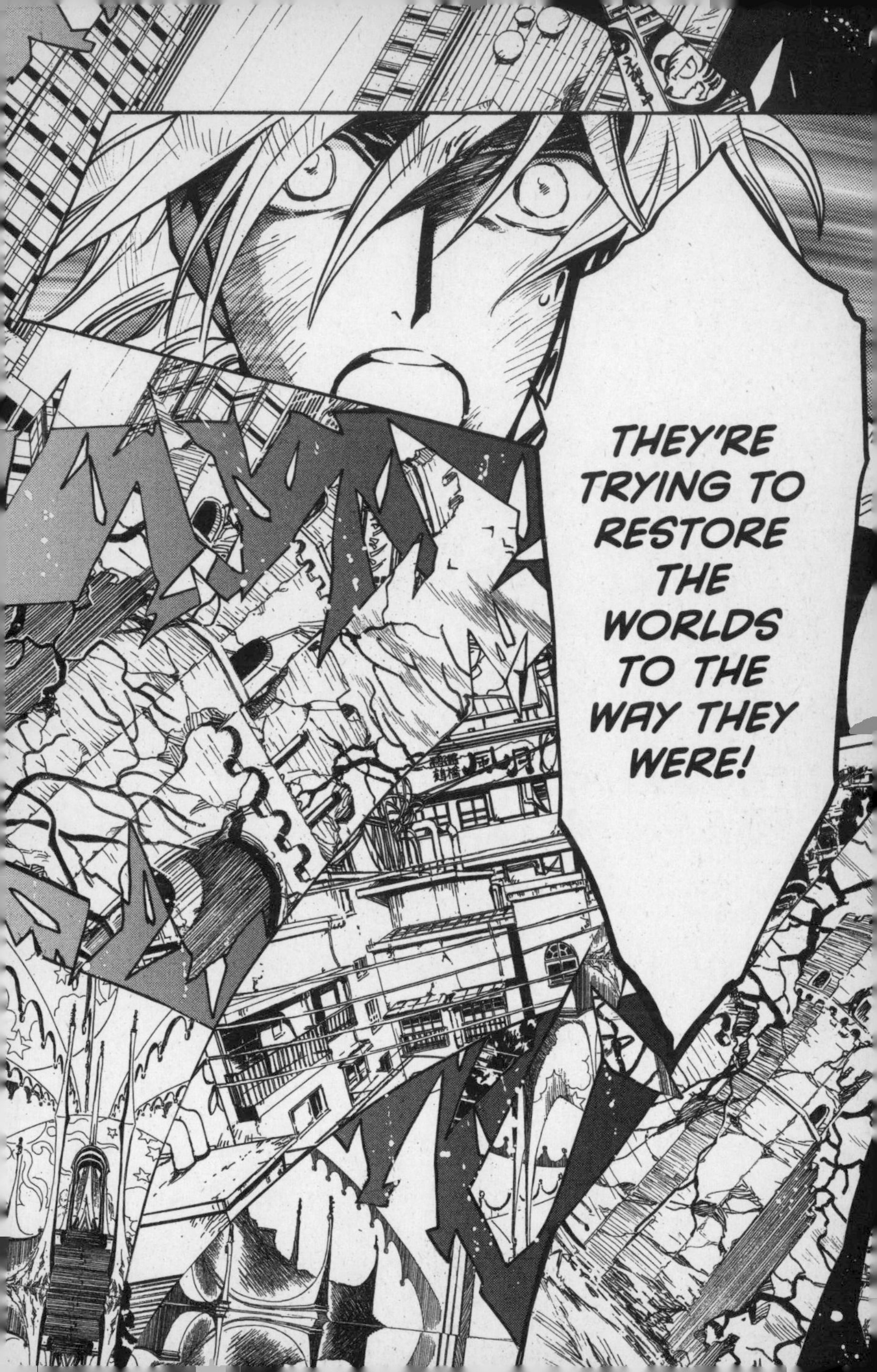
THEY'RE TRYING TO RESTORE THE WORLDS TO THE WAY THEY WERE!

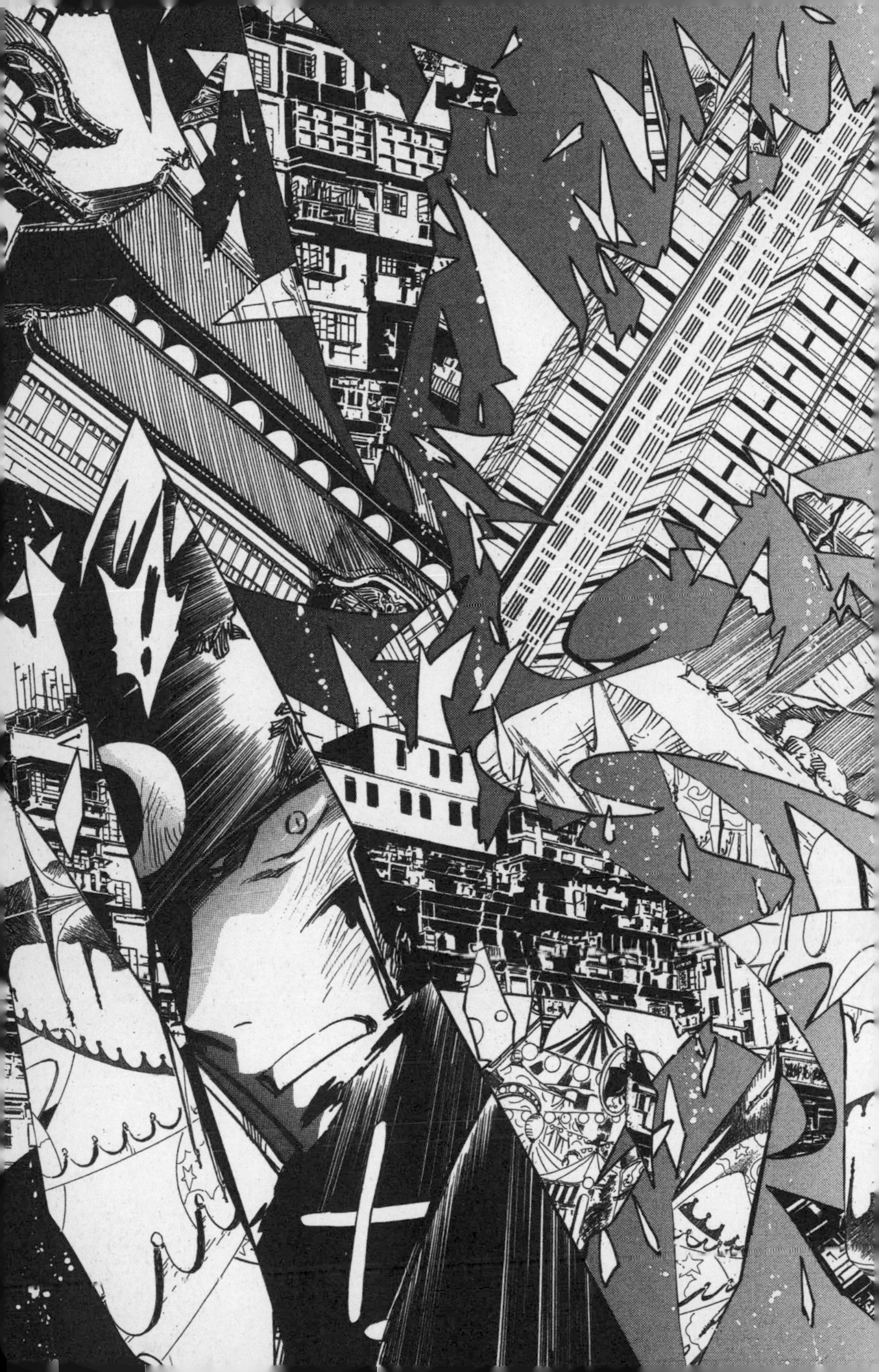

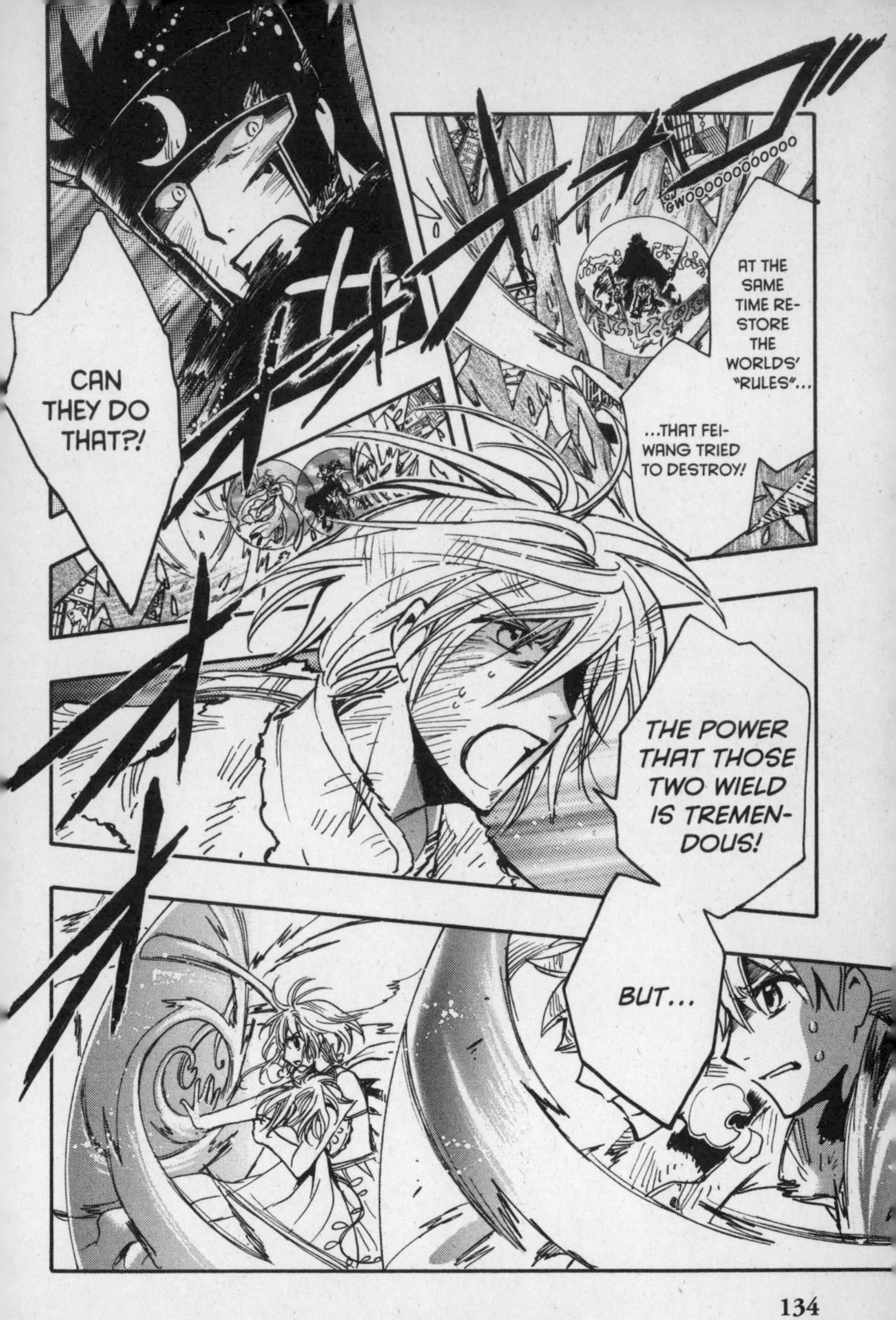
GWOOOOOOOOOOOO
AT THE SAME TIME RE-STORE THE WORLDS' "RULES"...
...THAT FEI-WANG TRIED TO DESTROY!
CAN THEY DO THAT?!
THE POWER THAT THOSE TWO WIELD IS TREMEN-DOUS!
BUT...

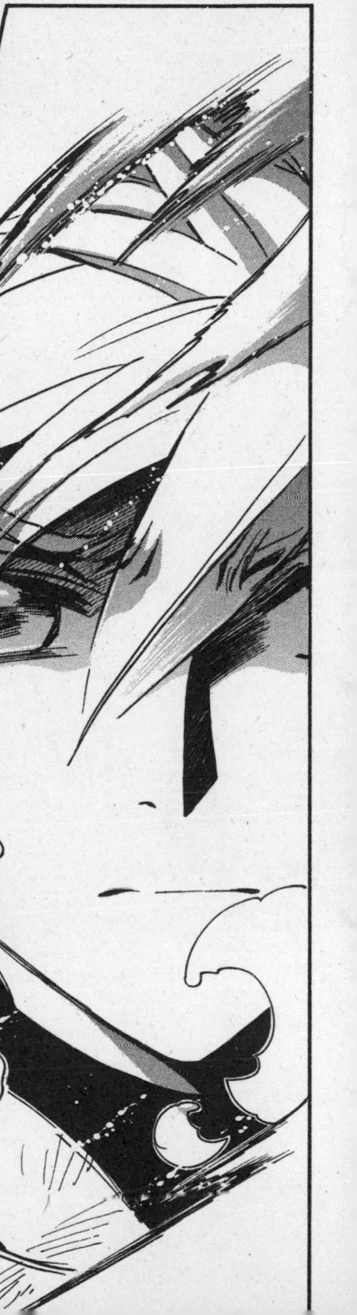
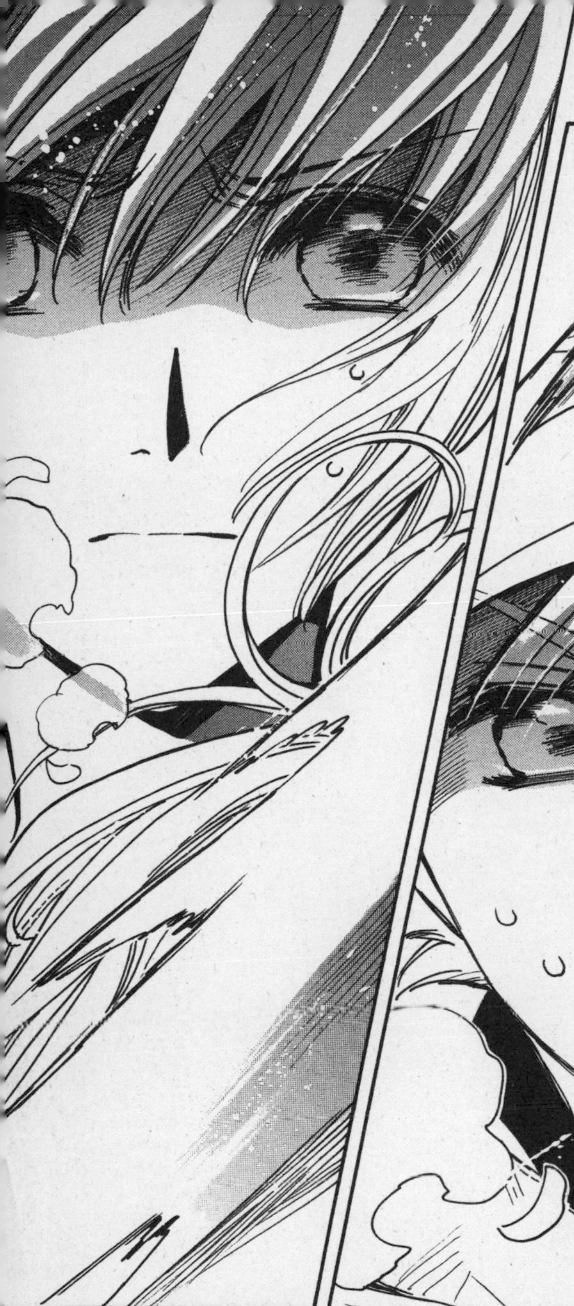

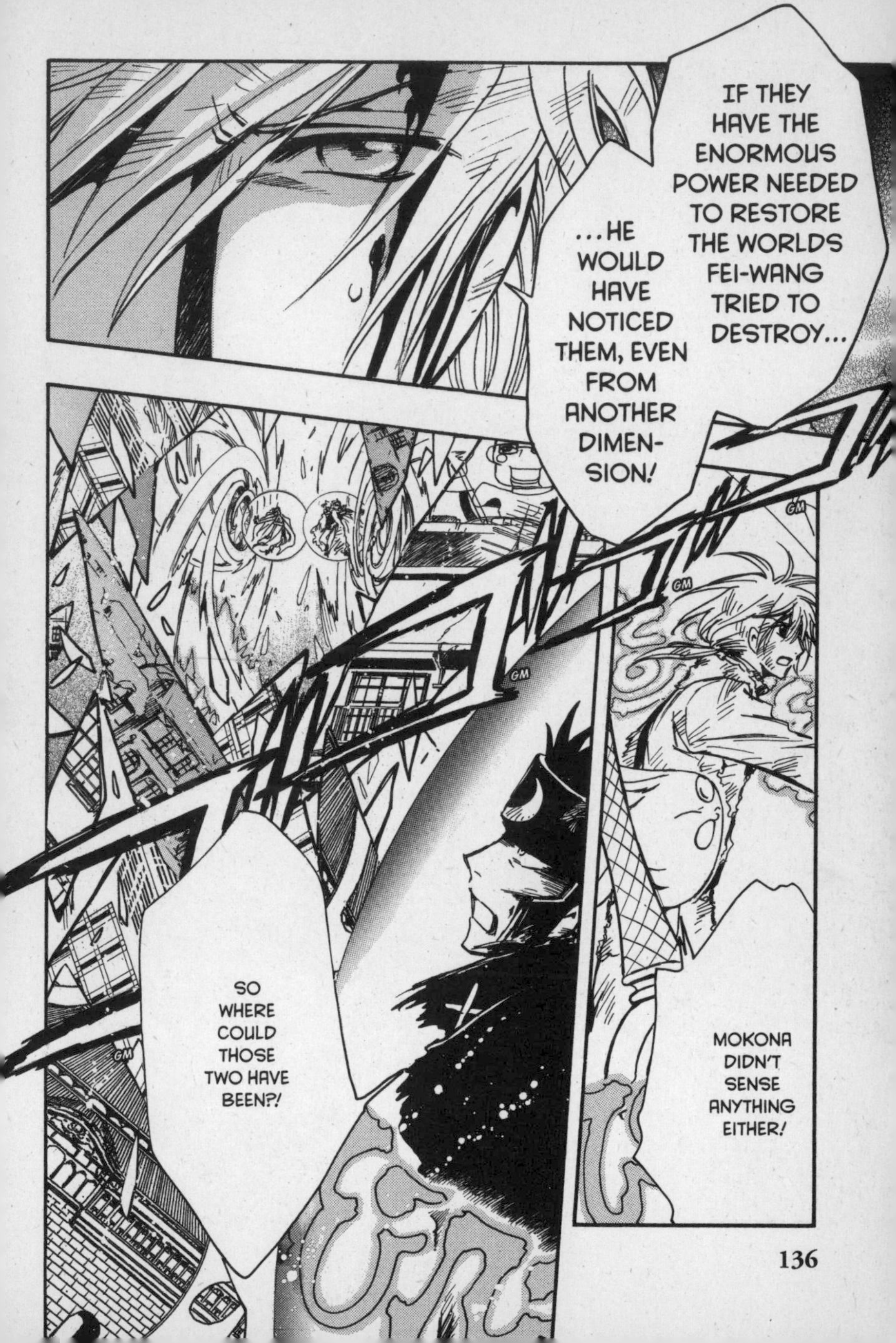
IF THEY HAVE THE ENORMOUS POWER NEEDED TO RESTORE THE WORLDS FEI-WANG TRIED TO DESTROY...
...HE WOULD HAVE NOTICED THEM, EVEN FROM ANOTHER DIMEN-SION!
GM
GM
GM
MOKONA DIDN'T SENSE ANYTHING EITHER!
SO WHERE COULD THOSE TWO HAVE BEEN?!
GM

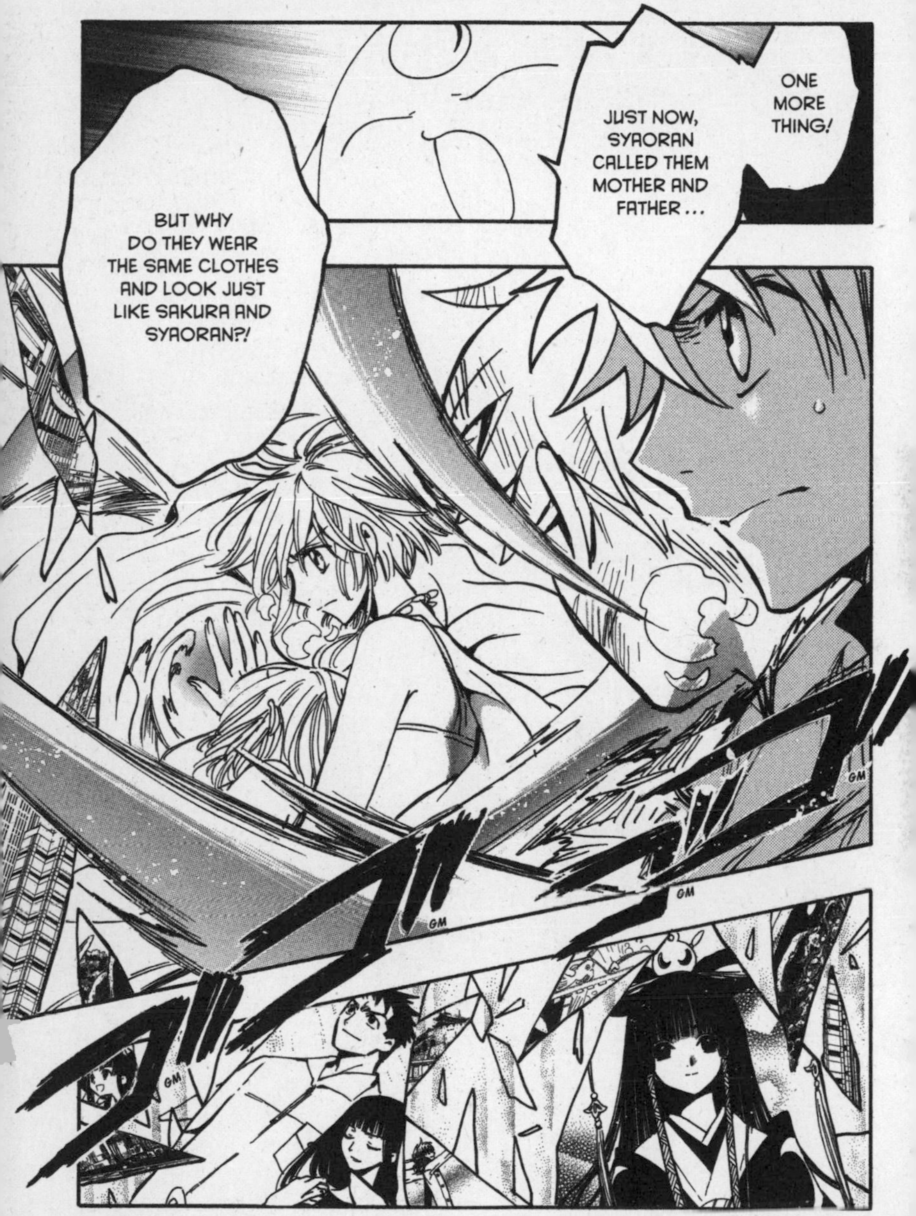
ONE MORE THING!
JUST NOW, SYAORAN CALLED THEM MOTHER AND FATHER...
BUT WHY DO THEY WEAR THE SAME CLOTHES AND LOOK JUST LIKE SAKURA AND SYAORAN?!

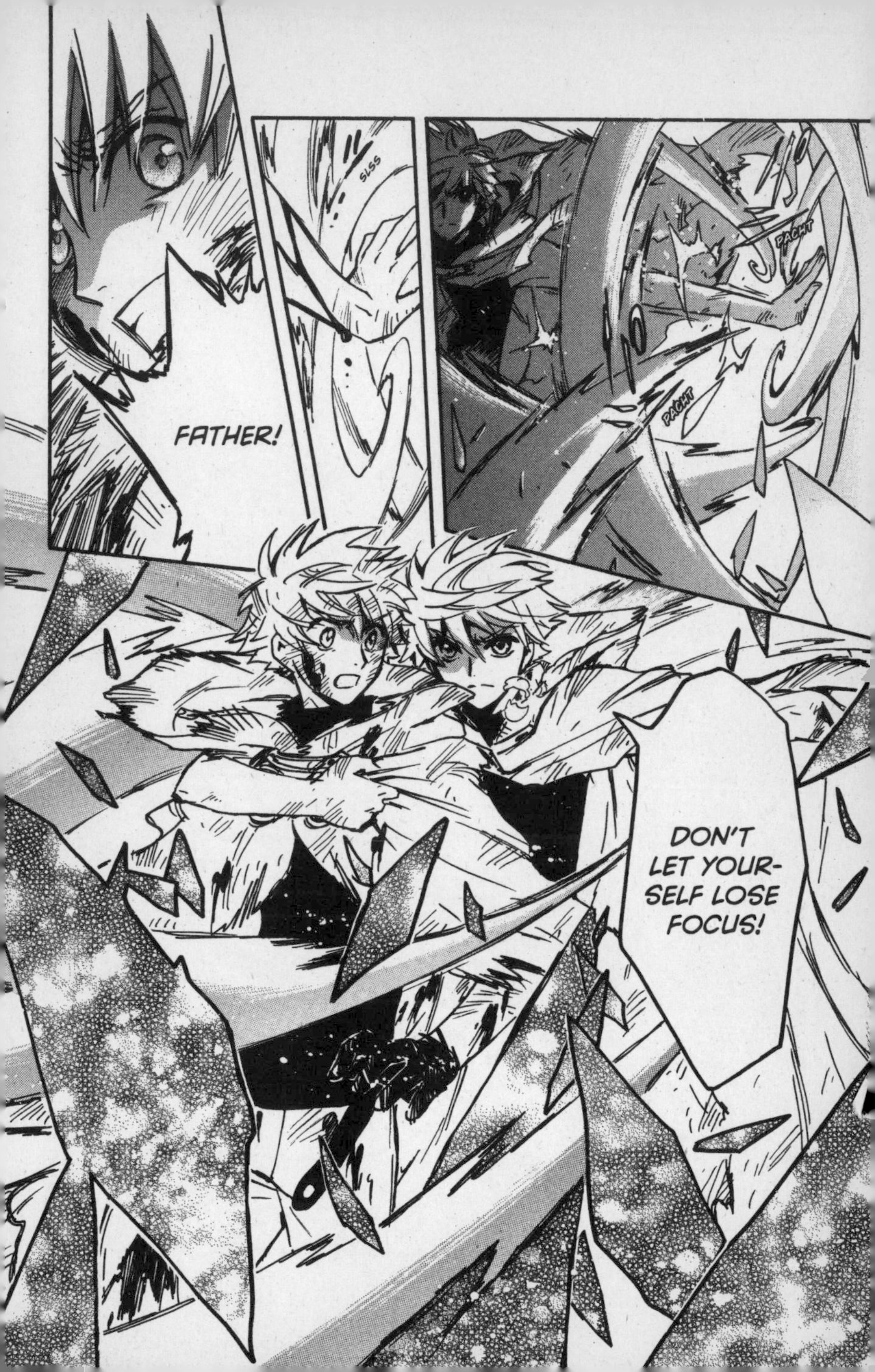
PACHT
PACHT
SLSS
FATHER!
DON'T LET YOUR-SELF LOSE FOCUS!

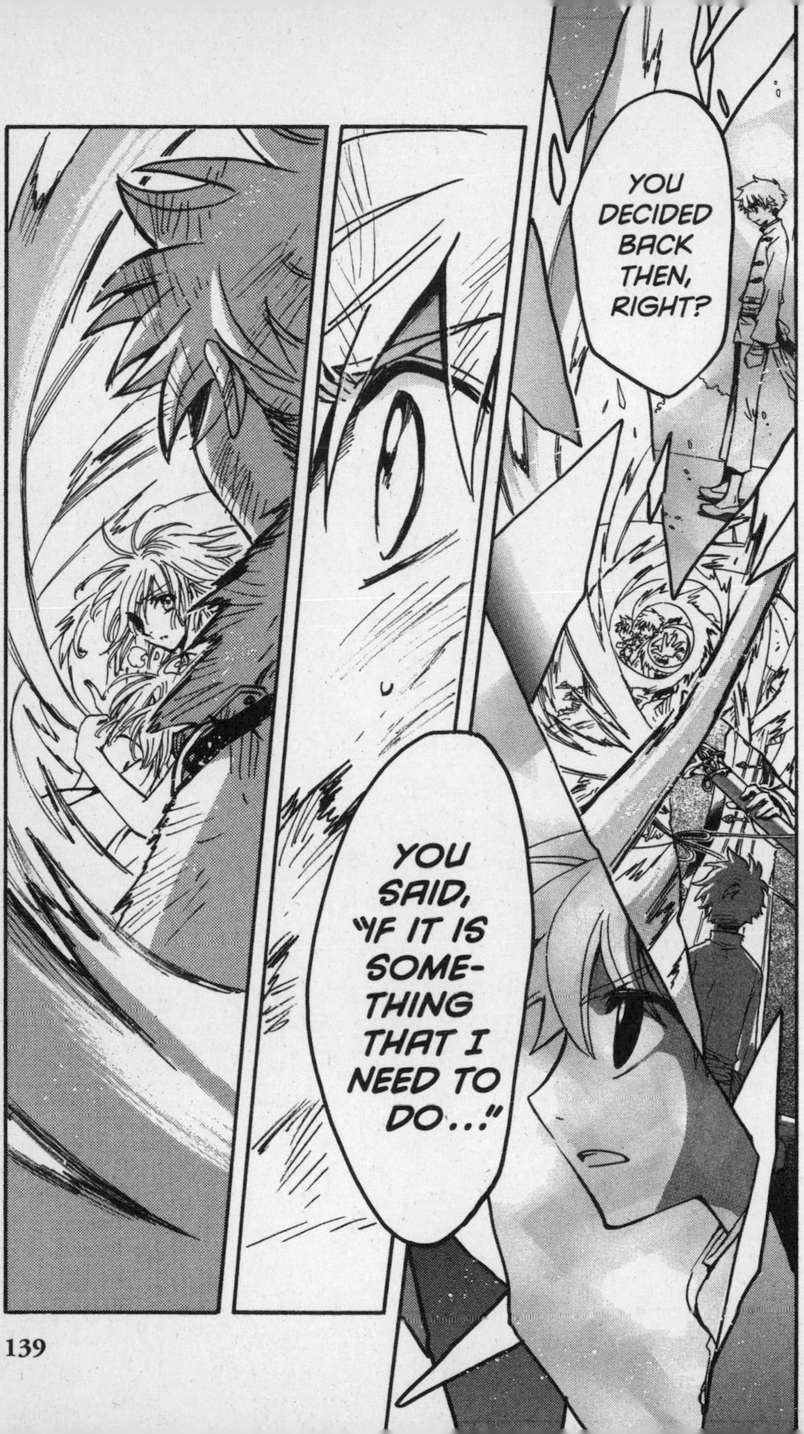
YOU DECIDED BACK THEN, RIGHT?
YOU SAID, "IF IT IS SOMETHING THAT I NEED TO DO..."

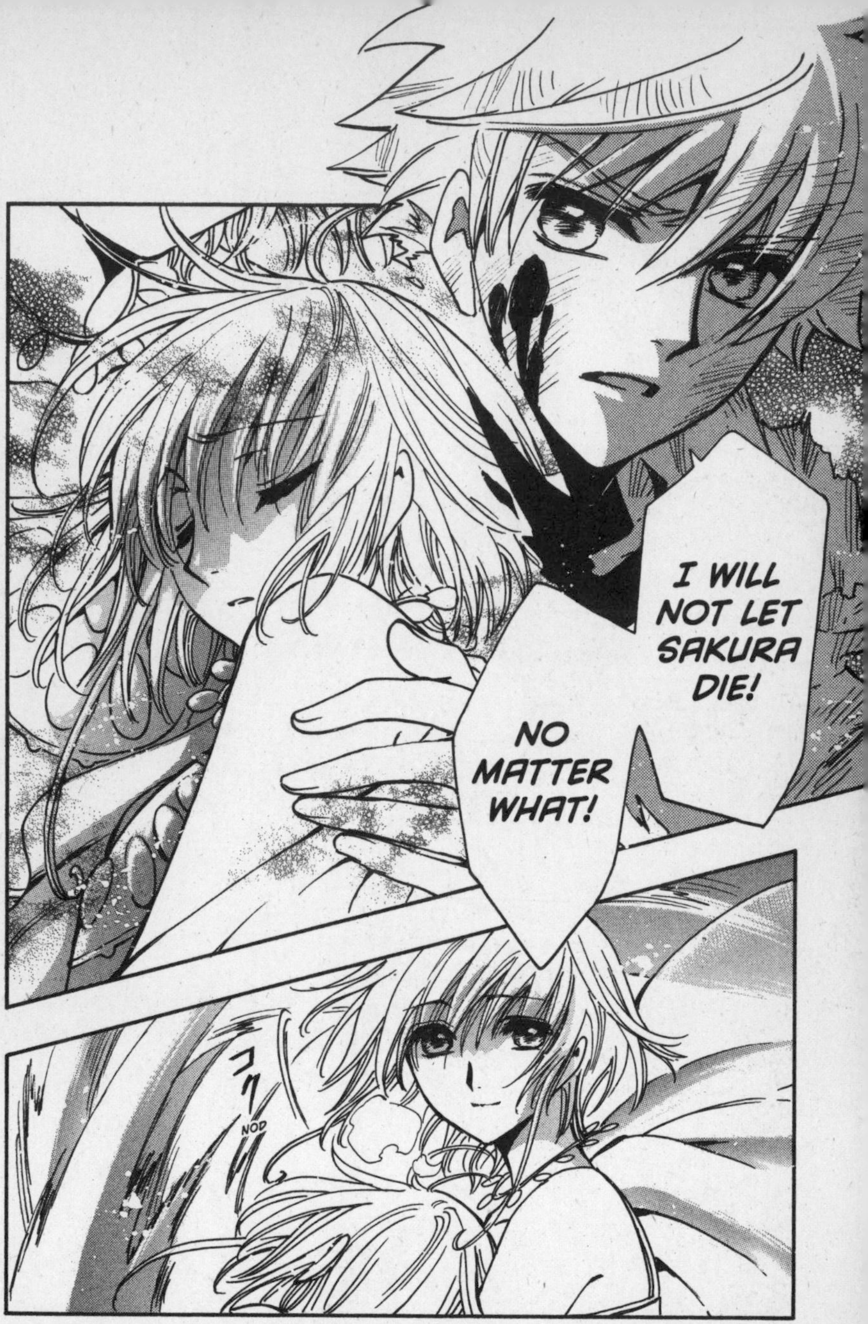
I WILL NOT LET SAKURA DIE!
NO MATTER WHAT!
コク
NOD

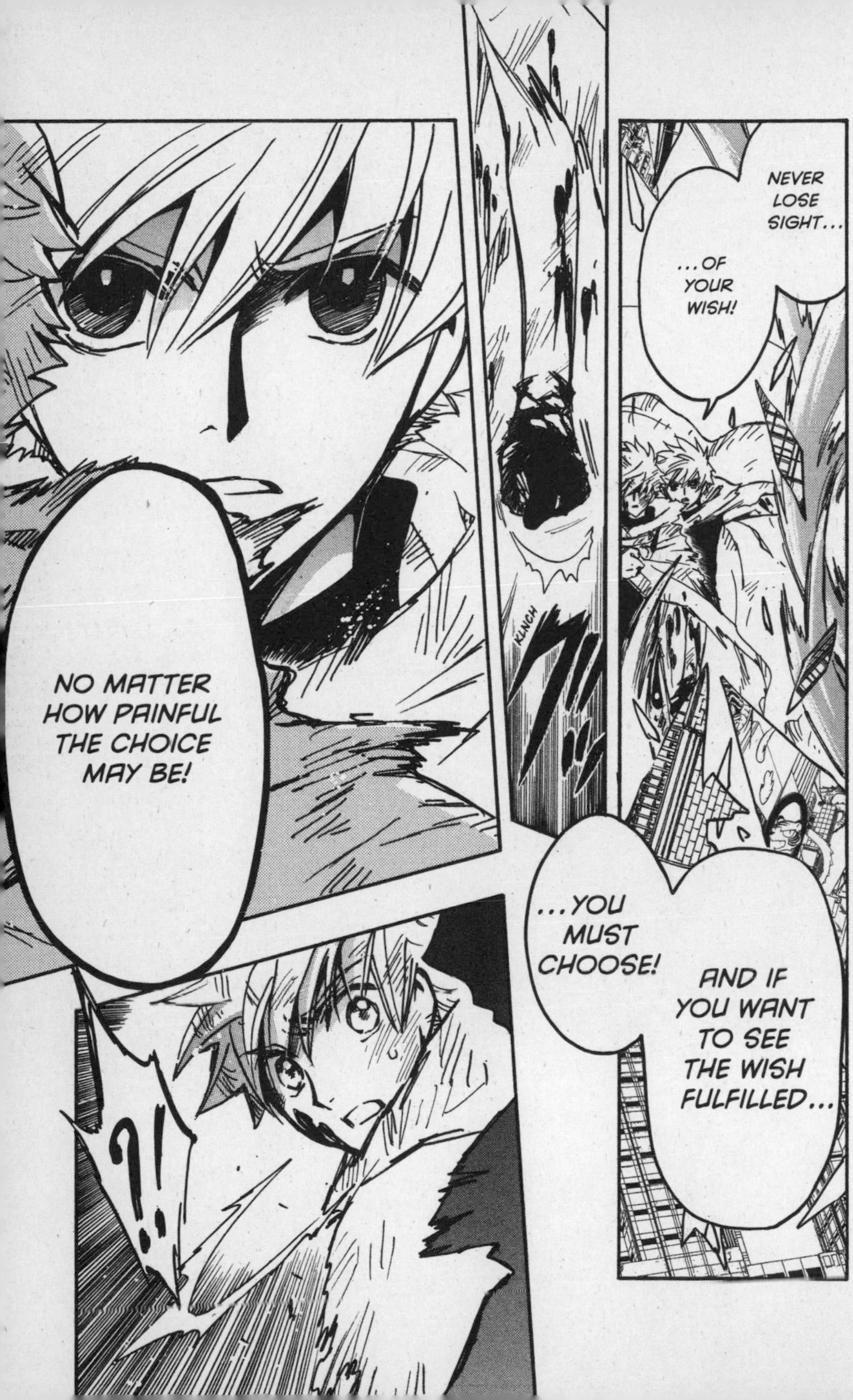
NEVER LOSE SIGHT...
...OF YOUR WISH!
KLNCH
AND IF YOU WANT TO SEE THE WISH FULFILLED...
...YOU MUST CHOOSE!
NO MATTER HOW PAINFUL THE CHOICE MAY BE!
?!

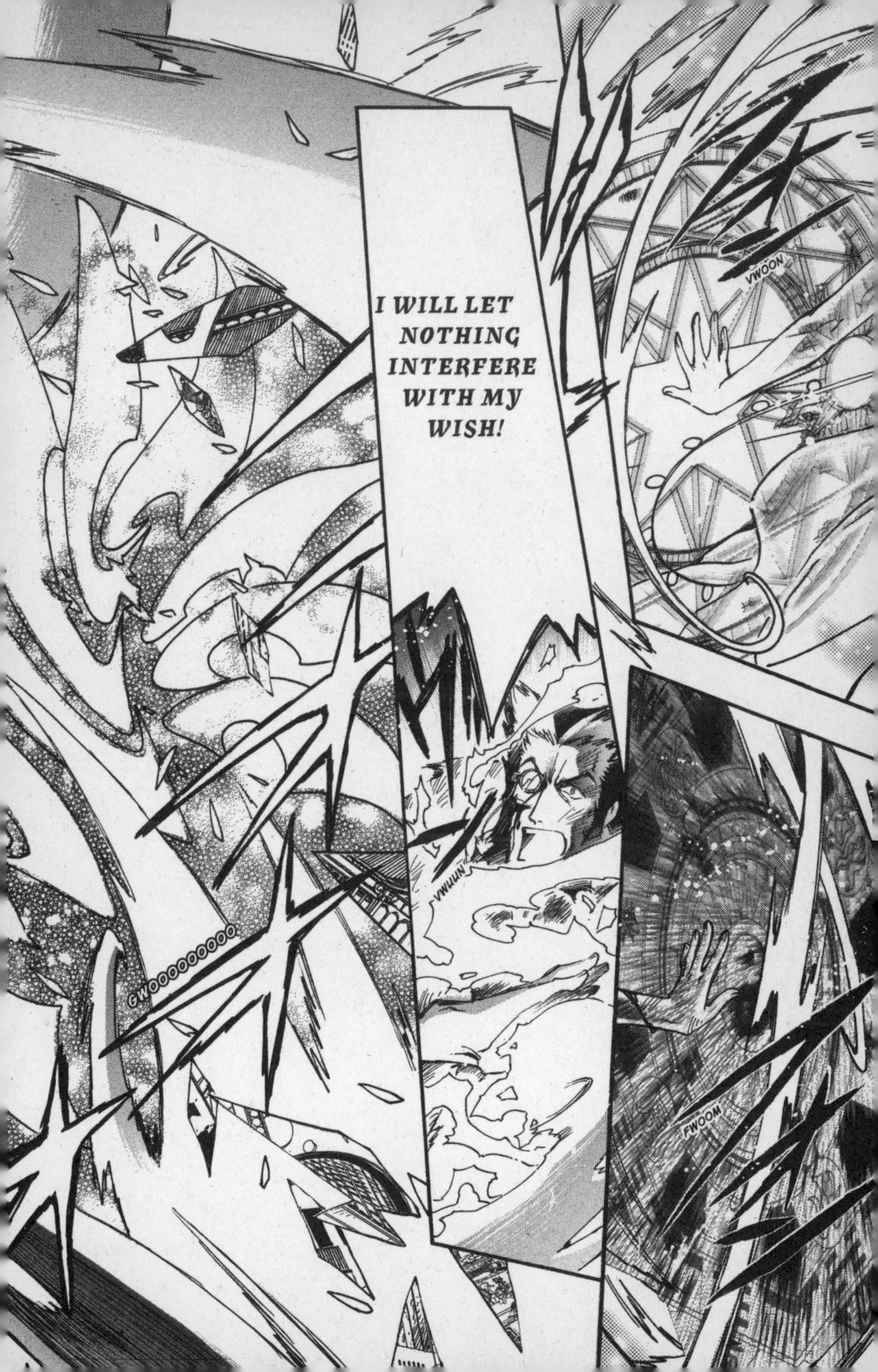
VWOON
I WILL LET NOTHING INTERFERE WITH MY WISH!
VWUUN
FWOOM
GWOOOOOOOOO

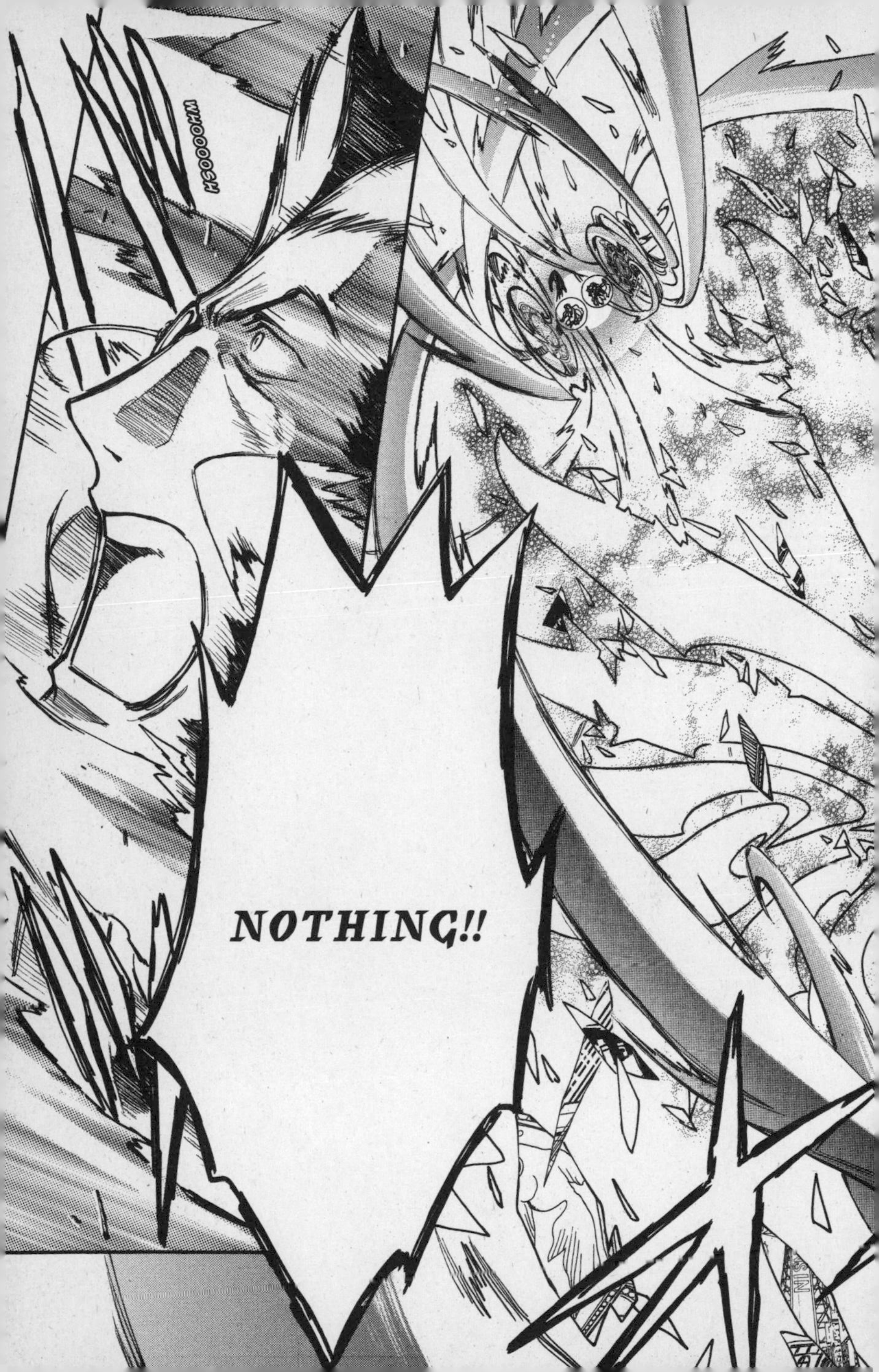
WHOOOOSH
NOTHING!!

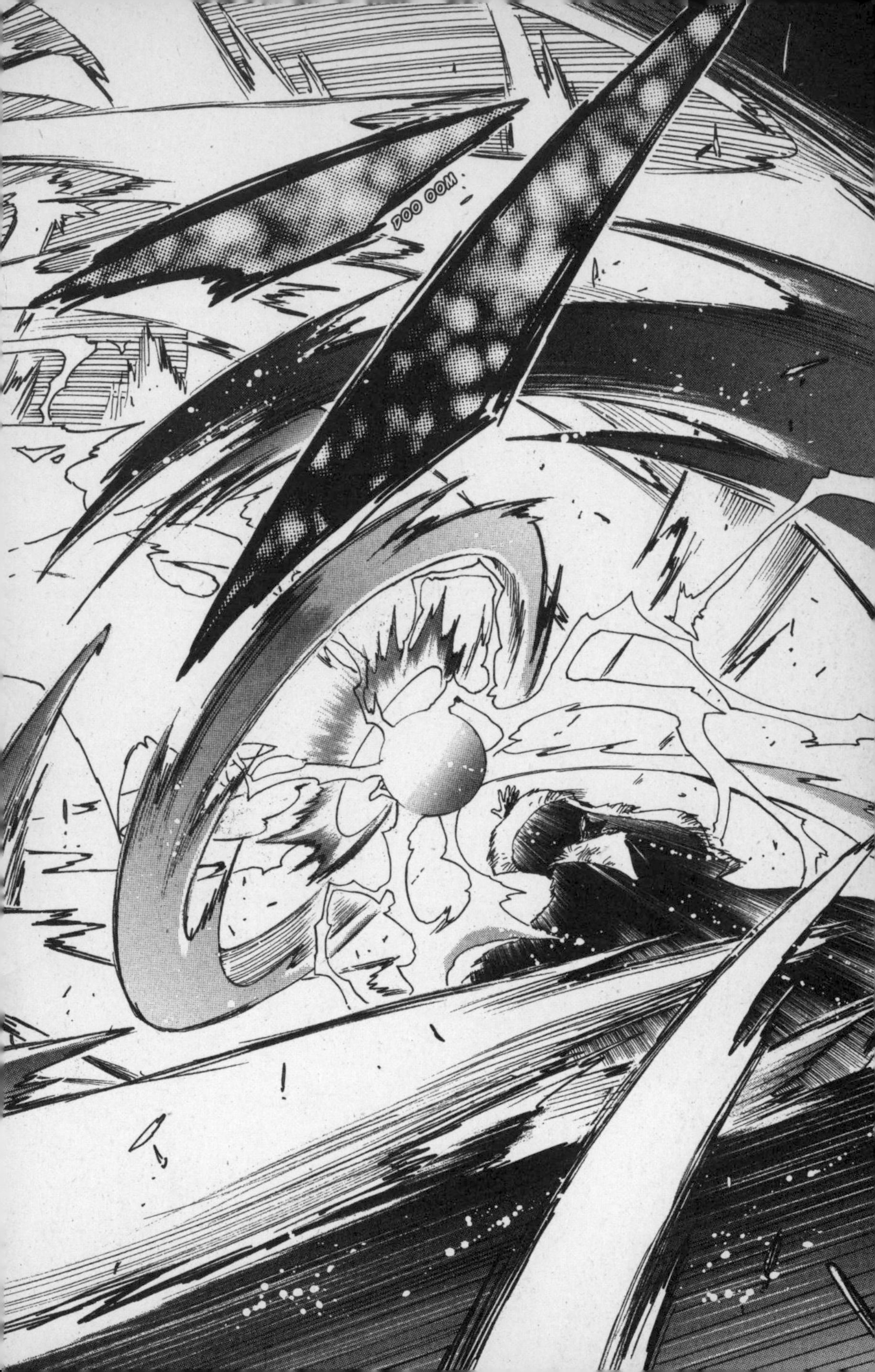
DOO OOM

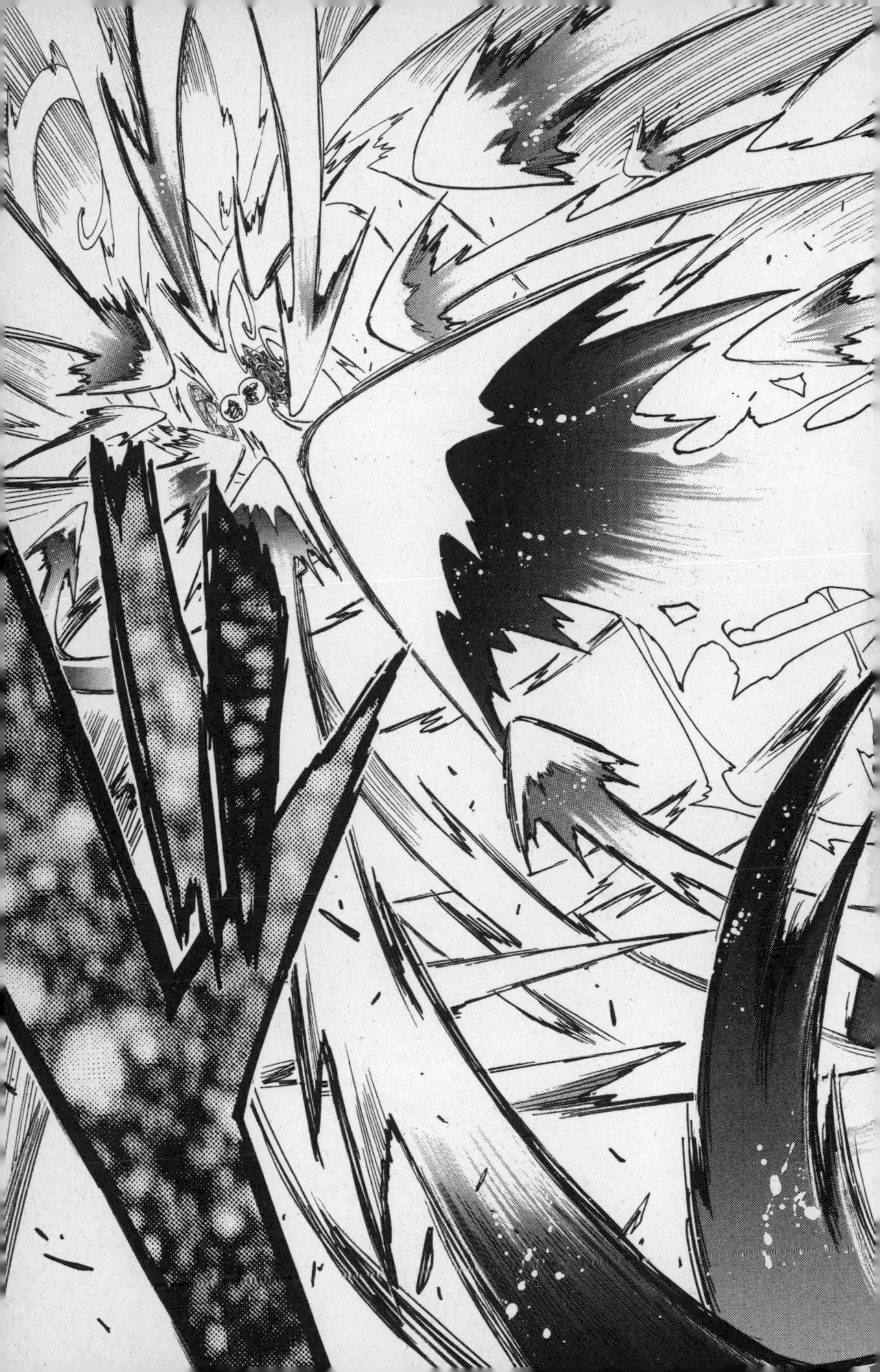

ツバサ

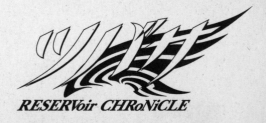

RESERVoir CHRoNiCLE

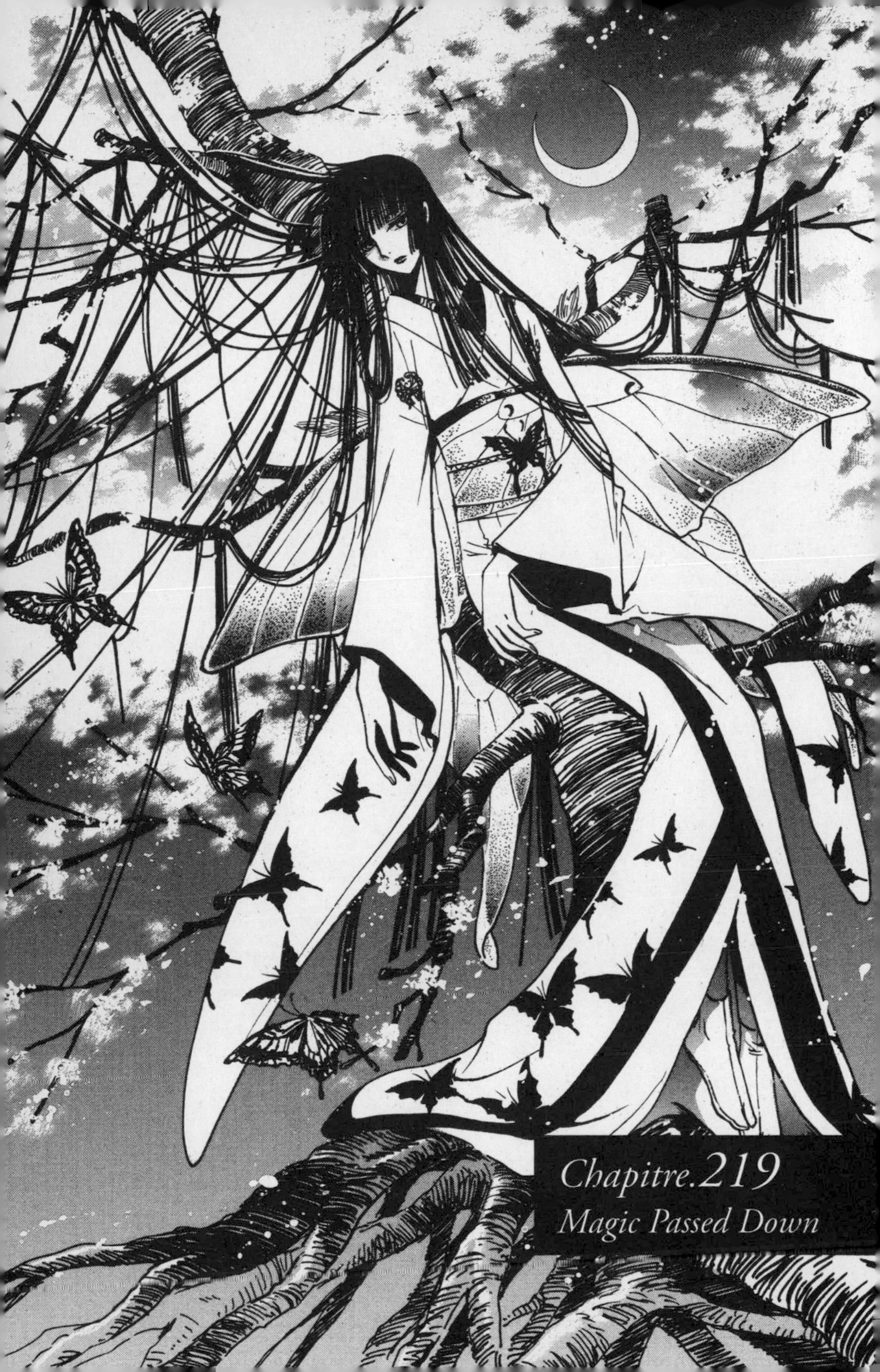
Chapitre.219
Magic Passed Down

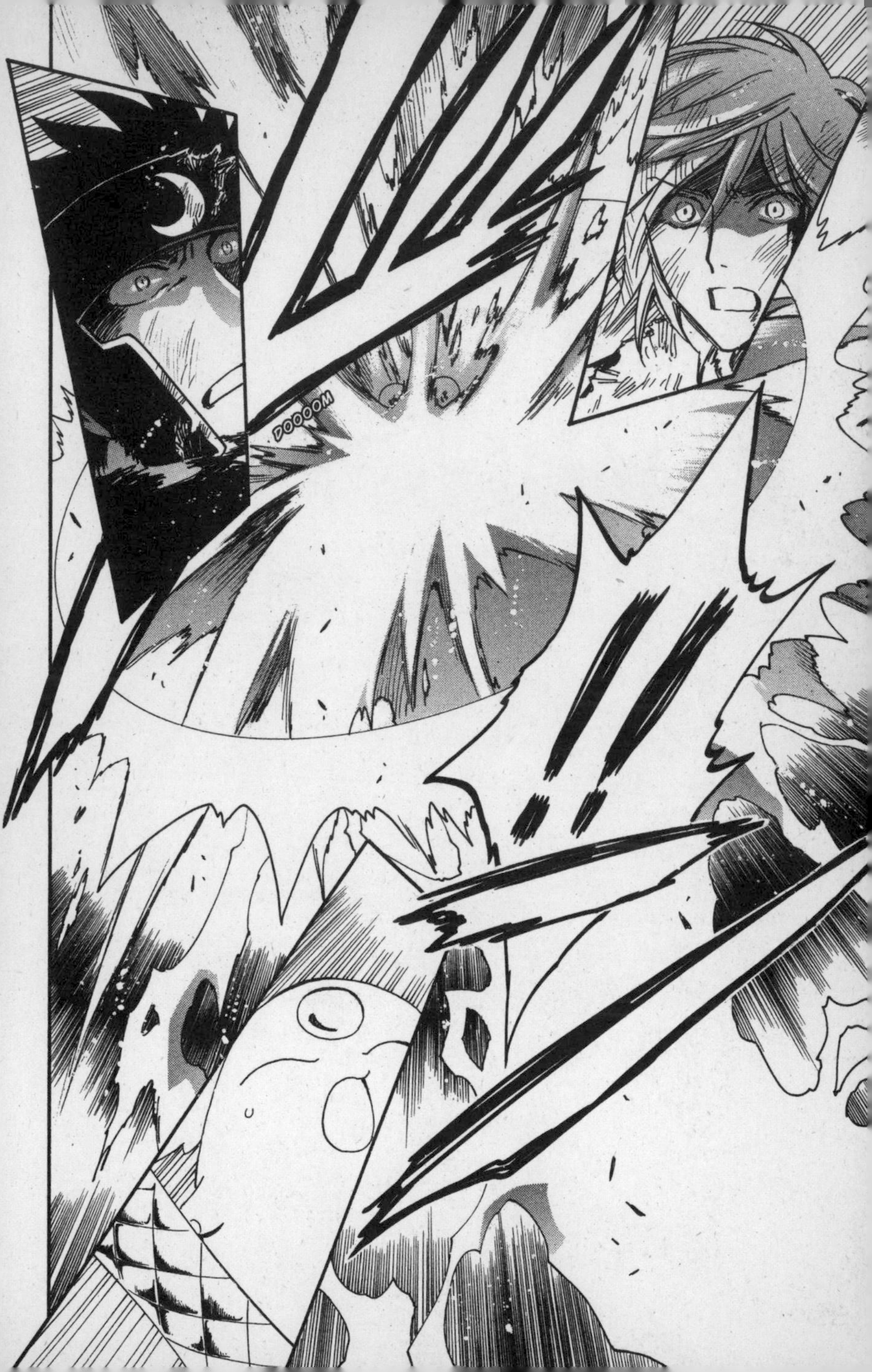
DOOOOM

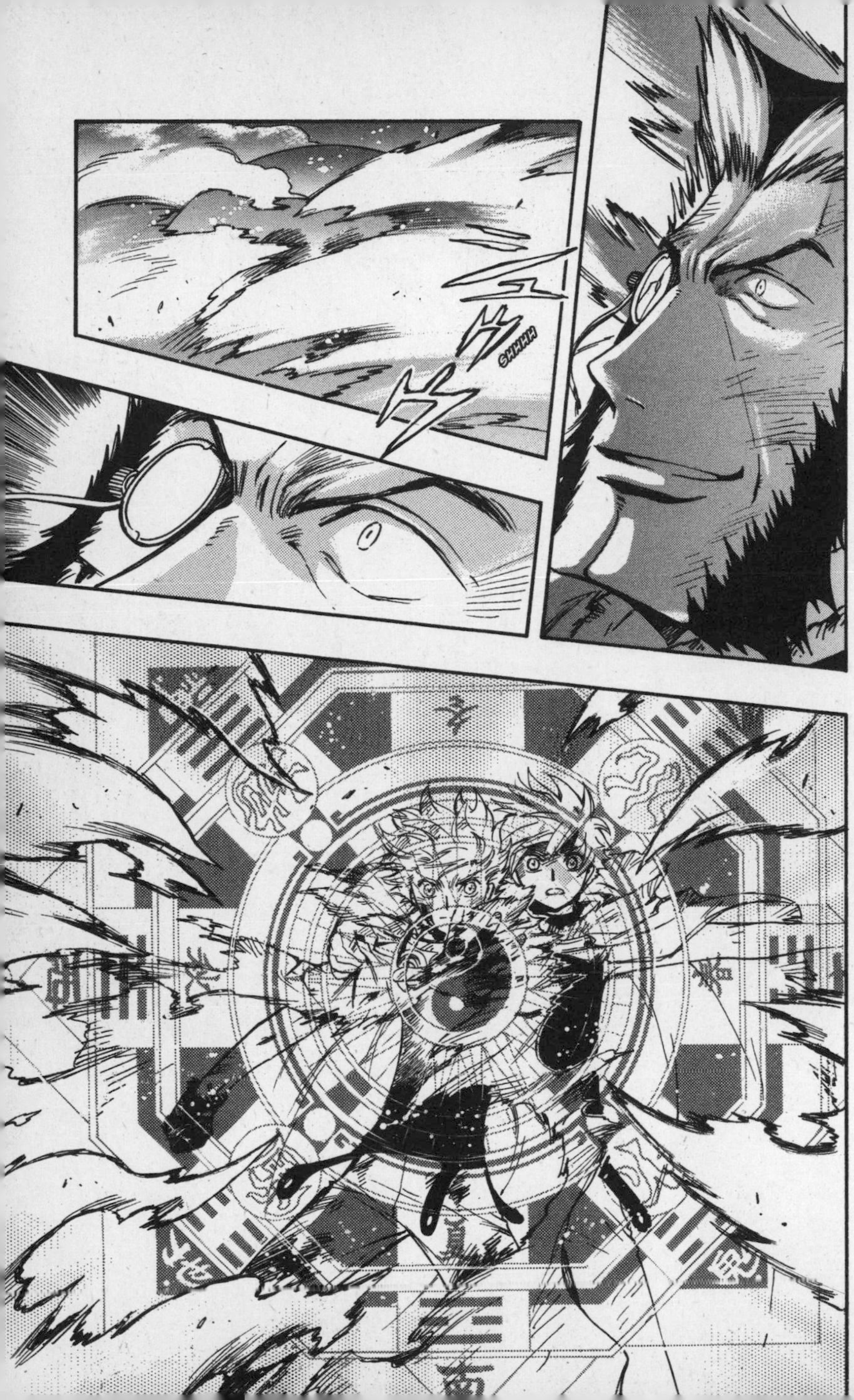
SHHHH

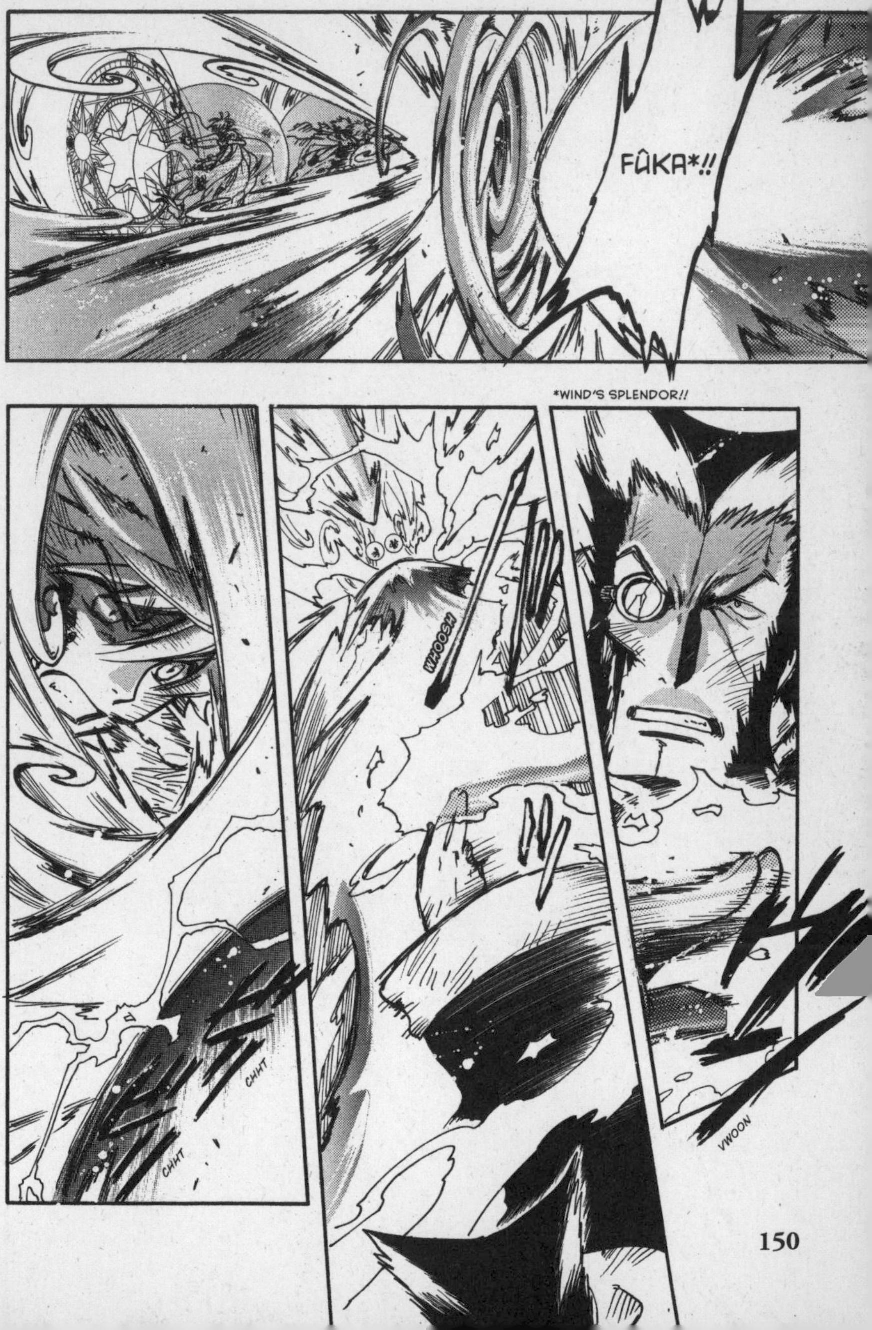
FÛKA*!!
*WIND'S SPLENDOR!!
VWOON
WHOOSH
CHHT
CHHT

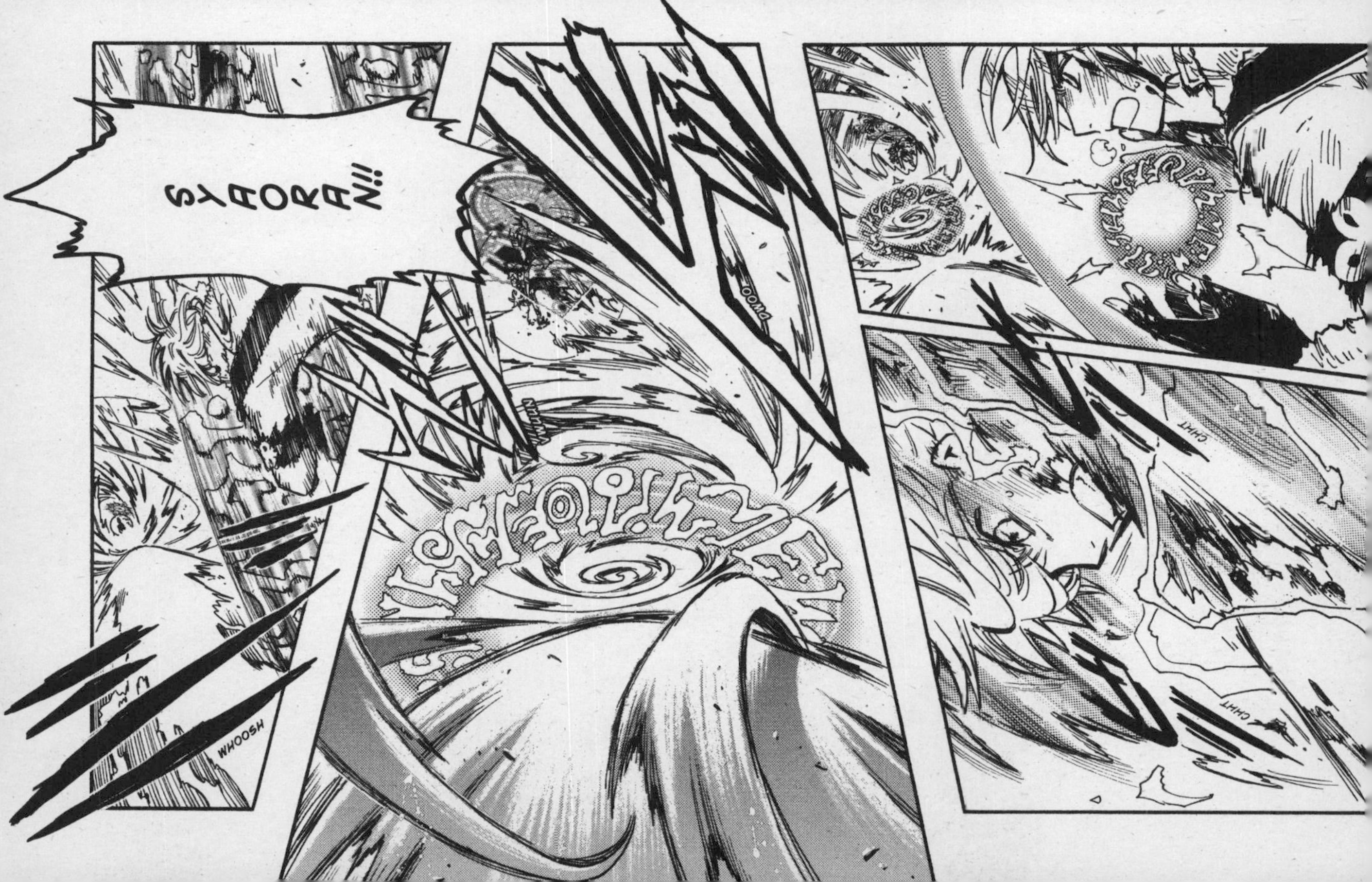
CHHT
CHHT
VWUUN
DWOO
SYAORAN!!
WHOOSH

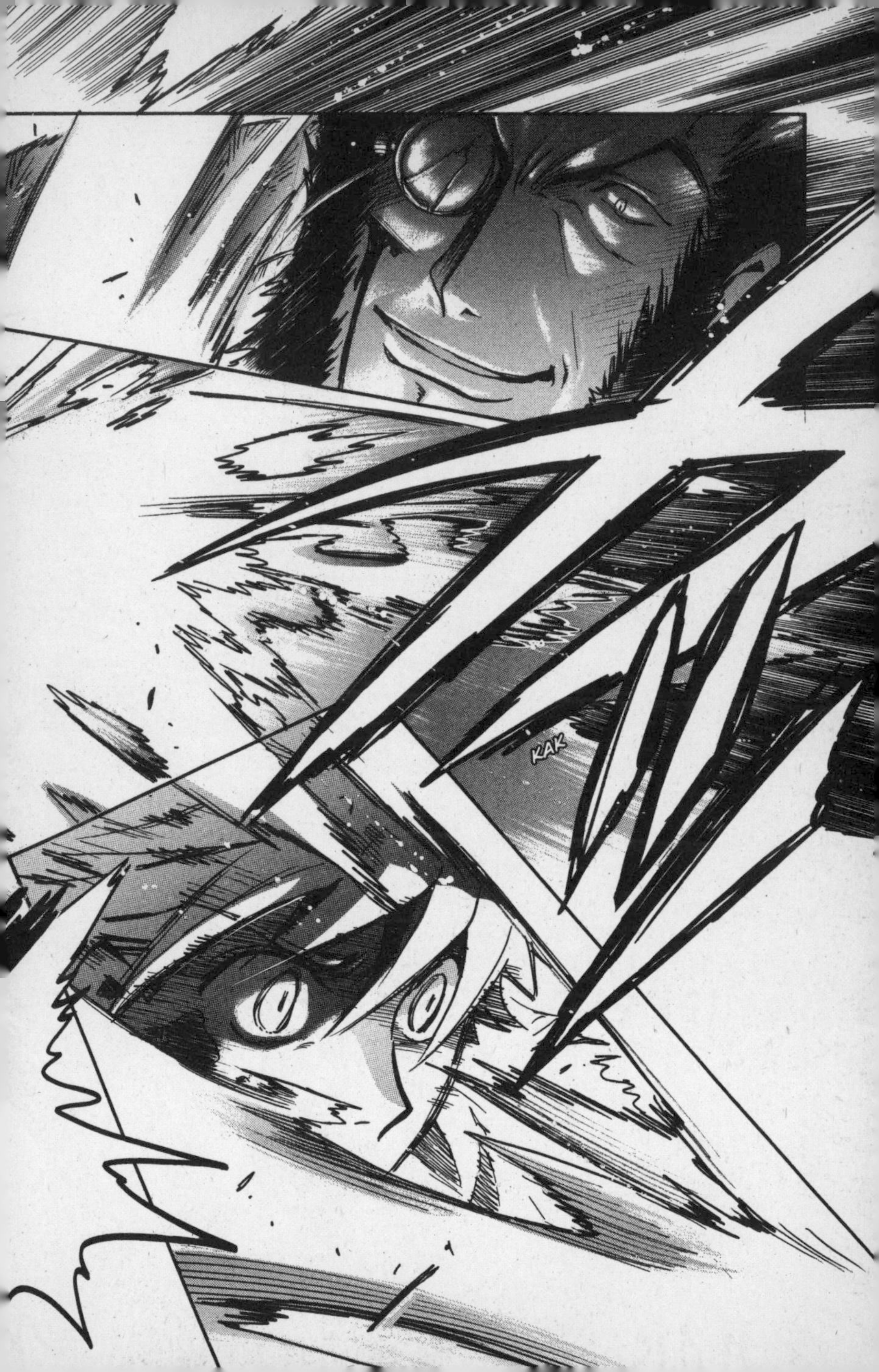
KAK

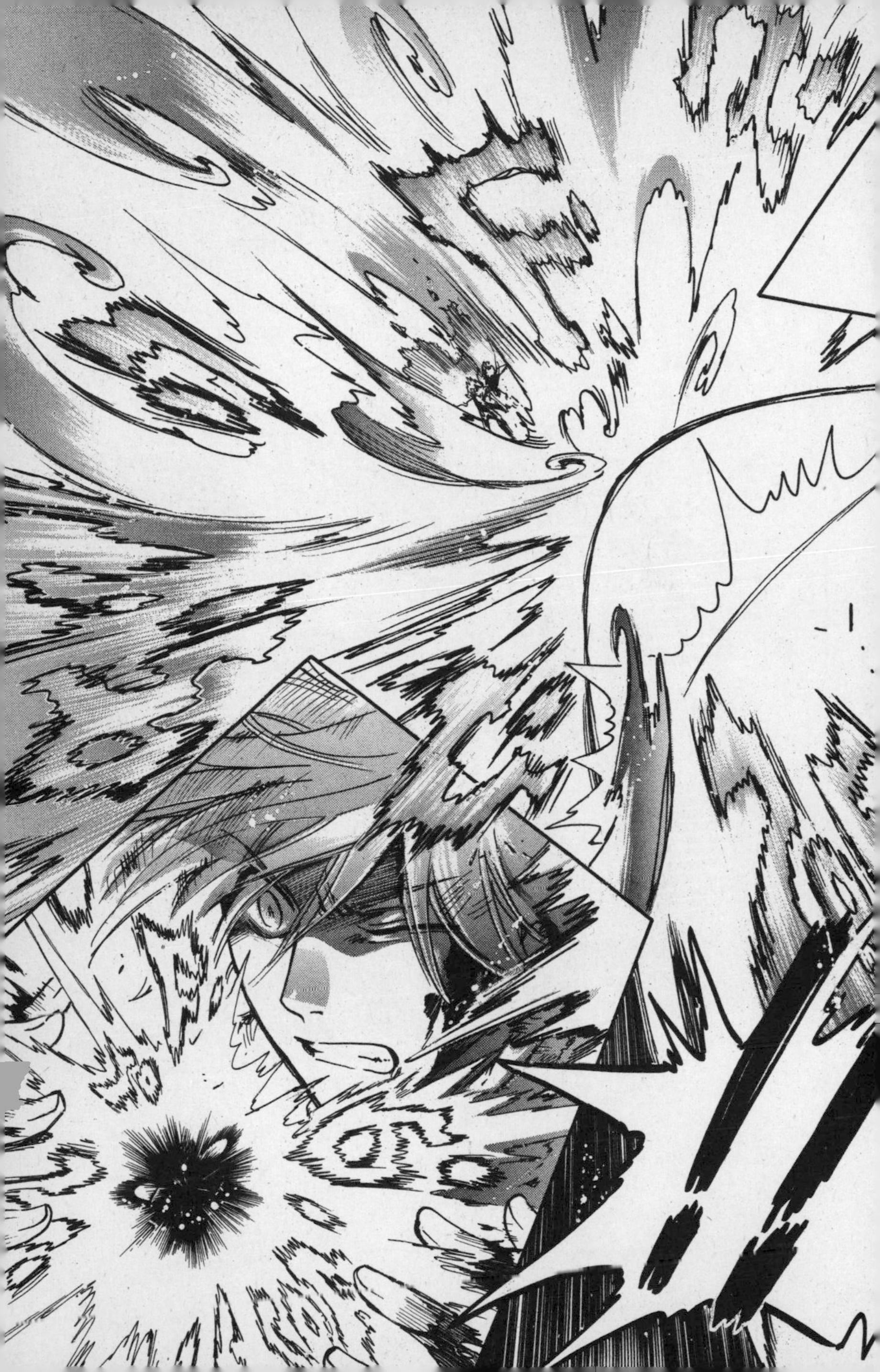

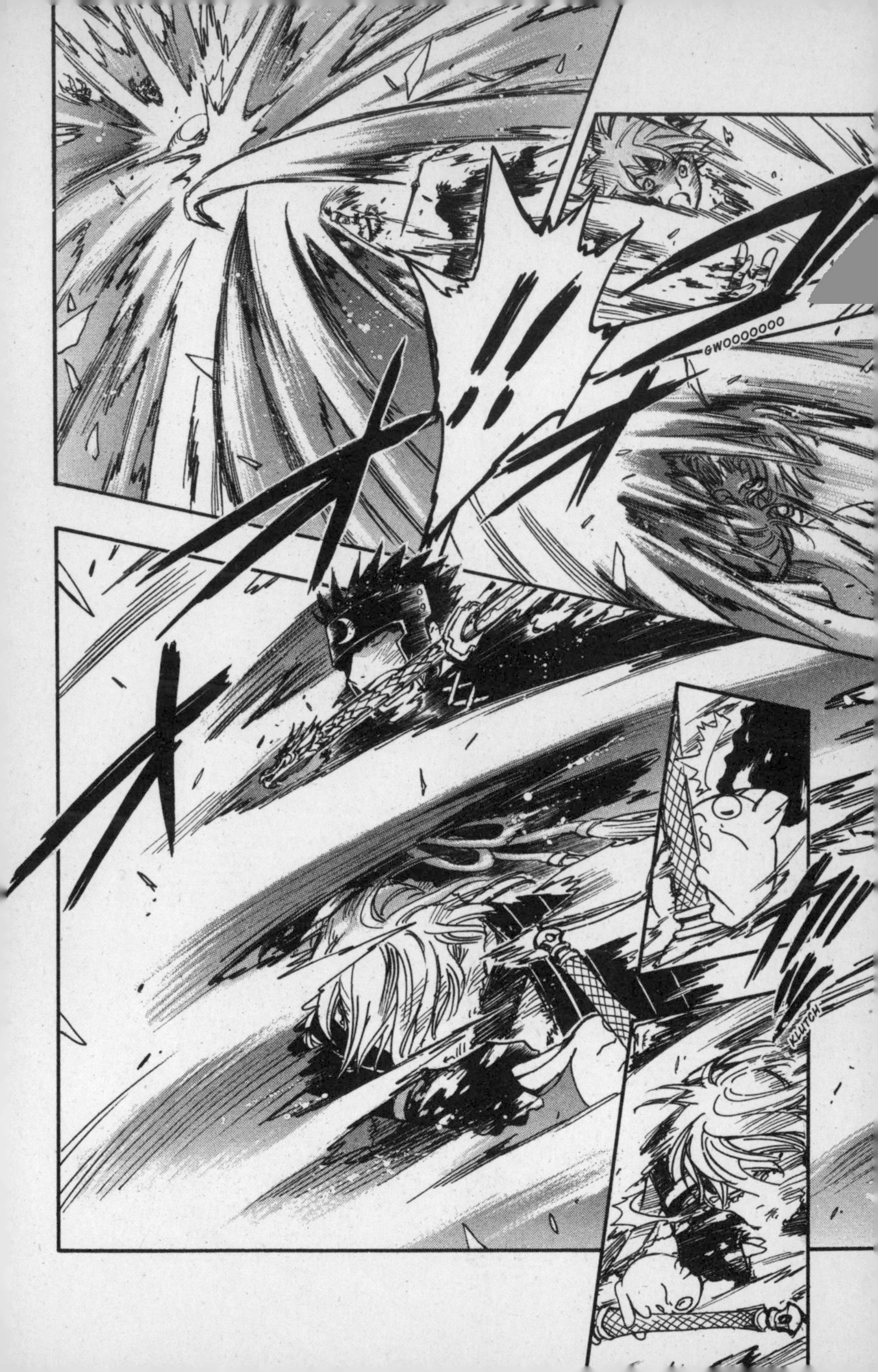
GWOOOOOOO
KLUTCH

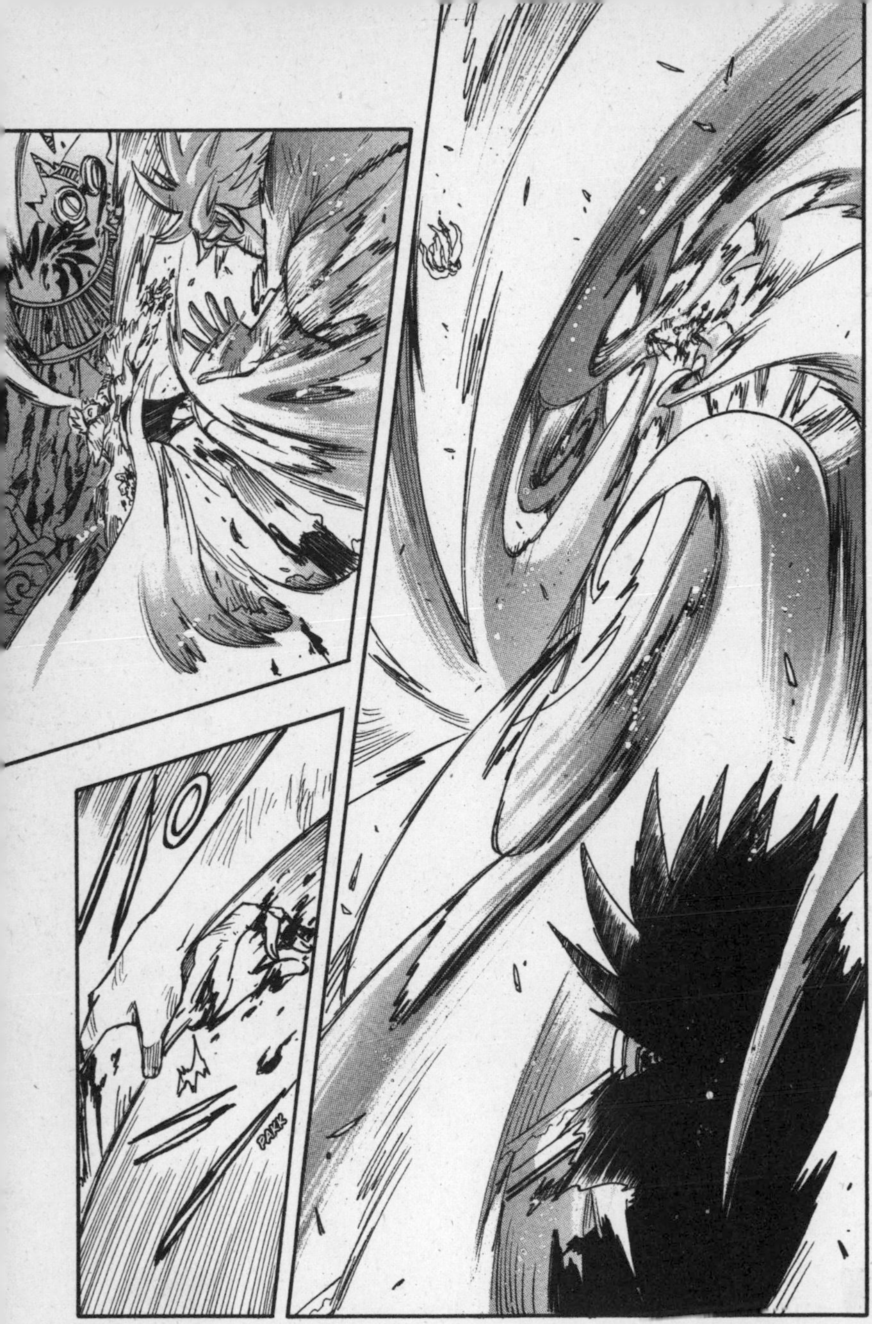
PAKK

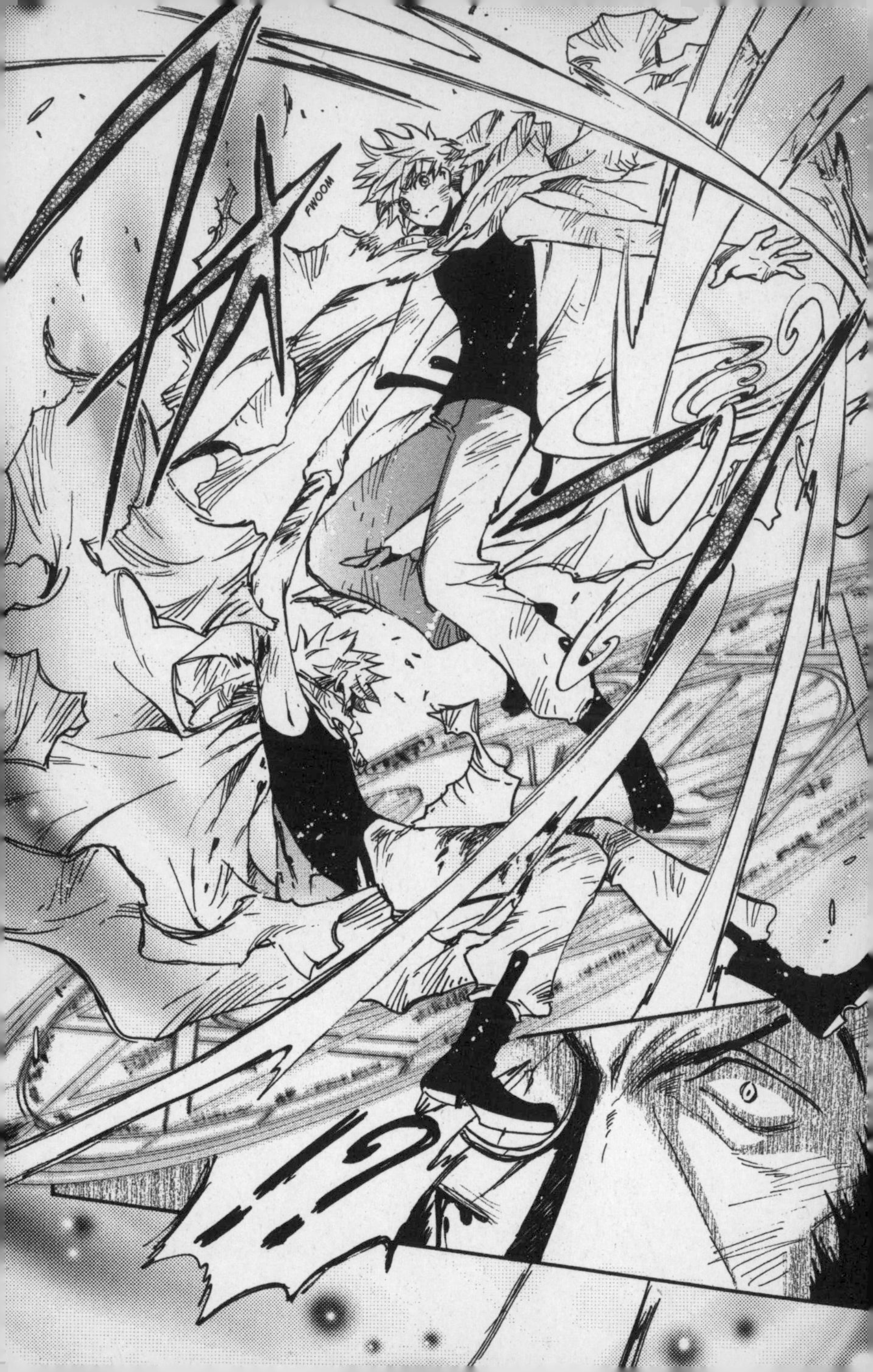
FWOOM
--!?

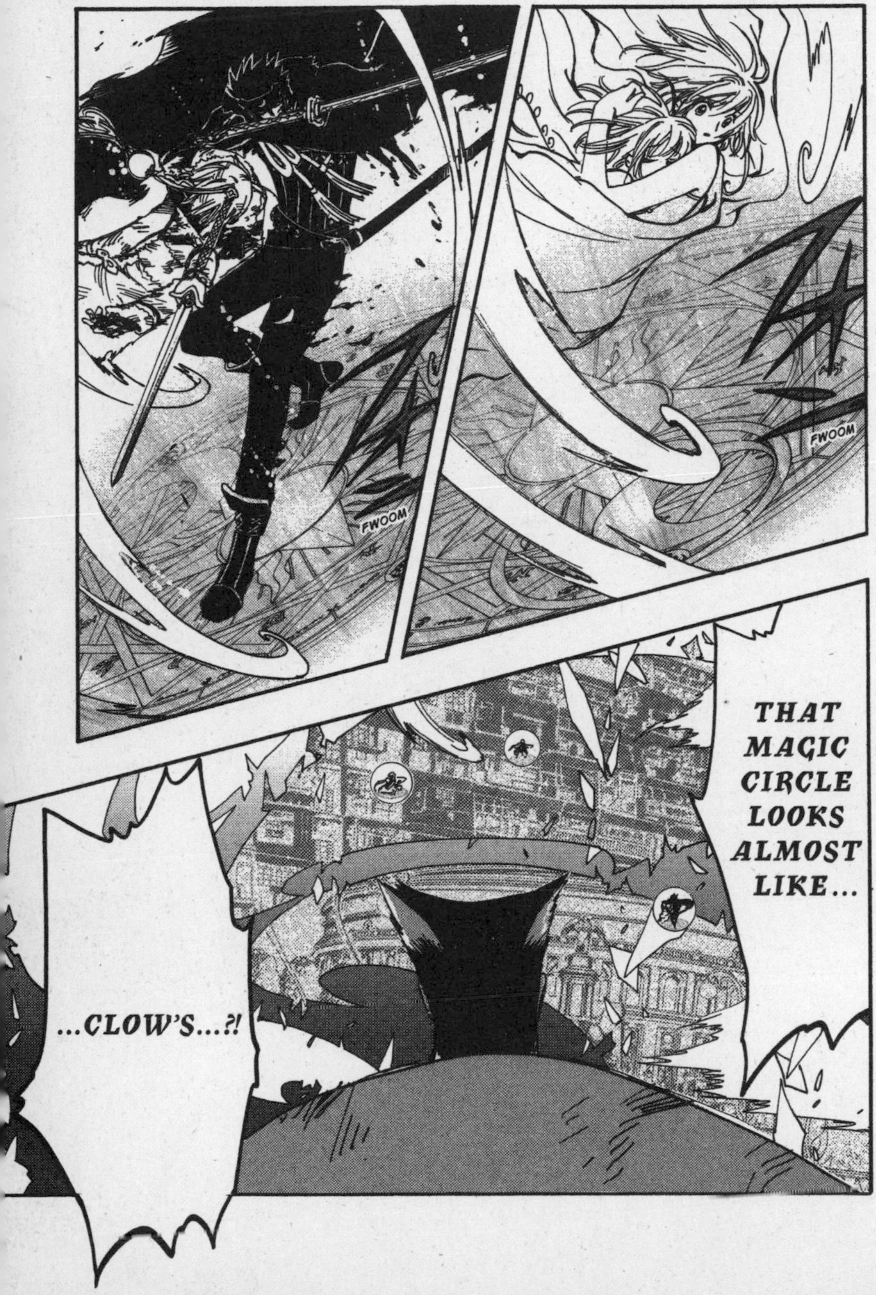
FWOOM
FWOOM
THAT MAGIC CIRCLE LOOKS ALMOST LIKE...
...CLOW'S...?!

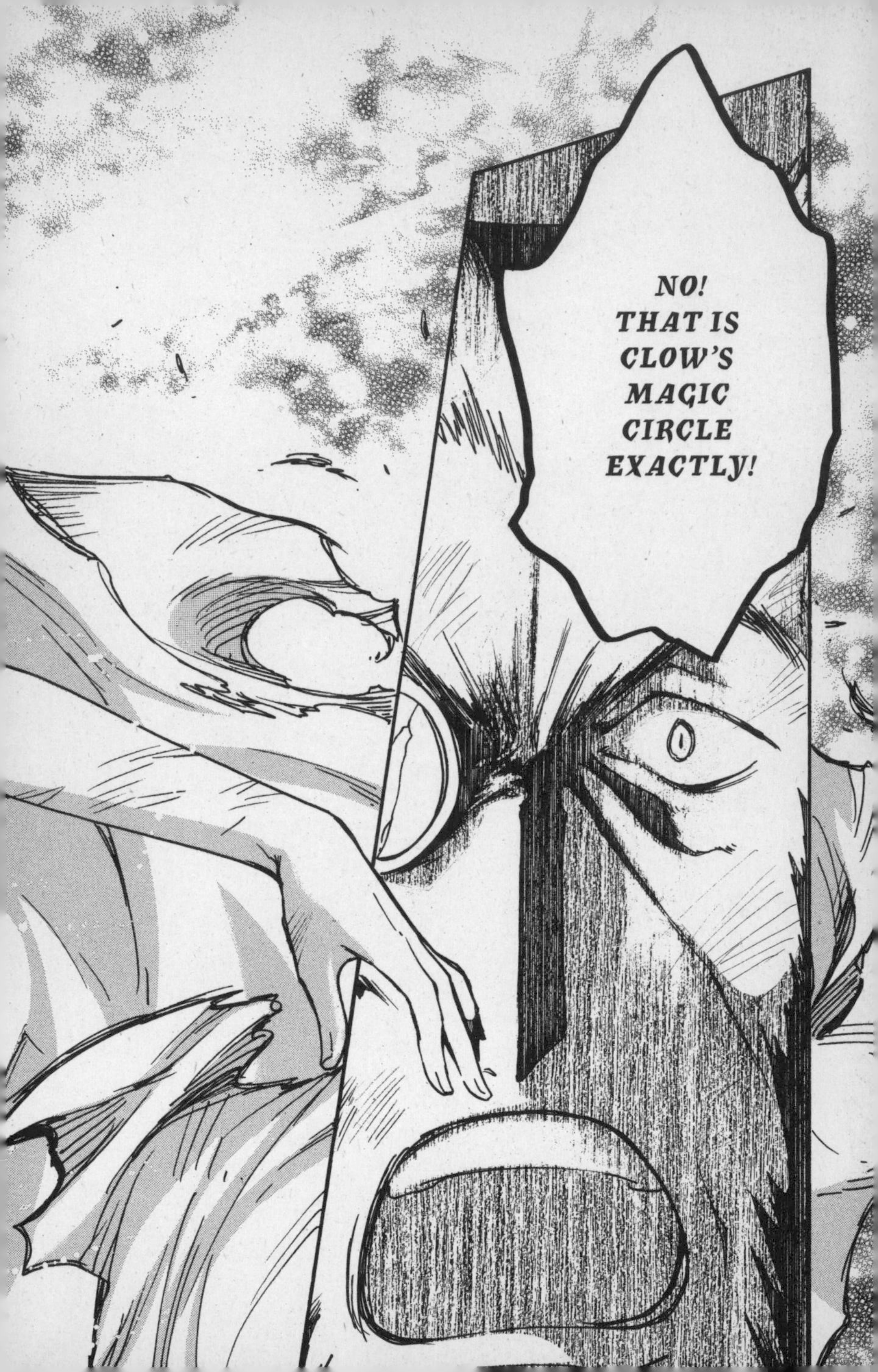
NO! THAT IS CLOW'S MAGIC CIRCLE EXACTLY!

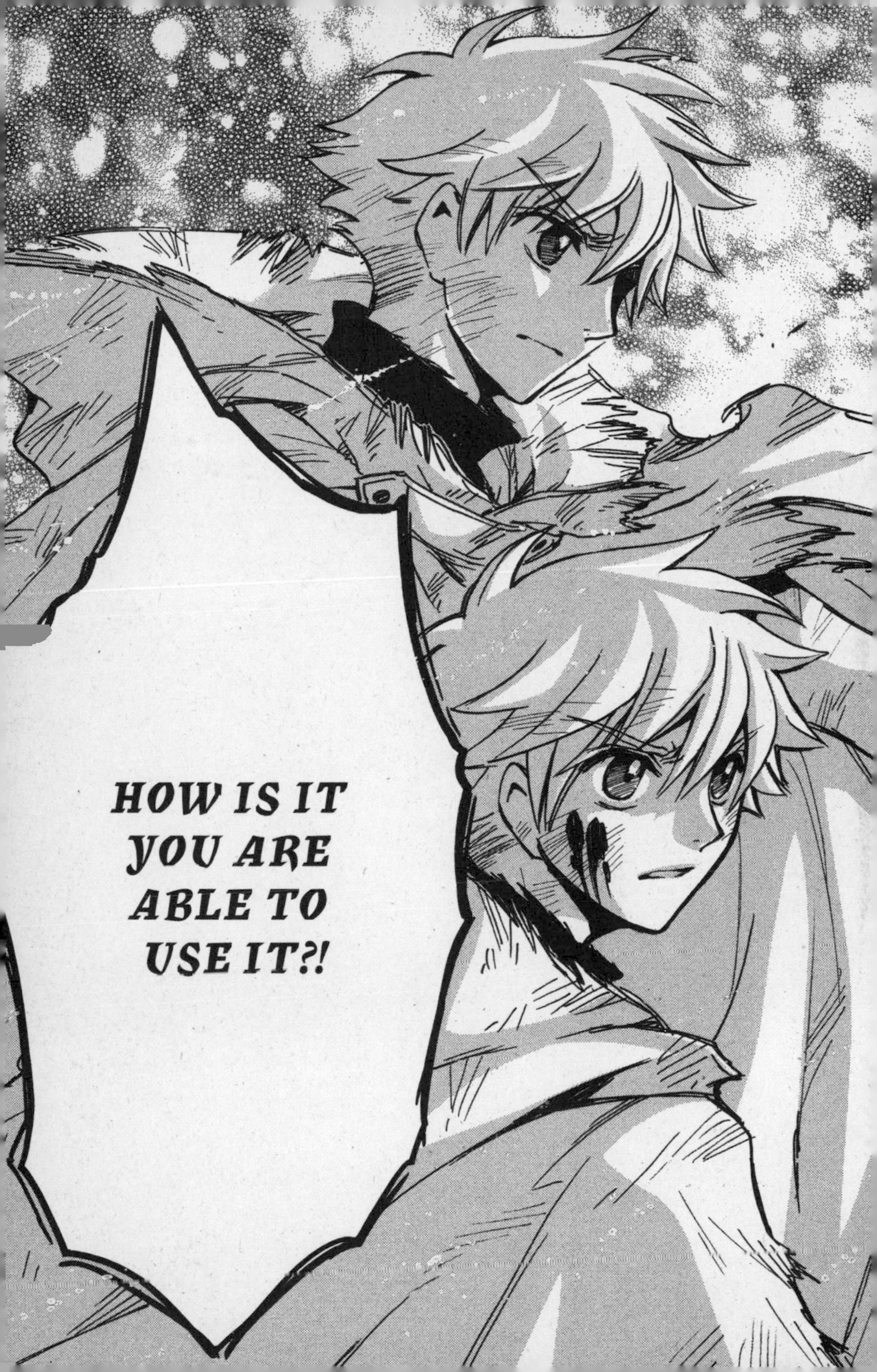
HOW IS IT YOU ARE ABLE TO USE IT?!

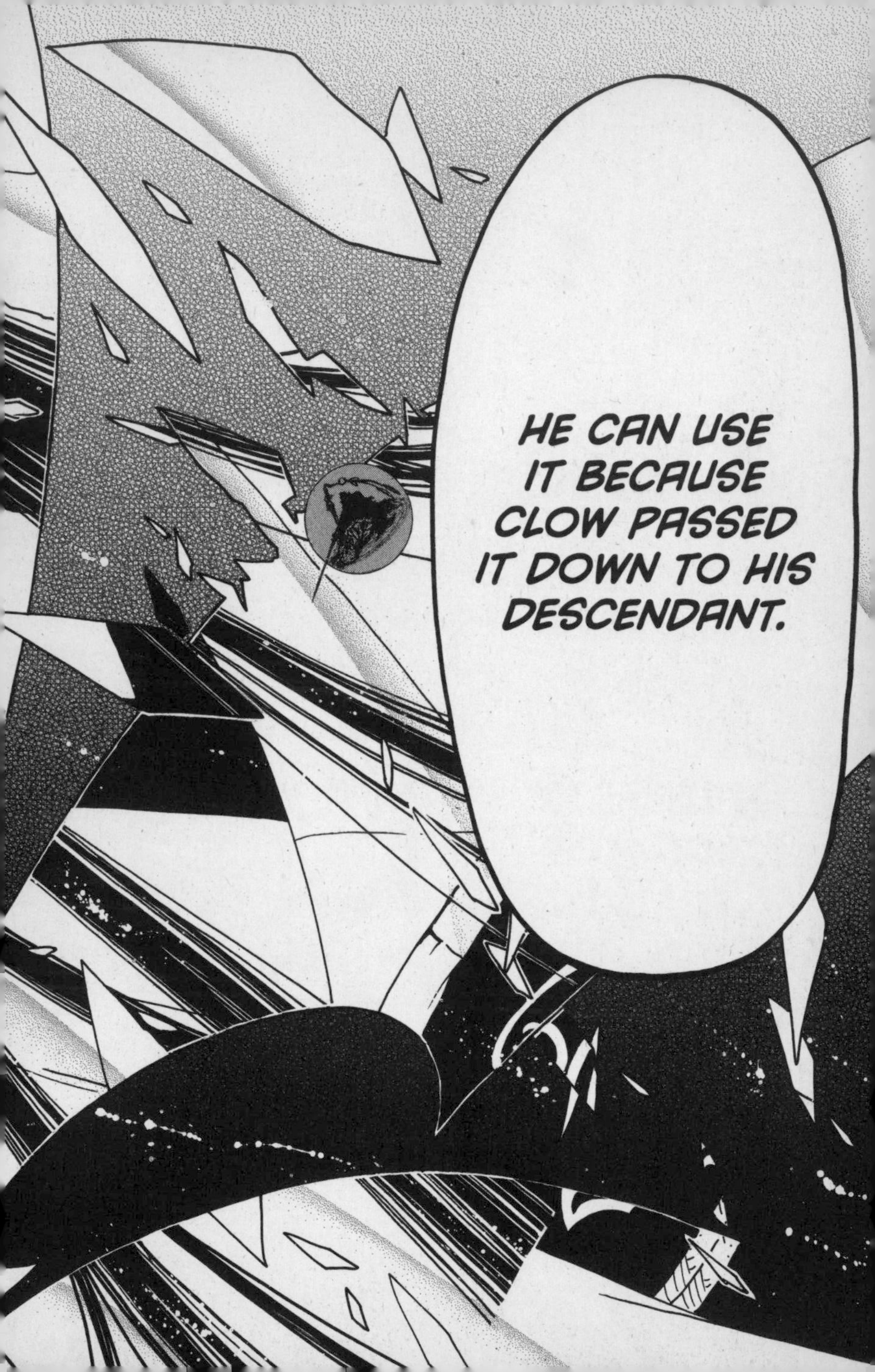
HE CAN USE IT BECAUSE CLOW PASSED IT DOWN TO HIS DESCENDANT.

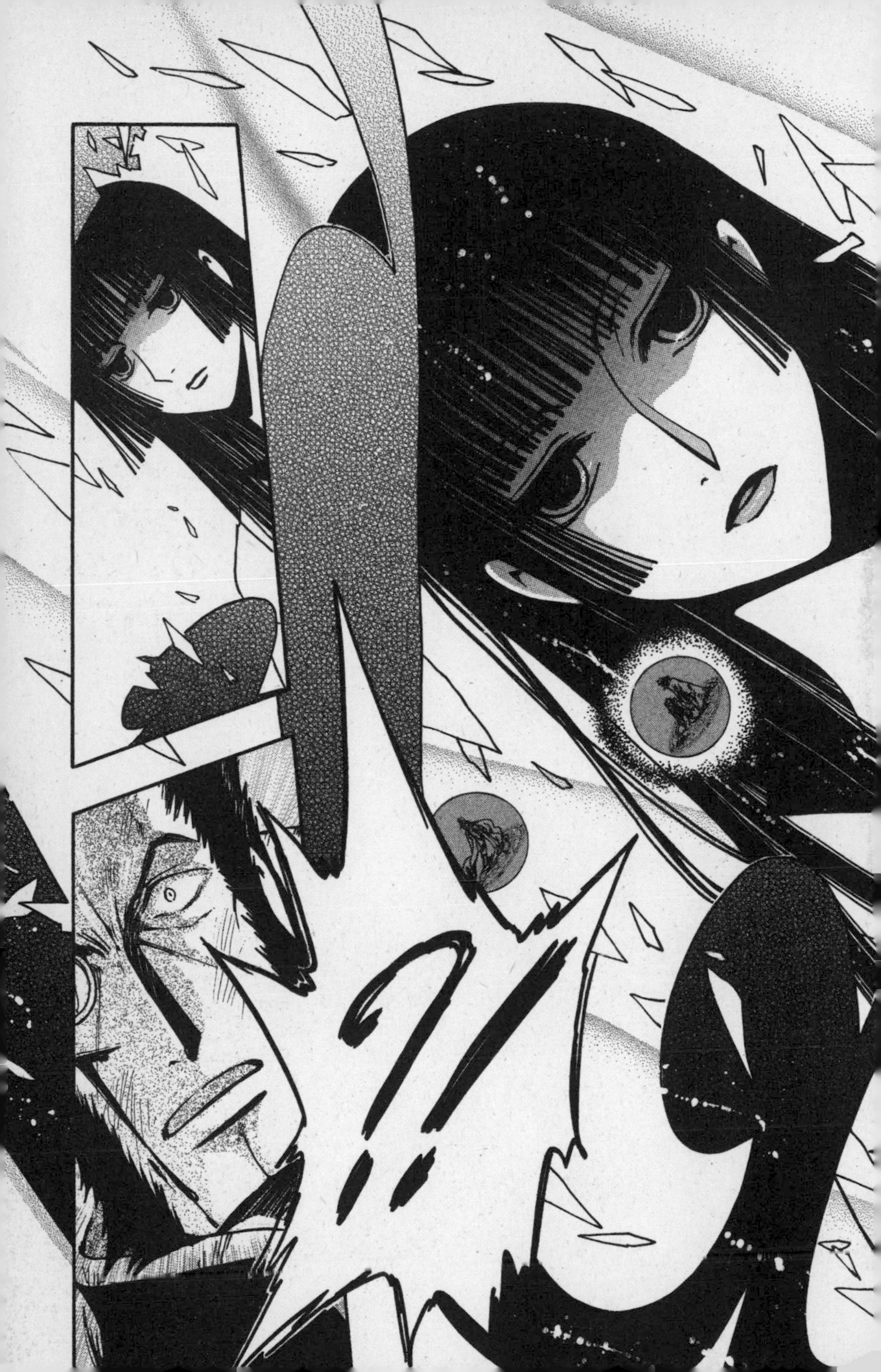

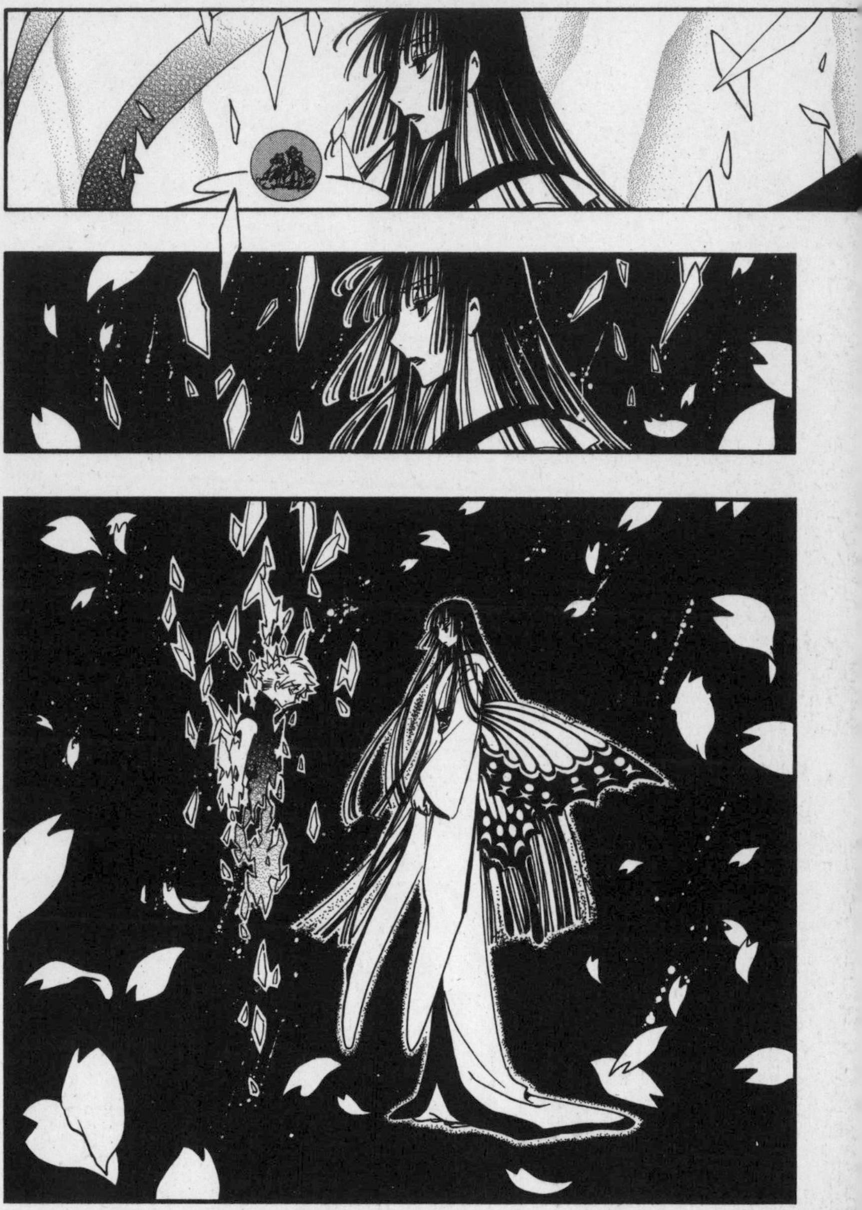

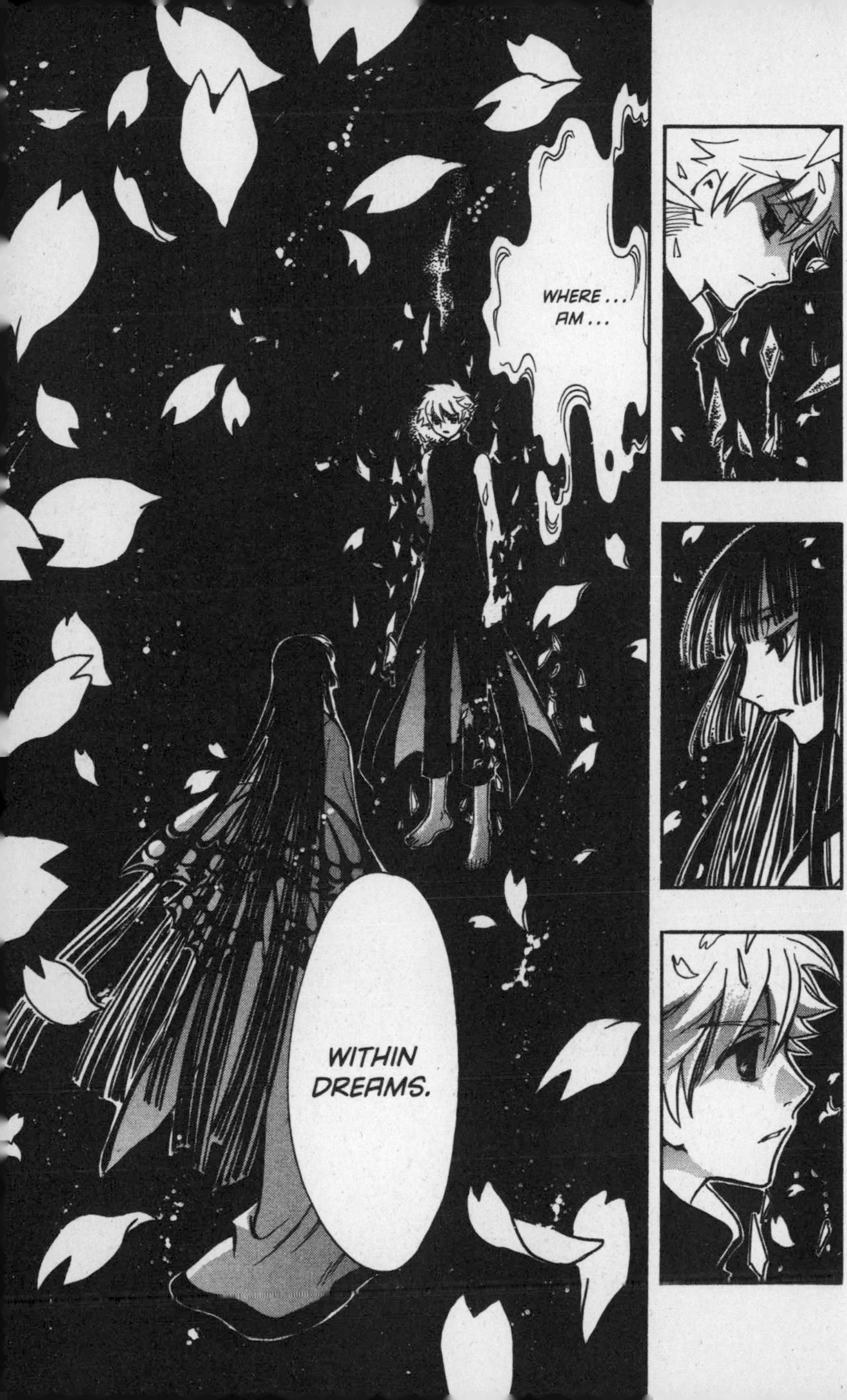
WHERE... AM...
WITHIN DREAMS.

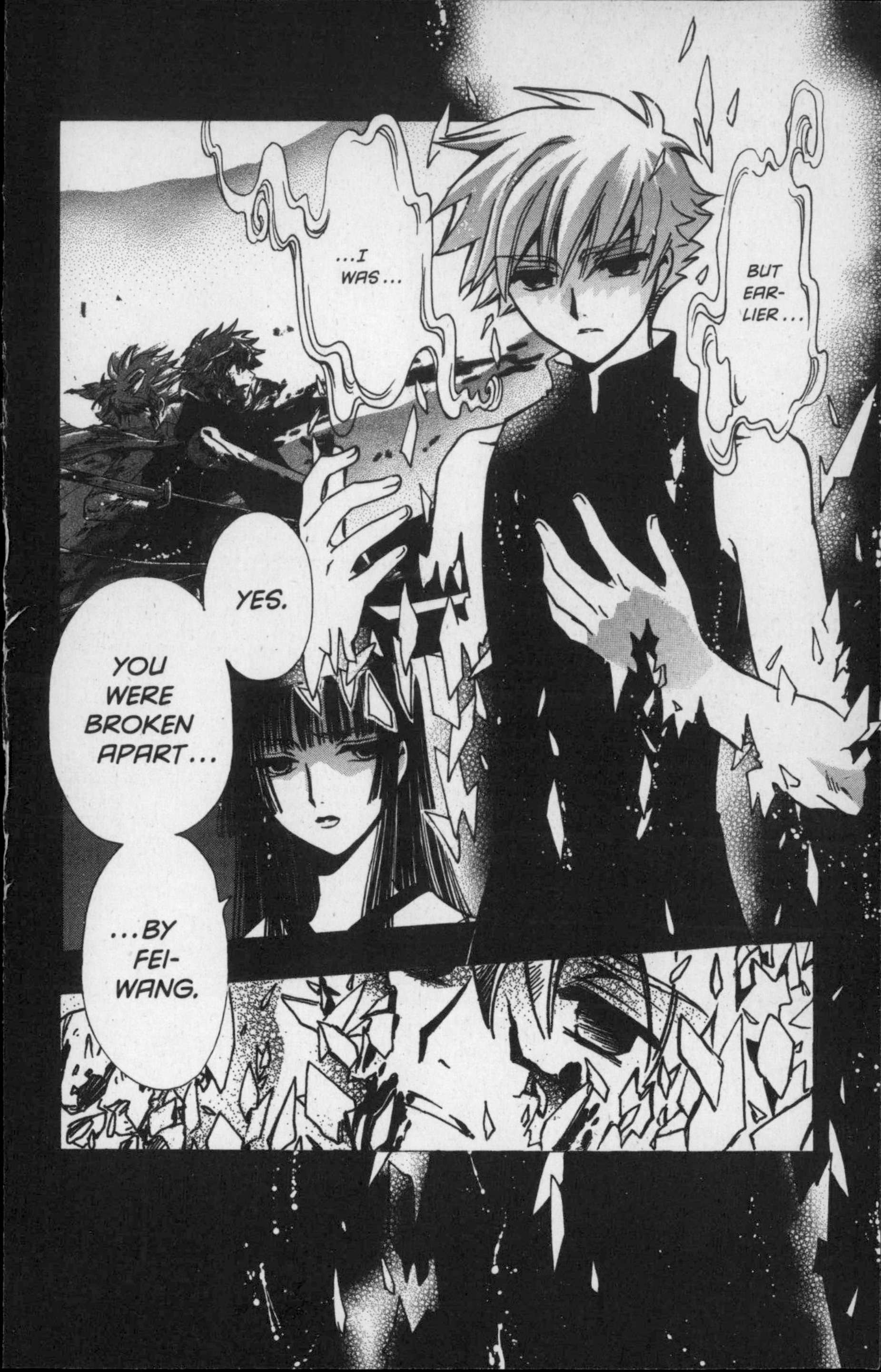
BUT EAR-LIER...
...I WAS...
YES.
YOU WERE BROKEN APART...
...BY FEI-WANG.

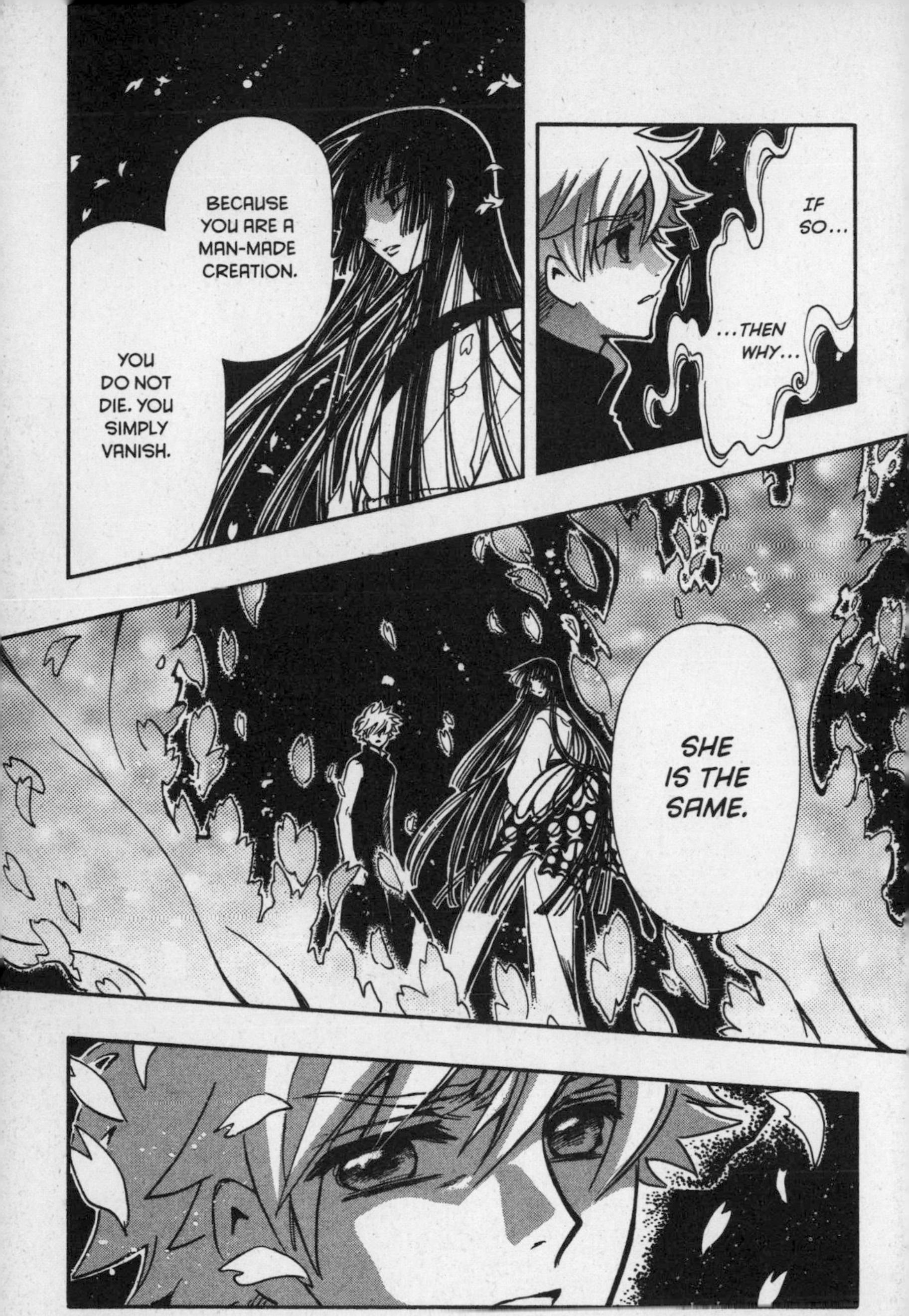
IF SO...
...THEN WHY...
BECAUSE YOU ARE A MAN-MADE CREATION.
YOU DO NOT DIE. YOU SIMPLY VANISH.
SHE IS THE SAME.

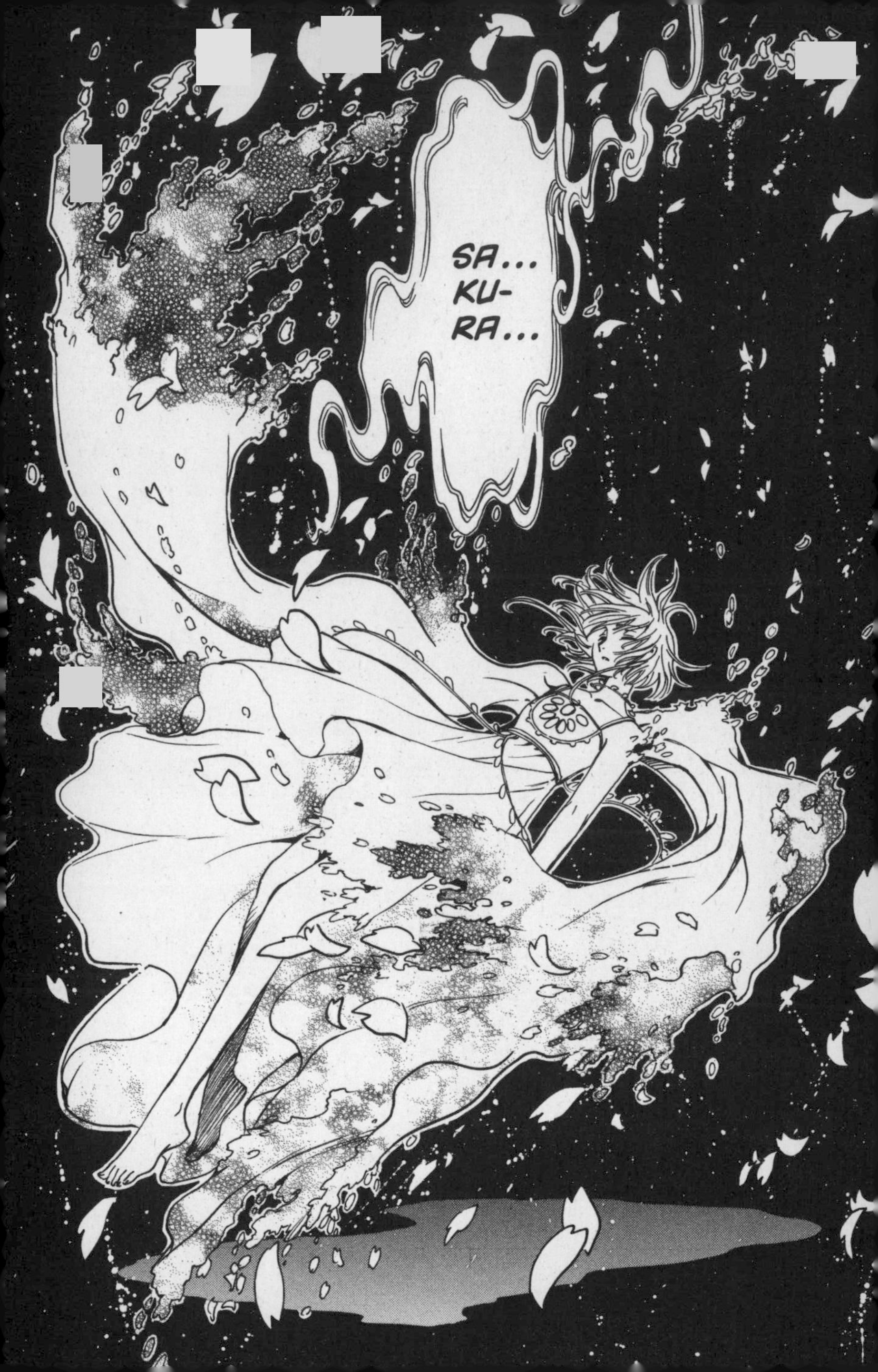
SA... KU- RA...

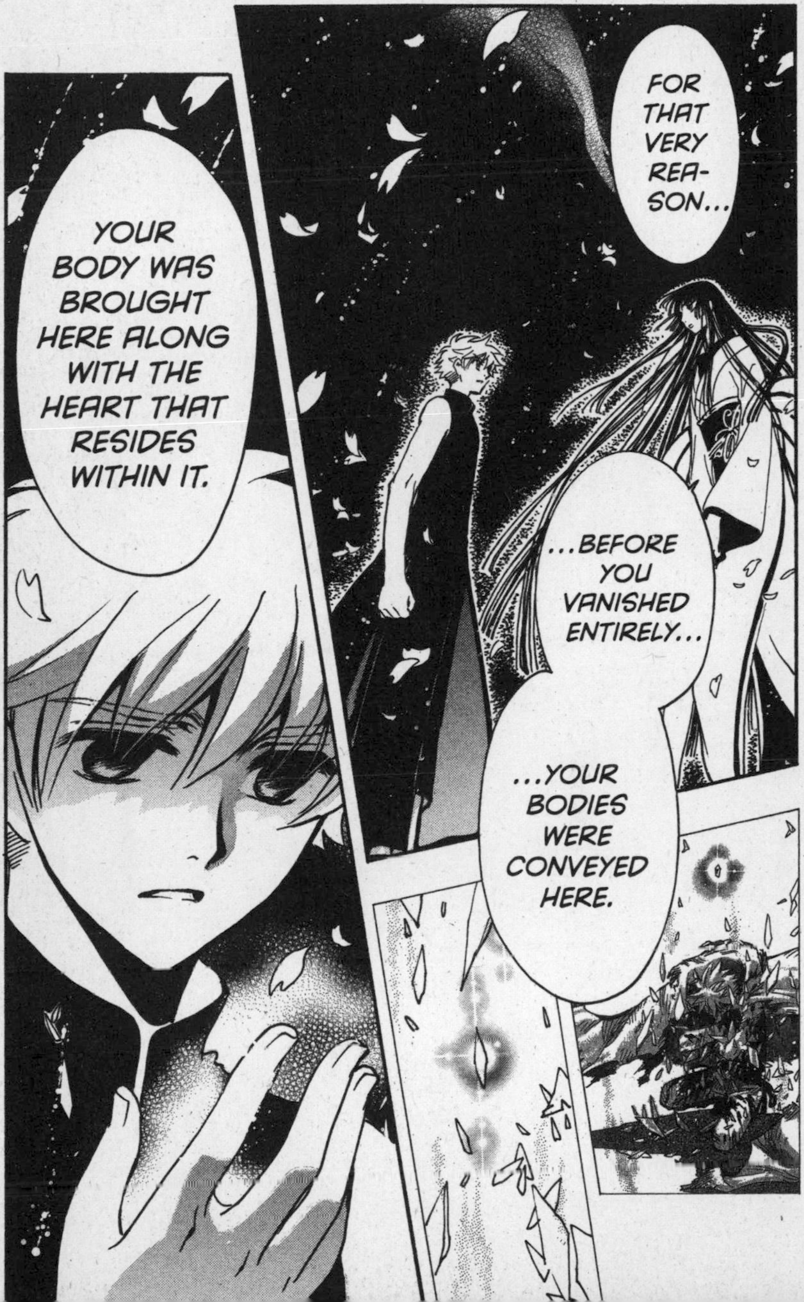
FOR THAT VERY REA-SON...
...BEFORE YOU VANISHED ENTIRELY...
...YOUR BODIES WERE CONVEYED HERE.
YOUR BODY WAS BROUGHT HERE ALONG WITH THE HEART THAT RESIDES WITHIN IT.

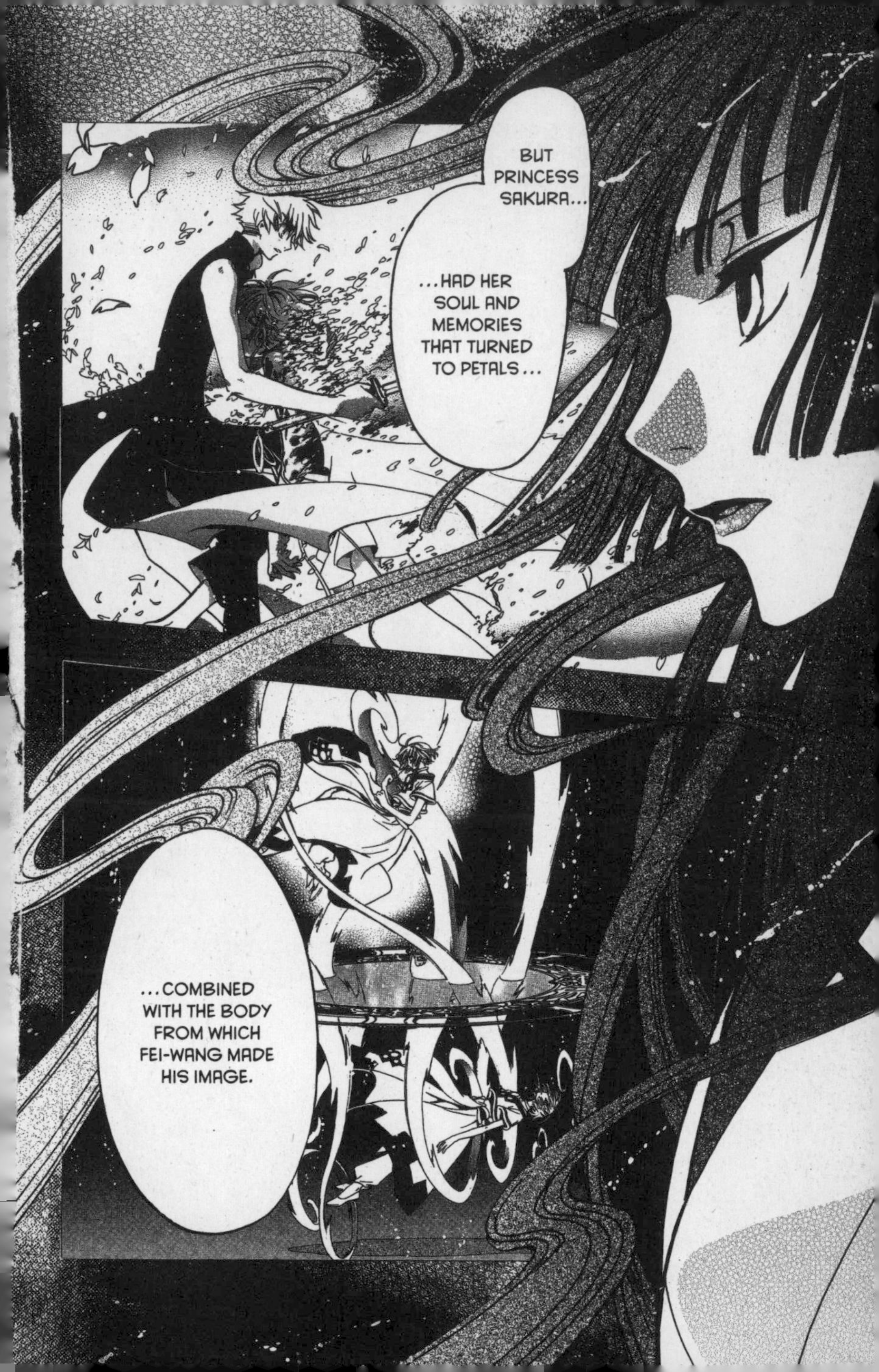
BUT PRINCESS SAKURA...
...HAD HER SOUL AND MEMORIES THAT TURNED TO PETALS...
...COMBINED WITH THE BODY FROM WHICH FEI-WANG MADE HIS IMAGE.

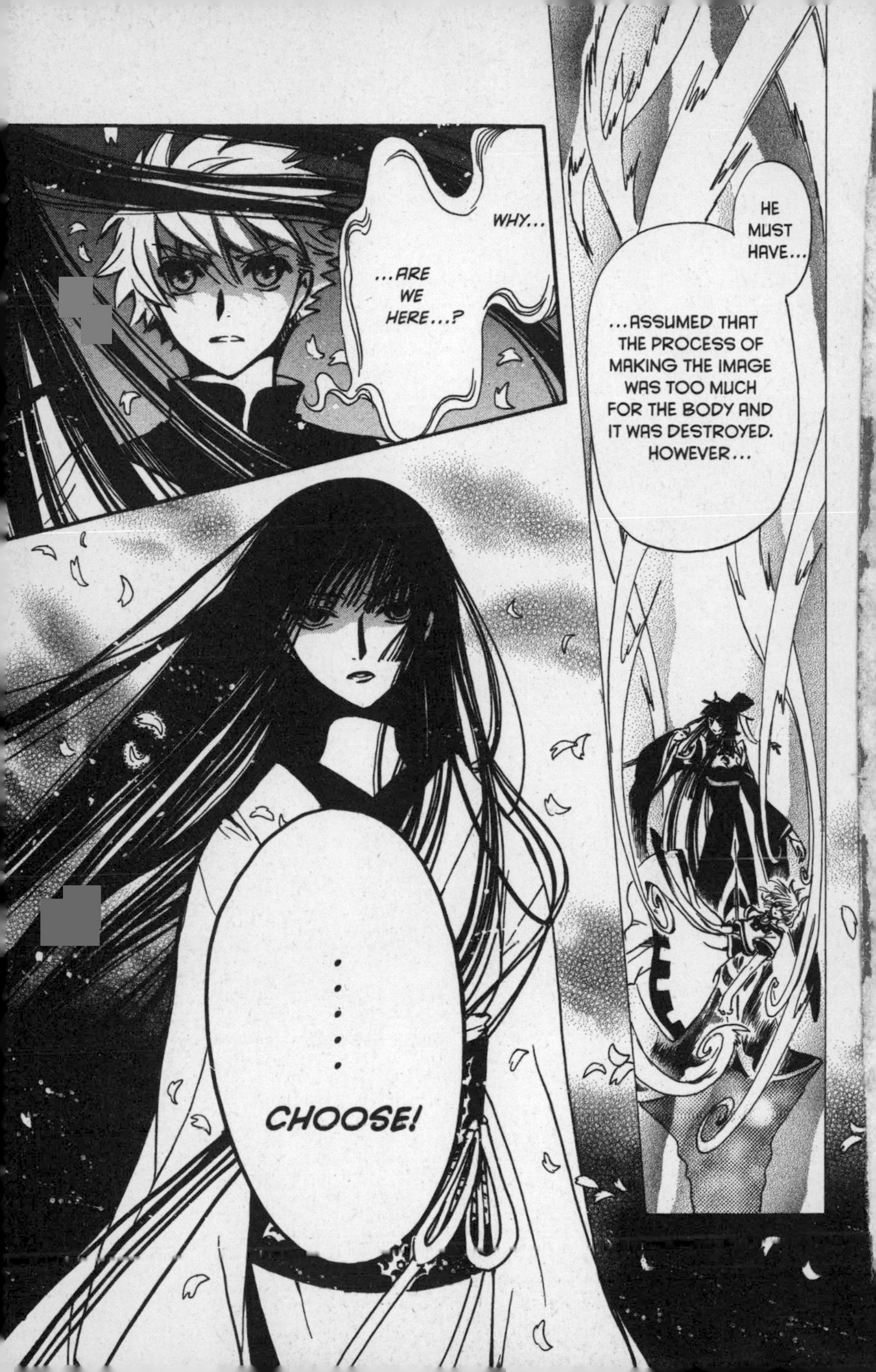
HE MUST HAVE...
...ASSUMED THAT THE PROCESS OF MAKING THE IMAGE WAS TOO MUCH FOR THE BODY AND IT WAS DESTROYED. HOWEVER...
WHY...
...ARE WE HERE...?
.....
CHOOSE!

To Be Continued

About the Creators

CLAMP is a group of four women who have become the most popular manga artists in America—Nanase Ohkawa, Mokona, Satsuki Igarashi, and Tsubaki Nekoi. They started out as *doujinshi* (fan comics) creators, but their skill and craft brought them to the attention of publishers very quickly. Their first work from a major publisher was RG Veda, but their first mass success was with Magic Knight Rayearth. From there, they went on to write many series, including Cardcaptor Sakura and Chobits, two of the most popular manga in the United States. Like many Japanese manga artists, they prefer to avoid the spotlight, and little is known about them personally.

CLAMP is currently publishing three series in Japan: Tsubasa and xxxHOLiC with Kodansha and Gohou Drug with Kadokawa.

Translation Notes

Japanese is a tricky language for most Westerners, and translation is often more art than science. For your edification and reading pleasure, here are notes on some of the places where we could have gone in a different direction in our translation of the work, or where a Japanese cultural reference is used.

Chapter title pages

Our editions of Tsubasa follow the format of the Japanese collected editions. In the Japanese edition of volume 27, the title pages for chapters 213–216 were omitted, owing to formatting issues. We have followed the format of the Japanese edition in our edition.

The Body-Double, page 20

The body double, also known as a "political decoy," has been used as a tactic to protect leaders and VIPs for millennia. Although the names and identities of most body doubles have been lost to history, a few, such as Clifton James doubling for General Montgomery during World War II in a successful mission to mislead the Germans concerning Montgomery's actual whereabouts, have been well documented.

THE CADENCE OF PEOPLE'S NAMES...

The Cadence of People's Names, page 37

In this line of dialog, Fei-Wang is talking about how the people of the Kingdom of Clow have such names as Yukito, Fujitaka, and Sakura. These are distinctively Japanese-sounding names.

The Magic Circle, page 104

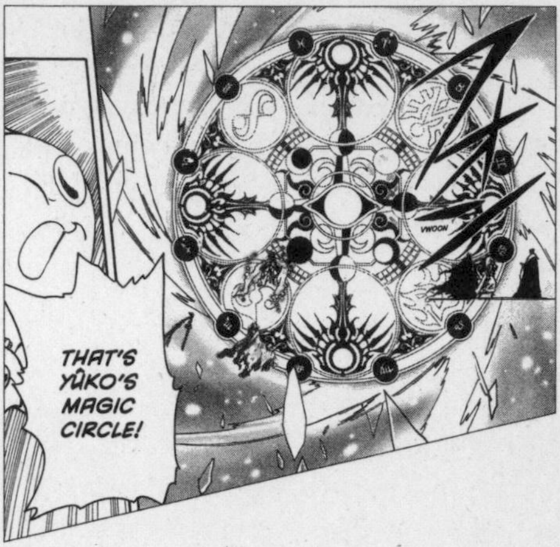
VWOON
THAT'S YÛKO'S MAGIC CIRCLE!

The magic circles in Tsubasa seem to be a cross between Asian and Western circles. The ancient Western magical art of circle casting reportedly dates back to Babylonian and Assyrian magic. That is combined with the Tantric Buddhist art of painting mandalas. The Western magic circle was once simply a protection—demons and other evils were said to be unable to enter the circle. Now it is said to be used in Wiccan and other pagan-based rites to contain energies within the circle until the rite unleashes them. In Tantric Buddhism, the mandala was an elaborate depiction of the universe from a symbolic perspective. CLAMP's elaborate magic circles seem to incorporate the Western ideas of protection and focus of energies, however the symbology is much like that of mandalas. The symbols on Yûko's circle represent the signs of the zodiac, while the *kanji* of Syaoran's mother's and father's circles are for the compass directions, seasons, elements (fire, water, wind, earth), and other mystic concepts.

Watanuki, page 110

While Kimihiro Watanuki's short cameo in this volume isn't explained (after learning Syaoran's story, does it really need to be?), it is replayed from Watanuki's perspective in volume 15 of xxxHOLiC. As always, the reader does not need to read xxxHOLiC to enjoy Tsubasa, but if one reads both, one may be able to understand the motivations and consequences of the characters' actions a little better.

Preview of Tsubasa, volume 28

We're pleased to present you a preview from Tsubasa, volume 28.
Please check our website (www.delreymanga.com) to see when this
volume will be available in English. For now you'll have to make do
with Japanese!

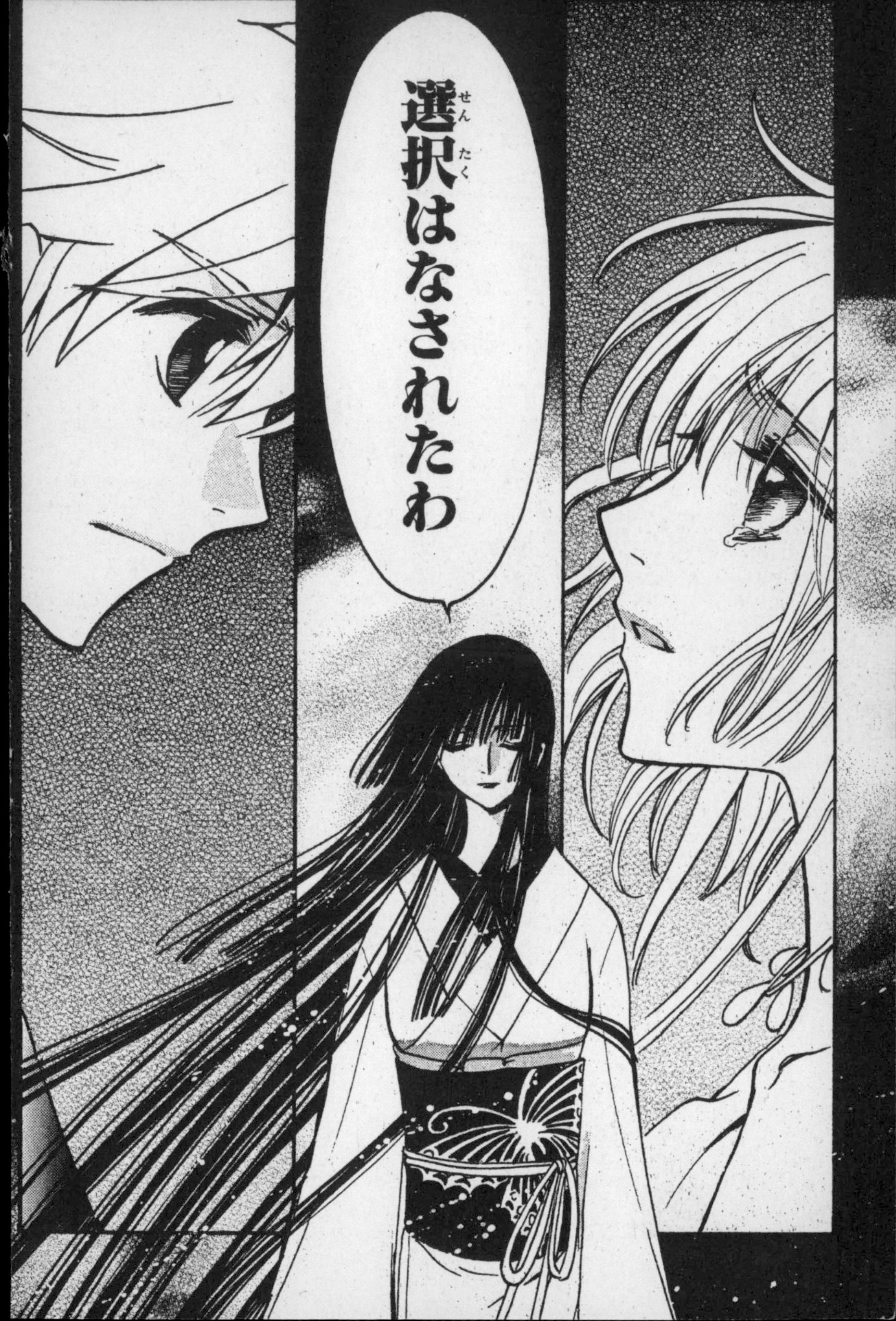
選択はなされたわ

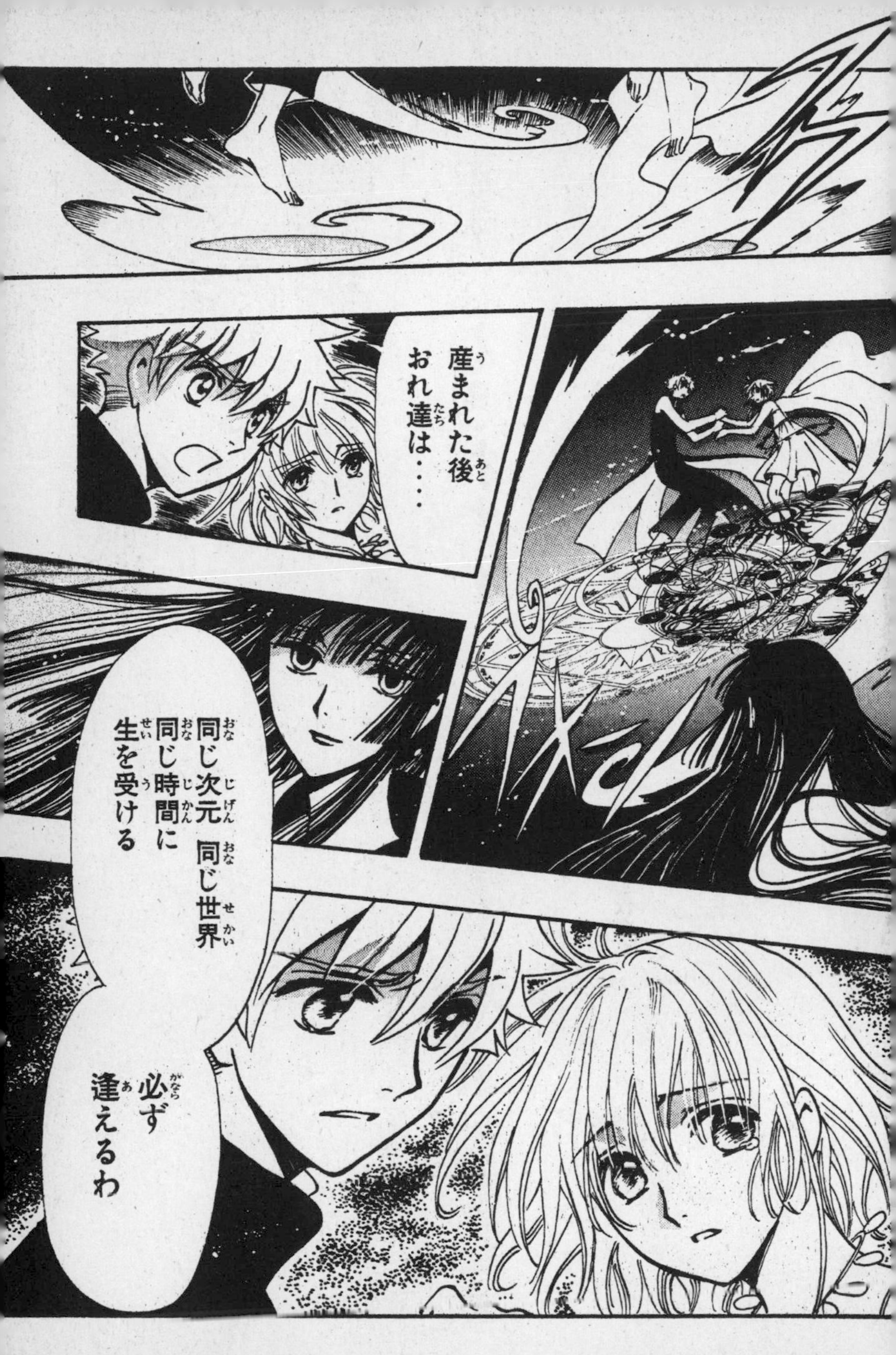
産まれた後 おれ達は‥‥
同じ次元 同じ世界 同じ時間に 生を受ける
必ず 逢えるわ

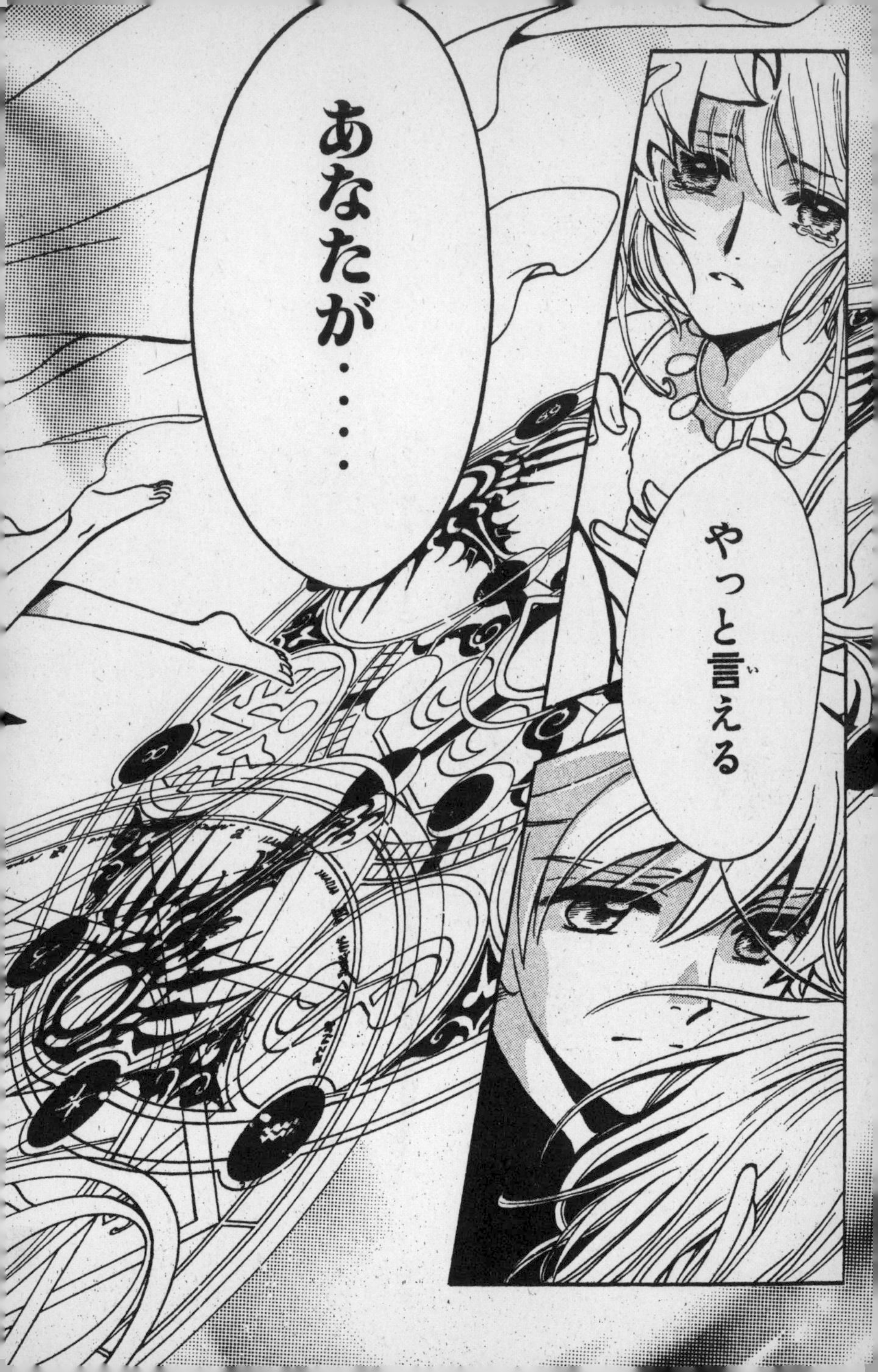
やっと言(い)える
あなたが・・・・

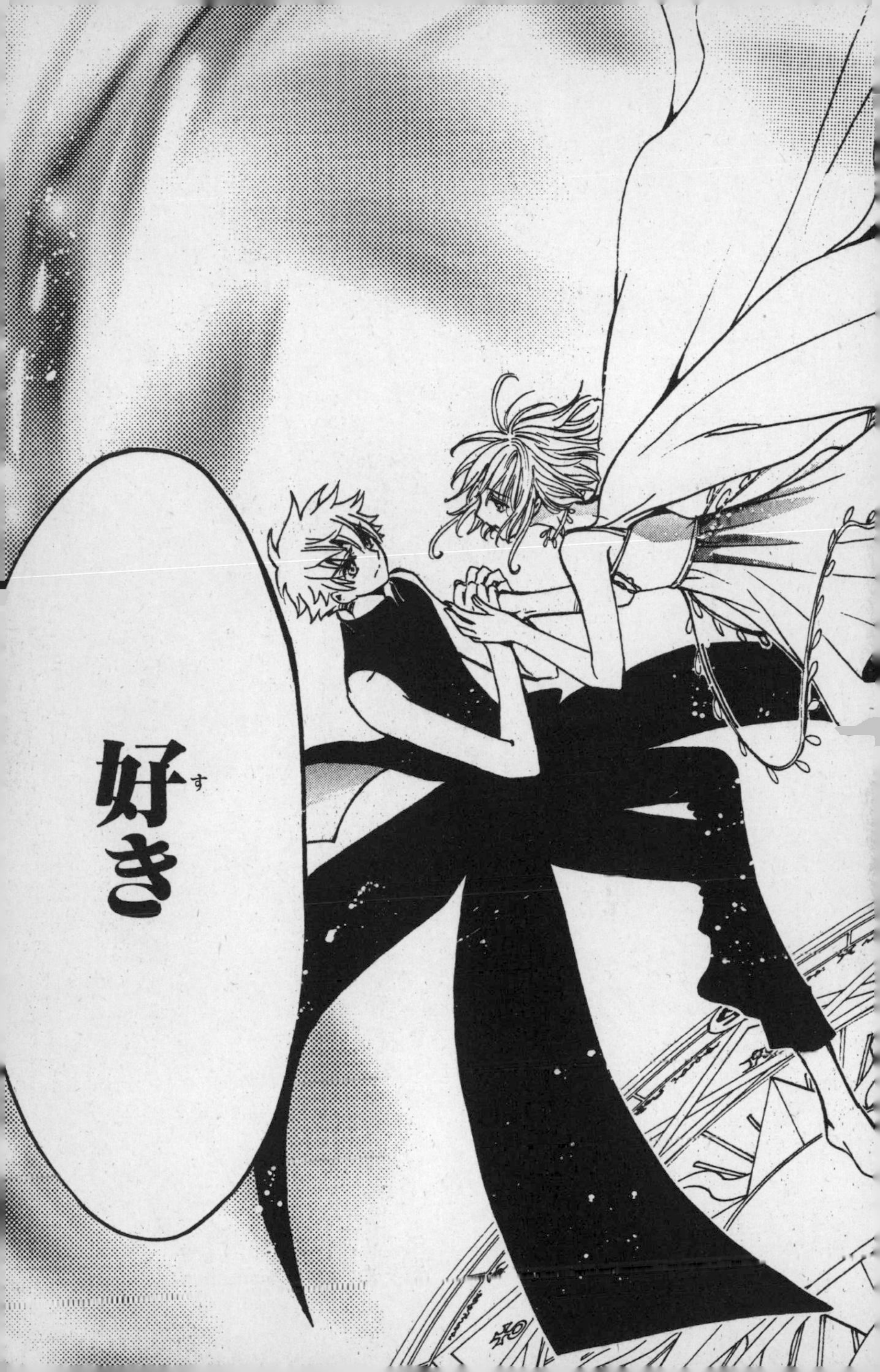
好き

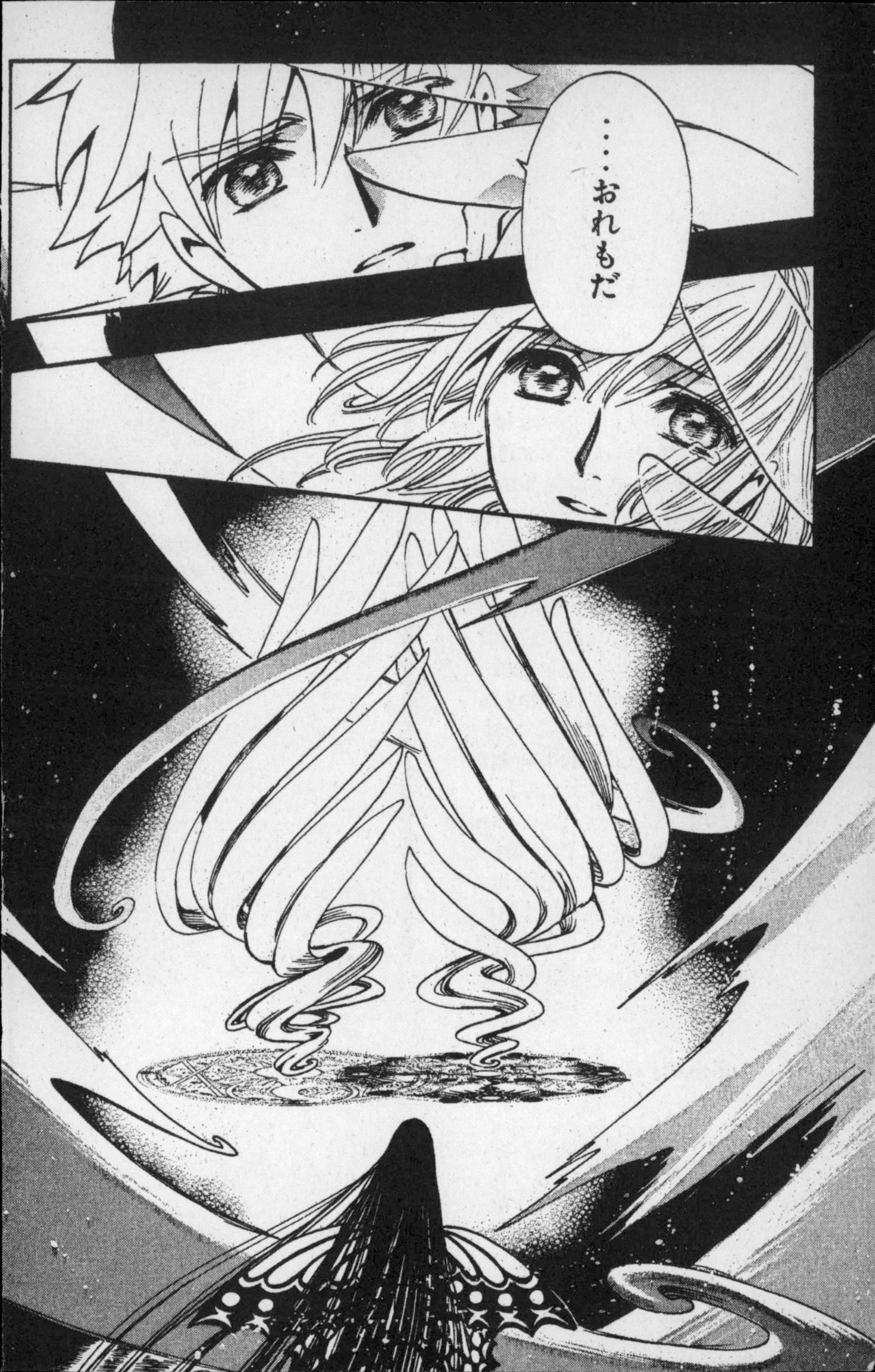
……おれもだ

xxxHOLiC™

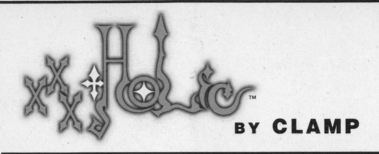

BY CLAMP

Watanuki Kimihiro is haunted by visions. When he finds himself irresistibly drawn into a shop owned by Yûko, a mysterious witch, he is offered the chance to rid himself of the spirits that plague him. He accepts, but soon realizes that he's just been tricked into working for the shop to pay off the cost of Yûko's services! But this isn't any ordinary kind of shop . . . In this shop, Yûko grants wishes to those in need. But they must have the strength of will not only to truly understand their need, but to give up something incredibly precious in return.

CLAMP
CREATORS OF CHOBITS!
1

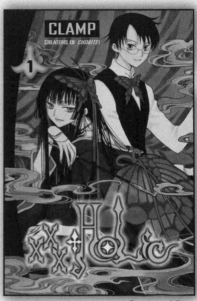

Ages: 13 +

Special extras in each volume! Read them all!

DEL REY

VISIT WWW.DELREYMANGA.COM TO:

- **View release date calendars for upcoming volumes**
- **Sign up for Del Rey's free manga e-newsletter**
- **Find out the latest about new Del Rey Manga series**

TOMARE!

[STOP!]

You're going the wrong way!

Manga is a completely different type of reading experience.

To start at the *beginning*, go to the *end*!

That's right! Authentic manga is read the traditional Japanese way—from right to left. Exactly the *opposite* of how American books are read. It's easy to follow: Just go to the other end of the book, and read each page—and each panel—from right side to left side, starting at the top right. Now you're experiencing manga as it was meant to be!